Klaus Schmidt

High Availability and Disaster Recovery

Concepts, Design, Implementation

With 83 Figures and 26 Tables

 Springer

Klaus Schmidt
Stockheimer Str. 20
60385 Frankfurt
Germany
klaus.schmidt@eds.com

ISBN-13 978-3-642-06379-4   e-ISBN-13 978-3-540-34582-4

Springer is a part of Springer Science+Business Media

springer.com

© Springer-Verlag Berlin Heidelberg 2010
Printed in Germany

Cover design: KünkelLopka Werbeagentur, Heidelberg

For Helga, Andreas, and Katrin

Preface

During the last 15 years I was involved in planning, deployment, and operations of IT systems for major companies. Those systems are mission-critical: the customers' business depends on their availability. The systems are required to be highly available and to protect against all kinds of problems, like hardware failures, software issues, human errors, through to physical disasters.

I learned that there are misunderstandings between customers, planners, and vendors about what high availability is, what can be achieved with IT systems, and where their limitations are. I also recognized that disaster recovery is only a feature of high availability, but is often seen as an independent topic.

This book addresses this area with an end-to-end view and makes it available as single piece of material: from requirements gathering to planning, implementation, and operations. Another missing piece is supplied, an approach to develop an architecture which leads to highly available systems that are robust and are able to recover from the relevant failure scenarios. But identification of failure scenarios is still a kind of art, mostly based on individual experiences. Selection of a solution is driven by a process, and not by products that claim protection but do not consider the whole picture.

With that end-to-end view, we get a structured approach that leads from requirements to possible failure scenarios to a successful solution. That was the motivation to write this book. It addresses these topics and is targeted at all parties involved, enabling them to speak a common language and manage their mutual expectations.

The goal of this book is to explain and discuss architecture, technology, solutions, and processes. Since products and features are too short lived for the aim of this book, it does not review, compare, or recommend any particular products.

I thank my employer Electronic Data Systems (EDS) for the excellent work environment that I have had over many years, for a very successful working relationship, and for support in writing this book.

I would like to thank the following friends and colleagues for their fruitful discussions, guidance, and reviews: J. Bankstahl (EDS), F. Haberhauer (Sun), H. Haupt (AES), F. Krämer (IBM), S. Krampen (EDS), F. Mittelbach (EDS), and Dr. F. Renner (Opel). I also thank all my many colleagues at EDS, especially from the Enterprise Technology Office. Their experience and insights helped me in understanding the full picture.

Special thanks to Joachim Schrod from Network and Publication Consultance (NPC). Without his significant contributions, this book would not have been possible.

Frankfurt, März 2006   *Klaus Schmidt*

Contents

1

Introduction

For information technology (IT), the last decade has been a revolution. Our lives and our businesses depend on IT to a magnitude that has not been seen as possible before. And even though there is a lot of fuss about this change, many people have still not realized their dependencies on functioning IT systems. But this book will not tell you how one preaches the importance of IT. Instead, it is for the situations where the importance is acknowledged in principle, and where we have to map business objectives to IT availability plans and execute those plans.

In other words, the mission statement of this book is

Show how it is ensured that IT services are available when they are needed, balancing benefit and costs.

The central question that will be answered is "how," not "why." We use a holistic view of that topic. When a solution is planned and implemented, every aspect must fit together and it is not sensible to restrict ourselves to certain areas.

Therefore this book approaches solutions to IT service availability and continuity from planning, via implementation descriptions, through to operations. This covers the whole range of work areas that are needed to establish and maintain a solution.

In addition, technical areas are covered too. We will discuss problems that hardware, software, infrastructure services, human actions, and company locations (sites) cause and the solutions that they can provide. We do not want to rest with descriptions that explain how one can ensure IT service availability in the case of hardware and software failures, but that do not mention floods or human errors by system administrators. Instead, the whole problem and solution range is accommodated, just like all work areas.

The book's goal is achieved with the experience that I acquired in planning and implementing successfully high-availability and disaster-recovery solutions in the last 15 years, for major international companies. The approaches and templates used have been successfully realized in many places and resulted in lots of practical experience about what works and where typical problems and stumbling blocks are – this book will make this experience available to you as well.

To achieve that goal, a solution-oriented presentation structure has been chosen. The first chapters will introduce the problem domain and will show the generic structure of possible solutions. The following chapters will present components of that structure, one after another.

But let us first describe the intended audience of this book in the next section. Then, Sect. 1.2 on p. 4 presents the book's roadmap in more detail, and Sect. 1.3 finishes the introduction with real-life examples.

1.1 Audience

In today's tight financial climate, business consequences of IT misbehavior or outages are often not realistically analyzed. Therefore the myth remains that high availability and disaster recovery is only something for large enterprises with an IT staff in the hundreds or thousands, big data centers, and established IT operations. But by now, solutions are mature and standardized enough to be able to be implemented in small work groups and with less formal processes. All that is needed is the intention to do good work and to care for quality.

We need to understand the link between business objectives and IT solutions. But we want to reuse existing design patterns; solutions that are created anew for each company's situation are too expensive. For that, we need to understand also the possibilities and limitations of typical IT solutions to high availability and disaster recovery. Only with that understanding firmly in place are we able to plan and implement properly a solution that fits to our situation.

The information from this book is not only of interest if one wants to implement high availability and disaster recovery in one's own company. Quite often, IT is outsourced, as it is not seen to be at the heart of one's business and one hopes to get better services from professional companies that concentrate on IT. Then one still needs the information from this book to negotiate contracts – in particular, service level agreements (SLAs) – with suppliers. Do not forget that one can outsource implementation and operations, but one cannot outsource responsibility.

That said, the book's main target audience is architects, system designers, and those who shall implement the systems. But it has also content for executive managers. For successful projects, one needs to look beyond one's own nose and read up on topics that are in other spheres of activities. This book will provide information about such adjacent areas, for each audience group. So let us have a look at the information you can get from it.

▶ *Executives – CIO and CTO*

For chief technology officers and for chief information officers who are interested in technical matters, the book delivers:

- An overview of IT availability and continuity. This will provide everything that an executive needs to know about high availability and disaster recovery.
- Technical information that is needed to communicate with architects and system designers.
- A link between business requirements and IT solutions.

It serves as the guide for how to give good objectives and guidance to the project team that has to implement high availability and/or disaster recovery. It also has information that allows us to judge the quality of their work, and to understand the technical reports that they are producing.

▶ *Architects and System Designers*

This audience group is those who are responsible for the actual system design and planning. This is the main audience of this book.

- A roadmap is presented that will yield a full-fledged architecture that goes beyond mere system design, including objective collection and business process architecture.
- A structured approach for solution finding and implementation is presented. This is the process that delivers the system design, together with explanations on how one can adapt them to local requirements.
- Solution structures are worked out, to help to divide the big problem domain into chunks that can be approached one at a time. This is the template where we can draw our system design from.
- Technologies are presented that build a toolbox for realization of high availability and disaster recovery.
- Adjacent areas that are not strictly part of the architect's or system designer's task are mentioned as well, and serve as an introduction. In particular, operational aspects are covered.

We take a broad view of the topics covered that caters for generalists and not for specialists who want to know the ins and outs of each bit in every configuration file. The book's content will help by providing an end-to-end view and not losing itself in the deep trenches of particularities of specific products or specific versions.

▶ *System Implementors*

Solution structures and technologies are the meat that make up the later chapters of this book. These parts of book cater especially for those system implementors who are interested in practical experience that they can use in their own environment.

- The central message for this audience group is how to implement a high-availability or disaster-recovery solution in such a way that it can be operated successfully and efficiently.
- To help with that, typical pitfalls and tricks are presented.
- Requirements are featured explicitly that help to trace back implementation plans to the system designer's work, and ultimately to the business objectives.
- The process of architectural planning is also of great interest as it enables better communication with one's colleagues.

In the end, as every implementor knows, failure will happen and cannot be avoided. It is necessary to plan for it in advance, both from a process and from a technical point of view, to take a broad view of the needs and the possibilities of implementation work. How this is done, both in principal and specifically for actual technology components, is an important aspect of this book.

1.2 Roadmap of This Book

We will start with the elementary concepts to get an introduction to the overall theme. Then two chapters will present the big picture: architecture and system design. After that, we will go into technical details and present categorized solution strategies. Each category will have its own chapter.

Within the technical chapters, we will present solutions that work for high availability and disaster recovery alike, but we will focus on high availability. A chapter on disaster recovery pulls together all parts from all solution categories and tells what is special about it.

The appendices feature a treaty on reliability and the math of it; we give an introduction to data centers and to service support processes. An index and the bibliography close the book.

That is the roadmap in general terms. Let us introduce each chapter with a short summary to give you more information.

▶ *Chapter 2: Elementary Concepts*

Business continuity is introduced as the overall goal of our activities. IT service continuity is our task to contribute to that goal. To achieve that, we need categorization of systems and outages, to leverage existing concepts. Minor outages are those that happen more often and do not do much damage; protection against or recovery from such minor outages is the task of high availability. Major outages are less probable and are covered by disaster recovery.

Quantification of availability is presented. We use them also in SLAs, which are part of (formal or informal) contracts between the IT department, IT contractors, and business owners.

The same basic approach is used to achieve high availability and disaster recovery: robustness and redundancy. With that tool in our arsenal, we are ready to design layered solutions that protect our services in depth – we can handle failures on several system levels.

▶ *Chapter 3: Architecture*

The architecture is described on those three abstraction levels: business objectives describe what shall be achieved. The conceptual model explains how the solution fits into business processes, and how it is connected to other IT processes. Furthermore, the architecture contains the system model that describes the technical solution strategy.

For each of these three abstraction levels, several questions are answered: What is the system concerned with? How does it work? Where is the data worked with, or where is functionality achieved? Who works with data and achieves functionality? And when is it done? Answering all these questions for each abstraction level gives us a structured presentation of the complete architecture.

▶ *Chapter 4: System Design*

The system design has the technical meat of our solution. It describes what systems are protected against which outages and how this is done. To achieve such a description in a structured way, we introduce the concept of the system stack, a categorization of those components that make up IT systems and services. The system stack is so important that we use it to structure the rest of this book when we present technological solutions for component categories.

We pick up the elementary concepts of robustness and redundancy and explain them in more detail. This cumulates in a solution roadmap that shows how we create a good system design that fulfills our requirements, starting from failure scenarios. As an illustration, we conclude that chapter with solution patterns and with the use case of high availability for an SAP server.

▶ *Chapter 5: Hardware*

Hardware is the component category where high availability was first realized; therefore, we find the most mature solutions in this area. First we look at all hardware components of a computer system and explain the technology that can be used for a high-availability solution.

Special focus is given to disk storage because it is very important – after all, all our business data is kept here. But we do not stop at the different technologies that make disks highly available, we also present storage subsystems, appliances that provide storage area networks (SANs) or network-attached storage (NAS).

Since we do not build our systems ourselves, we need to pay special attention to vendor selection. When the purchasing decisions have been made, installation, maintenance, and operation are also important, and these topics are handled in this chapter.

▶ *Chapter 6: Operating Systems*

High availability on the operating system level is the most widely used technology today. It is named host clustering and comes in two forms, as failover clusters and as load-balancing clusters, both are presented in this chapter.

Failover clusters make IT services independent of the computer system they run on. When a hardware error or a software crash occurs, the service is migrated to another computer system in the cluster. This cluster technology relies on disk storage that can be accessed from all systems and that is redundant in itself.

Load-balancing clusters distribute server requests over a set of identically configured systems. The distribution handles outages of one of those systems. This kind of cluster can only be used if the application has no state, since there is no shared storage between the cluster systems.

The chapter concludes with an excursion on the future of host clustering in the face of current trends towards server consolidation. Host clustering is based on the usage of extra computer systems, to get redundancy for failure recovery. Server consolidation targets the reduction of the computer systems used and has therefore the exact opposite goals. Host virtualization may help to combine both objectives, though today this remains a trend and future development cannot be assured.

▶ *Chapter 7: Databases and Middleware*

Middleware components are application-independent software products that are integrated as part of an application to realize an IT service. The prime example of middleware components is database servers: they are utilized in many mission-critical applications. Other middleware components are Web servers, application servers, messaging servers, and transaction managers.

This chapter presents the high-availability and disaster-recovery solutions that are available as features of middleware components. Most prominently, database clusters are introduced.

▶ *Chapter 8: Applications*

After all base components have been covered, it remains for us to describe how high availability is achieved for applications. Seldom will we implement full redundancy within an application – instead, we will utilize one of the high-availability options that we learned about in the previous chapters. But we have to decide which option to use, e.g., if we want to utilize a host clustering solution or if we want to use middleware clustering.

The solution approach chosen often has demands on the application, either on its realization or on its implementation. For example, one cannot use a failover cluster for any application, the application must fulfill some requirements. These requirements are spelled out in detail.

▶ *Chapter 9: Infrastructure*

Infrastructure is the set of application-independent IT services that are used by an application. Most important, this is the network and associated services like Domain Name Service (DNS), Dynamic Host Configuration Protocol (DHCP), or directory and authentication services.

This chapter will show how we create a highly available network infrastructure and will also present high-availability solutions for three important services: DHCP, DNS, and directory servers. It concludes with the influence of high-availability solutions on backup and monitoring.

▶ *Chapter 10: Disaster Recovery*

The previous chapters will have presented many solutions that apply both for high availability and for disaster recovery. But disaster recovery has specific important aspects that shall be presented in context; therefore, this chapter presents the overall approach, a conceptual model for disaster recovery, and the technology that is used to realize it.

A description of a prototypical disaster-recovery project rounds off the topic, as well as a step-by-step description of procedures that are used to activate backup systems in case of a disaster.

▶ *Appendices*

Reliability of components is an important property to achieve high availability. In particular for hardware components, reliability numbers are known and one can use them to assess reliability of combined systems. Appendix A introduces *reliability calculations and statistics*, the math that is necessary to do those assessments.

Data centers are the topic of Appendix B. We will not capture everything that is needed to create a top-notch data center – that goes beyond the book's scope. But a good data center is an important asset in implementing high availability, and we will see what aspects contribute to that importance.

Last, but not least, *service support processes* are described in Appendix C. The presentation orients itself along the categories of the Information Technology Infrastructure Library (ITIL), an industry standard of processes of how one operates IT systems properly. Good operation is very important for high availability and disaster recovery – all excellent implementation strategies and work will not help, if failures get introduced during maintenance operations. This appendix presents those parts of the ITIL processes that are especially relevant.

1.3 Real-World Examples

Before we start with business issues and elementary concepts in Chap. 2, let us entertain ourselves with some "war stories" of real-world IT problems and set the tone of issues we strive to avoid in our own installations.

Example 1 (Deferred overdue upgrade of legacy system). Over the 2004 Christmas holidays, Comair – a regional subsidiary of Delta Air Lines – needed to reschedule a lot of flights owing to severe winter storms. Reportedly, the aging crew management system software could not handle more than 32 000 changes per month. (Without knowing the cause exactly, let us assume that the real limit was $32 767 \pm 1...$) When this limit was exceeded for the first time, the whole system crashed on December 24 and return to full operations took until December 29.

This IT crash caused cancellations or delays of roughly 3900 flights and stranded nearly 200 000 passengers. The costs for Comair and its parent company, Delta Air Lines, were estimated to be in the $20 million ballpark, not counting the damaged reputation and subsequent investigation by the US Department of Transportation.

The reasons sound familiar to everybody who works in IT departments of large companies these days: Y2K, 9/11 fallout for aerospace companies, company acquisition by Delta, and a very tight lid on IT expenses brought enough workload for the IT department. The technical staff knew about the problem and management did not believe them. Replacing a supposedly working legacy system did not have high priority, and risk management was not prudent enough. Actually, the real issue was that they had no contingency plan for outages of that mission-critical system, and no means to create a quick workaround for the incident.   ∎

Example 2 (Network outage for a whole company). Flaky connections between network switches caused redundancy configurations to fail, turning the whole network unfunctional and thus almost all IT systems of a big manufacturing company unusable. Luckily, the actual manufacturing operation was not impaired, as the IT systems deployed there had their own separate network and were able to operate for several hours without connectivity to the company network.

The network used redundant lines between switches and relied on the Spanning Tree Protocol (STP) to create a loop-free topology that is needed for network operations. The flaky lines resulted in continuous recalculations of the minimum spanning tree, overloading the switch CPUs at one point. Owing to problems in the switches' operating system, a loop was formed and this error situation propagated to all other network devices, rendering them all unfunctional.

Before that case happened, there were anecdotal reports about problems with STP, but no real hard data about its reliability was available. Therefore this redundant architecture was chosen, not knowing that it does not scale well enough for big installations. Even though the network staff were able to remedy the deficiency quickly, a complete reimplementation of the network architecture had to be done later on. This raised the incident costs even more, beyond the actual damages that were caused by the nonreachability of all servers.

This is an example case of a technology that was not robust enough for the creation of highly available infrastructure designs. Only experience would have prevented such a design; the importance of experience is discussed in more detail in Chap. 3. ∎

Example 3 (Propagation of human error during upgrade). Even in situations where lots of effort was spent to create architectures that survive failures, there is always the last resort for error causes: our colleagues. A hierarchical storage management (HSM) environment implemented both the usual high availability and also intended disaster-recovery protection by placing backup tapes at a remote location, and running the HSM system as a metro cluster. This means that two HSM systems were placed at two different sites, with a high-speed network connection. Each system has a complete set of all data, on a tape library that is connected to it.

Upgrading a tape library and exchanging all backup tapes for new high-capacity tapes caused the complete erasure of all existing tapes. What happened is that cables got exchanged between two tape drives. Formatting of the new tapes was started in one drive. The exchanged cables only controlled the data transfer (write and read) commands; the load commands were transferred over another cable that was connected correctly. Since an HSM tape library is active all the time, new read or write requests led to loading of tapes into the wrong drive, where they were dutifully formatted. At the same time, all data access commands returned errors since they tried to access the new unformatted tapes; but some time was needed to detect this. In that time span, most of the tapes had already been reformatted.

By all accounts, this could be classified as human error and as software error. Of course, the cable should not have been exchanged. But such errors are so common that good software would take them into account and would not reformat tapes that are formatted already and which have data on them, without being told explicitly to do so.

Single point of failure analysis, as explained in Chap. 3, would have helped to prevent that failure.   ∎

Example 4 (Failover cluster rendered useless). A large business-important file server, with several terabytes of data, had a file system corruption that led to whole system aborts (colloquially called "system panic"). This file server was a highly available failover cluster system with two nodes; file system errors caused the file service to switch to another cluster node. The file system itself switches too, the error is not noticed during service initialization, and after a few minutes the new node panics again. The service switches continuously between the two cluster nodes.

Even though the switch ping-pong was noticed early, analysis of the problem needed a while. Then the decision had to be made to restore the whole file system. Such a decision could not be made by system administrators, as it leads to several hours of downtime. Instead the decision had to be escalated to senior IT management. After some time, it was decided to restore the system from backup tapes, and this was done.

In total, a downtime of 10 h occurred for that business-important service. Since 1000 office workers used that service and needed that service for their work, this lead to roughly 10 000 lost working hours, which is quite a feat. As a follow-up activity, proper disaster recovery for that service was established, to prevent such long outages in the future.

What happened here is that the marketing hype that high-availability clusters provide round-the-clock availability was believed. Even though the architects knew that there were still single points of failure – not least the files that exist only once in the cluster – management did not allocate enough money to protect against those failures. Only after a disaster happened, fault protection against data corruption was established.

Proper single point of failure analysis, as explained in Chap. 3, would have detected that design flaw. Chapter 6 details more limitations of traditional failover clusters.   ∎

Example 5 (System errors in SAP installation). Many medium-sized and large companies use SAP as their enterprise resource planning (ERP) system. Their whole financial and human resources departments depend on the functionality of those systems: purchasing, invoicing, inventory management, and other areas do not work without them. In addition, all financial planning data is kept in those systems; storing such data is subject to many regulatory requirements.

For a medium-sized business, implementation of a high-availability infrastructure for the SAP server was deemed too complex and too expensive. The system vendor sold a "4-h service contract" and management thought that this is sufficient outsourcing to mitigate outage risks.

After a hardware outage and subsequent database crash, it needed three business days to get a new system in place and up again. One had overlooked that the "4-h" time limit was about vendor reaction time, not about time to repair. Having all financial data not available for 3 days clearly did not satisfy business expectations. Luckily, postponing invoice creation for 3 days did not harm the company much.   ■

Example 6 (SAP installation that works). Owing to their importance for business finance, SAP installations are an area where cautious business owners spend money; therefore, they make up not only good examples for outages, but also for well-established and thoroughly engineered solutions that deliver high availability.

Outsourcing companies like EDS operate hundreds of SAP installations in a standardized manner and deliver highly available services for many companies' financial and human resources departments. They do so by using standardized templates for planning, implementation, installation, and operations. Up times of these services are measured in months or even years, and outages are in the small minute ranges.

Such design, implementation, and operation templates combine a multitude of methods that range from proper vendor selection, choosing the right hardware combination, using cluster technology to provide redundant solutions, and – almost most important of all – defining proper change and problem processes to keep the solution highly available over their lifetime.   ■

Example 7 (Disaster recovery for a snowstorm). On March 13, 1993, a data center in New Jersey became a casualty of the blizzard that was later dubbed "the worst storm of the century." A section of the roof collapsed under the weight of the snow and buckled the walls. Fortunately, nobody died and the operational staff were able to perform a controlled shutdown of all systems, and all employees were evacuated.

The outage of this site concerned 5200 automated teller machines (ATM), 6% of the ATMs nationwide. Execution of the disaster recovery plan was started immediately; that called for the creation of an alternative site and relocation of service to that place. First, a temporary data recovery facility with restricted functionality and performance was made operational; within 48 h relocation to a new permanent site had been done. In the meantime, prearrangements with dozens of regional ATM networks kicked in. These networks performed stand-in processing until IT systems and the network were up and running again.   ■

Examples Summary

Let us have a look at the examples with unnecessary outage problems, where we list the root causes for each one. One thing is clear from the outset: a recurring root cause is that there was a single point of failure, i.e., not enough redundancy in the implemented solution, or that redundancy was intended but was designed or implemented the wrong way.

Root cause	Example 1	2	3	4	5
Single point of failure			×	×	×
System used beyond design limits	×	×			
Software error			×		×
Human error				×	
Wrong design assumptions					×

Two other failure causes were close runners-up: that a system is used beyond the limits that it was designed for, and that software errors occur that make all other fault protection methods moot. In fact, many other examples show that human errors also cause major outages quite often; again and again Murphy's Law is proved true. Analysis of more outage examples brings into focus that we find the same fault causes again and again – and that is no coincidence. While there are many details that can go wrong, the basic reasons do not vary so much. Experience shows that the five reasons from the table are representative for a good part of many problems that we know about.

2

Elementary Concepts

The introductory examples set the stage for this book. This chapter shall give us the first course of our meal. It will introduce the most elementary terms and concepts that we need throughout the book. It is intended to set up a vocabulary that we can use, e.g., it defines *high availability* and *disaster recovery*. In addition, it explains principal problem categories and solution approaches.

This is done in the following order:

- **Business issues** are failure consequences, overall goals, and risk management; all of them are presented in Sect. 2.1.
- **System and outage categorization** and particularly the notion of minor and major outages are introduced in Sect. 2.2.
- **High availability** is defined in Sect. 2.3; definitions for other related terms (availability, reliability, and serviceability) are also introduced.
- **Disaster recovery** is defined in Sect. 2.4.
- **Methods to quantify availability** are presented in Sect. 2.5, and their problems as well.
- **Service level agreements** (SLAs) are the topic of Sect. 2.6; we concentrate on the technical stipulations that should be included in them.
- **Robustness and redundancy** are our basic approach that we use all throughout the book; they are introduced in Sect. 2.7.
- **Layered solutions** use this basic approach several times and establish multiple precautions against failures, as explained in Sect. 2.8.

This chapter has content for all reader groups, from executives and business owners, to project managers and architects, to system administrators. The basics are needed by all of them, otherwise communication about high-availability and disaster-recovery projects become impossible.

2.1 Business Issues

The need to protect against outage consequences seems obvious, but we should not take it for granted. Instead, we must be able to communicate the business needs that lead to the need for highly available systems and disaster recovery. For that, we need a structured view of the business consequences of outages. Only with money-associated references will we be able to justify the expense for fault protection.

For a business, an IT outage is not the real issue, but the consequences that are associated with it are. As Fig. 2.1 shows, IT outages affect either revenues or costs and we either can determine the effect directly or we can estimate it. Since costs are more easily determined and quantified than revenue effects, let us start with them.

Direct costs are associated with repair of IT defects, needed to continue IT operations. Devices need to be repaired, shipping has to be paid for, external consultants might be needed, etc.

  Other direct costs are contract penalties that have to be paid if an IT outage causes a delay in delivery of a service, beyond a contractual obligation.

Additional work hours are indirect costs that are attributed to any incident. IT staff will put work into remedying any IT problems, and that work has to be paid for by the company, in the end, by sales. Instead, improvements to IT services could be worked upon.

  But please do not make the error of considering *any* work that is done in incident and problem management as additional work. There is a base amount of work that has to be done in these areas in any case.

  Of course, IT outages may result in additional work hours in other areas of our company as well. Our delivery staff might need additional work hours if the inventory system is down. Our office workers will put up with evening work to get the work done that they could not do when they were not able to access any files, addresses, or emails during normal working hours. We can find examples for almost any branch of our company, as almost all business processes depend on some IT processes nowadays.

	Known	**Estimated**
Revenue	Lost revenue	Lost work hours
Cost	Direct costs	Additional work hours

Fig. 2.1. Business consequences of outages

Lost work hours are indirect indicators for lost revenue. When 1000 office workers cannot work for 2 h because some server is down, or when goods cannot be delivered, the sales that could have been made in that time span might be lost forever. After all, these thousands of work hours were good for some revenue, weren't they?

Lost revenue may also be directly attributed to an IT outage. This is the most important business consequence, but it is the hardest to measure directly. It is possible to estimate it though. If our point of sales systems is down, or if our company sells goods or services on the Internet, any outage in these systems will cause customers to go to competitors whose systems are still working. In the long term, many customer-visible system outages will damage our reputation and will result in loss of clients.

In the end, it is easier to specify costs than lost revenues as outage consequences. Costs can be identified and counted; lost revenues can only be estimated. Many experts try to make this up by taking lost work hours as a replacement for lost revenues. Do not make this error yourself – quite often, having no access to an IT service does not mean that the office staff cannot work at all. Instead, they will do different work. Similarly, the outage of a manufacturing line directly translates to lost revenue when the line runs at full capacity. But when there is still reserve capacity, the item will be manufactured and sold later instead. There will still be lost revenue, but it cannot be equated to full production capacity and can therefore only be estimated.

Of course, this also depends on the type of work. Call-center agents or CAD designers cannot work without their IT systems; in case of longer outages one might need to send them home. But these are occurring costs, and not revenues. In the end, the metric of lost work hours is important and interesting in its own right, but it is not *identical* to lost revenues, it just provides input for an estimation.

IT staff costs for outages are exaggerated sometimes, especially when all IT staff working hours are summed up as the cost of an incident. That is partly the job of these staff members, after all. But if the IT staff spend most of their time on sustainment work rather than on improving the IT services to create new business value for the company, it might be time to rethink our approach to implementation and operations. Many large companies report that 70% of their IT staff work goes into sustainment, and only 30% into development of new services – maybe it is time to consider some of that 70% that has gone into incident and problem management as additional costs that should be saved by better up-front work.

Do not kid yourself, this is not easy. As a colleague of mine recently mentioned, "Highly available solutions are easy to set up, but difficult to run over a long time." Properly done, one needs to design maintainability into the solution, and that costs additional setup money, i.e., one needs to spend short-term money to save more in the midterm or long term. And as long as middle or upper management demands tighter IT budgets now and caps IT investments, we will have to report multi-million-dollar damages like the Comair disaster that was mentioned at the start of this book, and we will have a vast amount of sustainment work not only for legacy installations, but also for new systems that were not done right.

For a full leverage of the solutions and tools that are presented in this book, one needs to establish an enterprise-class IT service. They are readily realized in data centers of larger companies where the availability demands are highest, potential losses are greatest, and the gain from availability improvements is best. But small and medium-sized businesses can utilize the same concepts, on their own system. Most of the technology can implemented in the server room of a small company as well as in a big data center.

Knowledge of solutions and technology for high availability and disaster recovery is also very valuable when one goes shopping for an IT outsourcer. Then it is a requirement for our ability to negotiate good contracts: it enables us to judge the proposals and proposed services properly.

2.1.1 Business Continuity as the Overall Goal

Most of the time, this book is about architectures and technology to achieve continuous operation in spite of IT outages. We must not forget that IT operations are a means to an end, and the actual objectives are something different. In the end, we need to support *business continuity*. Our whole business processes, not just the IT ones, must be anticipatory, adaptive, and robust in the face of ever-occurring problems. For this, business continuity is not just an aim, but instead becomes a tool that focuses on business processes and works on steady process improvements.

IT has to deliver its share of those improvements. As far as business processes depend on IT services, we have to manage their *IT service continuity*. As far as business processes do not utilize IT services, we have to check if we can improve their performance, their robustness, or their costs with IT support – again supplying IT service continuity for these new services as well. This way we are able to manage both risks and opportunities. We can maintain continuous business operations and enable growth.

Therefore, IT service continuity is the objective to work towards the goal of business continuity, and high availability and disaster recovery are two means to fulfill that objective.

2.1.2 Regulatory Compliance and Risk Management

The need for business continuity is not only justified on finance grounds. Companies must comply with legal regulations; multinational companies or companies serving multinational markets have to comply with several regulations from all over the world.

Most prominently, these are regulations for publicly traded companies, like the Sarbanes-Oxley Act (SOX) in the USA, or Basel II in Europe. There are other long-standing regulations, about workplace safety, environmental issues, and security exchange regulations; regulations for specific markets, like medical services and pharmacy and chemical products are also well known.

The need for compliance is not only created by public laws, but also by business partners. For example, in Europe Basel II is actually only binding for a few large businesses, in particular for banks. These large companies pass on the consequences of the regulations to their business associates. Banks demand Basel II compliance for good credit ratings; therefore, many more companies have to comply than the law itself requires.

Most compliance demands have two things in common: they demand that some behavior is followed and documented, and that risk is managed proactively. Risk management of business processes focuses on financial operations first, but IT services are not far behind owing to their importance for most business processes. Ensuring availability of IT services, both short and long term, is therefore important for regulatory compliance as well.

Well-run IT shops have realized this already, and have taken proactive steps to have well-documented processes for their service delivery and management. Beyond a single company's processes, the IT Infrastructure Library (ITIL) provides a framework that deals with the matter at hand, with processes for *availability management* and *continuity management*; these processes are the base for the following chapters. Other ITIL areas cover processes for proper operation of IT services, i.e., for service management, and will be presented in Appendix C.

2.2 System and Outage Categorization

The importance of IT services and IT systems is directly related to their business relevance. It depends on the revenue, which depends on their functionality, or on the amount of damage in case of an outage, or if there are regulations that demand their functionality. Since the importance of service varies a lot, the importance of their failures and service outage are quite different too. For planning and communication with different stakeholders – like management, clients, technicians, and others – the categorization of Table 2.1 on the following page has proven valuable. More fine-grained categorization is actually seldom needed; such categorization is overdesigned and not maintainable in usual business environments.

Table 2.1. System and outage categories. This book focuses on the *gray cells*

Category	Max. minor outage	Max. major outage
Continuous availability	1 min	2 h
Mission-critical	10 min	8 h
Business-important	1 business hour	3 days
Business-foundation	1 business day	1 week
Business-edge	> 1 week	> 1 month

For each system, we have to answer five key questions:

1. What failures should be handled transparently, where an outage must not occur? Against such failures we need *fault protection*.
2. How long may a short-term interruption be that happens once a day, once a week, or once a month? Such interruptions are called *minor outages*.
3. How long may a long-term interruption be that happens very seldom and is related to serious damage to the IT system? For instance, when will this cause a *big* business impact, also called a *major outage* or *disaster*?
4. How much data may be lost during a major outage?
5. What failures are deemed so improbable that they will not be handled, or what failures are beyond the scope of a project?

This book is concerned with solutions for the categories mission-critical, business-important, and business-foundation. Continuous availability is covered only in passing, and we look at the business edge only for disaster recovery. The former would need a book of its own, and the latter is not connected to high availability.

▸ *Fault Protection*

The first question asks for errors that must not be noticed by end users. Fault protection is the method use so that component failures do not lead to service outages at all. It provides continuous operation of a service in spite of those failure scenarios.

Only for a few components is fault protection available at reasonable rates. These are mostly hardware components, e.g., disk drives, power supplies, and I/O cards. This category is important nevertheless, as failures in those components happen often enough to make fault protection a standard solution.

For other components, especially for software, fault protection is very expensive and is used only in designs for continuous availability; we will come back to that later.

▸ *Minor Outages*

The second question intends to establish requirements for minor outages. We should not take the simple road and answer with the time span how long it takes until users cannot work anymore. Instead, we ask about the point where damage to our business is significant. Frankly, there are situations where some users not working is not identical to significant business damage – and small losses are not enough to justify the effort to establish a high-availability solution.

In this book, we are not interested in all kinds of minor outages for all kind of systems. Table 2.1 on the preceding page emphasizes our focus with a gray background – we are neither interested in continuous availability with its extremely high demands (more on that later) nor are we interested in the business edge where systems are just repaired, but no precautions are necessary to assure availability.

In fact, the techniques that are presented in this book are often not even necessary for outages in the business-foundation category. For many systems in that category, one can recover from an outage by having a support contract that assures repair of the system in the given time frame and this is not the type of technology presented in this book. But there are business-foundation systems that cannot be recovered in the given time period by repair actions alone; and then we need the high availability methods and technology.

▸ *Major Outages*

The third question intends to establish requirements for major outages. It anticipates the definition of *disaster* that we will flesh out in Sect. 2.4 on p. 26 and in Chap. 10. In this book, every major outage is a disaster, and not only a catastrophe in the physical environment, like a hurricane, a fire, or a bomb. Instead it is defined by the business-related damage that an event inflicts and where disaster-recovery actions are necessary to recover from it. After all, if some administrator deletes all our data, this human error *is* a disaster for our company. And then we need a prepared plan to handle this disaster, just like we need it after a hurricane.

The fourth question is only concerned with data loss in the disaster case. We assume that business data exists "in flight" and in a finalized form. That is, business data is acquired during a business process and entered into an IT system. As long as the process is not finished, the data is in an ephemeral state and there is no great business damage if the process is aborted and the data must be entered anew. When the process has been finished, the data is persistent and then they must not be lost because the user would not know that the process must be repeated.

Of course, there is more to it than just aborts of end-user sessions. When some batch processing of data is aborted in the midst of a long run, the application must be able to handle that and restart the processing. This must be done without repeating already finished actions, and no pending action must be forgotten. If we think about financial transactions, the objective behind such demands becomes obvious.

It is no coincidence that this concurs with the transaction principle that underlies most commercial IT applications and that is supported by many applications and middleware software products: a persistent state is important, an ephemeral state can be thrown away if necessary.

That end-user dialogs may be aborted without too much harm is a common-case assumption that might not be true in all circumstances. If we design a very busy business-to-customer Internet commerce site, aborting the goods collection and order process for thousands of potential customers might create relevant business damage as well, as many of those customers will cancel the order completely and will not come back owing to sheer frustration with our system. This example case shows that we have to think for ourselves about the constraints we use for minor and major outages for our use cases, and what consequences these outages will have.

▶ *Out of Scope*

The fifth question acknowledges that all IT services are designed and implemented in a business context. A risk analysis for some failure scenarios may decide that these failures shall not be handled, e.g., because these scenarios cause other failures that make the IT services not needed anymore. Or IT development plans or budget concerns may call for a project that realizes protection against some failure scenarios now and will look at the other scenarios later.

Actually, the latter is often the case: it is common to have a project establish protection against minor outages first and disregard major outage handling, which will be tackled in a later project. For the first project, all failure scenarios that lead to major outages will be out of scope – even though they are not from the business point of view, they will just be handled later.

The problem with this category is that it is much too often neglected and ignored. There are failure scenarios like fire at the same time in both primary and backup data centers – it is sensible to ignore them because risk mitigation would be too expensive. But we cannot lump all out-of-scope failure scenarios in this "obvious" category. Some decisions about failure scenarios must be made consciously, e.g., about protection against sabotage – is this out of scope, is this so seldom and improbable that it may lead to a major outage, or must this only lead to a minor outage?

It is not realistic to assume that one gets a 100% solution that either protects against or recovers from all failures. Economically, the quest for such a solution does not make sense, and also it is not possible – what about the failure scenario when all systems, including all backup systems at all remote locations, have outages at the same time? If we add another set of backup systems, what happens if they have the same outage at the same time? In the end, it boils down to our having to analyze carefully the risks for our IT services and IT environment and creating a good mitigation strategy, accepting existing residual risks.

Fine Points of Categorization

We do not need precise answers for our questions. To say that one system can be out of order for 2 h, and another for 3 h, is overspecification and is not of much practical use. Either one can take the thresholds from Table 2.1 on p. 18 or one chooses one's own thresholds.

Still, there are a few fine points in that table that need further elaboration.

- First of all, the outage times are per incident. For minor outage requirements, we will need additional values that will be discussed in Sect. 2.5 – these additional values will spell out the allowed cumulated outage times over a certain time span, e.g., over a month or a year.
- It must be emphasized that these are maximum outage times. This means that they are limits for the respective category. For example, the entries in that table demand that major outages for mission critical systems *must not* last longer than 3 days. Everything above 10 min is considered a major outage.
- The time spans are not just absolute times, they take into account if something happens during or outside business hours. Very few of our IT systems need to run all the time; often we were able to specify business hours where availability requirements are much more stringent than for the wee hours.
- There are two ways to approach this table. One might have a vague notion that some systems are very important, more important, or less important for one's company. *Analysis* of the situation helps to associate outage limits with that intuitive categorization. On the other hand, one might have several SLAs already that name such limits, then the table helps to *define* good categories.

Continuous Availability

Continuous operation is the ability of a system to provide nonstop, uninterrupted service to its users. *Continuous availability* is a special subset of high availability that combines it with continuous operation. The system must not have outages and service delivery must be ongoing, without interruptions.

This goal is very hard to achieve, as computer components – be they hardware or software – are neither error-free nor maintenance-free; therefore a system that needs continuous availability has to be *fault-tolerant*. Fault tolerance is often available for hardware components, but very seldom for software. It means that a failure does not become visible to the user, but is covered by internal protection mechanisms.

In addition, the need to realize maintenance activities in a running system is another differentiator between continuous availability and other categories of high availability. In such installations, one has to cope with installations that run multiple versions of the same software at the same time and get updated in phases.

Continuous availability concentrates on protection against failures, and discards user-visible recovery from failures as not acceptable. It is very rarely needed. In most situations, user sessions can be aborted and repeated without harm to the business or to people. Only in special application areas like airplane fly-by-wire controllers or nuclear reactor monitoring do we find the need for it; therefore, methods to achieve continuous availability will not be covered in this book, as we are concerned with classic enterprise applications.

But since this book is about high availability and disaster recovery, it is time to be more precise with our terms. What do they mean after all?

2.3 High Availability – Handling Minor Outages

High availability is one of those terms that everybody seems to know what it is but for which it is hard to find a widely accepted and precise definition. For the realm of this book, we use the following:

> **High availability is the characteristic of a system to
> protect against or recover from minor outages in a short
> time frame with largely automated means.**

It does not matter if the failures that cause minor outages are in the systems themselves, or in the environment, or are the result of human errors. In the case of such a failure, highly available systems have the option to abort current sessions, i.e., the user will notice the failure. But they are expected to make the service available again, in a short time frame.

It is important that our definition of high availability brings together three factors that must all be considered before we can speak of high availability:

1. **Outage categorization:** This is a precondition that tells us if we are in that problem and solution domain at all. We need to know potential failure scenarios for a service and the minor outage requirements for them. Only then can we start to talk about high availability.

2. **System categorization:** That tells us about requirements for maximum outage times. Only when those times are short do we speak of high availability. When a system can be down for a whole week, high availability is not involved. Typical high-availability system categories have a gray background in Table 2.1 on p. 18.

3. **Automated protection or recovery:** Technology and solution approaches also have an influence if we need high availability. The same requirement may be resolved for two different services in two different ways: one needs high-availability technology, the other does not. We will expand on this point below.

Minor outages have in common that one component or only a few components have failed and that these specific components are not essential to deliver the service – they are by design not a *single point of failure*. Most often, being nonessential is achieved by introducing redundancy for these components, by supplying several instances of the same component where one can fail and the other continues to operate. High-availability design ensures that as few resources as possible are necessary as single component instances.

We need to differentiate generic high availability from continuous availability which implies nonstop, uninterrupted service, as explained in the previous section. Continuous availability is a subset of high availability where every component failure is protected against, and no after-failure recovery takes place. As such, it is at the high end of a range that is described as high availability. But in reality, continuous availability is needed very, very seldom and is implemented even more seldom. This special system category therefore is not prominent in this book. While fault protection will be covered where it is mature and wide-spread technology, we will focus on fault recovery most of the time.

It was mentioned already that technology matters, that should be elaborated. Let us assume that we have a service that belongs to the business foundation and where the minor outage requirement is at maximum eight business hours per year. Often we can add the night for repairs, then there are plenty of services that can be restored on a spare machine from backup and where the service is soon available again. This would fulfill the requirements of outage and system categorization, but is not commonly regarded as high availability. To capture that understanding, we introduced the demand that recovery must be done by automated means, without or with little manual intervention.

On the other hand, the same requirement for a different service might need a different solution. When our data is so large that it cannot be restored until the next business day, we need to take precautions that the data is replicated in an automated way and also made available again in an automated way. Disk mirroring is a typical precaution for that. Or that recovery on the spare system is not done by manual backup but by automated procedures. With such solutions in place we already start to speak about high availability, though with restricted functionality.

Therefore the realm of high availability cannot be described more precisely. There is no undisputed availability limit where we can start to speak of a high-availability system. Also, there is no undisputed limit where one has to start using the approaches that are presented in this book. Nevertheless, it has to be said that usually high availability means availability numbers of 99.9%, measured yearly, and upwards.

Section 2.5 has more to say about availability measurements. But before we handle the measurement, we should consider the definition of *availability*. We will also look at definitions of the related terms *reliability* and *serviceability*. Together, they make up the acronym RAS that is used to describe the quality of IT systems. Reliability and serviceability contribute towards higher availability of a system.

Please note that there are several definitions of reliability and serviceability – we use one which best fits the purpose of this book.

2.3.1 Availability

Availability is the measure of how often or how long a service or a system component is available for use. Outage of a component is relevant for service availability if that component is needed to provide the service. For example, for a network service, outage of the sole network interface card terminates the availability, whereas for a local service on the computer it does not.

Availability also means features which help the system to stay operational even if failures occur. For example, mirroring of disks improves availability.

The base availability measurement is the ratio of uptime to total elapsed time:

$$\text{availability} = \frac{\text{uptime}}{\text{uptime} + \text{downtime}}.$$

The elapsed time includes scheduled as well as unscheduled downtime. A somewhat subtle point is if the elapsed time is meant as wall-clock time or service time (cf., Fig. 2.3 on p. 30). Both definitions are useful, but we need to be precise when we use the term. We use the wall-clock time, which is best for highly available systems. It has the effect that regular, preventive maintenance activities decrease availability.

The same availability can be expressed in absolute numbers (239 of 240 h last month) or as a percentage (99.6% last month); Section 2.5 on p. 29 presents quantification of availability in detail. It can also be expressed in user-related terms where the time span is multiplied with the number of users. For example, with our examples and 1000 users of this system, this would be "239 000 of 240 000 work hours" – which gives a better indication about the seriousness of that 1-h downtime.

This is the actual availability of a system that can be measured for its existence. For identical systems, experience with old systems can be reused as a planning guide. Otherwise, if one knows the *mean time between failures* (MTBF) and the *mean time to repair* (MTTR), one can express planned or expected availability as

$$\text{availability} = \frac{\text{MTBF}}{\text{MTBF} + \text{MTTR}}.$$

This formula also shows clearly how one can influence availability most easily: decrease the MTTR. Shortening the repair time to one tenth has the same effect as a tenfold increase in the MTBF:

$$\frac{10 \times \text{MTBF}}{10 \times \text{MTBF} + \text{MTTR}} = \frac{\text{MTBF}}{\text{MTBF} + \text{MTTR}/10}.$$

But it is usually much more expensive, sometimes impossible, to increase the MTBF by such high factors, whereas repair time can be improved by better processes, spare parts on site, etc.

2.3.2 Reliability

Reliability is a measurement of fault avoidance. It is the *probability* that a system is still working at time $t + 1$ when it worked at time t. A similar definition is the probability that a system will be available over a time interval T.

Reliability does not measure planned or unplanned downtimes; MTTR values do not influence reliability.

Reliability is often expressed as the MTBF. Make yourself aware that this is statistics, the science of big numbers. To really use the statistics, one needs to have a statistical sample. When we run thousands of disks, the MTBF for one disk becomes meaningful. But for computer systems, the MTBF has only a restricted value: you want to know the reliability of *your system*, not of a class of systems. Appendix A addresses reliability in detail.

Reliability features help to *prevent* and *detect* failures. The latter is very important, even if it is often ignored. The worst behavior of a system is to continue after a failure and create wrong results or corrupt data!

2.3.3 Serviceability

Serviceability is a measurement that expresses how easily a system is serviced or repaired. For example, a system with modular, hot-swappable components would have a good level of serviceability. (But note that implementing hot-swappable components contributes to all three qualities, not just serviceability.)

It can be expressed as the inverse amount of maintenance time and number of crashes over the complete life span of a system. For example, 1.5-h service in 720-h elapsed time (720 h is roughly 1 month). As such, it formulates how much sustainment work must be put into a system and how long one needs to get it up when it has crashed. Like availability, there are two measurements that are of interest: planned and actual serviceability.

Planned serviceability is a requirement that goes into the architecture as a design objective. A good architect will take Murphy's Law into account and use technology to make the actual serviceability much lower than the planned serviceability. For example, the planned serviceability of the same system might be 9-h planned service in 720-h elapsed time (i.e., around 2-h planned service time per week).

Good serviceability is directly coupled to good patch and deployment management. When upgrade processes and procedures are well thought out and do not need much manual intervention, we will have a lower planned service time and thus higher serviceability. Especially patch management has recently been given the attention that it deserved for a long time and is now commonly seen as an important activity as part of one's release management process.

Serviceability features help to identify failure causes, system diagnosis to detect problems before failures occur, simplify repair activities, and speed them up. A call-home feature and hot-swappable components are examples of serviceability features. Good serviceability increases both availability and reliability.

2.4 Disaster Recovery – Handling Major Outages

Disaster recovery is even harder to define than high availability. Traditionally, disaster recovery describes the process to survive catastrophes in the physical environment: fires, floods, hurricanes, earthquakes, terrorist attacks. While this is for good journalistic stories, it is not sufficient for IT planning because it does not cover all failure scenarios that describe severe damage to a company's business.

Therefore, current publications often emphasize the term *service continuity* and use that for coverage of all kinds of outages. In this book, disaster recovery is still used, but with an enhanced meaning that covers complete service continuity beyond high availability.

> **Disaster recovery is the ability to continue with services in the case of major outages, often with reduced capabilities or performance. Disaster-recovery solutions typically involve manual activities.**

Disaster recovery handles the disaster when either a single point of failure is the defect or when many components are damaged and the whole system is rendered unfunctional. Like high availability, it needs outage and system categorization as preconditions to describe the problem domain that it covers.

It handles the case when operations cannot be resumed on the same system or at the same site. Instead, a replacement or backup system is activated and operations continue from there. This backup system may be on the same site as the primary system, but is usually located at another place. Since this is the reaction to a major outage which is expected to happen seldom, disaster recovery often restores only restricted resources, and thus restricted service levels, to save money. Continuation of service also does not happen instantly, but will happen after some outage time, even in the restricted form. Full functionality is restored only later on in the process.

This book considers *major outage* and *disaster* as synonyms, i.e., they are the same in our context. But the definition of what constitutes a major outage or a disaster is obviously highly context dependent, with lots of gray areas. While destruction of a data center by an earthquake is clearly a disaster in the eyes of everybody, deletion of data by system administrators is a disaster for most companies, and system outages of a few hours may be a disaster for manufacturing companies when production depends on them. On the other hand, many clerical tasks can survive quite a few hours without computers. This is just as well, as disaster recovery is not a one-size-fits-all product either. Since different businesses have different notions of what a disaster is, recovery processes must be adapted as well.

Therefore, for each IT system, we need to define the situation of a disaster. For that, we utilize the system and outage categorization from Sect. 2.2 on p. 17 and introduce means to measure and describe the impact of major outages. The classification of major outage and associated data loss is used to describe the objectives of disaster recovery and these are so important that they have their own acronyms:

Recovery time objective (RTO): The time needed until the service is usable again after a major outage.

Recovery point objective (RPO): The point in time from which data will be restored to be usable. In disaster cases, often some part of work is lost.

But please note that we should use these acronyms only in the context of disaster recovery.[1]

Table 2.2 on the following page repeats the maximum times for major outages and associates them with the maximum data loss in that outage

---

[1] In particular, outside of disaster recovery, RTO most often refers to the Retransmit Timeout Interval (an essential part of TCP).

Table 2.2. Major outages and data loss

Category	Recovery time objective (max. outage)	Recovery point objective (max. data loss)
Mission-critical	8 h	2 h
Business-important	3 days	1 day
Business-foundation	1 week	1 day
Business-edge	> 1 month	1 week

category. As with the outage time, the important message of this table is not the actual values – they might differ from company to company, according to sensible business objectives. But one thing remains: we do not determine these numbers for every application and every IT service anew. We create sensible categories for our company, and then put IT services into these outage categories. This helps to select solution patterns for high availability and disaster recovery that may be reused for several IT services, where project synergies are put into place.

Declaring a disaster and migrating to the backup system has grave consequences. This is an expensive and sometimes risky operation, and migrating back to the primary system will be expensive again. Data loss might happen, in the realm of our RPO. Therefore one has to be very cautious about disaster declaration and triggering disaster recovery.

While high availability has a strong emphasis on automated protection and recovery procedures, disaster recovery takes a different approach. Here we face very uncertain and unusual circumstances and have to handle a wide variety of failures that happen seldom – if this were not the case, we would not have major outages. In such cases, it is better to rely on human intelligence and good processes. The processes provide guidance so that one does not forget actions, but the actions are done by IT staff that have the flexibility to react manually to uncommon situations. That is, disaster recovery gives room for "that's strange – let's check it first" situations, by design.

Disaster recovery is always associated with a bigger risk than high-availability precautions. It is rarely utilized, and is usually tested infrequently. That is not because it is not needed, but because the effort is not made since major outages happen so seldom. While the damage is often high, the probability is very low. Owing to the reduced testing, nonnegligible chances exist that some problems might occur during migration to the backup system. Proper preparation ensures that these are only minor issues that our IT staff will be able to handle on the fly, but nevertheless one must not ignore the inherent risks.

2.5 Quantifying Availability: 99.9...% and Reality

Another way to quantify the importance of our systems, and to characterize them, is *availability percentages*. This quantification appears in many contracts or outsourcing offerings, i.e., a WWW server hoster may promise 99.9% availability in its marketing material.

In contracts, such numbers are most often listed in the section *Service Level Agreement* (SLA). We will learn more about them in Sect. 2.6.

Such percentage quantifications are easy to write down and appear to condense the whole complexity into one single number. It also makes for great catchphrases, such as one can talk about "three nines" (99.9%), "four nines" (99.99%), and "five nines" (99.999%), each denoting higher availability classifications. Easy, isn't it? And in fact, it is really a good communication method – especially in executive summaries – but only if we use this single number during planning with very great care.

As the saying goes, the devil is in the small print. Always when one hears somebody talking of "percentages," one needs to ask "of what?" In theory, this percentage value is expressed over the whole time, 24 h a day, 365 days a year. This mode of continuous operation is commonly called 24×7: here, $n \times m$ means n hours of operations per day, and m days per week. Now we can determine combined maximum outage times over operational prime hours, and we can summarize them per month or per year.

When we negotiate SLAs, we should strive for absolute numbers in them. For all contract partners, it is clear what a summarized maximum of n minutes per month or x business hours per year means, whereas percentages must be translated first by each contract partner into such numbers, and different translations can lead to misunderstandings. We have to give absolute numbers anyhow in other parts of the SLA, e.g., in the specification of a maximum incident duration – then we can unify the way availability requirements in SLAs are done.

Table 2.3 on the next page does just so and illustrates different outage times for the same percentage value, differentiated by measurement intervals. The table also has four columns for the common situation where we can afford service times, i.e., do not work on weekends, or just have to support usual office hours (at maximum, from 06:00 to 20:00).

The numbers that are important for practical agreements are emphasized by a gray background. For example, round-the-clock operations for an Internet commerce site and a 99.99% yearly 24×7 SLA equates to a maximum outage of almost 1 h, which is reasonable if we do not plan eBay operations. Another possibility might by 99.8% with monthly measurement (i.e., 1.5-h downtime), whereas a 99.8% SLA with yearly measurement means 0.75 days of maximum total downtime, which might be too much.

Table 2.3. Maximum outage times as interpretation of availability percentages for different service level agreement (SLA) measurement scenarios. An additional 1 day per week outage time may be added to the $24 \times 6 columns$ (i.e., 6240 min/month or 74880 min/year) and more than 4 days per week may be added to the $14 \times 5 columns$ (i.e., 25530 min/month or 306360 min/year). Relevant numbers are emphasized by a *gray background*, and avoid other scenarios in the context of high availability

SLA (%)	24 × 7		24 × 6		14 × 5	
	Monthly	Yearly	Monthly	Yearly	Monthly	Yearly
99.0	7.3 h	3.7 days	6.3 h	3.1 days	3.0 h	1.5 days
99.5	3.7 h	1.8 days	3.1 h	1.6 days	1.5 h	18.3 h
99.8	1.5 h	17.5 h	1.3 h	15.0 h	36.6 min	7.3 h
99.9	43.8 min	8.8 h	37.6 min	7.5 h	18.3 min	3.7 h
99.99	4.4 min	52.6 min	3.8 min	45.1 min	1.8 min	21.9 min
99.999	26.3 s	5.3 min	22.6 s	4.5 min	11.0 s	2.2 min
99.9997	7.9 s	1.6 min	6.8 s	1.4 min	3.3 s	39.4 s

Do not underestimate these downtimes. A maximum of 1-h downtime per year is very hard to achieve for 24×7 operations because one must not have any downtimes for changes, or such downtimes must be included in that hour!

As a contrast, 99.99% availability during business hours (measured yearly, 14×5 coverage) is often suitable for a finance back office SAP installation – that demands a maximum outage time of approximately 20 min per year, but gives every day 10 h and additionally two full days per week for changes with planned downtimes. Restricting availability SLAs to business hours always means that the allowed maximum outage times become smaller than for continuous operations (since the total number of hours is also smaller), but it also means that one gains lots of freedom to plan operational changes. With them, more stringent requirements for business hours are much easier to fulfill.

▶ *Other Ways to Compute Outage Times and Availability*

Still, those high numbers are awfully hard to get by. When we have a look at 14×5 operations with 99.999% availability and yearly measurement, we get a maximum outage time of 2 min per year. Most technologies are not even able to detect failures and recover from them in that time span. Nevertheless those numbers are marked as relevant in the table, and even higher availability numbers like 99.9997% appear in practice. How are they computed then?

Well, what we did not capture in the table was that very high availability numbers sometimes are not even sensible per system and year. Enterprise-class computer systems are actually quite stable today and it is not uncommon to have uptimes of more than 1 year, without any outage. For such cases, where business owners expect less than one outage per system per year, the previous availability numbers are not usable and other ways to make measurements must be chosen.

In such a situation, one possibility is to distribute outages over a class of systems. For example, if we have five identical systems in five locations that provide a service, a possibility is to define an SLA that shares outage times over all systems. Then, a 5-min outage of one system would count as only 1 min towards the availability SLA. While this sounds impractical at first, there might be good business sense behind it. As an example, if one has five plants and respective computer systems that support manufacturing activities at each plant, the business owner might only be interested in the total outage of any plant, and not of a specific one. But if SLAs are made per computer system, it can be sensible to sum up availability SLAs per system to reach the overall availability goal.

Another possibility is to choose even longer availability measurements. If systems are expected to work longer than 1 year without any outage, this makes sense again. For example, a router might have an SLA of 99.9997% over 3 years; that makes 4.8-min maximum outage time – which can be realized with top-of-the-line equipment.

▶ *More Availability Metrics*

But maximum outage time in a given time period is not the only metric that is used to describe availability. For the business owner, it is not only of interest what the accumulated numbers are, single incidents are of interest as well.

So we introduce two other important metrics: outage frequencies and outage duration. The number of outages is of interest for the business owner; maybe 100 outages of 1 min are easier to endure and mainly a nuisance, but one outage of 100 min is already too much. After all, short outages are often not noticed by many users, they just wait a bit or they have to repeat their last action, whereas an outage of 100 min is probably noticed by all users and may impact our business. Other installations can handle one large outage of 1 h per month, but do not want to handle two short outages per day.

2.6 Service Level Agreements

There is the tendency to assert that all systems must be online and usable all the time in our new networked and interconnected world. The usual reasons are overseas contractors or clients, e-business, etc. Be advised that it is sensible to question such assertions and the associated costs. Business owners are sometimes inclined to raise the importance of

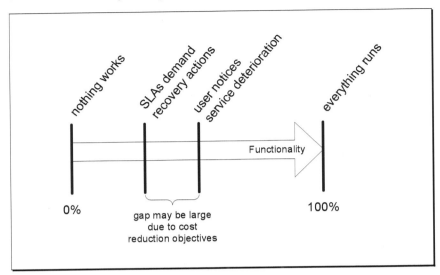

Fig. 2.2. Service level agreements (SLAs) and user notion of availability

their processes by asserting round-the-clock availability although it is not
necessary from the overall business viewpoint.

SLAs are the means to specify requirements for the delivery of IT services. They are a contract between the business owner and the IT department. If the IT services in question are outsourced, this is a real legal contract between two companies. But also in the common case that
the business owner and the IT department are from the same company,
a properly written SLA is an advantage for both parties – the business
owner knows what he or she gets and the IT department knows what it
must deliver.

With all this talk about measurement of availability, there must be
a reality check. For our end users, "availability" is often in the eye of
the beholder. If we have a scale from not working to fully working, SLAs
determine the limit where we *must* intervene. But for our users, service
will probably deteriorate earlier. Figure 2.2 illustrates that scale. It is a
matter of company policy if the users notion of "service is still usable and
thus available" is consistent with SLAs.

Often, cost-reduction objectives make them inconsistent – when the
SLA limit has not yet been reached, but users complain about unavailable
applications. There is no silver bullet for tackling this problem, but we
should make sure that our installations do not always wait for SLA limits
to be reached until corrective actions are taken. Instead, we should take
the user experience into account as well.

So, what are the agreements that should be specified in an SLA? Well, one needs to specify different SLAs for minor and major outages. The former will be fulfilled with high availability, the latter with disaster recovery. The specifications should spell out the following technical requirements:

1. **Minor outages** are caused by errors in ongoing operations. Specify:
   - Summarized maximum outage time over a defined time period
   - Maximum outage frequency over a defined time period, i.e., how often an may outage occur in a given time frame, independently of its duration
   - Maximum outage time per incident
2. **Major outages** happen very rarely and are situations that do not fall under the minor outage SLAs anymore. Nevertheless, we also want SLAs for them:
   - RTO, the time until the most important part of the IT service is usable again
   - RPO, the maximum data loss that may happen
   - Service recovery time, the time until full operations with all protection and redundancies in place are available again

It is important to separate SLAs for minor and major outages. If measurement and related contracts combined both, system designs would become too complicated and not realistic as it would be too expensive for the delivered functionality.

Maximum minor outage time can be specified as a percentage or as a specific duration. If possible, specific durations should be used as descriptions. Usage of percentages has the disadvantage that often the measurement time span is forgotten.

It might be that there are variants in those agreements; very often one number does not fit the business requirements properly. For example, probably there will be different service time recovery requirements for different outage scenarios – a physical destruction of a complete data center has a different full recovery time than the destruction of a set of computers that can be replaced relatively soon.

To specify those agreements, SLAs need also to include factual and process information. An example of factual information is how to measure the availability time period, i.e., if it is 24 × 7, or if it is not, what are the business hours, what is done on public holidays, etc.

Process information will make up the vast bulk of SLAs, and to list them all goes beyond the scope of this book. Nevertheless, we want to emphasize four descriptions that *must* be in an SLA, otherwise it cannot be fulfilled realistically.

1. The **escalation process** must be described. It must be formulated in a straight way after which time periods which kind of escalation is requested.

2. **Disaster declaration** is a process that is elementary and must not be skipped in an SLA formulation. It must be crystal clear how a major outage is detected and declared, to be able to start disaster recovery. Without such requirements, any disaster-recovery process is doomed to fail.

3. **Roles and responsibilities** must be spelled out, in particular the separation of work between department of the business owner and the IT department.

4. **Reporting** is often forgotten, but it is extremely important to specify this as well. What shall be reported, how often, and to whom are the questions that must be answered by SLAs.

If we follow these high-level guidelines, we have a good chance to get SLAs that actually mean something and help to define the expected interface to IT services clearly.

2.7 Basic Approach: Robustness and Redundancy

Our interest is the creation of highly available systems and to handle disasters, to continue eventually with providing the IT service. To do that we need to:

- Analyze our existing systems, their environment, and their usage
- Identify potential failure scenarios
- Design the future systems to continue operations in spite of these failures

On a very high abstraction level, our approach has two tiers that are simple to explain:

1. **Robustness:** We will minimize the potential for failures.

2. **Redundancy:** We will establish resources to continue operations when failures occur.

The first approach stresses *robustness* and *simplicity*. We will use a design that is as simple as possible and as complex as needed. If a feature is not really needed, it is shunned without mercy; even though some tool marketing specialist might have proposed it as the best thing since sliced bread. Let KISS be our guiding principle for system design – *Keep It Simple and Straightforward*.[2]

The second approach identifies single points of failure and adds *redundancy* to protect against or recover from failures of components.

---

[2] This is the modern euphemistic expansion. In the 1960s, when the term KISS was used heavily in the Apollo project, those down-to-earth engineers expanded that acronym to "Keep It Simple, Stupid."

Table 2.4. Categorization of components and failures

Component category	Typical failure
User environment	Data deletion or corruption
Administration environment	Data deletion or corruption
Application	Crashes, data corruption
Middleware	Crashes, memory leaks
(Network) infrastructure	Connection loss
Operating system	Crash, device driver errors
Hardware	Device defect
Physical environment	Power outage, fire, floods

These approaches are not independent; in fact, they conflict often enough. Adding redundancy makes a system more complex and usually reduces its robustness. That is because the redundant component introduces new dependencies; it must be operated, it can fail as well, its failure can propagate to other components, etc. It is a matter of judgment to balance these issues. For example, while hot-spare disks surely increase complexity, their gain in fault tolerance increase is tremendous and does well to offset any complexity questions.

Therefore, we need to take great care to design our redundancy and use it only where it makes sense. This needs judgment that comes with experience – this book will help you on your road to gather that experience, but it cannot substitute it. Enterprise-class system design has still many aspects of an art, and is not an engineering discipline.

But where do we start with the analysis of potential failures? As guidance, we utilize a scheme of component categories where failure may occur, from the physical environment to hardware to the user environment. For each component, potential failure causes exist that can be analyzed in turn. Table 2.4 presents those categories and typical failures. We refrain from exact category definitions at the moment, e.g., the difference between middleware and infrastructure will not be described here, but the respective chapters will provide the descriptions.

Components do not exist in an isolated space. Most of them depend in their functionality on another component. On a higher abstraction level, we can express that as a dependency between the categories. One can express such component relationships by dependency diagrams. These diagrams are not arbitrary graphs, instead they show a hierarchy of categories, where higher layers depend on lower layers. Concerning that dependency relation, the table lists higher categories above lower categories. The user environment depends on functional applications, they depend on middleware, which depend on infrastructure and operating systems, and so on.

Roughly speaking, these categories form a kind of layered stack structure – but we must take this layer idea only as an illustrative but coarse approximation that is suitable when we want to paint the picture with a broad brush. For one, this is not a strictly hierarchical stack; applications use middleware, infrastructure, and operating systems, administrators work on and with several components too. Second, (network) infrastructure services like routers, Domain Name Service (DNS), or license servers do not fit well into the stack picture either since they are usually deployed and planned independently.

Such a classification is extremely valuable, and it must not be underestimated. Table 2.5 on the facing page presents a list of failure scenarios that came out of a root cause analysis of previous outages; such a list is a good start. This list is presented here to illustrate the breadth that the spectrum of failure scenarios can take, from obvious failures like hardware failures to nonobvious scenarios like hanging Java virtual machines that are often forgotten.

But such a list has also too many ad hoc scenarios and does not structure any discussion about them. By making these scenarios more generic and placing them into the layered classification of Table 2.4, we further our work substantially. (Section 4.2.1 on p. 79 will present such a categorized list.)

We also need to select appropriate failure scenarios. As we have seen already, planning high availability and disaster recovery occurs in a business context. That business context also determines, or at least influences, the project's scope. By that scope, some scenarios might not be seen as relevant, maybe they will be handled in a later project phase, or not at all and their risk will endure.

We will have to select between several alternative solutions. This selection will be influenced by many factors, both hard ones and soft ones. The "hard factors" are those that can be easily counted and measured, "soft factors" are experience and judgment calls that can be specified but where measurement becomes difficult.

Soft factors are mostly human-related. Familiarity of our IT staff with certain solutions must certainly be considered. Setting up a high-availability system for a mission-critical server is no place to try out something completely new. On the other hand, most IT professionals are eager to learn something new, and a project for a crucial or an important server might very well be the place to try a variation or something completely new, to gain new knowledge and new insights. Other soft factors are vendor relationship – if we have a vendor that provides an excellent service, it makes good business sense to go with that vendor as long as it does not result in a vendor lock-in situation.

All those factors will have to be revisited and reevaluated regularly. Changing requirements, changing technology, and new possibilities all influence the decision process. Some time down the road, a formerly well

Table 2.5. Brainstorming result of failure scenarios

Corrupt database index	Denial of service attack on URL
Frozen process could not be killed (zombie)	Disk full (runaway process consumes all disk space)
LUN not accessible	Loss of shared network infrastructure
Last change generated run time issue not detected during preproduction testing	Synchronization to standby database hung, stopped primary database
Memory leak in application consuming available main memory	Flood in jobs caused system to stop
Memory failure	Disk failure could not be recovered by storage system
NIC failure, failover failed	DISK adapter failure, redundancy did not work
Switch interface failure	Storage switch interface failure
Network link failure not detected, no failover	Corrupt main memory caused system crash
Corrupt database index	Hung Java virtual machines
Corrupt data in database table caused application crash	Loss of access to primary LDAP server
Loss of network in the middle of a transaction	Network latency extended to 1000 ms
Loss of access to primary AD server	CPU failure
Unsupported browser access attempt	Log files out of space
Password fail on server-to-server communications	Two disks crashed, hot-spare disk did not work
Deadlock in database	Timeout of service
Repeated system crash after repair activity	Corrupt file
Corrupt database	File access security violation
AD directory corruption	Timeout on SAN disk
Application version/OS version incompatibility	Expired database password, application cannot access database
CPU load queue full (recursive spawned processes?)	Failover cluster switches back and forth in a loop
Bus error	Lost connection to DNS server
Message queue overflow	

reasoned decision might need reworking. This leads to a spiral model of requirements analysis, design, development, utilization, and review that is illustrated in Fig. 2.3 on the following page. Of course, in software engineering that model is well known and tried, but it is important to point out that IT system design will gain from that model as well.

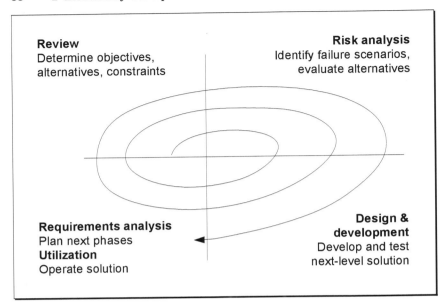

Fig. 2.3. Spiral model of high-availability and disaster-recovery implementation

2.8 Layered Solution with Multiple Precautions

Our analysis of component and failure categories, and our basic approach – increasing and balancing robustness and redundancy – lead to a layered solution. Table 2.6 on the next page takes up the failure categories again. Table 2.4 introduced them and presented typical failure situations – now we associate typical fault protection methods for each category that protects against or recovers from such failures.

We can have fault protection in several components at the same time, of course. Fault protection here means that there is an explicit process or procedure, be it automated or manual, that handles faults of that component and restores functionality. We say that we have redundancy on some level if all dependent components are available multiple times or are redundant themselves and if failover in the case of errors is managed on that level.

For example, when one has a backup system at a different site where the failover is controlled manually, this is redundancy on the user level. It delivers fault protection against all errors if the switch to this backup system works smoothly. But this is often not the case. Therefore, we usually want a *layered solution* where we employ protection by redundancy for several component categories at once. We will have redundant hard-

Table 2.6. Layered fault protection

Component category	Fault protection
User environment	Disaster-recovery processes
Administration environment	Disaster-recovery processes
Application	Distributed application, failover, clustering
Middleware	Clustering
Infrastructure	Independent high-availability architecture
Operating system	Clustering
Hardware	Redundant components, hot-spare disks maintenance contracts
Physical environment	UPS, backup data center

ware components, deploy a clustering solution for some components, and provide backup systems at a different site to handle disasters.

As mentioned, in theory we would need only protection methods on higher levels. If the application is fault-tolerant, recovers from user and administration errors, is distributed over several sites from the start, runs on different hardware, and does transparent failover and clustering, then that is sufficient. No other fault protection is needed anymore.

In practice, the higher-layer-only approach is too brittle and introduces too much risk. Component failures should be handled near the cause of the problem. When a disk fails, we should handle that disk failure, and should not be forced to move to a whole different system for that. Such broad-sweeping service migrations are always associated with more risk than replacing a disk – in particular, if that disk is redundant anyhow.

2.9 Summary

Failure scenarios, outage categorization, and specific availability and continuity requirements lead to a layered solution that will deliver the needed value to business:

- Failure scenarios are used to analyze what can happen to our IT systems.
- The resulting potential outages from such failure scenarios are categorized, according to probability and damage. Some failures must only result in minor outages, some failures may result in major outages, and some failures are not covered at all – we will live with the residual risk.

Example scenarios	Category

Server crash
Operating system panic
User error destroys data

Minor outage:
covers "normal operations"
High availability required
Availability SLA:
e.g., 99.99% per year
Frequency SLA: e.g., max.
2 incidents every 3 months
Outage SLA: e.g., max. 15 min
per incident

Administrator error destroys data
Software error corrupts data
Environment failure destroys
server(s)
Catastrophe destroys environment

Major outage: "disaster"
Disaster recovery required
Recovery time objective:
e.g., 1 h
Recovery point objective:
e.g., 8 h
Service recovery time:
e.g., 2 weeks

Fire in primary and backup site at
the same time

**Not applicable,
no recovery provided**
Outside project scope

Fig. 2.4. Combining failure scenarios, outage categories, and requirements

We have thus three outage categories:

1. Minor outage requirements
2. Major outage requirements
3. Not applicable

Each of these categories has:

- A fault-protection or failure-recovery strategy
- Associated SLAs

This clear separation of concerns gives us the opportunity to plan our projects properly and communicate them to our peers and to business owners.

If we put these items together, we come up with the summary in Fig. 2.4. There are also some example scenarios and example SLAs in that figure for better illustration.

3

Architecture

An architecture is often seen as the artifacts that describe the structure and high-level workings of a system. Is the architecture of a house the drawing that describes where the walls are and how high the ceilings are? Well, surely that drawing is an important artifact of an architecture, but it is not representative of an architect's work. An architect is responsible for gathering and documenting the objectives, planning the work, organizing stakeholders, designing the system, and providing the means to control the implementation. Thus, describing the "system structure" and "system functionality" is only part of an architect's work.

We approach the architecture topic in the broader sense. Of course, we are concerned with high availability and disaster recovery for systems, with their structure and functionality; this is the topic of this book, after all. Therefore, the design of the system structure is an important part. But we also take the view beyond the system and look at the other parts of an architect's work, at the objectives for high-availability systems and how they are gathered, and at the business reasons and conceptual model that guide the system design.

Without the objectives and a grounding in business processes, any system design will "float in the air." For example, we might implement features that are not required at all, or we might even miss features. In order to spend our money in sensible ways, it is mandatory that we anchor the architecture to our business and justify its business value.

This chapter will present the information that we need for an architecture in a structured way. An architecture is a set of documents that describes that information – we will see what documents should be written, the structure of these documents, and proposed content for each section of the documents.

The target audience for this chapter is:

- IT architects who have to design high-availability systems
- Managers who have to set objectives (planners)

- Managers who manage business interfaces (business process owners)
- Developers who want to know what demands they will get "from above"

This chapter will not go into technical details though – that is what the following chapters are for. Instead, the aim is to get a feeling for our undercurrent beliefs, and how we approach this area of work.

The presentation follows roughly the *Zachman Framework for Enterprise Architecture* [15, 8]; as far as it is sensible, as it is not our goal to create an architecture for the whole enterprise. Instead we want to create an architecture template for the domain class high availability and disaster recovery, i.e., a specific IT architecture for specific IT requirements. Zachman is a very strong proponent of the view that architecture is more than system design. For him, an architecture is a two-dimensional endeavor where certain aspects are described for different scopes or different abstraction levels.

The aspects are:

Data: *What* is the architecture concerned with, on the respective abstraction level?

Function: *How* is the data worked with, or how is a functionality to be achieved?

Location: *Where* is the data worked with, or where is the functionality achieved?

People: *Who* works with the data and achieves the functionality? Who is responsible, who approves, who supports?

Time: *When* is the data processed, or when is the functionality achieved?

Each aspect can be described for each of the following abstraction levels that make up the structure of this chapter:

Objectives: What shall this architecture achieve? How shall it be done, on an organizational level? Which organizations are responsible? Section 3.1 describes that level.

Conceptual model: Realization of the objectives on a business process level. Explanation of how the business entities work together in business locations on business processes, using work flows and their schedules. Section 3.2 explicates the content of this level.

System model: The logical data model and the application functions that must be implemented to realize the business concepts. The roles, deliverables, and processing structures to do so. Section 3.3 introduces the abstract content of such a model. The "system what" and "system how" descriptions are the artifacts that are commonly designated as *architecture documents* but are better named *system design*.

In fact, Zachman's framework has an additional aspect (motivation or rationale), and two additional abstraction levels (technology model and detailed representation). We do not need this aspect and these very low level abstractions for our presentation, so we leave them out.

Table 3.1 on the next page gives an overview on our architecture, using the familiar layout of the Zachman Framework. A table is created where the abstraction levels are rows and the aspects are columns. For every abstraction level, each aspect is summarized in a few words. The next three sections will look at the abstraction levels and present each aspect in more detail. Thereby, the table is a one-page summary of the whole architecture.

The table emphasizes two cells that make up the system design. For a technically oriented book such as this one, these are the most important part of the architecture. They are presented with a special focus as we concentrate on these two cells in Chap. 4.

▸ *Architecture Deliverables*

As mentioned already at the start of this chapter, the deliverables of an architecture are documents. That means that the complete architecture is made up by several documents that describe each architecture level and each aspect. But distribution of the architecture's description over documents is often more a matter of organizational processes (authorship, reviews, approval, release cycle, etc.) than of content.

Very often, the objectives and the conceptual model are described in one document. This is especially sensible when the same authors are responsible for both. It might be that these two parts are written at different times: first the objective part is written, approved by business owners or executive management, and then the conceptual model is added to the document. But in very large projects, these two parts will be written by different authors and thus will probably be separate documents.

For the system model two approaches exist. In companies that are more process-oriented, projects create one document that describes the whole system model, including the complete system design. As the other possibility, often done in projects in technology-oriented companies, the system model gets its own document or is added to the conceptual model document. In this case, the system design part of the system model (that is the "what" and "how" cells in the Zachman table) are only described at a very abstract level, because the system design gets its own document. This is propelled by the conviction that the system design is actually the only part of the architecture that counts for implementation because it describes the technological aspects of the solution.

So we have a choice to create between one and four documents. The parts are:

1. Objectives
2. Conceptual model
3. System model with a high-level description of the system design

Table 3.1. Overview of high-availability and disaster-recovery architecture. Abstraction levels are from top to bottom and aspects are from left to right

	Data "what"	Function "how"	Location "where"	People "who"	Time "when"
Objectives	Business continuity, IT service continuity	Identify business processes and relevant IT services, set SLAs (RTO and RPO), measure	IT department, outsourcing	Business owner, business responsibilities	Time frame for implementation
Conceptual model	Overall availability of mission-critical and important services, no edge systems; not servers, but services	ITIL processes, IT processes, projects	Data center, backup data center	IT department, CIO	Outage event categories, scenarios
System	Component categories (hardware, operating system, infrastructure, physical environment, …), dependency diagrams	Design patterns; redundancy, replication, robustness, system-independence, virtualization; plan RAS, availability tests	All systems, all categories	IT management, project manager, architects, engineers, system administrators	Local failure, change, incident/problem, disaster

System design artifacts

4. System design

The best advice for most projects is to create two documents, one with objectives and a conceptual model and one with the system design. The system model is either described in the first or in the second document – that choice depends on the project team, if it is more process-orientated or more technology-oriented.

Each document thus consists of one row or several of the rows in the Zachman table. Each row is one major document part. The aspects (the table columns) become the sections of that document part. In the rest of this section we will have a closer look at those sections and what should go in them.

3.1 Objectives

Since the whole of the first chapter was concerned with the reasons why we want and need high availability and disaster recovery, this section can remain short and will present the known facts in a structured manner. The main target audience for this section is business managers who set the objectives and project managers who need to gather objectives for a project proposal, or who need to specify requirements since they started with vague objectives only. Of course, the topic is of interest for developers too.

What

Business continuity is the overall business objective that we need to meet. It is met by a process that ensures that we can continue with business operations regardless of any incidents, interruptions, and problems. The business continuity process is at its heart one of the central risk mitigation activities of any company. In many publications, the term business continuity is used both for the objectives and for the process; in this book this is done as well.

It is not only there for incident and problem avoidance. While it is traditionally its main goal to prepare against failures so that they do not have consequences, business continuity as a modern process also includes adaption to changing requirements and realizing opportunities. As such it is one of the main tools of the agile enterprise that does not only adapt to changes, but rides the waves.

IT service continuity is the derived objective that applies as a business goal to a company's IT environment. The same term is used for the process to achieve the objective, as with business continuity. This process must manage IT services that are relevant for important or mission-critical business processes. It must ensure that incidents do not impair service delivery and that users can use these relevant IT services within chosen service levels.

How

IT service identification is the first thing one has to do. If you do not have a list of your IT services, now is a good time to start one. But a list alone is not sufficient. You also need a categorization of your services, as explained in Sect. 2.2 on p. 17.

If your company has proper business process documentation, that is your best bet to start. This documentation should have associated assessments that make clear which are the mission-critical business processes, which are important, and other appropriate categorization. If such assessments are not there, you discovered a job half done – do not let yourself get immersed into business process definitions, this is not your task. Your task is using those definitions to create proper objectives for IT service continuity.

If there is no business process documentation, or if the assessments are missing, you need to take stock of your IT systems and check what runs on your systems. This is a good thing to have anyhow, and most IT departments have that information at least in large parts.

A configuration management database (CMDB), an asset management system, or an inventory system may provide information about your IT systems, often without information on the services that they are hosting. Ideally, they would include that information as well, since it is very valuable for change, problem, and incident management. But many CMDBs tie configuration information to specific systems and cannot capture services that run distributed over several hosts or may migrate seamlessly from one host to another. Therefore, in most companies the CMDB is not the right place to look for such information – though it may be a start, it may list system-bound services.

For each service, you need to specify its outage category, as introduced in Sect. 2.2 on p. 17. Is it mission-critical, business-important, or a business-edge service? Problems from the past and associated consequences are good indicators of its real importance. This is a business judgment, of course. Many project and department leaders will be quick to assert the importance of "their" processes and needed IT services. But eventually the real question is: How much money does your company lose when an IT service is not available anymore. This must be answered – and the answer to that question will be the main input to determine the need for high availability and disaster recovery.

It is very valuable to be able to measure the availability of a system. If you are able to specify what shall be measured from a business perspective, the technicians will have a chance to actually deliver this measurement to you. Otherwise they will not test at all or will make up a test –

and then you have to rely on your luck and their intuitive understanding of the business process to get the right checks. An end-to-end test is ideal. This sounds easier and more trivial than it is. One needs to identify the essential functionality of each service and set up the objective to test for that functionality. Much too often, functionality tests are designed from a technical point of view, and miss the mark in testing business-relevant functionality.

Where

Your list of IT services that you have or have started, must have two columns among others: (1) the location (site, building) in which the service is running and (2) the location of its users. Remember that this is not a 1 : 1 relationship even if it seems so for simple services: eventually, some services will be used at many sites, or will be provided at many sites.

This information is important as it provides the objectives for availability and disaster recovery of the IT infrastructure that connects users and servers. All your precautions at a site will not be enough if your users at another site cannot access the service and they need it urgently for their work.

You should also add information about locations of outsourced IT services. This sets up the objectives for the service provider and can be used by you to formulate your requirements better and audit their service delivery.

Who

Responsibility for high availability and disaster recovery is located in the IT department. If we have outsourced our IT services, we might be inclined to think that we have outsourced the responsibility to the service provider as well – but this is never the case. One can outsource architecture creation and operations, but one can never outsource responsibility.

The business process owners need to honor their responsibility too. They must not take for granted functionality and availability of IT services, but must be aware that it takes earnest, dedicated work to provide them. This work can only be done properly, if changes in processes are communicated properly and in a timely fashion to the IT staff. It happens much too often that process changes become too expensive because related IT service changes were only implemented as an afterthought, and not planned from the start.

In the end, one of the main demands is "work together, communicate requirements, problems, and changes." Easy said – but the larger your company is, the harder this is to do.

When

An important objective is the expected time frame for implementation of high-availability or disaster-recovery services. Of course, the estimation depends on several important factors:

- Are your service information and associated service level agreements available or not? If you have to compile them first, a few weeks can be easily added to the time frame.
- Are requirements clear enough or is it part of your project to determine the requirements? The latter situation is not bad – in fact, it is the common case – but it will prolong the duration of your project and that must be taken into account when time objectives are set.
- The experience of the IT staff to create high-availability and disaster-recovery solutions. If they have done it a dozen times already, they will have created templates and can reuse their solution. If they do it seldom, they will need longer. If they are doing it for the first time, you should seriously consider help from the outside; that money for technical consultants is well spent.

Sadly, this book cannot provide good estimations of how much time will be needed in your specific situation. Dependency on the widely varying factors listed above results in time ranges that go from a few weeks to several years, and such information is not really valuable for you, is it?

But maybe an example from one of our projects can illustrate realistic time spans. For a multinational company with thousands of servers, the complete project needed 2.5 years. The following time ranges were used for intermediate process steps:

- Six months to set up big rules and accomplish the information exchange between business organizations and the IT department
- One year for implementation of (1) disaster recovery for mission-critical IT systems and (2) high availability for business-important services
- One year for smooth integration of these solutions into IT processes and operational procedures, also with tests to check if the disaster-recovery implementations really work.

In the specific case, almost all the effort concentrated on disaster recovery, as high-availability solutions for mission-critical services were in place already.

3.2 Conceptual Model

This section will guide IT architects and project managers to the topics that should be included in the conceptual model of high availability and disaster recovery for a company. Our goal is to provide the ability to connect the system model (that comes later) to business processes and business objectives. This will give you the opportunity to capture the business need for technical solutions and also to explain them to auditors, those responsible for budget, and other managers.

What

The objective is provision of business continuity and IT service continuity. Conceptually, this means providing improved overall availability of IT services, both in normal operation and in disaster situations. Therefore this part of the architecture is a list of all relevant services, systems, and their categorization.

As it fits the theme of this book, we will concentrate on mission-critical and business-important IT services that run on servers. The services will be the focus of our attention; servers (i.e., specific hardware systems) are only a means to our end and are only mentioned in passing. We will also consider availability issues of service-independent infrastructure, e.g., the network and associated services.

Edge systems, i.e., desktops, workstations, and small department servers, are not part of an architectural model for high availability. Depending on the objectives for disaster recovery, they might be part of the disaster-recovery architecture.

How

On the conceptual level, processes are at the heart of objective fulfillment. All technical considerations, all technology, and all tools will not help if they are not properly used. Only processes make usage reliable and repeatable. It is not enough that one has a guru who can build and fix almost everything – if that guru is on vacation, or has an accident, the rest of the company must be able to continue working on IT services as well.

In the past, provision, delivery, and management of IT services were organized methodically. This has changed in the last few years, starting with work in the UK. There, the Information Technology Infrastructure Library (ITIL) was developed in the late 1980s. It describes common IT processes in service management (delivery and support), infrastructure management, security management, and application management. Sadly, the IT world needed 10 years and the dot-com crash to catch on and see the importance of these processes – and now they overdo it sometimes.

In our context, the processes for service delivery are the most important, among them availability management and IT continuity management. The former provides the process framework for high availability, the latter the framework for disaster recovery. The task of this part of the architecture is to write up the business processes

When one realizes these process frameworks, it is important to do it one step at a time. Plan small steps, with known deliverables that have a measurable return of investment, and where the reason for process changes is well known. Much too often, process changes are done for their own good, or because they shall conform to some arbitrary set standard. Do not make that error in your organization, instead cherry-pick the changes that will give you an advantage in your IT service delivery.

Where

Our processes and also our system work are concerned with the place where delivery of mission-critical or business-important IT services takes place: enterprise-strength data centers and associated locations. This also includes the network that connects data centers and office or plant locations.

Plant locations merit some additional remarks. Factory IT installations must fit to the mindset of manufacturing departments, and they are used to having every relevant infrastructure on-site, including backups. They have backup power generators and backup machines, everything to run the business at this location in the case of failures. The IT systems that control plant elements are only of use if the plant is still functional. This is relevant as no off-site backup locations are needed for plant IT systems, on-site backup systems are sufficient.

Since single business-edge systems and services are not our concern, we do not need consider availability of office systems and end-user desktops in our high-availability architecture. In the disaster-recovery part of the architecture, when we choose to include destruction of office environments, backup locations for office space should be planned for, of course. This is especially sensible for areas where natural disasters like floods, hurricanes, or earthquakes are expected.

While one can use most of our high-availability and disaster-recovery concepts also for mid-sized businesses and the small office/home office (SOHO) market, we should be aware that only an enterprise-class data center will be the real McCoy. It simply is not possible to realize genuine complete high availability without such an infrastructure, since some redundancy demands (e.g., multiple power grid connections and careful cabling) can only be realized there.

Who

Chief information officer (CIO) and chief technology officer (CTO) are the executive positions that plan and supervise establishment of high-availability and disaster-recovery measures. Eventually, they have to decide what projects will be established and which services are important enough to spend the money available on.

The IT department is in charge of fulfilling that demand. It realizes the processes, and also works on the formulation and implementation of the system model.

To achieve that goal, external companies will contribute. This may start with consultants who bring in external experience or help to translate between the technical staff and business owners. It may also mean whole outsourcing of IT system management or even IT processes to external companies. Then the task of the IT department concentrates on formulation of processes, service level agreements, and architectural goals that must be obeyed by the outsourcer.

When

One of the tasks of the IT department and its executive management is to come up with a list of outage event categories and scenarios that might happen. For each category and for each scenario, it must be specified how availability and disaster recovery have to be handled; with manual workarounds, quick fixes for an incident, or complete problem analysis and resolution.

Reaction to failures differs between outage categories, and the task of the conceptual model is to give guidance about expected properties of processes. That establishes requirements that the system model must fulfill. The processes have already been expressed in the "How" aspect, and are usually subsumed under the categories *incident management*, *problem management*, and *availability management*. This part of the architecture describes the events that trigger the start of such processes and failure scenarios that must be covered.

3.3 System Model

As mentioned at the start of this chapter, the system model is the artifact that is the beef of architectural work. This section has information for IT architects, project managers, and developers. We will see now the high-level overview of the system model; the next chapter will then dive into the details of the system design.

What

Realization of high availability and disaster recovery is concerned with IT services and systems, i.e., services are delivered by systems:

- Running on hardware
- That are controlled and managed by an operating system
- Where application-independent software supplies a middleware layer of functionality
- That are used by application software
- That are maintained by IT staff and used by end users
- That run in a physical environment
- That use application-independent infrastructure services like networks, directory services, and maybe authentication or license services

These services are realized by system components like the CPU, memory, storage, database servers, application servers, and a set of applications. These components can be categorized to deliver a service or functionality from one of the items above. For example, database and J2EE application servers are in the category *middleware* and the CPU and memory are in the category *hardware*. Components depend on other components for their functionality. On a higher abstraction level, one can also express dependencies between component categories, e.g., one can say that the application category depends on the middleware category.

For each system, we can pin down a diagram with dependencies of components or component categories. For most systems, this dependency diagram of component categories looks similar or even identical. The category dependency diagrams often form a hierarchy that we call the *system stack*, even though it is not a stack in strict computer science terms. Section 4.1.1 on p. 56 presents the system stack in more detail.

How

High availability and disaster recovery are primarily realized with redundancy and robustness. This book is mostly concerned with the system model; therefore, the rest of it will present that one sentence in intrinsically deep detail.

Redundancy often means replication of functionality or data over several system components. To be able to do that, functionality or data storage must be independent of the actual system component at hand. This leads to the demand of system independence that is often realized by virtualization.

Design patterns may be used for high-availability and disaster-recovery realization. They are the foundation to plan and create appropriate levels of reliability, availability, and serviceability (RAS). In addition, rigid test approaches are described that can be used to assert that our redundant and robust systems are really that, and work to deliver the chosen objective. These design patterns are not on the code level though. They are methods and plans of solutions that fit scenarios.

Where

In theory, redundancy at some high layer in the system stack is sufficient, as it covers all lower-level failures as well. But this is not practical. Higher stack layers come with raised complexity, and this implies higher risks since more things can go awry without dedicated countermeasures available. This is not a simple and robust solution anymore.

Therefore, we feature the approach that redundancy and robustness must be designed on several stack layers of a system. Only then will we get services that deserve the label *highly available* and that survive disasters.

Who

Senior management has to set up the projects for implementation. Project managers and architects are responsible for planning, production engineers and system administrators for realization.

External consultants and vendors will help to achieve that goal; they are also a valuable source of technical information that is needed during implementation.

When

The system model is concerned with failure events and their categorization in scenarios. This is the case for both local failures (the domain of high availability) and nonlocal failures (the domain of disaster recovery).

Such failures do not only happen by accident or because some hardware or software component is erroneous. Quite often, they happen during standard service management procedures. Therefore we will pay special attention to events that happen during changes, and during incident and problem management. For example, incident management is only concerned with quick fixes that may cure a current symptom, but may reduce redundancy or robustness as it happens. We must plan ahead for that symptom and look after it throughout the life of our IT systems. For example, in the incident process, a problem analysis and robustness analysis may be added, and should be done after the quick fix.

4

System Design

The system design is the part of the architecture that explains what components a system consists of and how it works, i.e., how high availability and disaster recovery are realized for that system. It is a document or a set of documents that describe the system's structure, potential failures, and how requirements are fulfilled.

To be able to create a good system design, we need to know a few basic concepts first that help us to communicate our design clearly and guide us towards a good solution; thus, the chapter starts with this explanation:

- **Base concepts** are means to analyze a system and categorize its components, as well as helping to synthesize a good solution. Section 4.1 elaborates on these topics; it builds on the basic approach that we have met already in Sect. 2.7.
- The **solution roadmap** is a process description and a check list to achieve good high-availability and disaster-recovery system designs that is presented in Sect. 4.2.
- **System solution patterns** are common scenarios that can be reused in other contexts and serve as example system designs. We will learn about them in Sect. 4.3.

All these descriptions have a focus on technical questions. The system design has the actual computer system at its heart and covers the technology that is used for implementation. It does not cover the processes that are used to create or maintain the systems.

4.1 Base Concepts

The last sections presented the architecture in terms of objectives, the conceptual model, and an overview of the system model. The system model is at the focus of this book; its artifacts are emphasized with a gray background in our overview in Table 3.1 on p. 44. This section has a closer look at the concepts that are used to realize high availability and disaster recovery on the system level.

Good processes, solid architecture, careful engineering, and consideration of details is all it takes to successfully realize high-availability and disaster-recovery solutions. The main stumbling block is that details matter. When you get a detail wrong, your system might stand still and your availability objective has dropped dead on the floor; that is the discrete nature of IT systems.

As usual, the basic recipe for problems with lots of details is "divide and conquer." Compartmentalize the problem and the tasks, name the dependencies, and tackle each subproblem one after the other. All our concepts and actions can be reduced to four key abstractions and principles. The first abstraction delivers the categorization, the other three are principles that are applied for each category:

1. **System stack** is a component categorization that is an important weapon. The categorization will partition the overall problem into divisions that can be handled separately.
2. **Redundancy** is the hallmark principle that may be applied in each layer.
3. **Robustness** is the corrective check that prevents us from going overboard with our redundant designs.
4. **Virtualization** allows for flexible mapping of IT services to IT systems or IT components, thus earning us fewer dependencies.

4.1.1 System Stack

The system model in Sect. 3.3 on p. 51 already presented a categorization of system components that is the base for our term *system stack*. Figure 4.1 on the next page takes it up and presents it again: eight component categories with typical dependencies.

The system stack is the dependency diagram over components or component categories. At the top of the stack are the components on which no other components depend. At the bottom of the stack are components that have no dependencies. Let us have a look at each component category first, and then at notations and dependency diagrams.

User Environment

User environment is the category that combines everything user-work related that is not part of any software or hardware. First and foremost, it includes the user as a kind of "component," and thus captures all human user errors and related fault protections. Second, this category is there to express dependencies on infrastructure services that are not accessed by the application software, e.g., authorization and authentication services.

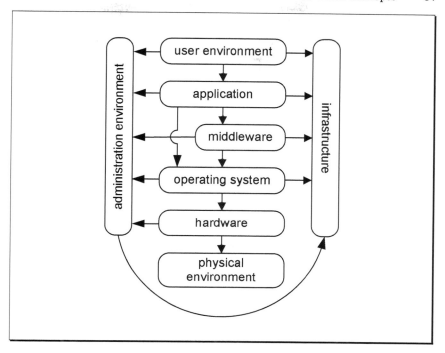

Fig. 4.1. System stack. *Arrows* are dependency relations

Administration Environment

Administration environment is the category that combines everything administration-work related that is not a software or hardware component, but human work. This category consists mainly of the components "system administrators" and "operators", but also security administrators and other administrative tasks are captured in this stack layer.

This category is there to capture all human administration errors and related fault protections. Second, this category is there to express the importance of administrative work in the dependency diagram and how much can go wrong if administrative or operative work is botched.

Application

Application is the category of software components that make up our system or service. Very often, this whole category will be just one application; here the distinction between components and their category becomes blurry. But also it is not seldom that a service is delivered by a combination of applications, e.g., a design and engineering workplace service may consist of a CAD application and a product data management application.

Middleware

Middleware is the category of service-independent software components that are integrated into the application. Database servers, application servers, Web servers, messaging servers, and transaction managers are all available independently of a given application or service. But they need to be adapted and configured specifically for that service. That is, something is middleware if we can get it independently of the application software but it has to be configured to be an integral part of the service delivery.

Databases are an illustrative example: while we talk about the database software in terms of the producer's brand name (Oracle, DB2, etc.), when it is used in an SAP installation, one talks about the "SAP database" and drops the brand name because the database schema and configuration is more important for the service.

Infrastructure

Infrastructure is the category of service-independent software and hardware components that are used by application, middleware, or other categories, but are not integrated. The whole network (routers, switches, cables), directory services like the Domain Name Service (DNS) or Microsoft's Active Directory (AD), license servers, and authentication services are examples of components in this category. They are used by the service, many components depend on them, but they do not get to be part of it.

Operating System

Operating system is the category of software components that control and manage hardware resources and provide an abstract interface for other services to run on. This category includes also management components that are standardized (e.g., by POSIX) or are delivered by the hardware vendor.

Interestingly, the difference from middleware and infrastructure is sometimes difficult to express and is not always made for technical reasons, but is used to express organizational relationships. As an example, the job management system *cron* is seen as part of the Unix operating system since it is standardized and delivered together with the hardware, whereas other job management systems (e.g., LSF) are seen as middleware because they must be bought independently.

Hardware

Hardware is the category of components from which our systems are created. It includes not only the core computer components like CPU, backplane, and interfaces, but also storage – both internal and external storage subsystems.

The latter categorization is done for ease of presentation: external storage subsystems are actually computer systems in their own right, but they are better modeled as black boxes in the hardware stack layer.

Physical Environment

Physical environment is the category of components where we operate. Our data center with rooms, power supplies, air conditioning, and the river nearby that might flood our building all belong to the physical environment. For that component category, "failures" usually result in major outages as they have consequences for many systems at the same time, maybe rendering them unusable at the same time.

Notation for Components and Dependencies

Figure 4.1 on p. 57 introduces a graphical notation for components, component categories, and their dependencies. Within that notation, we do not differentiate between components like CPU or memory and categories like hardware. They are named and put into boxes. Dependencies are expressed by arrows between those boxes, where an arrow expresses the "depends-on" relation.

In fact, the differentiation between components and component categories is negligible in practice. The context provides the abstraction level we want to discuss at the moment, and we simply select an appropriate term, either on the component or on the category abstraction level. In addition, components sometimes consist of other components (e.g., the storage unit may have a CPU itself); there we have already an abstraction layer that expresses the consists-of relationship. Therefore, in the rest of this book we will ignore the fine-grained terminology difference and use the term "component" for components and categories alike.

The notation in that diagram is not complete. We will enhance it with redundancy and repetition information in Sect. 4.1.2 on p. 63.

Dependency Graphs and Diagrams

A component depends on another component if there is a direct dependency or if there is any dependency between subcomponents. All dependencies of a system form a graph, named a *dependency graph*. This graph must be acyclic; the system architecture must be changed if it is not.

Cyclic dependencies cannot be resolved with existing high-availability solutions. The picture that shows a dependency graph is called a *dependency diagram*.

If we ignore the infrastructure and administration environment components, we see that components in the dependency graph form a total order: there is a unique order of all components c, so that c_i depends only on c_j, with $j < i$. In other words, for every pair c_i and c_j we can determine exactly if c_i comes before c_j in the dependency graph or not. The infrastructure component introduces a partial order, as we cannot determine any transitive dependency between it and hardware or the physical environment.

Please note that this dependency order lists more independent components first, i.e., hardware comes before operating systems, which come before applications. The list is from top to bottom in Fig. 4.1 on p. 57.

Since we have mostly a total order, we can see the dependency graph as a sort of linear hierarchy and use the term *system stack* for it. We say that a component c_i is on a higher stack layer than c_j if there exists a transitive dependency $c_i \mapsto c_j$ and $j < i$.

Of course, strictly speaking the system stack is not a stack in the computer science sense. There, only dependencies to the next-lower layer would be allowed, but we also have dependencies to arbitrary lower layers. Nevertheless, the common English usage of *stack* covers our model as well and it is a very illustrative usage of that term.

Getting a Project-Specific System Stack

Now that we have seen a generic system stack, we need to instantiate it for our specific system model. For each component category, we check if our application has such components, determine their dependencies, and add them to our graphics. Up front, it might be that certain component categories are not used at all, e.g., there might be no middleware (databases, application servers) in our system. We can then discard those components from our specific system stack immediately.

Next, we take the preliminary system stack and use it to create failure scenarios. For each component we make a list of what problems could appear. Eventually, the goal is to determine the exact scope of our project and thus of our architecture. Some failure scenarios will be outside the scope of our project – e.g., a bomb at our data center. If *all* failure scenarios for one component are considered outside the scope, that component can be eliminated from the specific system stack as well.

This elimination often hits components at one of the ends of the stack. Most often, failure scenarios for the physical environment or infrastructure are considered beyond a project's scope. Also, failure scenarios in the user or administration environment are often not considered. In fact, this is the cause for the distinction between high availability and disaster recovery: in principle, both are concerned with the same task, service continuity and fault protection. In practice, protection against building outages (e.g., fire, hurricanes), user or administrator errors, and infrastructure outages are handled in disaster-recovery projects, while protection against outages of computers and databases is handled in high-availability projects.

As an architect or a project manager, be careful to document that elimination. In fact, this elimination must be made on the level of the conceptual architecture model and must be consistent with the objectives model. If that is not done you will likely get into trouble if a failure happens that you just declared to be outside your scope. If the objectives or the conceptual model does not record a sign off of this view, you might be held responsible for the failure consequences nevertheless. After all, these scope exclusions must be recognized during risk management and might need to be handled in separate projects. You might also want to make sure that the scope exclusions are documented in your company's SOX, Basel II, or other risk management documentation, as demanded by regulations.

Finally, we have a high-level system stack for our specific system. It consists of all relevant components, excluding those that are not used here and those that are beyond the project's scope. The next thing will be to refine it by adding details and zoom into components to name subcomponents. Eventually, we will achieve high availability and/or disaster recovery for this system's stack by assuring redundancy through component replication.

Division of our complete problem into these stack layers gives us the opportunity to think about potential problems and their solution separately. This separation is so important that it builds the base for the whole book structure: the four stack layers from hardware to applications are covered by Chaps. 5–8, the user and administration layers are handled in Chap. 10 on disaster recovery, Chap. 9 is on infrastructure, and Appendix B is on data centers.

4.1.2 Redundancy and Replication

High availability is fault protection against minor outages; disaster recovery is fault protection against major outages. Both objectives are actually two sides of one coin: incidents and problems happen, and we need to cope with them. Redundancy is the ability to continue operations in the case of component failures with managed component repetition.

Providing a backup component or system for the error case is the basic precaution. This can be a duplicated part, an alternative system, or an alternative location. There can be just one duplicated backup component or there can be several components. Therefore we cannot use the term "duplication," so we call this backup approach *repetition*. All component repetitions have one goal in common: they avoid *single points of failure*. If we succeed in this, we will have achieved a fully redundant installation that will provide both high availability and disaster recovery if needed.

But simply adding a backup component is not enough. This backup component needs to be *managed*. There must be a third component that looks to see if one component is faulty, prevents its usage in that failure case, and makes the backup component do all functionality. For example, if we have two network cards, this is not a redundancy in itself. Only if some component notices that one network card is not functional anymore and uses the backup card for all traffic, then we can name that configuration redundant. This component can be the operating system (so-called "multipath configuration") or it can be a human being that reconfigures the network card.

Also, if the component has a persistent state (i.e., stores data or the configuration somehow), the backup component must be kept in the same state, otherwise it cannot take over the service in the case of failures. This requirement is loosened sometimes, and some data loss is accepted to continue with the service. This is usually the case for disaster-recovery scenarios, where major outages are associated with a recovery point objective, a point in time when data must be restored again. Therefore *replication* of the state is a precondition. But please note that the state is not data alone; the configuration must be replicated to the backup component as well. This can be files or registry entries in the case of software components, or firmware releases in the case of hardware components.

Replication can happen in two ways. A one-way replication is the case where data is first written on a "primary" component and then copied to a "backup" component. A two-way replication is the case where data (i.e., persistent state) is written to the duplicated components at the same time, controlled by the management component. Two-way replicas are better known as *mirrored components*.

In summary,

Redundancy = repetition + management,

where

Management = replication + fault handling.

This principle leads to an essential part of our terminology. It is not sufficient to say that we have two redundant components, we must also name the management component. We express this as

Components *foo* are **redundant via** component *bar*.

Example expressions would be "*disks* are redundant via the *volume manager*" (in the case of mirroring) or "*primary and standby databases* are redundant via the *system administrator*" (in the case of human failure handling).

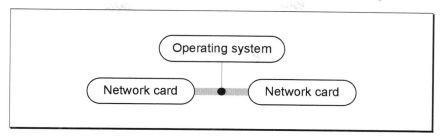

Fig. 4.2. Graphical redundancy notation: basic managed repetition without replication

There might even be the case that management is done with several components. For example, there might be one component that does the replication and another one that does fault handling. This occurs sometimes on higher levels in the system stack, when manual fault handling is involved. Replication might be handled by some software or system component, but activation of the backup component is handled by processes. For the sake of conciseness, this fine distinction is not mentioned throughout this book. Instead we always talk about *the* management component and recognize that it could be several components.

The point with manual fault handling is also worth emphasizing: on lower system stack levels, fault handling is often based on technology and is automated, but on higher levels, fault handling is dominated by processes and most often is not automated. We do *not* want an automated system to take the decision about disaster recovery and trigger its execution; that would be much too risky. Instead, humans should be involved in the decision and in executing such an important step.

Dependency and Redundancy Diagrams

Figures 4.2–4.5 introduce a graphical notation for redundancy that enhances dependency diagrams:

- Thick gray lines are used to denote repetition.
- One-way replication is involved if the gray line has one arrowhead.
- Two-way replication (mirroring) is involved if the gray line has two arrowheads.
- The managing component is connected to the gray (repetition) line and ends with a dot on that line.
- Redundant components have double-line borders.

This notation completes the dependency diagrams.

Sometimes, the redundancy management line would make the diagram unreadable owing to too many lines. Then we leave it off and add a legend to the diagram that explains the management relationship.

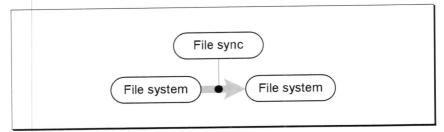

Fig. 4.3. Graphical redundancy notation: one-way replication

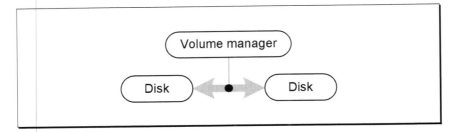

Fig. 4.4. Graphical redundancy notation: two-way replication

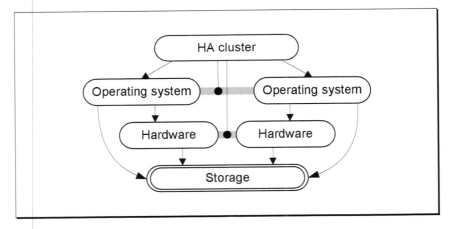

Fig. 4.5. Graphical redundancy notation: dependency on redundant system

Dependency and redundancy diagrams are means for communication, they are not standardized circuit diagrams. They are used to emphasize the essentials to our fellow coworkers – drawing them requires design decisions, e.g., to which level of detail we go for the component in the diagram. For the sake of readability, we just name them dependency diagrams in the rest of this book and drop the qualifier that redundancy information may be included.

Also, dependency relations are sometimes difficult to express. Consider the case where both the administration environment and the infrastructure are part of our project-specific system stack, i.e., they are in our dependency diagram. The infrastructure and administration components are supposed to be redundant themselves. This means that we have two components in the diagram (with double-line borders) where dependency arrows point from almost any other component in the diagram to them. That information brings us almost nothing and adds lots of arrows to the diagram, making the rest of the picture hard to understand. In such a case, it can be best to add these two components at the bottom of the diagram and to add a legend that all other components depend on these two. No information gets lost, but the rest of the diagram (where our high-availability and disaster-recovery design decisions are) is suddenly much more readable.

Another technique for better readability is zooming. Dependency diagrams on high-abstraction levels present coarse granularity of component abstractions and show the overall picture. Subdiagrams zoom into components and show internal dependencies and redundancies.

Objectives of Dependency Diagrams

Dependency diagrams are used to communicate dependencies and redundancies to other workers and auditors, and are a help during discussions. In particular, they are used to detect and highlight the places where the system design is *not redundant*, also called *single points of failure* (SPOF).

> **All components that do not have a double-line border, have no repetition (gray) lines, and have dependency arrows pointing to them are *single points of failure*.**

For each of those single points of failure, we need to decide if the risk is bearable or if we have to introduce fault protection in our system design. This is mostly a judgment call, on p. 75 this issue is discussed in more detail.

The highest-level stack components, i.e., those diagram components to which no dependency arrows point, are very often single points of failure. When we have full system coverage, we have to look at user and administration errors. And these two "components" can always cause big trouble by deleting or changing data. It is not possible to devise technical protection against all such errors. Here fault protection does not mean introducing redundancy (after all, how will you make users redundant), but means designing policies and mechanisms that will help to cope with such errors after they have happened and repair the damage in acceptable time frames.

It is possible to devise a system without any single points of failure. But note that this is rarely really needed; maybe it is necessary for emergency communication lines where human lives depend on their functionality. (And note also that even such installations are known to have long outages during major disasters, like the Indian Ocean tsunami of 2004 or the New Orleans flood of 2005.) Practically, such extreme precautions are sometimes not worth the money. Instead of such extreme high-availability fault protection, it is often more sensible to provide adequate disaster-recovery mechanisms and deal with the fault after it has happened.

A Closer Look at Redundancy and Repetition

Managed repetition of a single component is often not sufficient to achieve redundancy on a higher system stack layer. Let us look again at the dependency and redundancy diagram in Fig. 4.5 on p. 64. Just installing the operating system twice on a given piece of hardware would not bring us redundancy on the operating system layer. Instead, the hardware must be duplicated as well, and this repetition must be managed too. Without repetition of the hardware, duplication of the operating system would be futile – we could simply restart the system to get it running again, whereas the storage subsystem does not need to be duplicated as it is redundant already. Incidentally, Chap. 5 will tell you that the assertion of a redundant storage system is often wrong – both the disk repetition management component in the storage box and the file systems are usually single points of failure.

You might notice that the example does not include the physical environment and the user environment. That is intended: redundancy is an attribute that refers to a specific scenario, a project-specific system stack as outlined in Sect. 4.1.1 on p. 60. When our project is not concerned with failures in the physical environment, the example shows a redundant operating system. If it were concerned, the hardware would need to be placed at two locations to achieve redundancy.

Eventually, this leads us to the point where we are able to formulate in more exact terms what we mean by *redundancy*: a system has a redundant component on stack layer i when all components of layer j with $j \leq i$ are (1) either redundant themselves or (2) are available multiple times and the repetition is managed (i.e., the state is replicated and failover in the case of outages is handled) by another component.

The first condition is introduced to capture the dependency of components that are already redundant, like network infrastructure, DNS servers, or some network storage subsystems. That is not to say that they cannot or should not be replicated anymore – quite the contrary, it is common to introduce multiple redundancy by replicating SAN storage systems that are already redundant. But that definition gives us the opportunity to describe exactly when we have single or multiple redundancy.

The second condition stresses the independence of dependent component replication. To achieve a truly redundant database solution, it is not sufficient to replicate the database on the same server, we need to replicate those servers as well. Either the middleware layer must manage outages in that replication, then we name this a database cluster and call it redundancy on the middleware layer, or we have one database component on a redundant operating system layer (e.g., managed by a failover cluster component), then we call it redundancy on the operating system layer.

In theory, this means that if we have the choice between a middleware cluster and a failover cluster, we should always choose the middleware cluster. In practice, the choice is not always as easy. It might be that the middleware cluster software is not mature enough, or is too complex and operations are error-prone. It might be that we have a failover cluster already available where the database will be included. We need to take into account experiences that tell us about the quality of a solution; on p. 75 we will discuss this consideration in more detail.

Redundancy Is Expressed in Project-Specific System Stacks

It is important to emphasize that this redundancy definition depends on the pruned system stack that was adapted to our system and our project, as explained in Sect. 4.1.1 on p. 60. For example, when our project ignores failures in the physical environment, we can talk about redundancy on the middleware layer even though both systems might be in the same data center (and thus have a dependency on the same physical environment). This single point of failure still exists but is masked out of our project's objectives and conceptual model. Figure 4.6 on the following page illustrates that scenario.

This is so important that it must be repeated: good pruning of the generic system stack is essential. We simply might not have the resources to cover failures for some components or there are business objectives why it is not sensible, but we might also be too lazy. For example, if a plant is destroyed and the controlling computer is in that plant, it does not need to be replicated at a backup data center – that is common business

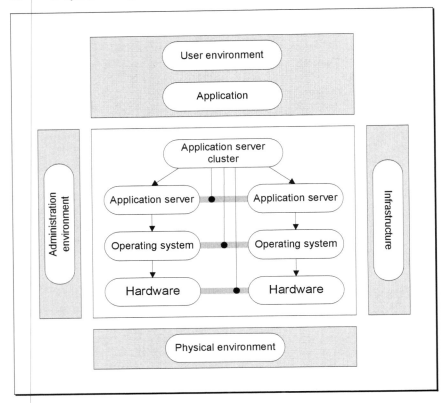

Fig. 4.6. Masking out components that are not in project scope. Components in *gray* are identified as being outside of the project's scope

sense and sensible pruning. But if we simply ignore the possibility of user, administration, or application errors and confine ourselves to redundancy on the middleware or operating system layer that is harder to judge. If we cannot afford a backup system, OK. But if it is just because "that's the way we did it in the past" then you should think about updating the set of methods in your toolbox.

Figure 4.6 is also of interest because it illustrates the "traditional" scope of high-availability projects that do not have disaster-recovery objectives. Applications and infrastructure are simply taken as is, since the project probably cannot change their deployment anyhow. Human errors and physical disasters are ignored; fault protection for them is often the task of another project.

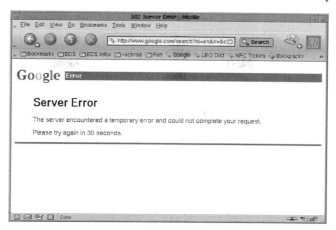

Fig. 4.7. Google outage message

Redundancy on Several Stack Layers

As already mentioned in Chap. 2, redundancy should be approached on several stack layers. Even though it is possible to build a distributed redundant application that would cover all failure cases in duplicated lower layers as well, it is not practical. First, we cannot rebuild all applications and have to live with those that we must deploy today. Second, on the application layer we do not have sufficient information about failure causes on lower layers anymore to trigger sufficient corrective actions. For example, while we might get notice of I/O errors, we will not know which erroneous disk must be replaced right now.

Google is sometimes cited as an example of such a distributed application that does not care for lower layers and handles all outages on the application layer. But this is not true, quite the contrary. The Google engineers went so far to create their own highly redundant file system to achieve better redundancy on the operating system level. Google is redundancy on many layers in action, as proposed above. Incidentally, Google does not cope with errors on *all* layers, so we still get to see outage messages like the one in figure 4.7 from time to time. (In that case, the outage lasted several minutes and also was not a single-server error, the retry 30 s later was not successful, nor were explicit queries to different Google servers.) Please note that this observation does not denigrate the quality of Google's IT architecture or IT staff; they do an outstanding job of running the world's largest computing grid today; their architecture is as highly available as it gets in that application context. The exception from the rule "Google is always available" is the reason that we reference it here.

Having replicated components complicates systems though. If data is stored persistently, e.g., on a disk, that must be taken into account during write and read: write must replicate the data to all components, and read must select one of the components to take the data from. Even if no data is involved, component usage must be aware that there are multiple instances to choose from, which complicates usage as well.

While it is clear that replication is involved in the case of redundant data storage systems, this is also the case for redundant hosts or redundant data centers. If one operates a backup data center as a precaution against disaster, the whole data center is a redundant component and replication needs to be established and managed properly to get it working.

Redundancy with Cheap Components Is Not Easy

Again, it is important to emphasize one crucial issue: our goal is high availability and disaster recovery for a complete system, not for single components. We utilize component redundancy, on several stack layers, to achieve that goal. This may also allow us to save some money for components: sometimes it is possible to use cheap multiple components and that may be good enough and less expensive than using high-quality components. On the hardware level, the concept of redundant array of independent disks (Raid) storage pioneered that approach; we describe it in more detail in Sect. 5.2.1.

An adjacent and intriguing idea is the usage of that "cheap redundant component approach for hardware components other than storage and on other system stack layers as well," as one of the book reviewers put it. But we have to be careful with that. For hardware components, such an approach is not a simple task of plugging together available components – it demands new designs from the ground up. It is not sufficient to just cobble together two memory banks without error correcting code (ECC) error correction to be able to use them redundantly; that usage must be designed up-front. This sometimes implies adaptations on higher stack layers too, e.g., special hardware drivers are needed in the operating system for redundant network cards. "Just" using cheap components, without proper design, will simply lead to inferior availability owing to reduced quality, that is all.

In addition, it is hard to define what such a "cheap component" is on higher stack layers. Let us take a database or any application software as an example. Cheaper – does that mean it is tested less, has less of the needed functionality, is more unstable, does no proper resource management, and crashes from time to time? Well, if that is the case, remember that this application holds and manages data that is important for your business and ask yourself if you want to trust that data to such an application. Remember, combination of cheap components in a redundant

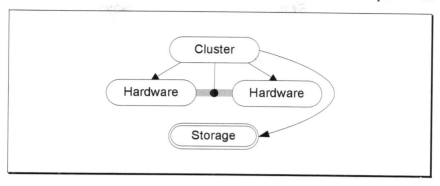

Fig. 4.8. High-availability (*HA*) cluster dependency diagram: marketing information

way must be designed up-front, and that would mean that the application software would have to be written with partial failures in mind and would have to cope with such failures. NASA software is often written in this way (for other reasons), and as we can see there, writing failure-tolerant software with such an approach is anything but cheap.

In general, computer science has experimented with *n*-version programming for some time, where independent groups implement solutions for the same task. The goal of that research was to raise availability and correctness by comparison of the outputs against each other. This research has shown that many independent implementation groups make the same errors for the same tasks. Many problem domains have obvious solutions where the same subtle errors can and will be introduced by most realizations. In summary, "cheap redundant components" will not work in the predictable future for higher stack layers.

Almost-Redundant Components

When our dependency diagram shows no single point of failure, this does not necessarily mean that there *are* no single points of failure. Detection of single points of failure depends most often on the granularity of observation, i.e., on the detail level in which we analyze a component.

This is particularly true for components that are touted as "redundant" by vendors. Let us take the prototypical example of a high-availability failover cluster that comes with a marketing-level diagram as illustrated in Fig. 4.8. The cluster is said to be redundant (of course, that is the whole purpose of it), the hardware is redundant via the cluster, and the storage subsystem is redundant as well.

But if we look into the redundant components, a different picture emerges, as shown in Fig. 4.9 on the following page. In this diagram,

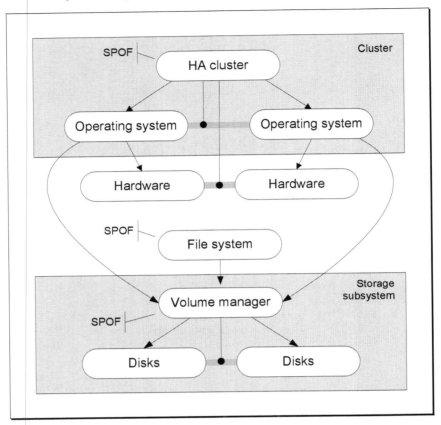

Fig. 4.9. HA cluster dependency diagram, reality check. *SPOF* single point of failure

we have zoomed in on the redundant components cluster and storage. A high-availability failover cluster consists of the operating systems for each node and a cluster software component that is distributed over all nodes and has a shared state and shared configuration. An external storage subsystem consists of disks that are redundant via a volume manager. Neither the cluster software nor the volume manager is redundant in itself. (They cannot be, no managing component for them would be available.)

In fact, there is an additional component, the file system on the storage subsystem, that is not shown in the marketing diagram, but is not redundant either. Many publications on and discussions of high-availability software ignore the problem that persistent data exists only once in such a system. The data is switched from one cluster node to the other and any logical damage to the data cannot be recovered. For example, errors in the file system code, or human errors, or errors in the application software. All of them will render the whole cluster unusable. Chapter 6 reflects more on the matter of high-availability failover clusters on the operating system level.

This means that a fault in the high-availability software, faults in the storage subsystem's volume manager, and faults in the file system might all render the cluster unusable. Management components are often the culprits when we discover single points of failure. This does not mean that we cannot use that design; first of all, it means that the marketing information is not the whole truth. We have (at least) three single points of failure in each standard cluster setup – the real question is how we cope with them.

There is the simple possibility that we can accept the remaining risk and live without protection against the faults. Remember that high availability is fault protection against minor outages, and faults in these components will cause major outages since they are single points of failure. Protection against major outages is possible in the form of disaster recovery. In fact, you are well advised to plan for it, at least for your mission-critical and business-important systems. This is an advantage of dependency diagrams. By zooming into supposedly redundant components, we are able to detect single points of failure and we can decide if we need disaster recovery or if we take the rest risk. Then this decision is made consciously, and not because of unavailable information.

Storage subsystems and failover clusters have been presented here as cases for almost-redundant technologies. These are standard technologies to realize high availability for the operating system level. That shows that almost-redundant solutions happen to be accepted quite often; this also appears in many cases in this book. There is a basic truth behind this:

Full redundancy is very hard to achieve!

Therefore many almost-redundant architectures are tagged with the label *redundant* even though they still have single points of failure.

In summary, when you analyze a dependency diagram, you will have to decide if you can trust any outside information about components that are "already redundant," or if you need to zoom into these components and have a deeper look at their parts. In addition, when you discover single points of failure, you need to decide if you will leave them as is and handle faults by disaster recovery (or not at all) or if you will handle them in the high-availability design. On p. 75 criteria for such decisions are discussed in more detail.

4.1.3 Robustness and Simplicity

Keep It Simple and Straightforward (KISS) was the guiding principle of the Apollo project that took humans to the moon. This engineering principle also underlies most Internet technologies, founding the networked world at the end of the twentieth century. It encourages the construction of robust architectures that have as few elements and interdependencies as possible and as many as needed.

It is worth pointing out that existing technology has a tendency to forget this principle and that it becomes more complex over time. A prime example is today's Internet technology. Early Internet protocols prided themselves on being simple and have that in their name: Simple Mail Transfer Protocol (SMTP) still rules our mail transfer and Simple Network Management Protocol (SNMP) is ubiquitous in network management products. And these protocols are really simple, one can debug them easily, they are easy to implement and have simple semantics.

Modern Internet protocols do not follow that pattern anymore. Even though the Simple Object Access Protocol (SOAP) still has the word "simple" in it, it is a layered specification that reminds us of baroque ISO/OSI specifications. Several layers in this specification are not even used in normal applications and are only there to satisfy potential requirements that are not needed for real-life environments.

To make KISS your guiding principle, you need to ask yourself three questions all of the time:

1. Is this really needed?
2. Which requirement is fulfilled here?
3. Is there another, simpler, way to do it with sufficient quality?

where "it" and "this" are the component or configuration that you are designing right now, or where you are working.

When we design something, a few basic principles should be used as guidance:

High intra-component abstraction strength: Make a component do one thing and do it well. Each component must have a clear objective; you should be able to express it in one or two sentences. If you cannot do that, your architecture is probably wrong. This objective is the responsibility of that component, do not water that down.

Low component coupling: Components depend on others to do their work. Try to keep these dependencies as few as possible. Do not just access another component "because it is there." For every dependency, there must be a real functional need that is solved and that cannot be solved internally or with fewer dependencies.

If you have dependencies anyhow, it is better to introduce another in an already-existing dependency relationship than to create a new one. That is, if two components had no dependency relationships up to now, think hard about adding one.

Create interfaces and obey them: There is a common problem on all system stack layers above the hardware level – engineers tend to access internals of other components and depend on implementation details in the component's usage. It might be that internal storage formats or storage technology is visible at the interface, or that access cannot be traced, audited, and debugged properly (e.g., access to internal variables instead of using services or functions). This seriously hinders future development of your architecture, when the requirements change – and requirements will change, all the time.

Therefore, each and every component must have a documented interface, and that interface should be used solely for access to that component. While it seems to be a lot of up-front work, it will result in big advantages in the midterm and long term.

These questions and principles will enable you to create robust architectures that will stand the test of time. Of course, they are good advice for any architectural development, not just when you target high availability and disaster recovery. Nothing here is specific to high availability and disaster recovery, but it is worth repeating nevertheless as it is forgotten or ignored so often.

Redundancy and Simplicity – Contradicting Goals

We have maneuvered ourselves into a contradiction: on the one hand, we promote redundancy to achieve protection against component failures; on the other hand, we argue for simplicity since less complex system designs tend to fail less frequently. But redundant designs have more parts and the additional burden of a management component, and are therefore by definition more complex than nonredundant systems. These two goals obviously contradict each other.

Sometimes the solution consists of managing the failures. When we can devise a repair or workaround action for a failure, we can handle incidents that are caused by it, even automatically. For a component, one might not manage all failures the same way: some failure scenarios are handled automatically because they will lead only to minor outages; for some failure scenarios, it is accepted that they lead to major outages, then failure management often becomes manual.

Looking at practical experience, it is not possible to tell outright if one has to prefer one goal over the other:

- Network interface cards can be made redundant by supplying multiple cards and managing the duplication in the operating system by a "multipath configuration." For many operating systems, current multipath configurations are more prone to error than the network card itself. In such constellations, it is better to leave the card nonredundant and just go on with the simple solution and the remaining risk. In particular, if some redundancy is planned at a higher level anyhow, only multipath configurations known to be stable should be used.

- Disk failure is so probable and failure consequences are so grave that one needs fault protection in any case. Enterprise-class storage subsystems provide reasonable redundancy: the disks are redundant, the volume manager is not. The probability of a volume manager error is usually negligible.

  But this example also shows that one must not make simplistic recommendations. If you have the requirement that disks shall be redundant and just go out and buy an arbitrary "Raid storage controller" for disk mirroring and think you have succeeded, you might be in luck or you might be in for a bad surprise: Some Raid controller/operating system combinations just do not work well enough, e.g., you do not get proper notifications about disk outages, or the controller microcode can crash.

- Database clusters are a technology that is not mature for many products, or where not enough experience exists in many companies. While one company might choose to utilize redundancy on the database level by introducing database clusters, other companies are reluctant.

  Another choice is database failure management: there are failures with high probability and low damage, notably not or slowly responding server processes. Failover clusters can be used to manage such failures and try several error recovery strategies automatically, among them restart of the server or switch to another computer system. For the rest of the failure scenarios, disaster recovery by any means might be an acceptable solution.

Looking at these examples, a question raises itself almost immediately: How does one know which variant and which technology to choose? Well, the answer is straightforward, although not very easy: experience is the key to success.

Experience Gathering

Either the architect or other subject matter experts have enough experience themselves to know what works. Or they need to tap the experience of others and try to capture the "common knowledge" that is available about technology and components. For example, this book provides a collection of such experience, among other content.

If you have the experience already, that is best, of course. It is quite natural that experienced architects are drawn to design the mission-critical systems of a company, and that people with less experience first need to work in many projects to gain their own experience. But what if one arrives in a situation that goes beyond one's past work scope and where one has to tackle new dimensions?

One method to handle such situations is to work with consultants that one trusts. They have the advantage that they do similar work for several clients and in many environments and can leverage that past experience for your situation. You should make sure that their design process and design rationales are transparent for you. It is a very bad situation if the consultant left your company and you have to cover failure situations without having realized the trade-offs that were made during the design.

Another method is to look for experience reports. They can be in technical magazines; the better ones are well known. Or they are personal war stories from past or current colleagues. That is especially the raison d'être for user groups that exist for almost any vendor product. To be a member of such a community gives access to a wider range of experience than you can have personally. Other experience reports are published and discussed in Usenet and on Web sites. Usenet is a particular place where a plethora of technical information can be found, both good and bad. The good information is in FAQs, or is accompanied by a discussion where the most sensible arguments in the discussion thread agree with that opinion.

It goes without saying that one has to judge the quality of the information source – there are fans out there who will praise a product unrealistically, as well as those who bear a grudge against the vendor and will denounce the product at every opportunity. But both types of person are mostly easy to detect and their advice can be outrightly dismissed or at least taken with a very big pinch of salt.

Marketing material and vendor appraisals are never a good source for experience information. No vendor will tell you that their goods are not good; they will all tout their own products as the best thing since sliced bread. You can get factual information from the data sheets, and even they must be read with caution. Often it is more telling what the data sheet leaves off than what is on it.

4.1.4 Virtualization

Virtualization is a topic that has accompanied computer system designs since the start. Depending on the time, most people associated different things with the term:

* In the 1950s, it was usage of computer systems by more than one program: time sharing comes along.
* In the 1960s, it was usage of more memory than is available in the computer system: virtual memory becomes common.
* In the 1970s, it was independence from the hardware components: UNIX was rewritten in C, the first portable operating system in the world.

- In the 1980s, it was independence from algorithm implementations: software architectures evolved with new programming paradigms that encouraged creation of ever-higher abstractions. On the hardware front, the idea was dormant; this was the age of the PC with its software installations bound to specific drive letters.
- In the 1990s, it was independence from computers: the Internet took off and networked environments were en vogue.
- In the 2000s, a 1960s idea has reappeared with full force and it is virtual computer systems all over again: virtual hosts promise to remedy the problems that we introduced with the PC architecture in the 1980s.

But basically, it is all the same.

Virtualization is building abstractions and using them, instead of the real things.

This concept is important, not the specific products or technology that is associated with it.

We need virtualization to implement redundancy. It establishes independence from specific components and allows us to exchange them as needed, or to locate the service at a different component that provides the same virtual interface.

When we introduce redundant components into an architecture, we do it to cope with potential failures of one component. This means that our component usage must not be bound to a specific instance, otherwise outage of that instance would render our complete system unusable. Instead, a virtual component must be created that conceals the real thing. That virtual component takes requests and dispatches them; it is able to change the dispatching according to availability or functionality of the real system.

Please note this is not only the case for hardware. We use the term *component* in a very broad sense. A component is also an operating system abstraction like a process or network interface. It may be a logical database space, or an abstract identifier for a Web service that is mapped to a specific service end point by some directory system. We meet virtualization in many variants, all over the place on all system stack layers. In fact, as we have seen, virtualization is one of the basic computer science principles that permeate all good designs and will appear in high availability and disaster recovery as well.

4.2 Solution Roadmap

Up to now, we have learned about the basic principles of good system design for high availability: categorization in the system stack, redundancy, robustness and simplicity, and virtualization. But what does this mean for you if you are responsible for producing a solution and want to create the technical system design? Let us assume that you have written down the business objectives and the business processes that are relevant for your system architecture. If you want to produce the *what* and *how* cells of the system architecture, you need to proceed in the following steps:

1. List failure scenarios
2. Evaluate scenarios, and determine their probability
3. Map scenarios to requirements
4. Design solution, using the dependency chart methodology
5. Review the solution, and check its behavior against failure scenarios

These steps are not just executed in sequence. Most important, solutions, requirements, and failure scenarios are not independent. If one has a different solution there might well be different failures to consider. Also, different solutions come with very different price tags attached. Business owners sometimes want to reconsider their requirements when they recognize that the protection against some failure scenarios costs more than the damage that might be caused by them. Therefore, during each step, we need to evaluate if the results make it necessary to reconsider the previous steps' results. These feedback loops prevent the consistent-but-wrong design syndrome.

With this iterative approach in mind, let us have a look at each of those steps in more detail.

4.2.1 List Failure Scenarios

It is not realistic for us to list each and every incident that can render such complex systems unusable. For example, one can have an outage owing to resource overload that may be caused by many reasons: too many users, some software error, either in the application or the operating system, a denial of service attack, etc. It is not possible to list all the reasons, but it *is* possible to list all components that can fail and what happens if they fail alone or in combination.

So we start by writing up the specific system stack without any redundancy information. Then we list for each component how that component can fail. The system stack already gives us a good component categorization that will help us to categorize the failure scenarios as well. First we will write up high-level failure scenarios, and then we will iterate over them and make them more precise by providing more detailed (and more technical) descriptions of what can go wrong.

Sometimes the owner of a business process has its own failure scenarios, e.g., from past incidents, that it wants to see covered. Usually, it is easy to add them to the list of generic failure scenarios. That is a good thing to do even if they are there already in a generalized form – it will bring you a better buy-in from that important stakeholder.

Example 1 (Failure scenario for an engineering system). The following list is an excerpt from failure scenarios for an engineering system that also utilizes a database with part detail information. This is the second iteration, where high-level failure scenarios (marked with bullets) are dissected into more specific scenarios (marked with dashes). The iteration process is not finished yet; the failure scenario list therefore is not complete and covers only exemplary failures.

But if you compare that list with the one from Table 2.5 on p. 37, it is clear that this is more structured and oriented along the system stack. It is the result of a structured analysis, and not of a brainstorming session:

- User- or usage-caused failure
  - Deletion of a small amount of data (up to a few megabytes)
  - Deletion of a large amount of data (some gigabytes, up to terabytes)
  - Utilization of too many resources in a thread-based application
  - Flood of requests/jobs/transactions for a system
- Administrator-caused failure
  - Deletion of application data
  - Deletion of user or group information
  - Change to configuration or program makes service nonfunctional
  - Incomplete change to configuration or program that makes failure protection nonfunctional (e.g., configuration change on a single cluster node)
- Engineering application failures
  - Aborting of application
  - Corruption of data by application error
  - Loss of data by application error
  - Hung Java virtual machines
  - Memory leak consuming available main memory
  - File access denied owing to erroneous security setup
- Database failures
  - Database file corrupted
  - Database content corrupted
  - Index corrupted
  - Database log corrupted
  - Deadlocks
  - Automatic recovery not successful, manual intervention needed
- Operating system failures
  - Log files out of space
  - Disk full
  - Dead, frozen, or runaway processes
  - Operating system queues full (CPU load queue, disk, network, ...)
  - Error in hardware driver leads to I/O corruption

- File system corruption
  - Recover by journal possible
  - Automatic file system check time within the service level agreement (SLA)
  - Automatic file system check time beyond the SLA
  - Manual file system repair needed
- Storage subsystem failure
  - Disk media failure
  - Microcode controller failure
  - Volume manager failure
  - Backplane failure
  - Storage switch interface failure
- Hardware failure
  - CPU failure
  - Memory failure
  - Network interface card failure
  - Backplane failure
  - Uninterruptible power supply (UPS) failure
- Physical environment destroyed
  - Power outage
  - Room destroyed (e.g., by fire)
  - Building destroyed (e.g., by flood)
  - Site destroyed (e.g., by airplane crash)
  - Town destroyed (e.g., by hurricane, large earthquake, war)
- Infrastructure service unavailable
  - Active Directory/Lightweight Directory Access Protocol (LDAP) outage, not reachable, or corrupted
  - DNS not reachable
  - Loss of shared network infrastructure
  - Network latency extended beyond functionality
  - Virus attack
  - Switch or router failure
  - Email not available
  - Backup server not reachable
  - License server outage or not reachable
- Security incidents
  - Sabotage
  - Virus attacks
  - Denial of service attacks
  - Break-ins with suspected change of data

You might have noticed that some failure descriptions are quite coarse and do not go into much detail. Failure scenario selection is guided by experience, and in particular by experience with potential solutions. When one knows that all faults that are related to processes will have to be handled the same way (namely, the system must be restarted) it does not make much sense to distinguish whether the CPU load or the memory queue is full.   ■

4.2.2 Evaluate Failure Scenarios

For each failure scenario, you have to estimate two properties:

1. The probability of the failure
2. The damage that is caused by that failure

Chapter 5 has a section on computation of probability of hardware failures. But in practice, we cannot determine numbers, neither for the probability nor for the damage. If we have a similar system running and have had incidents there, we can use this data for better approximations.

What we can do is to determine the relative probability and the relative damage of the scenarios and map them on a two-dimensional graph. Figure 4.10 on the facing page shows such a mapping for selected scenarios.

4.2.3 Map Scenarios to Requirements

Scenarios with high probability must be covered within the SLA requirements. All these failures must lead only to minor outages, i.e., to outages where work can continue in short time frames. Protection against this class of failures falls in the realm of high availability.

Usually, some of the failure scenarios are expected to lead to no outage at all, also to no aborted user sessions. In particular, this is true for defects in disk storage media that happen quite often. When disks fail, backup disks must take over functionality without any interruption and without any state changes beyond the operating system or the storage subsystem.

Our knowledge of business objectives and processes, i.e., about the requirements, gives an initial assumption about maximum outage times per event and maximum outage times per month or per year for this class of failure scenarios. For example, business objectives would strive for at maximum 1 min per incident and 2 min per month, during 14 × 5 business hours. (As mentioned already in Chap. 1, such measurements are more illustrative than 99.99%.) Later, when we have seen the costs for such a solution, the business owners might want to lower their requirements, then we have to iterate the process described.

There are failure scenarios with low probability and high potential damage that should be considered as major outages and will not be covered by SLAs. If we choose to protect against these failures as well, we need to introduce disaster-recovery solutions.

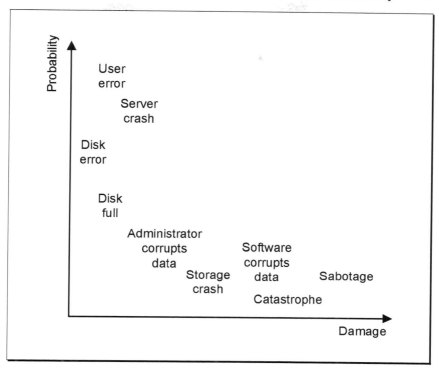

Fig. 4.10. Scenario mapping on probability and damage estimation

Again, requirements for disaster recovery come from business objectives and processes. The requirements are expressed in terms of recovery time objectives and recovery point objectives. For example, requirements might be to achieve functionality again within 72 h of declaring the disaster, and to lose at most 4 h of data.

At the very end, there are failure scenarios that we choose not to defend against. Most often, these failure scenarios are associated with damage to non-IT processes or systems that is even larger and makes the repair of IT systems unnecessary. It might also be that we judge their probability to be so low that we will live with it and do not want to spend money for protection. For example, while coastal regions or cities near rivers will often find it necessary to protect themselves against floods, businesses in inner areas will often shun protection against large-scale natural catastrophes like hurricanes or tsunamis.

Eventually, such scenario/requirements mapping means categorization of our scenario map. We color different areas and tell which kind of protection we want for these failure scenarios.

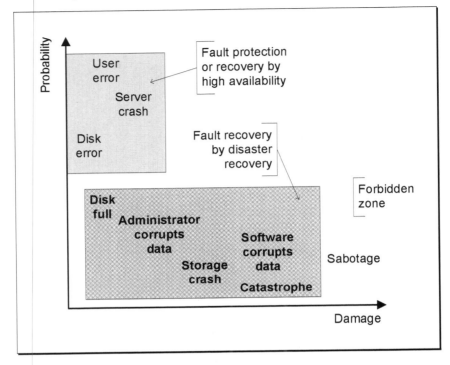

Fig. 4.11. Requirement areas added to scenario mapping

Figure 4.11 takes up Fig. 4.10 and adds those areas. We can also have two other, similar, figures where we exchange the meaning of the x-axis. In the first one, we use outage times. Then we can have two markers, one for the maximum minor outage time and one for recovery time objective. The locations of some failure scenarios in this graph will change, but the idea is the same: We can show which failure scenario must be handled by which fault protection method. The second additional figure would use recovery point objectives on the x-axis and would show requirements on maximum data loss.

It is important to point out that the chart has a large area where no scenario is placed and which is not touched by any of the requirement areas. We call this area the *forbidden zone*, as failure scenarios that appear subsequently must not be located there. If they are, we have to remap the scenarios and redesign our solution.

There exists the possibility that there is a failure scenario with high probability and high damage, where the protection cost would be very high as well. For example, if an application allowed a user to erase several hundred of gigabytes of data without being able to cancel the process, and without any undo facility, this might very well lead to a major outage. In such cases, the only possibility might be to change the application's code, or to select another application that provides similar functionality.

4.2.4 Design Solution

We started with a first approach at a specific system stack and its dependency diagram when we looked at failure scenarios. This diagram is now developed further:

- Either products for the components were chosen up-front by the business owner, or you are able to choose them at will now.
- Each product might introduce new dependencies, in particular, to infrastructure services. Do not forget to note them.
- Some products are promoted as redundant. For example, many storage subsystems have mirrored disks (or at least Raid5) and therefore the vendor names them redundant. For a first analysis, one can mark these components as redundant in the dependency chart.

    Later, one has to draw from one's experience if one is willing to live with the single points of failure that are invariably in such components. In our storage subsystem example, that is most often the internal volume manager and the microcode controller.
- Do not forget that there is a difference between storage media (disks) and storage data (file systems, databases). Making the media redundant still leaves the data unique in your system. While databases are seldom forgotten, file systems are often seen as a part of the operating system, but should be seen as separate components from the start.
- Next, we need to determine the single points of failure. For each single point of failure, we must decide if we want to protect against its failure and add appropriate redundancy to our system design.

    This redundancy often comes in the form of added products that must be added to the chart as new components. We need to pay particular attention to the management component of the redundancy relation which is very often not redundant in itself. For example, if we introduce a failover cluster for redundancy on the operating system level, the cluster management component is distributed over all cluster nodes and is not redundant; its failure can bring down the whole cluster.
- The newly introduced dependencies and components will add additional failure scenarios. Selection of products might also mean that some failure scenarios apply only partially. For example, while we might have "disk failure" as one scenario at the start, we need to distinguish between "disk media failure" and "disk subsystem failure" (meaning failures in the volume manager or microcode controller) now.

We need to go into an iteration of our solution design and write up those new failure scenarios, evaluate them, and map them to our requirements. This might lead to detection of additional single points of failure, where the iteration starts again.

- Finally, we need to check the costs of our solution against the benefit that it will bring. If we do not do so, there might be a chance that we will have designed a system that fits described specifications, but not real requirements. Here is the point where a business owner might want to lower or raise its SLAs, depending on the value of the business process and the available budget.
- For the remaining single points of failure, we need to prepare and get management sign-off that the business owner is willing to live with the remaining risk.

4.2.5 Review Selected Solution Against Scenarios

We had several solution candidates and chose one of them. Now is the time to check that in order to develop the solution we have not lost sight of our requirements. Before we start to implement it and invest lots of resources, we need to review whether the selected solution really fits.

It would be possible to test this, after a solution has been built, but we get best value for price if we do such a check up-front theoretically, without any practical tests. A good method to do the check is a review.

Best practice is to let the review be made by an independent party that was not involved in solution selection or solution design. The reviewer may have been involved in other areas of the architecture, e.g., in formulation of objectives or the conceptual model.

The reviewer will look at each failure scenario and will check if the selected solution protects against or recovers from those failures. Part of the review is also to check if the time ranges are realistic, i.e., if the selected fault recovery can really be done in the required maximum outage time. For that, the reviewer must be acquainted with the technology of high-availability and disaster-recovery solutions, otherwise he or she would not produce realistic assessments.

4.3 System Solution Patterns

Securing IT services against failure cannot be done without considering the whole IT process that is needed to keep a service alive.

Enterprise-class IT processes require complex system architecture solutions. Decisions about high-availability usage must consider the whole set of systems involved throughout the process. To find adequate high-availability solutions for your own IT infrastructure, it is necessary to evaluate two aspects:

1. Which categories of systems are involved in the complete IT process for a service?
2. Which level of importance or which category of availability is needed for a service?

With these questions answered, it is possible to follow recommended patterns about usage of high availability for the categories of systems involved.

4.3.1 System Implementation Process

System architecture solutions for services follow the demand of IT processes. Enterprise-class IT processes cannot only focus on operations of a service, but must consider all other parts of a software life cycle as well.

The specific system requirements will vary depending on the business, application and technical demands of a service. In-house development certainly requires additional extensive IT infrastructure.

However, no complex IT service runs out of the box. Even for commercial products, the IT department will have to implement a service based on the software bought, which includes configuration, integration into other business solutions, establishment of data backup, operative backup solutions, tests, and release cycles.

Though the number of systems may differ, the tasks, the actors, and therefore the categories of systems involved in establishment and operation of a service stay the same:

- Development and configuration for new and for upgrade versions
- Tests
- Acceptance by business owners
- Integration into operative environment
- Establishment of failover/backup/disaster solutions
- User training
- Operations

4.3.2 Systems for All Process Steps

As stated before, an IT service depends on more than just its operative servers. The following categories should be considered for keep-alive scenarios of services:

Development systems provide a platform for software development, modification, and configuration that is completely separated from production.

For complex services, the architecture may differ from the production setup:

- Service components may share systems that are separated in production: e.g., a database is on the local system instead of a central database host.
- Service components may use different systems that are on the same host in production: e.g., a central database host is shared by development systems for different services.
- Service components may be missing: e.g., test of backup mechanisms is not possible.

Functionality and acceptance test systems provide a platform that is used for testing the application at stable development points. Usually, one will work with systematic test scenarios here, to cover a specific range of functionality.

Integration test systems provide a platform for integrating a new release into the productive environment. The systems must therefore be as similar as possible to the production systems. Failover and disaster-recovery tests should be possible, as well as access to copies of live data.

Staging systems provide a platform for introduction of new releases, especially to train users. Some functionalities may be deactivated or simulated only (e.g., billing, accounting, alerting).

Staging systems will often be unified with the integration test systems, though the two tasks may need careful synchronization (user activities may prevent system-level tests, backup/recovery tests may lead to user irritations, etc.).

Production systems run the current release of a service. This includes failover systems, load-balancing systems, etc. that are operative or in hot standby.

Disaster-recovery systems take over the services when the production systems fail. They may have reduced performance, functionality, and complexity.

In the past, establishing these systems for each project was very expensive and was only done in special circumstances for mission-critical services.

But advances in host virtualization and hardware performance make it possible today to introduce virtual hosts for each system category on a small set of hardware systems. One can also easily share a computer system to run virtual hosts for many projects. Therefore, one can assume that proper system categorization will become a commodity and will be used for many more situations in the future.

Table 4.1. Solution approaches for system type and outage categorization. *HA* high availability, *S* standalone, *SB* has standby

	Mission-critical	Business-important	Business-foundation
Disaster recovery	SB	S	S
Production	HA+SB	HA	SB
Staging	HA+SB	HA	S
Integration test	HA	S	S
Acceptance test	S	S	S
Development	S	S	S

System Type Selection

We introduced system classes in Sect. 2.2 on p. 17 according to their allowed outage times, i.e., mission-critical, business-important, and business-foundation. Each of our system types can appear in one of these categories, and for each combination we have to select if we really need high availability for that system, if a standalone system is sufficient, or if we also need a standby system as a disaster-recovery precaution.

Fault-tolerant deployments of production systems often change the environment in which an application operates. For example, failover clusters come with requirements for applications that we will present in Sect. 8.1 on p. 217. Quite often, application developers are not aware of those requirements or do not obey them consistently. It would be very nice if the application development happened under circumstances that are similar to those in production.

On the other hand, operating high-availability environments is additional work, even with virtual host technology employed. Since such work is expensive, development-near systems are seldom operated under high-availability conditions. Table 4.1 presents typical selections for a combination of system type and outage categories.

4.3.3 Use Case: SAP Server

Finally, to finish this chapter, we look at a possible high-availability system design for an SAP server. This scenario combines several often-used methods and technologies that will be covered in detail in the following chapter.

We will have a look at a modern SAP installation that includes a Web front-end and is not restricted to the classic R/3 client. Figure 4.12 on the next page introduces the three-tier model that underlies such a server installation. In fact, that model is the basis of many current applications; therefore, the approach from this scenario can be utilized for many other scenarios as well.

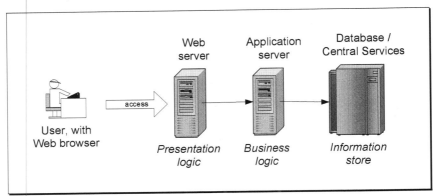

Fig. 4.12. SAP server introduction. *Arrows* between servers show request flow

Users access the SAP server with a browser. There is also the possibility to access it by a client program: this utilizes a subset of the same server installation and can be subsumed in the realm of our example scenario.

Web server is used to realize the *presentation logic*. It is also known as the *WGate* component of the *Internet Transaction Server* (ITS). No data and no state are kept here. All user requests are forwarded to the SAP Application Server, and results are returned and turned into Web pages to represent them. Of course, these Web pages also have forms with user actions (buttons, links) to complete the dialog component.

Application Server is used to realize the *business logic*. It is also known as *AGate* for ABAP-based SAP environments, or as *SAP Web AS* for Java-based SAP environments. For this scenario, the *Replicated Enqueue Server* also belongs to the Application Server.
No persistent data is kept here, but user sessions and their respective transient states are managed. Functional requests are received from the Web server and results are computed, depending on past actions and business rules. The computation utilizes the database server and retrieves or stores persistent information there.

Database server and Central Services are used to store all persistent information in a relational database and hold the message queue. SAP supports the usage of a wide range of database products, ranging from the open-source SAP DB to IBM's DB2 or Oracle. In some SAP variants, the enqueue service also is part of the Central Services, when no Replicated Enqueue Server is used.

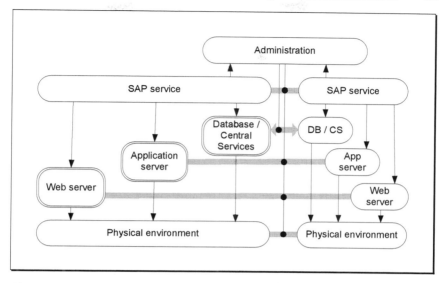

Fig. 4.13. SAP server system design overview. Not all dependencies to Administration are shown

High-Level Design Decisions

Since the SAP server keeps the financial information of the whole company, it is a mission-critical system. We do not postulate specific maximum outage times or availability SLAs for this scenario; they can be tailored to typical ranges for that type of application.

Since SAP software does not allow a user to destroy a lot of data, the business owner decides that errors in the user environment are not covered. All components depend on the infrastructure environment. That is seen as redundant already; its failures are beyond the scope of that project.

Therefore, we can discard any dependencies from or to components *user environment* and *infrastructure* from our specific systems stack. On the other hand, administrators can do a lot of damage to an SAP server, so they are in. Also, failure scenarios with the physical environment (fire, floods, earthquakes, terrorist attacks) will be handled.

Figure 4.13 gives an overview of the resulting dependency diagram. Basically, the server installations are at two sites: the primary site is on the left, the backup site on the right. Server installation at the primary site shall be redundant as well; this redundancy shall be good enough to handle minor outages. There will be single points of failure on the primary site that can lead to major outages; we will have a look at them later.

The redundancy shown in this diagram is there to handle major outages and is managed by administrators. Since several of the components involved are themselves redundant, we have to leave more detailed description of this redundancy until we describe the respective components. Only for the database server must data be replicated. For all other components, redundancy is achieved by synchronizing software installation and configuration.

The dependency diagram shows one single point of failure: the administration. For our example case, the remaining risk associated with administrator failures is judged acceptable. Of course, administrators are required to be careful in their work, but additional safeguards (e.g., mandatory four-eyes principle for every configuration change) are not established. Their associated costs are deemed too high.

An important tidbit of this dependency graph is the way that we represent the dependency between the three SAP server types. The obvious choice would have been to take the request flow arrows from Fig. 4.13 on the previous page and use them literally as dependencies. Instead we introduce a new component named "SAP service" that depends on all servers. This way the dependency diagram represents directly the fact that an outage of one server makes the whole SAP service unusable and that all server configurations must be orchestrated to match the demands of the SAP service. It also gives us the opportunity to express the management of redundancy for the SAP service – administrators might need to change the overall configuration to make the SAP service functional on the backup site.

Last, but not least, it gives prominent notice that this is about the SAP service in the end, and not about three servers that are dependent in some way. Failure in the SAP service component occurs when the orchestrated "working together" of the three server components is not done correctly, supposedly through a software error. For example, though it is not probable, an error in the code could delete the whole database, leading to a major outage that cannot be handled by the database server redundancy anymore.

To handle failure in this component completely and achieve full redundancy, care must be taken that the same software error is not repeated at the backup site; this will be the responsibility of the administrators. That failure scenario illustrates why switches to the backup site often need some time and are *not* a matter of simply switching on the backup system. When a major outage happens, one needs to analyze the failure situation and understand what has happened and why. Otherwise that failure situation could be repeated at the backup site – and we do not yet have another backup; utilizing the existing backup site for disaster recovery will be the first and last attempt that *must* succeed.

A Closer Look at Server System Design

In our overview dependency diagram, we noted that each server on the primary site is redundant itself and has a nonredundant server on the backup site as redundancy for major outages. Let us have a look at each of those servers in more detail.

When we zoom into these redundant components, we will see that each and every component will have single points of failure. In fact, we could subsume them all under the heading of *almost redundant*, as discussed on p. 71. On the other hand, when we look at the higher-level design decision that the redundancies at the primary site shall protect against minor outages and that a backup site is available for disaster recovery, we can achieve failure handling for the remaining single points of failure in that way. Of course, the remaining single points of failure are named for each specific system.

Web Server

Web servers in an SAP installation do not hold any state. That is the ideal situation to utilize load-balancing cluster technology. That technology is described in Sect. 6.2 on p. 176. It protects against outages on the operating-system and hardware level. When an outage occurs, the load balancer notices the nonreachability of the respective computer system and does not forward any requests anymore. Appliances are used as load-balancer components, to protect against their outages, and appliance-specific redundancy is utilized. This means that an appliance cluster manages the Web server cluster.

Figure 4.14 on the next page illustrates that design. Remaining failure causes could be in the Web server's code or configuration, and in the load-balancer cluster management itself. Outages in one of these single points of failure is extremely seldom and therefore a risk that can be taken for normal operations. When it happens, it will be a major outage since it will bring down the whole Web server as well, and disaster recovery shall kick in. For that case, we introduce redundancy for the Web server via administration. In the case of outages in this device or software, administrators will have to look at the failure causes and will have to bring the Web server at the backup site up and running – without running in the same failure situation.

Please note that we do not use redundant hardware. Since the Web servers do not have any data or state, we can utilize several cheap installations and let the load balancer handle outages. In fact, such designs often involve more than two Web servers. This is not taken up here since it would complicate the presentation without any additional benefit.

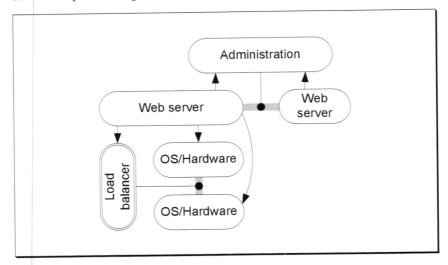

Fig. 4.14. SAP Web server design

Application Server

Both SAP AGate and SAP Web AS have built-in cluster capability. They are examples of middleware software products that deliver fault tolerance without the need for third-party software. Such fault-tolerant middleware software is the topic of Chap. 7. Figure 4.15 on the facing page illustrates that design choice.

Usage of that technology protects against failures on the operating-system and hardware level. Within limits, it also protects against errors in the Application Server, namely, when the failure is caused by previous application states and can be remedied by starting the session anew. This is handled in a transparent way by SAP, the end user does not notice reconnection of the client and restarting of the session.

There is a variant of the SAP Enqueue Server with built-in clustering capability too. If that product is used, it belongs to the Application Server as well from a system design point of view, as its high-availability tech-nology is the same. It also has fully transparent support for transaction resets in the event of enqueue service failure.

Other issues with the application server software will lead to a major outage; our disaster-recovery solution must handle these cases. For that, we introduce backup servers and manual management of that re-dundancy, as with the Web servers.

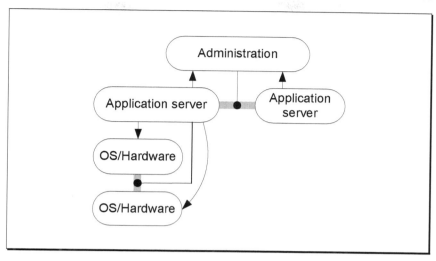

Fig. 4.15. SAP Application Server

Database server and Central Services

For the database server and the Central Services, a failover cluster on the operating system level has been selected. For Central Services, there is no other possibility. Since one uses it already, one can handle the database server redundancy with it as well.

If performance is not sufficient, usage of a specific database cluster would be possible, but most of the time, the simple failover cluster is sufficient.

An external storage subsystem is used that is already redundant. Figure 4.16 on the next page presents the resulting design.

Failover clusters on the operating system level protect against failures in the operating system, the hardware, and against some database errors. The are discussed in detail in Sect. 6.1. As with the Web and application servers, disaster recovery is used to protect against the remaining failure scenarios. Since storage is so important, disk failures are very probable, and redundant storage subsystems are a commodity nowadays, we also use them on the disaster-recovery site.

There remains the question of data replication to achieve redundancy for this part of the architecture. The storage subsystem is deemed to be redundant. But the caveats from p. 72 that those systems still have their single points of failure remain; therefore our design does not utilize a storage-based replication technology like WAN mirroring. Instead, database data are replicated logically by redo-log shipping that is applied with a delay to be able to skip commits of faulty transactions. The messages

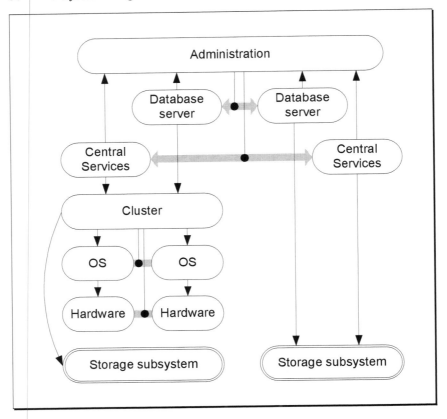

Fig. 4.16. SAP database server

that are maintained by Central Services are also stored in the database; therefore, no special replication method is needed for them. If the print output spool (e.g., invoices) is placed on file storage and not in database tables, we can utilize file replication for them.

Therefore, actual disaster recovery involves database administrators who will analyze the redo logs and make sure that the error situation of the primary site is not replicated at the backup site. Chapter 10 presents this method in more detail.

SAP Server System Design Pulled Together

Finally, Fig. 4.17 on p. 98 pulls together the high-level and the detailed design decisions that were presented in this section. This diagram is not complete and shows the problems of large dependency diagrams that shall present the essential points without getting bogged down in details.

- Some dependencies are not shown. In particular, there are many more dependencies to administration than the diagram is able to express and still be readable. After all, almost *every* component in that diagram must be administered somehow, even the physical environment. Only the most crucial dependency is shown that is specific for this installation.
- Some redundancy relations are not shown. For example, the Web and application servers on the primary and on the backup site are redundant via administration. Only the redundancy that involves data replication is shown.

According to this dependency diagram, the only remaining single point of failure is the *administration* component. However, more detailed analysis of the products used would be needed to confirm that there are no hidden single points of failure. There are still remaining risks with application errors that software problems will occur both at the primary and at the disaster-recovery site. But the remaining risk is very small and we have here a very sound system design that will provide IT service continuity both for minor and major outages.

One can go even further and tackle the remaining risk that lies mainly with potential failures of system administrators. That can be done with skill assessments, only letting people with a proven good track record do administration work, better work procedures, establishment of the four-eyes principle for changes, and other process-oriented improvements. With proper processes in place, and good people working as administrators, the remaining risk is negligible.

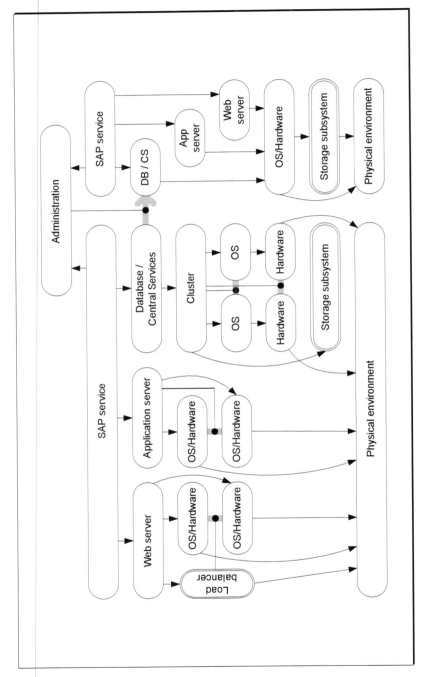

Fig. 4.17. SAP server dependency chart (incomplete, some dependency, and redundancy information is missing)

5

Hardware

In this chapter we talk about hardware, how to protect against failures or how to minimize them if total protection is not possible. We obviously do not build any hardware, but we select products and components which we configure to build our systems.

Hardware components are the most basic building blocks for computer systems. Handling their failures and outages was the first objective that was realized in high-availability installations, when failures in other system-stack components were not (yet) handled. Therefore it is also the most mature technology with the most widespread availability of ready-to-buy solutions and products.

As with all other component categories, redundancy and robustness are the basic approaches that are used to achieve high availability for hardware components. Both approaches contribute to increase the reliability of those components and complete systems, realizing high availability and disaster recovery.

The maturity of the system-stack hardware layer can be seen in the fact that hardware is the only area where quantification of reliability is available. This is the only area where we can really compute the probability of failures and plan in advance how to handle them and which resources must be made available for that. Appendix A introduces the theory behind reliability computation and shows how that can be used in real environments.

Another sign of that area's maturity is that it not only concentrates on recovery from failures, but also on protection against failures. This is particularly true for disk drives, which are the most probable source of failures, owing to them being high-end technology and having moving parts. For them, standard technology allows disk failures to be handled in a way that is completely invisible for the end user: no outage is recognized. Most other redundancy technologies do not protect against systems or application crashes and "just" realize proper continuation of service after a restart.

This chapter introduces the most important hardware components and also management and operational issues that are needed to achieve high availability on the hardware level:

- **Components and computer systems** will look at the different hardware components in computer systems and will show high-availability options that are available for them, in Sect. 5.1.
- **Disk storage** is presented in Sect. 5.2 and will pull together all information about that area. That will not only cover disks themselves, but also complete storage systems as well as a discussion of storage area networks (SAN) vs. network-attached storage (NAS).
- **Virtualization** is a property that is needed all the time to realize high availability for hardware components and is presented in Sect. 5.3.
- **Vendor selection** is the topic of Sect. 5.4; while it is not possible to recommend specific vendors in this fast-moving industry, we will see general criteria that help with purchasing decisions.
- The **system installation** can make a computer system available in the long run or can cripple its reliability; that is explained in Sect. 5.5.
- **System maintenance** is the next straw, after a successful installation. As Sect. 5.6 shows, it can make the difference between keeping a system running or seeing it fail all the time.
- High availability is also the quest for ongoing improvements. **Own statistics** are a prerequisite for qualified decisions and Sect. 5.7 shows how to gather them.

But before we go into the details of high availability for hardware components, let us review the evolution of systems and their features. The two driving factors are improvements in silicon technology (i.e., chips) and disk drive technology. Both show exponential increases of several features over the last few decades. The best-known example is *Moore's Law*, which was stated by Gordon Moore in the 1970s. Moore observed that the number of transistors in an integrated circuit doubles every 24 months.[1] He analyzed future potential improvements and predicted that this growth will continue in the foreseeable future. The amazing fact is that his prediction has held pretty well for more than 30 years until today. Moore never named his prediction a "law," but today it is always referred to as "Moore's Law." To illustrate its power, the first microprocessors came out in the 1970s and had a few thousand transistors, whereas today chips have billions of transistors, a factor of millions in complexity!

A similar observation was made by Kryder about the information density of disk drives (bits per area). He saw an even faster growth rate than Moore did for chips.

---

[1] His statement is sometimes cited with a doubling rate of 18 months; however, the exact number is not important to our discussion.

Table 5.1. Comparison of different growth rates based on Moore's Law and Kryder's Law.

	Yearly increase (%)
CPU complexity	50
Memory capacity	60
Memory speed	10
Disk drive capacity	60
Disk drive speed	25
Network bandwidth	40
Network latency	0

So far so good, we should be happy that everything gets faster, bigger, and cheaper. The important point is that different features have different growth rates, which lead to a change in bottlenecks and overall system behavior. Table 5.1 shows some features with different growth rates. The growth rates given there could be debated – they depend on the time interval considered. For our context the results do not change if the numbers change by some percentages.

Let us first consider CPU complexity, memory capacity, and memory speed. More memory allows us to work on larger amounts of data or could be used to improve disk performance by using it for caching. The higher CPU complexity allows for faster CPUs. But the issue is that memory speed does not grow evenly fast. That resulted in large memory caches which sit between the CPU and the main memory. Some systems have a three-level hierarchy of caching, where the first two levels are mostly located on the CPU chip. This led to the fact that most of the transistors of a CPU chip were used as a cache. Over time the gap grew so much that a different approach was chosen: instead of "wasting" all the transistors as cache, multiple CPUs were built into a chip. The idea behind this is when one CPU waits for data coming from memory, the chip switches to the next CPU to execute other code. This works well when the workload can be parallelized (i.e., multiple processes or threads which can be executed independently) and if the requirements for memory bandwidth are small. That concept allows us to limit the size of the caches and lets the single CPU wait longer as more data need to come directly from or go to memory (i.e., worsening memory latency), but the waiting time is used for work by other CPUs in the chip. How far this concept works is unknown today; however, vendors experiment with chips that have many CPUs.

There is an imbalance between capacity and bandwidth. The chips deliver capacities that cannot be used to their full extent because the interfaces and bus systems do not have enough bandwidth to access all transistors as needed. This introduces the tendency that we will change buses and add more memory chips just to get more and wider interfaces, to yield higher bandwidths. These additional chips will add even more capacity that we will not use properly, but that is not the point. Adding these chips is triggered by the hunger of the CPU chips for memory bandwidth, not by the additional capacity.

Of course, adding more components increases also the probability of errors. This is not made smaller by the capacity increase of each chip that is realized by increasing the density. Just by the nearness of the transistors on one chip, the probability of failures on the transistor level is increased. Chip vendors conquer that problem by better production quality management and by adding internal redundancy, to get a reliability that is as high as or even better than that of chips of previous generations.

A similar effect comes from the imbalance of disk speed versus disk size. Relative to their capacity, drives are becoming slower and slower. This means that the time to write or read a whole drive is getting longer and longer. Also the larger amounts of data (coming from bigger memory as explained earlier) require more disk speed than the individual drives can provide. This leads to the need for wider and wider stripes, with the negative consequences for reliability as discussed in Sect. 5.2.1 and App. A.

A consequence of this trend is that components change their roles over time. Let us compare servers 20 years ago with those of today:

Disks ⇒ tape: They have become more and more sequential devices which store bulk data. Their random access time has become worse; their bandwidth has increased by utilizing striping. Many databases are stored in memory to a major extent – access to the disk is only seldom needed, like for a full table scan. Because of the long access latency, sophisticated read-ahead and write-behind algorithms are used to "hide" disk access by utilizing the high I/O bandwidth.

Memory ⇒ disk: Random access latency and huge size allows memory to play the role of disks 20 years ago.

Cache ⇒ memory: But only caches have an access latency of a few CPU cycles which gives them the role memory had before. Because the relative size of a cache compared with that of main memory gets smaller over time, other technologies are needed, like multicore CPUs or multithreading.

Figure 5.1 on the facing page illustrates the power of exponential laws and how the imbalance between size and speed grows over time. It shows that the time to read or write a whole disk drive takes exponentially longer over time: If a disk bought at year 0 takes time 1, then the newest model bought in year $n + 5$ will take 4.5 times longer. With memory it is even worse: here the factor after 5 years is 7.6.

Finally, let us see what consequences this development has for high availability of hardware components, and their realization by redundancy and robustness:

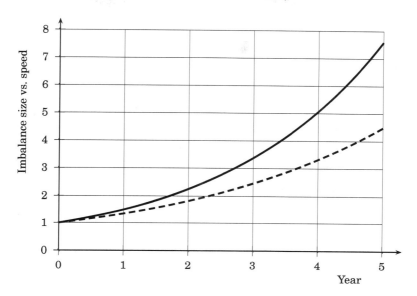

Fig. 5.1. Evolution of imbalance between memory capacity vs. memory speed (*solid line*) and disk capacity vs. disk speed (*dashed line*)

- Redundancy for disk drives means replication of data. But when a disk drive is replaced after a failure, that data must be restored to the new disk. Since the time to read and write whole disks gets longer every year, the resynchronization time will be longer as well – this means we will need longer to achieve redundant operation again. In effect, this means that the mean time to repair increases and the availability decreases.
- To compensate for the (relatively slower) disk speed, the data on one storage volume is distributed over more disks. This is called *striping* and is explained in more detail in Sect. 5.2.1. Utilizing more disks for one volume increases the probability of failures for that volume and thus decreases the overall reliability.
- A similar argument holds for memory chips. As outlined before, more memory chips and more connections are needed to feed CPUs with data. More parts increase the probability of failures.
- Larger memory capacity requires more time to read the whole memory. This will slow down the boot process if memory checking is enabled, and increase the time to write a dump after a system crash.

We see that improvements in chips and disk drives change the behavior of computer systems. This requires rethinking of configurations and operational procedures over time.

5.1 Components and Computer Systems

Even in today's state-of-the-art computing systems there are single points of failure like CPUs or the backplane.[2] The memory can be made redundant. The reason why they cannot protected by redundancy is that there is no independent management component available which could discover failures and activate backup components, see Sect. 4.1.2. For example, there is often no layer between a CPU and the operating system.

If we plan to purchase a new system, failure scenarios need to be considered and reviewed with the vendor's documentation to determine how they can be approached. Different vendors have different reliability features implemented in their systems; therefore we need to walk through the major components and point out the most important high-availability features to look for.

▶ *CPUs*

Some systems have a layer between the CPUs and the operating system, and this is sometimes called *hypervisor*. In this layer some errors can be managed and a CPU can be deactivated without a system crash. The application that uses the CPU at this time will probably crash nevertheless; that failure must be handled on a higher level in the system stack. But if the failure happens when the CPU executes operating system code, this failure scenario usually cannot be recovered at all, and the whole computer crashes.

Hypervisors do not provide fault protection or transparent failure recovery. If there is a CPU error, the end user will recognize it, because either the application or the whole system aborts. The goal of hypervisors is to restart and continue operation after such a failure has happened. For instance, such a system can reboot in a "degraded mode" after a CPU failure, with the failed CPU deactivated.

▶ *Memory*

As discussed at the beginning of this chapter, chip density is increasing exponentially. The number of memory chips in a system might increase as well to adapt to raising bandwidth demands – of course not as fast as chip density. This gives an increased number of failure scenarios from

---

[2] There are some exceptions which can partially deal with such failures, like HP NonStop servers or IBM mainframes, but even these are not protected against all kinds of failures, and they are not the subject of this book.

single bit errors to chip failures. Vendors have added error detection and correction mechanisms to their memory subsystems. This is done with technologies similar to redundant array of independent disks (Raid) for disk drives.

All systems should detect and correct single bit errors and detect multiple bit errors.

Modern computers can survive failures of a whole row or column (memory is organized as a matrix of bits), a whole chip, and sometimes a whole memory card (dual in-line memory module, DIMM). This requires the use of parity bits on multiple levels up to mirroring of the whole memory.

A technology called *memory scrubbing* tries to identify soft errors by reading in the background while memory is idle. If a threshold of soft errors is exceeded, the part affected can be deactivated before a real error happens.

We strongly advise reviewing the memory redundancy features of a system, especially if it has high capacity.

▶ *Backplane and System Bus*

These are the connectors at the heart of a system. Their ability to recover from failures is limited; a failure in the backplane typically causes a system crash. A reboot is often not possible, as there is no "degraded mode" possible without the backplane.

The only thing we can look for to identify a stable backplane or system bus is simplicity and robustness. This means no active components (this is commonly called a *passive backplane*), no cables, and mechanically robust connectors with a limited number of pins.

Systems which do not pass these criteria cannot be expected to run reliably over a long time. To illustrate the point we look at a negative example (the vendor is out of business today). The connection between the active backplane (bad) and the CPU and memory cards was implemented via cables (bad), which had several hundreds of connections (bad) on an area of about $4 \times 10\,\mathrm{cm}^2$. Many maintenance activities are required to unplug and plug these connections (bad). This system had a rating of four "bads" and never ran stably.

▶ *I/O and Network Cards*

Now we have arrived at the less critical components. I/O and network cards can be made redundant. The operating system manages redundancy and handles failures at that level.

Such cards can often be replaced without service interruption (hot plug), but this feature does not appear to be robust yet. We propose testing it under load conditions before we need to do it in production environments without experience.

▶ *Power Supplies*

These devices should be simple, robust, and easy to make redundant – a no-brainer. Servers have more than one power supply. They are typically installed in an $n + 1$ configuration, where for n active power supplies, one additional backup supply is available. With such a configuration, one productive supply can fail without service interruption.

Power supplies need heat dissipation, which is today mostly done with fans. Because fans have moving parts, they happen to have a lower reliability than many other hardware components; causing power supplies to fail as well more often. In the end, they can cause system crashes, or even smoldering fires. For mission-critical servers, $n + 1$ configurations are often not deemed reliable enough, and $n + 2$ configurations are used. Here, two backup power supplies are available and the whole component remains redundant even when one productive supply fails.

It is important to realize that power supplies can cause problems if they are not properly installed (e.g., not connected to independent power sources), failure detection does not work well (e.g., it is detected that one supply failed but not which one), or if one electrical short circuit can destroy multiple supplies.

We can expect that mature products should not show such problems anymore. It should be verified that the identification of a failed supply works and is integrated into our monitoring procedures.

▶ *Cables and Connections*

Cables and connections are the enemy of reliability. They are the place where intermittent problems or repeated problems with different failure patterns appear that are a horror to analyze and repair. They are very hard to identify, especially as every activity on the hardware could change the failure pattern. A good measure of the quality of a system is therefore how many cables it contains (internally and externally).

Our only advice is to look for systems with the minimal number of cables and simple connections.

If we work with clusters of systems, the situation with cabling can become worse. When many nodes reside in one rack, the amount of cabling can become enormous. Here specially prepared clusters can simplify the cabling significantly. Such cluster systems are called *blades*.

They are marketed with the argument of higher computing density per room space, but from the high-availability viewpoint their real advantage is the severe reduction of cabling in their installation.

An example of a problematic configuration is the *card-on-card architecture*. In that architecture, interface cards are not connected directly to the backplane. This might be because they are too small, e.g., Fibre Channel cards. Or one wants to use standard Peripheral Component Interconnect (PCI) cards, and the backplane of high-end servers have no PCI bus.

Then an intermediate (big) card is attached to the backplane, and the actual (small) interface cards are connected to this intermediate card. Such a configuration often comes with problems in failure identification when some connections do not work as intended. It needs very high production quality and the simplicity of the connections must be sufficient, otherwise such systems must be rated as bad.

When we have eventually decided on a vendor and a configuration, the next challenge comes up: system installation. We will have more to say on this in Sect. 5.5 and will just mention the important issue of cabling here. There is an incredible spectrum of quality in technicians who install systems, even if they come from reputable vendors. Both a good and a bad installation work in the beginning, but the bad one can and, according to Murphy's Law, will eventually make trouble.

Therefore we need to review the installation using the following little checklist:

- Do the cables have the right lengths (not too short, not too long)?
- Are they labeled?
- Do the texts on the labels have a meaningful scheme?
- Are the labels properly mounted (or do they fall down after a few weeks)?
- Do the cables have proper strain relief?
- Is the cable routing done properly?

All these questions sound obvious and trivial, but reality has proven, they are not!

Hardware Repair Activities

All hardware repairs can solve problems and create new ones. Especially work on productive system which are not redundant is a big risk. Take replacement of a failed power supply in an $n + 1$ configuration as an example. With no redundancy available anymore, the technician can pull the wrong (still working) power supply, and that will crash the system.

Another frequent source of errors is carelessness, e.g., when cards are not pushed straight on their connectors. Pushing them slanted may destroy some connector pin, again rendering the replacement component or even the backplane connection unusable.

The only thing we can do about this is to only let well-trained technicians do the work. Some companies do a "skill assessment" before they let somebody do work on their systems. This is similar to a driver's license. Unfortunately there is no generally accepted certificate for technicians; we are on our own with this risk.

5.2 Disk Storage

Disks are one of the most important parts of a computer system as they store the data, application programs, and operating systems. Owing to the data storage they are the most important hardware component of all – without that information, no IT-dependent business process can continue. Disk drives have moving parts and are high-end technology. Therefore they are the hardware component with the lowest reliability. That means most hardware errors are disk errors.

Since disk errors are so probable and disks are so important, the early users of the relevant high-availability technology thought that failure recovery was not sufficient and strived for fault protection instead. Redundant disks provide multiple storage of data, and that is discussed in the following sections. If a disk drive fails and is replaced with a new one, its content needs to be copied to the replacement disk. It requires somewhat complicated mechanisms to handle disk failures transparently to the upper levels in the system stack.

Before we discuss the various protection methods, let us consider the two major categories of disk storage:

Data disks This is where all our application data is stored. They are located in files which reside in file systems.[3]

Data disks have the special property that their replication and thus their redundancy has limits. Information that is stored there is only available once, and must be changed consistently. Therefore even with replicated data, some mechanism must exist that manages that replication. When this mechanism fails or some other failure happens on a higher level in the system stack, the content of the data disk can become corrupted and unusable. Therefore data disks carry always one of the highest risks in any system.

An important question is how large should the file systems be? We should always consider that a file system might crash and cannot be recovered. If we have a logical copy on another system (like a standby database) this failure should not be an issue. But if we depend on that file system, we need to recreate and restore the data from a backup, which also can cause data loss. This will mostly end up in a major outage. Therefore the file system size must be small enough that the restoration time is acceptable. Even with a high performance backup/restoration system, it is not advisable to go over a few terabytes.

The use of snapshots can also help with this issue.

Operating system disks Todays disk drives are far too large to only hold the operating system; therefore, it makes sense to use the same

---

[3] The use of a raw device to store databases is being used less and less. It is more difficult to operate and brings only a minor performance advantage.

disks for the root file system and the swap space. A typical configuration contains four disk drives: disks 1 and 2 for root/swap and its
mirror, disk 3 is a hot spare and disk 4 holds another copy of root/swap
for testing purposes (e.g., to test a new patch).

Mirroring root disks is sometimes tricky on some systems. It must be
possible to boot the system with only one disk, if it crashed during
a nonmirrored situation. This is mature technology, but needs to be
prepared and tested.

We propose always using local disks for the operating system. It is
possible to boot via a SAN or over the network using Internet SCSI
(iSCSI). However, for real missing critical servers the simplest and
most robust solution is the best.

There is an exception if a vendor provides an integrated solution with
this functionality, especially for small and medium-sized systems. Another reason to use a SAN or an iSCSI connection is the extensive use
of host virtualization. Then we typically have to manage many operating system instances, all with their own operating system. In this
case we need a management function for all the images, and often
works using a SAN or iSCSI. This technology provides lots of flexibility and many other advantages, but the additional level of complexity
needs to be understood.

5.2.1 Raid – Redundant Array of Independent Disks

Disk drives used to be large (some hundreds of kilograms), expensive
($10 000+), and had little capacity (a few gigabytes). The disks were often
not protected and if one broke, data needed to be restored from tape. In
accordance with Moore's Law, disks became small, cheap, and of high capacity. The concept of a *redundant array of inexpensive disks* (Raid) was
invented.[4] This technology, combining multiple disks to improve redundancy (and also performance), is a key technology nowadays – we need to
understand it in some detail to configure our systems. Several physical
disks are combined to build a "logical" one, often named a *Raid group*.
Figure 5.2 on the next page illustrates how the logical disk is seen by the
computer system; it is a layered model, as we find it in many other places
in this book.

There are different Raid configurations (sometimes called *Raid levels*)
which need to be discussed, before we explain the risks and pitfalls we
need to overcome in practice. They all follow the same idea: the data of
one I/O request (*read* or *write*) coming from the computer system are sent
to the Raid group and are distributed there to multiple disks enriched
with redundant information to provide protection against disk failure(s).

---

[4] Later renamed to *redundant array of independent disks*, which sounded more
respectable.

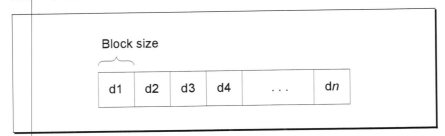

Fig. 5.2. Illustration of a virtual disk with its blocks, as seen by the computer system. Redundant array of independent disks (*Raid*) levels differ in how these blocks are mapped to blocks on the physical disks

If a disk drive fails, the redundant Raid group is able to reconstruct the lost information. It does this on-the-fly without disruption, but possibly with performance degradation. During this time the Raid group runs in a *degraded mode*, because now there is no (or less, in the case of Double Parity Raid, RaidDP) protection. To minimize this time, so-called hot-spare drives are used. Those are disks which are already installed and running, but they are not used and have no data on them. Their only purpose is to immediately jump in if a productive drive fails. Now the information on the failed disk needs to be reconstructed by using data from the surviving disks. Of course, the hot-spare disk will not be ready immediately and redundancy will only be reestablished after the reconstruction. This will take several hours for current disks.

Example 1. To illustrate how the reconstruction of data works, let us take a Raid group consisting of four disks for data and a fifth one storing the redundant information, called *parity*. The parity is calculated by using the *exclusive or* (XOR)[5] function between the corresponding bits on the data disks and storing the result on the parity disk.

In Fig. 5.3 on the facing page we show the parity calculation for 1 byte of data on each disk. How can we reconstruct the data if a disk fails? We just calculate the parity between the remaining disks plus the parity disk. If, for example, disk 2 fails, we see on the right-hand side of Fig. 5.3 how it works. ■

One advantage of using parity for redundancy is that it works with an arbitrary number of data disks. The disadvantage is that after a disk failure, all remaining disks need to be read in order to rebuild the data and write it to the hot spare.

---

[5] XOR is calculated by counting the number of 1's. If this is odd, then the result is 1, otherwise 0. For example, 1 XOR 0 XOR 1 XOR 1 = 1.

Disk	Byte							
1	1	1	0	0	1	0	0	1
2	0	1	1	0	1	1	1	0
3	0	0	0	1	0	0	1	1
4	1	1	1	0	1	0	1	1
Parity	0	1	0	1	1	1	1	1

Disk	Byte							
1	1	1	0	0	1	0	0	1
Parity	0	1	0	1	1	1	1	1
3	0	0	0	1	0	0	1	1
4	1	1	1	0	1	0	1	1
Reconstr. 2	0	1	1	0	1	1	1	0

Fig. 5.3. Parity calculation of four bytes (*left*) and reconstruction of data on disk 2 using the parity information (*right*)

Let us now take a look to the relevant Raid configurations.[6] Appendix A.4 goes into much more detail, and there we will learn about the influence of different disk configurations on reliability computation.

► *Raid0 – Striping*

Raid0 is not one of the original Raid levels. It is not a configuration for redundancy but for performance. In fact a stripe has a worse reliability than a single disk. It is advisable to use stripes without further protection only for temporary data like scratch files. This combines several disks to one stripe with the goal that the I/O load is evenly distributed between the disks. There two parameters which describe a stripe: the number of disks (also called *stripe width*) and the number of bytes written to a disk as a chunk. Those chunks are distributed between the disks. Figure 5.4 on the next page shows a four-way stripe (a stripe with the stripe width of four disks) and how the blocks of the corresponding virtual disks are mapped to the physical disks. The stripe size is a parameter for performance tuning; it typically can vary between 2 KB and some megabytes. Its influence on overall performance is significant; differences between a bad and a good stripe size can be an order of magnitude. The optimal value for the stripe size depends very much on your load profile, mostly on the size of the I/O requests, random vs. sequential I/O, and concurrent vs. single-threaded I/O.

Example 2. Assume we have a stripe of four disks and want to store files of sizes between 4 and 400 KB. The I/O size from the computer system is 16 KB. See Fig. 5.5 on p. 113 for a comparison of two different stripe sizes (8 and 64 KB). The 8-KB case has the advantage that all disks are mostly evenly used, and the disadvantage that file f2 is spread in four slices on each disk (in the case of 400-KB files each file would be split into 50 chunks). At a stripe size of 64 KB, file f1 is on one disk only and file f2 is split onto two disks. The advantage of this configuration is minimal

---

[6] We leave out Raid2, Raid4, and proprietary Raid levels, as they are not relevant for this book.

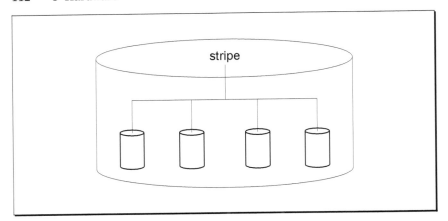

Fig. 5.4. Four-way stripe. Mapping of the virtual disk to the physical disks

head positioning overhead; the disadvantage is that the disks are not evenly used (file f1 is on one disk only, file f2 uses two disks). In this case the optimal stripe size would be somewhere in-between; we would chose 16 KB. ∎

To identify the optimal stripe size we need to find a compromise between minimizing positioning overhead (large stripe size) and transfer bandwidth (small stripe size). If we have lots of concurrent I/O requests, a too small stripe size would create too much disk positioning, as most file access would access multiple disks. If we have only single-threaded I/O requests, the stripe size should be the I/O size divided by the number of disks; this configuration is sometimes called *thin stripe*. The I/O size is another tuning parameter which is set on the computer system (at the volume manager, database). Its default value is often too small, and too many small requests create an unnecessary overhead.

▶ *Raid1 – Mirroring*

This is first – and simplest – level for redundancy: all data is written to two drives as shown in Fig. 5.6 on p. 114. Mirroring is a simple and robust technique – all I/O requests are just duplicated; this minimizes overhead and provides good performance.

Mirroring can decrease write performance slightly as twice the amount of data needs to be transferred. Read performance is increased, close to doubled, as two disks are available for reading – this helps mostly for concurrent small requests.

If one disk fails, performance is degraded to one disk. Mirroring shows a quick rebuild; the remaining disk just needs to be copied to the hot spare. Write requests improve rebuild time.

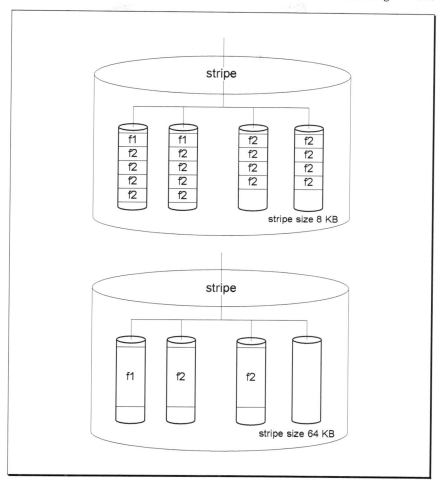

Fig. 5.5. Four-way stripe. Data layout of two files f1 (14 KB) and f2 (120 KB). Comparison between two stripe sizes: 8 and 64 KB

▶ *Raid3*

Raid3 uses so-called byte-level striping with a dedicated parity disk.

Each single I/O request is distributed over all data disks. This can be seen as a stripe with stripe size 1 byte (sometimes a few bytes) plus the parity.

The performance of Raid3 is very good for large, single requests, as all disks are used equally. On write, parity information can always be calculated using the data of the I/O requests – no information needs to

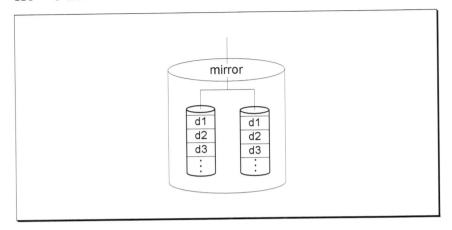

Fig. 5.6. Mirror of two disks

be read from the disk. On read, the parity can be read together with the data and used to verify data integrity; this does not cause an additional delay.

On small and concurrent I/O requests Raid3 becomes very slow, as it uses all drives for each single request, and no load balancing between requests can take place. If requests are small, the disk positioning time can dominate, as it needs to wait until the last disk drive has processed the data.

Raid3 is very good for media streaming, backup-to-disk, and file serving of very large files.[7]

To reconstruct a failed drive, all the data needs to be read, which makes reconstruction much slower than with Raid1. The combined bandwidth of all disks is so large that it is larger than available bus bandwidth. Even though all disks are read in parallel, the slower bus will cause wait states that lead to much longer times than if a single disk must be read. Furthermore, the disk array will be in use during redundancy recovery. Every I/O operation will contend with the recovery process for disk access, because that process accesses all disks all the time, whereas in Raid1 only one disk is used and access to other disks does not lead to contention.

---

[7] There are special arrays with synchronous rotating disk spindles to minimize positioning time.

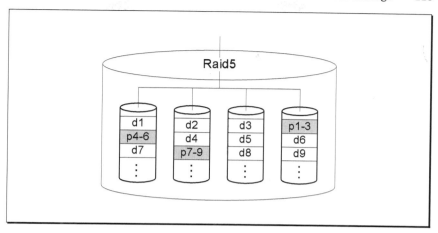

Fig. 5.7. Raid5 configuration consisting of four disks. The data blocks d are striped over the disks as well as the parity information p

▶ *Raid5*

Raid5 implements block-level striping (we just named it striping before) plus parity information which is distributed over the drives, illustrated in Fig. 5.7.

Similar to normal striping, the stripe size (or block size) needs to be defined. A block is also the unit for parity calculation.

Raid5 has the best performance (same as a normal stripe) for concurrent read requests, as the load is balanced between the drives. This is the most common load pattern, which makes Raid5 a widespread solution. On small writes, Raid5 is inefficient. Each time a block is written, first the old data block and parity block need to be read (they are needed to calculate the new parity), then the new data and parity blocks can be written. This means for each block to be written, two blocks need to be read and written. As read and write cannot be done in parallel, Raid5 is very slow for small synchronous write operations.

For large writes, the controller can coalesce all data blocks from one stripe (e.g., d1, d2, and d3 in Fig. 5.7) to calculate the new parity without reading any old data.

Like Raid3, Raid5 has slow redundancy recovery times, since all the data needs to be read in order to reconstruct the lost data. During reconstruction, writes are very slow (as first the whole stripe needs to be read to reconstruct old data), but reads are unaffected if the requested block is not on a failed disk.

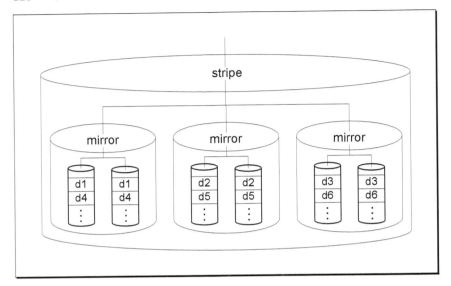

Fig. 5.8. Raid10 configuration consisting of a stripe of three mirrored disks

▸ *Raid6 – Double Parity Raid aka RaidDP*

RaidDP works similar to Raid5 but uses two disks for parity information; therefore, two simultaneous disk failures can be recovered. Some implementations use two dedicated disks for parity, others distribute the parity information over all disks.

On read, RaidDP has the same performance as Raid5 (and striping); on write it is slower than Raid5 because two parities need to be calculated and written. The reconstruction time is also worse than Raid5

However, RaidDP is being used more and more because of the advantage of surviving two disk failures.

▸ *Raid10 and Raid01 – Combining Stripes and Mirrors*

Sometimes it is useful to combine multiple Raid groups with different Raid levels. Typical combinations are a Raid level to provide redundancy combined with striping to improve performance. These nested constructions are labeled by joining the numbers of the individual Raid levels: Raid10 means a stripe of mirrors, see Fig. 5.8; Raid01 means a mirror of stripes, see Fig. 5.9 on the facing page.

In practice, Raid01 and Raid10 are often confused; for high availability only Raid10 is of interest, one should never use Raid01 at all. Disk outages in the Raid10 configuration leave the mirror intact, though without redundancy. The stripe that includes that nonredundant mirror is

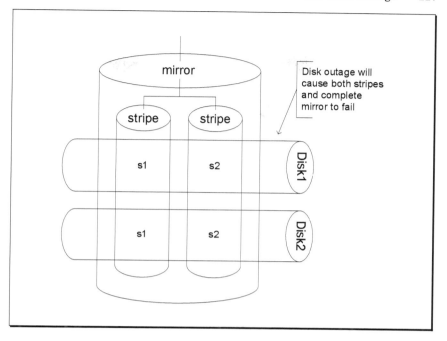

Fig. 5.9. Raid01 configuration consisting of a mirror of two stripes from two disks

still functional, whereas in Raid01 configurations, a disk outage causes the failure of all stripes on that disk and that can render whole mirrors defective. Appendix A.4 explicates the reliability difference between those two configurations.

▶ *Summary*

This concludes the discussion of Raid levels. There are more Raid levels and we left them out because they are used less or are proprietary to one vendor. Table 5.2 on the next page provides a summary of our discussion.

   Appendix A.4 has an in-depth analysis of the reliability of different Raid levels. At the end on p. 371, you will find also some selection and configuration guidelines that result from that reliability analysis.

Volume Managers and Software Raid

If our computer system has multiple disk drives connected to it, all the aforementioned Raid configurations can be implemented using functionality of a so-called *volume manager*. This is a piece of software running

Table 5.2. Summary comparison of redundant array of independent disks (*Raid*) levels. Please note that the evaluation is only a rule of thumb; it depends on many parameters which are not taken into account. *DP* double parity

Raid level	Storage efficiency	Reliability	Recon-struction time	Performance			
				Seq. read	Random read	Seq. write	Random write
0	n	$--$	NA	$++$	$+$	$++$	$+$
1	$n/2$	$++$	$+$	$-$	$-$	0	0
3	$(n-1)/n$	$+$	$-$	$++$	0	$++$	0
5	$(n-1)/n$	$+$	$-$	$+$	$++$	$-$	$-$
DP	$(n-1)/n$	$+++$	$--$	$+$	$+$	$-$	$--$
10	$n/2$	$++$	$+$	$++$	$+$	$++$	$+$

as part of the operating system and is a layer between the physical disks and the logical devices which are used to build file systems.

The volume manager's function is to implement all the functionality needed for Raid configurations. Originally, they were the only way to do so. In the meantime, that functionality has been taken over more and more by specialized hardware (called *Raid controllers*) or storage appliance systems that we will meet in the next section. But volume managers are still in use to manage small Raid configurations with a couple of disk drives.

Even if most, if not all, functions are available from storage systems, a volume manager is often still needed as a layer between the storage system and the raw devices and file systems in the computer, see later. This has historical reasons and is nowadays an unwanted complication.

The volume manager's configuration stores the information on how the individual disks (or logical units, LUNs, if a storage system is used) are connected to build the raw devices. If this configuration is lost, no data can be accessed anymore; therefore this configuration is stored in multiple copies on different disks, or at other places. It is important to fully understand how and where this information is stored, to prevent unwanted corruption or deletion. For example, sometimes it is stored on a piece (slice) of the root disk(s). In this case, we cannot easily have a copy of the root disk(s) to boot from in if there are problems. They could contain an old version of the configuration and could corrupt data, or make it inaccessible, at least.

If we are careful, we should do the following test, before a system goes into production: we should delete the whole volume manager configuration and recreate it. This activity will not destroy any data (please verify this with your vendor) and makes sure that you can recreate the data if it is needed.

The volume manager is a single point of failure, also in a failover cluster. There it is a little more complex, as we have two instances running, one on each node. They typically build a type of application cluster themselves and synchronize configuration changes automatically. This leads to problems if the configuration needs to be changed if one cluster node is not available. We need to check this scenario before we go into production.

An interesting use of volume managers is to mirror between two independent storage systems (this is called *host-based mirroring*).

This provides protection against the failure of a whole storage system. The idea might sound a little paranoid at first hand, as the storage systems should be fully redundant. But they can fail, mostly because of misfunctions in their system software. After all, storage systems are specialized computer systems, including the operating system, the disk driver, and the internal volume manager. That software is the most critical single point of failure in many storage systems!

5.2.2 Storage Systems

Historically, two evolutions led to the emergence of independent *storage systems*:

1. **Limitations of volume managers:** the volume manager functions are executed on the computer's CPU, and caused a performance bottleneck – especially the calculation of parity information and reconstruction activities. They were limited in scalability to manage a large number of disk drives, both in terms of easy configuration and performance. Many implementations were of poor quality, which decreased their reliability – specialized products had better quality and performance. Functions like snapshots were not available with volume managers, but were available from storage subsystems. However, today not all of these arguments are still valid.
2. **SANs enabled new functions:** multiple computers could easily share drives, which allowed there to be a pool of disk space for many computers. Data can be copied directly between storage systems over long distances, which allowed for new disaster-recovery solutions.

What is a storage system? It is basically a hardware box which contains disk drives (typically up to some hundreds), a specialized storage processor, specialized firmware to execute its function, cache storage, and Fibre Channel connections to the SAN. The vendor tries hard to provide reliability, performance, flexibility, and ease of operation with such a system. Indeed there are many good products on the market, which eventually enabled the utilization of Moore's Law. On the other hand, there are bad products as well, which needed years to become mature or disappeared from the market. Let us describe the basic components and functions together with some recommendations (Fig. 5.10).

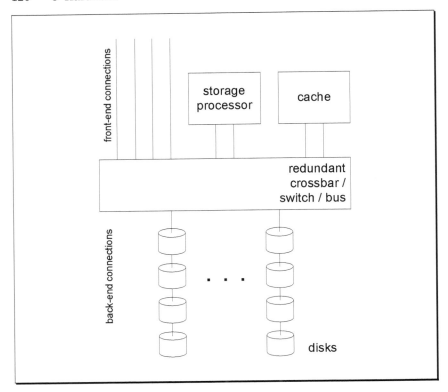

Fig. 5.10. Typical layout of a storage system

▸ *Disk Drives and Back-End Connections*

Disks are often physically grouped in *shelves*, sometimes called *trays*.[8] Then it is important that the different shelves are independent of each other, e.g., have independent power supplies and independent connections to the storage processor(s). Systems which do not fulfill this requirement should be avoided.

In a mirrored configuration, the two disks which build a mirror should be in different shelves to prevent single points of failure. This sounds obvious, but we saw several products where this is not done automatically.

The shelves are connected to the storage processor via so-called *back-end connections*. This is typically done via Fibre Channel (sometimes other connections like SCSI, even if the front-end connections are Fibre

---

[8] Disks are grouped in most systems, even if this is not visible by physical inspection. How these groups are set up needs to be understood by reviewing the system's documentation.

Channel connections). We need to review the redundancy of these connections. If many disks share the same connection (e.g., are members of the same Fibre Channel Arbitrated Loop), then one single disk can bring down the whole connection in the case of a failure. These shared connections can also be a performance bottleneck – we might need to distribute each Raid group over multiple shelves.

▶ *Storage Processor and Cache*

The storage processor is the heart of the system:

- It implements the Raid functions (today's systems provide most or all Raid levels explained in the previous section).
- It provides additional functions like remote mirroring and snapshots.
- It manages drive errors and hot-spare functions; it masks disk errors (and corresponding SCSI error messages) from the computer system, handles other failure situations like timeouts, and can initiate a "call home" to order a technician for repair.
- It manages the cache to improve performance.
- It provides a management interface.
- It moves the data from the back end to the front end.

The storage processor need to be highly available – better fault-tolerant. Some vendors use off-the-shelf hardware components and use operating systems like Linux or Windows. This gives some kind of failover cluster with all its complexities and limitations. An additional issue is that a storage processor needs real-time features to handle failure events properly, which creates another complication in this case. Other vendors choose a proprietary solution with microcode instead of an operating system and a cluster. This needs more effort and cost, but seems to be the more suitable solution for the task.

We conclude that both solutions have their pros and cons, which can lead to philosophical discussions. We need to carefully review the approach and do tests. We need to evaluate the patch strategy: How are patches and new releases to be installed? Is it possible during operations? How can we back-out a patch? How often does the vendor bring out new patches, and is there a release strategy?

Where is the operating system or microcode stored? Some vendors use small pieces of the data disks. This is not a good and low-cost solution, because it creates additional complexity and dependency.

The cache is another core component. As write cache, it hides performance penalties of the mechanical disks and some Raid configurations like Raid5, by immediate acknowledgment of write requests from the computer. As read cache it can implement clever strategies of read-ahead to also hide disk wait times. Some implementations detect even complicated read patterns like full-table scans of databases, and read ahead. However, the cache function needs to be coordinated with the cache on the computer system (operating system and application) to avoid double caching, which would decrease performance and waste hardware resources. The write cache holds data that has not yet been written to disks; it needs to be protected very well against hardware and power problems.

Most systems have a battery to store the cache to disk before the system needs to be shut down (which happens automatically). Those batteries need to be tested every few months.

▸ *Front-End Connections*

These are the connections to the servers, often via a SAN. They are Fibre Channel connections (sometimes also FICON for mainframe connections). A storage system has typically between four and up to 100 connections. The connections provide redundancy and load balancing together with special drivers which need to be installed on the computer system.

▸ *Logical Units*

From a logical view, the objects which made available are *logical units* (LUNs). They look like a disk from the viewpoint of the computer system. The volume manager can combine several LUNs or split LUNs to build multiple file systems on one LUN. This brings additional flexibility, but makes the whole configuration more complicated. We propose doing the disk configuration only in the storage system and not using the features of the volume manager, unless there are good arguments to do it differently.

What is the best size of a LUN? This is a difficult question as we need to find a compromise between simplicity, performance, and reliability. Very large LUNs lead to a simple configuration and provide better performance if the underlying Raid group is configured right. But it would take a very long time to restore too large a LUN if the LUN is destroyed or corrupted. We need to take the performance of our restoration from the backup system into account to find the maximum size of a LUN. As an alternative an independent copy of that LUN could do the job. As a rule of thumb, LUN sizes are between 100 GB and a few terabytes.

Remote Mirroring

Remote mirroring is a feature that allows LUNs to be mirrored between two storage systems over a SAN (sometimes also over a TCP/IP network). A typical configuration is shown in Fig. 5.11 on the facing page. In two data centers a server and a storage system are installed. The production system runs in the first data center, and uses the "primary LUN." The second location acts as a standby. All changes to the primary LUN are copied to the "mirrored LUN" in the standby storage system. The mirrored LUN can be accessed as read-only (if at all) during normal operations. In the

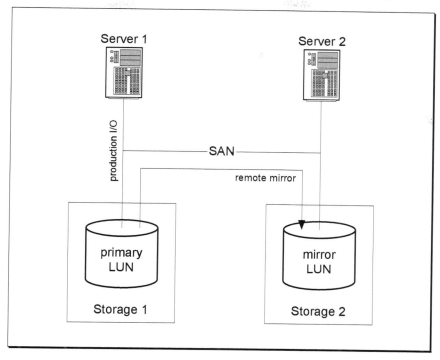

Fig. 5.11. Configuration for remote mirroring

case of a disaster, the mirrored LUN needs to be reconfigured to become the primary one and can be accessed read-write by the standby host.

This looks like a failover cluster spanning two sites. But there is a drawback: with today's technology the long distance and the combination of failover software (running on the servers) and proprietary copy function (runs on the storage systems) is not well integrated. Manual steps are often needed to activate the standby systems. Therefore such a "cluster" is not as good as a normal failover cluster at one site only and an additional server and storage system for manual failover in the case of a physical disaster or other kind of major outage.

The distance between the two locations can be very long, up to many hundreds of kilometers. This distance injects additional latency for the remote mirror function. If it worked synchronously (a write to the primary storage system is acknowledged after it is also written to the second system) the performance would be very bad over long distances. Therefore an *asynchronous copy* mode was introduced. Here, the state of the second system follows that of the first one with a delay. It is as consistent as on the primary system; write operations are not interchanged, they are just delayed. In most applications, such a delay is perfectly OK, but that needs to be checked.

Snapshots

A snapshot is the capability to instantly create a frozen copy of a LUN, also called *point-in-time image*. When the LUN is changed via subsequent writes, the snapshot stays in the state it was when it was created.

There are two implementations for snapshots: split mirror and copy on write. A *split mirror* snapshot is an additional mirror connected to the LUN, on top of Raid protection. When the snapshot is created, the mirror is detached and is available from now on. This technique has no performance impact after the split and the data is available on independent storage devices. But to create such a snapshot all the data needs to be copied. One also needs enough storage capacity to store the whole LUN; that is not necessary with the other snapshot technology.

Copy on write is a technology where an (initially empty) region is used to store all changes to the LUN. Then, the system can create both "views" to the data by using the old data or the data with the changes. Such snapshots are mostly read-only. If the rate of change is very high, then the region which holds the changes can be very large. With the copy-on-write technique it is possible to create many snapshots (like every hour) with limited additional disk space.

Snapshots can be used to create consistent backups to tape. They can be done more frequently than a normal backup and could even replace incremental backups.

They can also be used "go back in time" if data corruption or deletion occurred. This is a very useful high-availability feature that helps us to recover easily from several failure scenarios.

5.2.3 SAN vs. NAS

Storage area networks (SANs) are designed to connect storage systems, tape drives, and computer systems. They are optimized for disk type I/O, redundancy, and robustness.

If we compare SANs running over Fibre Channel with IP networks running on (ten-)gigabit Ethernet, there are no significant differences in the requirements for such networks. It is therefore unclear if SANs are really needed besides some special cases like connection of tapes or very high performance databases, especially if we notice the additional cost (cabling, switches, and people). Many features which have been available on IP networks for many years have been reinvented for SANs, for unknown reasons (e.g., flow control via buffer credits).

Another issue of the SAN world is compatibility: In classic IP networks, the standards are strong enough that we do not need to check if an arbitrary system can connect to a gigabit Ethernet network. This is different for SANs: here even today point-to-point compatibility needs to be checked and storage vendors provide big "compatibility matrices" to ensure that their box can connect to computer system X with interface card type Y.

However, today SANs are widely used and have reached a good level of maturity. They can be built fully redundant and with very high reliability. Their biggest risk is people skills for monitoring, incident handling, and reconfigurations.

On the basis of these observations it is unclear if SANs will hold their market share or become more and more a niche solution. So let us look at their biggest competitor: *network-attached storage* (NAS). NAS is a file level protocol (vs. SAN, a block level protocol). NAS runs over a normal TCP/IP network and has two competing protocols: *Network File System* (NFS), an Internet standard originally developed at Sun Microsystems, and *Common Internet File System* (CIFS), a proprietary protocol from Microsoft. The focus of CIFS is the sharing of file systems to end-user devices. NFS is a little more general; it can be used similarly to CIFS, but also to attach servers to storage devices.

The current challenge for NAS solutions is if they will successfully serve database files in mission-critical environments. Many people believe it works well, but a breakthrough has not happened yet.

5.2.4 Journaling Is Essential for High Availability

Journaling is a property of file systems or storage systems where changes are first written to a nonvolatile area before the I/O operation has finished. That restricts very aggressive caching strategies, where write operations just place the changes in RAM and rely on the cache management to write the data to disk eventually. Instead, it is a compromise that allows still heavy caching for current disk structures while ensuring the safety of the data. In the case of a system crash, the changes will still be available and can be replayed.

Journaling in operating systems is implemented in the file system drivers; here disk storage is set aside for the change information. Sometimes explicit mirroring of this *journaling area* is necessary to achieve high availability. Otherwise, a disk error of that area would render the journaling functionality void. Very often, only metadata changes are recorded, i.e., only creation and deletion of files. Good journaling file systems have the opportunity to demand journaling of file content changes as well, though this has to be configured manually.

Storage systems implement journaling as well. They often use battery-buffered CMOS for the journaling area. For NAS systems, this ability is similar to the journaling file systems on the operating system level. For SAN systems, journaling resembles more the redo logs of databases; see Sect. 7.2 for more information.

For files, journaling should be used all the time, otherwise, restart times after a crash are too long. For databases, journaling should be turned off since the database servers handle the storage themselves. There we must pay attention instead to ensure that no write caching is used for the redo-log areas.

5.3 Virtualization of Resources

Virtualization is the hallmark of modern IT systems. They supply resources in logical units to application programs and free them from reliance on specific hardware or hardware configurations.

Virtual CPUs

Virtual CPUs mean that each application thinks it has the CPU for itself, even though it is sharing it with others, i.e., the capability of multiprocessing. For most people, multiprocessing is so elementary that they do not even mention it anymore. In this book, we should remember that they are a virtue that are engineered and that this capability is available in different qualities, depending on the operating system.

That a service needs a CPU is often neglected, much to the chagrin of those who have to handle real-world problems of computer systems. If a service is made up of multiple processes, or if several services run on one physical host, it can well be that one process runs amok and usurps lots of CPU time. The other process may now react so slowly that services are not functional anymore and are migrated to another node.

Being able to supply time slices to processes in a fair way, even under very high load, is a sign of a mature enterprise-class operating system. Mainframes, but also proprietary UNIX systems like Solaris and AIX, shine in this area, whereas Windows and Linux both have their problems here, at the time of this writing.

More and more, operating systems also add quality of service approaches to CPU virtualization. They guarantee that processes or groups of processes will get a minimum of available CPU power, or they set an upper limit on the number of CPU slices that are scheduled for these processes. While this capability has started to appear on symmetric multiprocessing (SMP) systems, where whole processors are allocated to process groups, newer operating systems also make it possible to allocate parts of a CPU. This decreases the likelihood of damaging interdependencies between processes and builds an important base for enterprise-class host virtualization, as explained in Sect. 6.3.2 on p. 184.

Virtual Memory

Virtual memory is as old as virtual CPUs, and as mature. In contrast, administrators are often more aware of it, as they have to configure the amount and location of swap space. But as with multiprocessing, the implementation quality of virtual memory management differs from operating system to operating system.

Memory leaks in application programs are a well-known and often-occurring problem for services. Regular restarts help to confine that problem. Most operating systems have another problem: overcommitment of storage allows applications to allocate more memory combined than is actually available as virtual memory. This is due to many processes not using all their allocated virtual memory – especially Fortran and Java programs are prone to heavy preallocation of memory that might not be used in the end.

When virtual memory is exhausted, a failure might occur in a different application from the one that is actually exhausting it, owing to overcommitment. The memory exhausted error does not appear when an application requests the memory, but when an allocated memory page is used for the first time, without available space in virtual memory. Operating systems have different strategies to handle that situation, which all boils down to aborting arbitrarily chosen processes. This is relevant for our high-availability topic as it is another illustration of dependencies between several applications or services running on one host that seemed to be independent before.

As with virtual CPUs, quality of service based memory resource management is starting to appear in some UNIX operating systems, though it is not yet available in Windows or Linux. This resource management is being introduced for enterprise-class host virtualization, but will be put to good use for running several highly available services on one server as well.

Virtual Storage

Much of the topic of storage virtualization has been described already in Sect. 5.2; we do not need to repeat it here.

The specialty of storage virtualization is that data disks in high-availability environments must be accessible from several servers. As we have explained already, data disks are crucial because they keep all the business information and that information exists only once. If any computer system has an outage and the service is now continued on another system, that backup system must have access to the data.

If we use such *shared storage*, we need to pay attention to the restriction that a disk can be allocated to only one system at a time. To achieve that, the volume manager is used. Disks are combined into *volume groups*, and the volume group is the unit of virtual storage that is managed. Volume groups with application data are associated exclusively with services, and are reallocated to servers as needed for service migration.

Virtual network interfaces

Virtual IP interfaces, also called *alias interfaces*, make it possible to provide a "network identity" for every service. This allows services to be moved between servers. These alias interfaces are supported on all operating systems.

To make that work, virtual interfaces must be complete and also include the Ethernet level (that means they must have their own Media Access Control (MAC) address) or if they share the MAC address with the underlying physical interface, traffic must be routed properly to the new node after service migration and Address Resolution Protocol (ARP) caches must be updated.

5.4 Vendor Selection and Purchasing Decisions

Working with the right vendors, using the best products, and running them using the best teams are key ingredients for highly available systems and their operation. But the selection cannot be static: vendors change their product plans, perform restructuring activities, and execute mergers and acquisitions. All those changes can happen in a short time frame of a few years. They can change a good choice of a vendor and its product to a bad one and vice versa.

Therefore we cannot provide a list of the best vendors and products. Instead we present a list with the most important criteria and considerations for your guidance:

▸ *Product Line*
This is decided by carefully reading the technical product descriptions.

- How flexible is the product line with different options (i.e., different models in the product line)?
- How scalable are the products (e.g., numbers of CPUs, memory, I/O cards)?
- Are the main features state of the art (e.g., speed of internal buses and external connections)?
- Do they provide quantitative features like performance numbers?

The key features for high availability are quality, robustness, and service-ability, as explained in Sect. 5.1 on p. 104.

It is always good to compare similar products from competitors. Take some time to review the market space of the product line. Is it in a niche market, because of its very special features? If you plan to purchase such a product, carefully check why you really need it and be aware of the risk in purchasing a niche product.

▶ *Product Roadmap*

After we have analyzed the current product line, we need to understand how it evolves over its lifetime and what its future is expected to be. Most hardware vendors publish roadmaps that explain what we can expect to see from them in the midterm. It is often worthwhile having a roadmap presentation by one of the vendor's presales engineers. Sometimes such presentations only provide in-depth information when you sign a nondis-closure agreement.

There is a wide spectrum in the quality of such presentations. Some show mostly vision and hype – with only little specific and useful information for your future planning. This can be translated to a bad roadmap or a less skilled presenter. We propose to openly bring up your concerns and give them a second chance.

A really good roadmap starts in the past, shows how the current product line developed, and goes a few years into the future. Further on it talks about potential future product lines and the company's vision of how the the technology will evolve. This discussion can be vague but should be grounded by specific arguments and trends.

One topic which vendors do not share is product announcement dates, unless they are only a few days ahead. But they might share dates with the precision of a quarter or even a month. To make a purchasing decision, you need to get this information, as you do not want to purchase a system just before its successor is announced. We propose having an open discussion around this potential issue to prevent any surprises.

The typical timeframe for which a vendor has an oversight of its products is about 1–2 years. It does not make sense to ask for a much longer roadmap.

▶ *Vendor Visit*

There are multiple places which you should visit. First the laboratory; some vendors might allow a sneak preview of the next product generation. This is a very good opportunity to check the reality of the new product is and in which state of development it is. Is it still only one box or even only components, or are they already performing integration tests with other products from other vendors? If you have the opportunity to talk to a development engineer, you can gain insight into which challenges they are fighting with.

In the manufacturing plant where the final assembly is done, you should concentrate on the vendor's approach for quality. How do they test for bad systems? How is burn-in executed (see also Appendix A.6)? Do they stress-test all systems they deliver or only samples? If systems fail early, how do they analyze the root causes? What equipment do they have for this analysis? Some vendors are proud of their quality system and show you their efforts; others might give you some vague talk about six sigma. You need to accept that high quality has its price – you can only expect such efforts for high-end (and therefore high-price) systems.

A visit to the vendor's "Executive Briefing Center" must be properly prepared for. Without such preparation, the chances are high that you will get only lots of marketing material. Furthermore, it is likely that you will speak to marketing people who will not go beyond the information that is already in those brochures. If you plan such a visit we propose specifically asking for in-depth technical information and carefully checking the agenda for your visit. If you have questions about the competitiveness of the products, this is the place to do it. You might inform the vendor about this intent in advance to allow preparations to be made.

▸ *Cross Platform Support*

Most sites have a heterogeneous environment and deploy systems from several vendors. What is the vendor philosophy about openness? Can documentation be provided like "compatibility matrixes," which tell exactly which combinations with other vendors' products, configurations, and releases work and have been tested?

▸ *Alliance Partners*

In today's world, most vendors need alliance partners to be competitive and to supplement their product suites. Therefore we need to review the alliances the vendors have. What is really meant if your vendor claims that company X is an alliance partner? Potentially, alliances are a win-win situation both for vendors and for customers – as long as there are comprehensible plans behind the partnership. For example, good signs are shared product development or tight integration of products; bad signs are when they only buy equipment from each other. Other criteria can easily be found and are common sense in the assessment of vendors.

▸ *Maintenance Concept*

Review the vendor's concept for maintenance activities. Are they done in-house or are they outsourced to another company? How are your calls handled? Review the call-handling process. Ask the vendor how the ticket system is organized. Do you have online access to your own tickets?

Is there active notification of changes and notification triggered by time passed? Or do you need to phone in yourself every hour and ask what is going on with the open call that you have for your mission-critical server? How is second-level and third-level support organized? Where is the next depot with spare parts? Often it is in another country or state, for tax reasons. This is important for the mean time to repair; sometimes spare parts must be fetched several times (because they were the wrong part, or because they are "dead on arrival").

▶ *Reference Installations*

Visiting a different installation can provide very good information and can limit the risk. The vendor should provide you with a list of at least three reference clients that you can choose to visit. During the visit you can get all kinds of insight, including good and bad configuration options, quality issues, and outages. Many reference clients are very open in sharing their experience, but they naturally have a positive bias as they want to defend their decision for choosing that vendor.

▶ *Client Councils*

Many vendors organize so-called client councils or user groups. This is a win-win situation for the customers as they can share information and experiences, and for the vendor who can efficiently communicate marketing and sales messages. It is worthwhile investing a few days per year in such miniconferences. If a vendor does not support such activities at all, he wants to overly control communication, or if the meeting contains more incentives than information, caution is advised.

▶ *Financial Situation*

We do some simple checks, like the company's rating and its base financial indicators. On the basis of our experience it is very hard to get deeper insight and predict the company's future. Even insiders typically do not know about important announcements and mergers and acquisitions until they really happen. Therefore we limit our time to basic checks.

▶ *Local Team*

Beyond product features and quality, the performance of the vendor's local team is crucial. It consists of three roles:

The *sales representative*, who is also the informal team leader. He (or she) is also your first point of escalation in case of problems. But not everything can be an escalation – then nothing would be!

The *presales* and *postsales engineers* are consulted for all technical questions and make sure that you purchase a good configuration. Their most important attributes are technical qualifications and experience. Such roles cannot be done by a newbie.

The service manager is responsible for all operational questions. This role is important as a consultant for proactive maintenance activities and in case their are problems (problem and incident management in IT Infrastructure Library, ITIL, terms).

You need to build a mutual trust relationship, which takes some time to get established – therefore vendors who often change their staff cannot be rated as good!

We see the vendor selection and relationship to the vendor as a long-term activity. Working with the vendor and being its partner is much better than a simple buyer-seller relationship. This should not be a hurdle for tough price negotiations – therefore the partnership should not become too personal, which can only be achieved if some distance is retained.

If the vendor struggles with delivery or if there are issues with a product, do not just switch to another vendor – be loyal and give him a chance to fix the problems. But after multiple bad experiences it is time to consider a change. This is obviously a tough decision and needs to be thought through. If the decision is made, it needs to be communicated properly to all parties involved, to allow there to be a graceful breakup between you and the old vendor.

All these topics and scenarios should be considered when selecting a new vendor!

With how many vendors with a similar product portfolio should we have relationships? We believe that two, perhaps three, is a good number. Only one is not a good choice – that vendor could become a single point of failure very soon. If we have more than two or three, we would lose our focus and this would cost us too much time for all the activities previously described.

For us, in order to stay long in our business, we should write notes about products, features, and experiences. This helps later on when making technical and strategic decisions.

5.5 System Installation

The time between delivery of a system and its *start of production* (SOP) is thrilling – on one hand, we need to cover a tough schedule, on the other, we need to identify and resolve all potential problems for the future. In order to manage this successfully, we need to develop a good plan which usually consists of the following steps:

▶ *Preparation*

We need to prepare our computer room for the new system. If our organization is big enough, we will have a data center (see also Appendix B). Then we need to plan the exact location on the raised floor (including maintenance areas), feed through of cables, verification that the raised floor can hold the weight, etc. In any case, power cabling, network cabling, and SAN cabling should be installed in advance. IP addresses, host names, and configuration management database entries need to be defined and entered into the appropriate databases. A time plan for the following steps needs to be developed and the various tests need to be prepared (see the following). The overall plan needs to be reviewed and approved by the internal departments and all vendors.

The following sections until p. 139 provide you with further information needed for the preparation.

► *Installation*

The installation is done by and under the responsibility of the hardware vendor. We need to provide support and make sure that all connections needed to our data center (power, network, etc.) are available in advance. We also monitor the installation process and review that all cables are installed and labeled properly. The assumption that hardware vendors have mastered these topics might be wrong. That is why we need to do many of the tests described in the following.

► *Declaration of Operational Readiness*

This task is done by the hardware vendor. Until the vendor declares the operational readiness, he is responsible and liable for the system (i.e., if the system creates a fire, he is liable if it happens before that point). If it is declared, than we take over responsibility and we own the next steps.

► *Functionality and Performance Tests*

For the context of this book, functionality is the delivery of high-availability features. Therefore this phase needs to test that the planned fault protection and failure recovery works. In addition, the tests should try to discover the behavior of failure scenarios that have not been planned for. It is less of a problem if they are noticed before the whole system goes into production; later it cannot be changed anymore.

We need to develop a test plan during the preparation phase to know what we want to test later on. We propose following the process described in Chap. 3 to design your system. This gives us a list of failure scenarios and the expected behavior of your system. Another artifact which came out of the architecture planning is the dependency chart. It helps to identify all relevant components in a structured way.

It is not practical to verify all possible scenarios; we need to select the most important and most critical ones. We start with a review of the tests that the vendor has already executed. Most vendors have a process for their testing to verify their system and its installation. Our task is not to blindly execute the same tests again – we should see our role in a control situation as following the four-eyes principle. We can expect that the installed system works, but sometimes the technician did not configure it in the most redundant way. An example is that a disk and its mirror are on the same Fibre Channel loop (or in the same storage tray) – such a failure can be detected best by pulling a disk and looking at the LEDs on the disks. Then we easily see the location of its mirror. Another example is that two redundant network interfaces are connected to the same system bus. Finding such configuration failures is one of the main targets, besides a set of standard tests.

The vendor oversees only his part of the overall system. We need to make end-to-end tests to make sure that the integration works. Consider as an example a server, a storage system, a network, a SAN, and an application. Those components could come from five different vendors – it is our responsibility to develop the right tests to cover all possible scenarios. This is where the dependency chart helps us.

The next question is how should we document our test plan? It is our experience, that some people do all the planning in their heads only (i.e., no documentation); others develop large text documents. Both extremes do not work well. We propose using a simple spreadsheet like the example shown in Table 5.3 on p. 136. This can be easily managed and all parties involved can read and understand it. It is also designed for two further jobs: reuse for other systems you will install in the future, and proof of what worked in the beginning (in case we need a root cause analysis if an unexpected outage happens in future).

In the following we describe the most important columns; you might add more depending on your needs:

Component: The affected component from the dependency chart. The level of detail should be limited and so should the total number of different components. We might sort by this column to see all tests for one component together.

Scenario: The scenario for that test based on our developed architecture.

Objective: Which feature of the system is the subject of the test.

How: A simple and explicit description of how this test should be executed. If applicable it should contain host names, paths, command names, etc.

Expected result: A description of what we expect to happen. This is the last chance to verify the system design against the requirements.

Downtime: The expected downtime, or other relevant times like time to do a failover. It is a good exercise to predict the times. It shows how good our information about the different components is and how well we thought through our design.

Execution time: The expected time to execute the test. This is important for the resource and time planning. The sum of all execution
times gives us a hint for how long all the tests will take.

The test plan should also contain performance tests. To measure the
performance of infrastructure components (i.e., I/O, network, CPU, memory) is straightforward. Lots of tools are available to measure all kinds
of values. The challenge is more to define requirements on the infrastructure level and to predict the values for the configuration chosen. We
should work with the particular hardware vendor and ask him what performance numbers can be expected. This is the point where marketing
messages meet reality...

Overall system performance is most important; it should be seen as
a feature that needs to be verified. However, such tests are often complicated and not easy to do, as it is not easy to artificially create sufficient
load. Load-generator software can be a useful tool to create production-
like load. However, such tools are somewhat complicated to use, and it is
not possible to verify or falsify the results before we can compare them
with those for with real production load. Therefore we should considered
involving a specialist, often a consultant from the software vendor.

After we have finished the test plan, it should be reviewed and approved by all parties involved.

Now it is the time to verify that the new system works as designed.
We execute the tests according to our plan and document the results in a
table which corresponds to the one from our planning. Table 5.4 on p. 137
shows an example. In the best case all tests are successful, and all predicted behaviors and times are met. However, if a test fails, then our plan
was also successful; we have the chance to fix failures before the system
goes into production. If the root cause of a failed test is obvious and can
be fixed by a small change (e.g., fix a typo in a configuration file), then
it is advisable to immediately fix the problem and rerun the test. But if
the root cause is complex or cannot identified in a short time frame, we
should step back before we spend all our time in fixing this single problem. We might decide to continue with other tests, if that makes sense,
and let another team work on finding the root cause.

If a root cause can be found and it requires a complicated change, we
should not immediately start working on that change. The risks are that
we lose too much time and might not identify other problems. We also
might need to rerun other tests because of that change – this needs to
be thought through very well. It would be more than disappointing if we
fixed one problem, but created another one by the fix!

If the new system is sufficiently complex than it is advisable for one
person (or one team of people) to execute the tests and another person
to manage the tests. This includes documentation and decisions and provides an independent look at problems.

Table 5.3. Table for test planning with example entries

No.	Component	Scenario	Objective	How	Expected result	Downtime (min)	Exec. time (min)
1	All	Power cycle	Maintenance activity: verify that all components can be gracefully shut down and restarted	Shut down computers, storage, switches. Switch off, switch on	System available	30	60
2	Storage	Single disk failure	Redundancy of storage configuration, hot-spare functionality	Pull disk from storage array. Locate mirror disk and hot-spare disk, verify that mirror disk is in a different storage tray. Measure time to sync hot-spare disk	Hot-spare disk is activated and data is synced to the hot-spare disk. No impact seen on server and application	0	200
3	SAN	Interswitch link failure	Redundancy of SAN fabric, failover functionality of SAN switches, automatic reactivation of "repaired" link	Locate interswitch link on SAN switch. Pull Fibre Channel cable, push Fibre Channel cable	No impact. Link becomes automatically active after push	0 (2 s to reactivate link)	20
4	Server	Server crash	Functionality of high-availability failover	Enter shutdown -q on console	High-availability software activates failover and successfully executes failover. During failover, application not available, after it works again	15	60
5	Database	Database listener crash	Verify high-availability functionality	kill -9 listener process	High-availability software detects the problem and restarts the listener. No failover	0.5	20
6	–	–	–	–	–	–	–

Table 5.4. Table to document test results related to test planning (Table 5.3) with example entries

No.	Status	Observed result	Action	Measured downtime (min)	Observed exec. time (min)	Who
1	OK	Works as expected but shutdown took too long (20 min). Unmounting file systems is the assumed reason	Needs further investigation. Opened problem ticket #12321	40	120	...
2	FAIL	Time to sync to hot-spare disk OK, (95 min). Mirror disk is located in wrong tray	Storage system needs to be reconfigured. Mirrors need to be in different trays from their pairs. Opened change ticket #32186	0	200	...
3	OK	Works as expected. After pushing in the link worked instantaneously (less than 1 s)		0	10	...
4	FAIL	HA software immediately observed problem and initiated the failover. Mount of the file systems on standby node took longer than expected (7 min). Application startup failed – configuration problem? Log file contains further information, stored at /local/pretests/sap.log.20060402	Investigate application configuration. Opened problem ticket #37632. Rerun the test	12	210	...
5	OK	HA software observed problem after 10 s. Restart successful		10	10	...
6	–	–	–	–	–	–

▸ *Reliability and Stress Tests*

At this stage we hopefully have verified that our system works as designed. Now it is time to freeze the system configuration, let it run, and see its stability.

Depending on our buying power, this can be a step before system acceptance. If we do not have a strong position with our vendor(s), or if there is no time, or the system is not seen as so critical, we skip this step. Then we rely on our monitoring during production and have to document and follow-up on all irregularities.

If we plan for a reliability phase, how should we do it? The first question is when: before start of production, after, or a mixture? Because the lifetime of a system is normally about 3 years, we should put it into production as soon as possible. It depreciates every month by around 3%; for financial reasons we *cannot* do testing prior to production for a long time. Therefore we propose a mixed approach, if there are not good reasons against it: a very short period of a few days where the system runs under artificial load and stress tests. If the system survives this period, it will go into production. The reliability test phase still can continue, also from a contract and payment viewpoint with our vendor(s).

What are the right conditions for this phase? We definitely do not have enough time to get statistically meaningful information. In our experience the following approach works best. We chose a time interval when the system is not allowed to fail. A typical duration would be 4 weeks, but it could be a good strategy to let the vendor propose a duration. As the vendor needs to say how long he expects his system to survive, he cannot come up with a very small number. If a failure occurs during this interval, then we start from the beginning. Depending on our negotiating power, we can connect penalty payments with each such failure, up to the right to give it back after a predefined number of failures during the reliability test phase.

If our system contains parts which do not cause an outage if they fail (e.g., disk drives which are mirrored), then we can use an alternative (or additional) approach: we can specify a number of such failures which can be calculated in advance from value of the mean time between failures (MTBF) given by the vendor. Example 3 on p. 373 in Appendix A shows such a computation.

▸ *System Acceptance*

System acceptance is a project milestone, often connected with payment to the vendor(s). Unless we negotiate and contract differently, a system is accepted implicitly if we start using it in production. Sometimes it makes sense to pay some of the purchase price (e.g., 50%) when the system goes into production. The remaining price – possibly reduced by a penalty – will be paid after successful completion of the reliability test period.

▶ *Start of Production*

The start of production is a milestone which needs approval by all stake-holders, foremost the system owner and the business owner. It usually follows a successful *user acceptance test* (UAT), which is not the subject of this book. The user acceptance test is about application functionality; it is not a statement about reliability, quality, or probability of failures.

5.6 System Maintenance and Operations

An exhaustive description of how to organize and manage system opera-tions would go beyond the scope of this book. We provide some guidance about the most important aspects to optimize system reliability.

▶ *Monitoring*

System monitoring has many aspects and we need to cover them all to achieve reliable operations. Let us start with the environment. We expect that power, temperature, and humidity are monitored by our data center. If our systems are not in a data center, we need to install sensors and record the values. Second is the internal environment of our system. This is mostly the temperature inside the system rack and inside the system (i.e., temperature on the CPU or system board).

Next is the operating system. There are many commercial and open-source systems available which can do this, mostly out of the box. But we need to set sensible thresholds: a compute server, for example, al-ways runs at 100% CPU utilization; a database server should not run above 80%. Middleware and applications, on the top level, need to be mon-itored as well. Most monitoring tools provide the capability to develop our own agents for this purpose. Many tools deliver agents for the most com-mon applications, like databases. The development of such agents needs some experience and a good understanding of the application's behavior and system requirements.

When do we know that we measure and monitor all relevant in-stances? We propose using our dependency chart to verify that all compo-nents of our system stack are covered. An example of a common failure is missing monitoring of cluster activities. Many tools monitor all kinds of operating system variables but are not cluster-aware. They see clus-ter activities like a failover as reconfiguration, which sometimes creates a (misleading) alarm, and sometimes they are just ignored.

If we have now implemented monitoring of all components of our sys-tem stack, what can we do with it? Besides reacting to alarms which are automatically created if thresholds are exceeded, the different specialists should regularly look at the evolution of the values to detect long-term trends and to proactively prevent problems. In ITIL terms, we are in a gray zone between monitoring and capacity management.

Another activity is the detection and analysis of correlations of values from different layers: if the transaction rate of our database increases, what is the influence on our storage system? Does the I/O wait time go up (which could indicate an upcoming bottleneck) or stay constant?

Those end-to-end views are important for us to understand the whole system and to detect problems early, before there is an impact on business.

Review of log files is the other component of system monitoring. First we need to discover which log files exist and are important. The operating system logs are obvious, but there can be many more components which might create their own logs, like volume manager, cluster software, middleware, applications, and infrastructure services. Here again, we use our system stack and dependency diagram to find all relevant logs. There are tools available for automatic log scanning and analysis. It is proposed to use such tools, but to not only rely on them. We also need to review all logs manually, to get a better understanding of our system, and to inspect the work of the automatic tools. Many tools for log scanning are highly configurable. We should use our experience from the manual log inspection to constantly improve the configuration of our tool(s).

On the basis of experience, more than 30% of system outages could have been prevented if all logs had been inspected properly!

▶ *Vendor Maintenance Contracts*

We propose regularly reviewing our contracts and optimizing them according to our real requirements. We found that very often systems miss an appropriate maintenance contract: some have a too high level and too much money is paid; other – critical ones – have a contract with too long reaction times.

Three aspects need to match: the business requirements, our operating concept, and the maintenance level of the vendor contract. It does not make sense to pay for a 7 × 24 contract, if our own team does not monitor the systems over the weekend and would not notice a problem at that time.

And sometimes systems run out of maintenance unnoticed, which will significantly increase the time to repair in the case of an incident.

We need to gain a clear understanding of the conditions of the contract, in particular what is the meaning of the term *reaction time*. Often this is just the duration until when we are contacted by a call agent after we have opened a problem ticket, with no further commitment of when and how fast the vendor will work on the problem.

The best case is when the vendor guarantees a time to repair; most vendors decline such a contract clause. However, even if we do not get such a time in writing, we should have a discussion with our vendor to match up our expectations.

Another important topic is the vendor's concept for problem resolution. First, how does the vendor get access to information about the system and its problem? There is a wide spectrum of approaches, the worst one is unfortunately widespread: some call-center agents ask for information via email and we enter in a loop of sending mails back and forth, which could take forever. The best approach is when the vendor has the capability to remotely access your system (under your control) and he holds your detailed system configuration in his database. Second, how is his first-, second-, and third-line support organized and how does this fit with 7 × 24 availability ("follow the sun")?

If there are questions or concerns, we propose placing a bogus problem call during the night and seeing what happens. After the call has been closed we should review the activities with our vendor and ask for an extract of the vendor's call tracking database.

In future we expect more and more data sharing with the vendors about problems and configuration changes; XML could be the enabler.

▸ *Team Approach*

Our system is operated by multiple parties: vendors, other companies, and multiple departments of our own institution. We need to prevent all these people working only in their "silo." Therefore it is advisable to schedule operational meeting regularly where all the parties come together and discuss all kind of activities, like planned changes and other observations. This will lead to better responsibility and accountability for the whole system, not only the individual piece of the puzzle.

▸ *ITIL – Information Technology Infrastructure Library*

ITIL is the globally accepted process-oriented approach to system operations; refer to Appendix C. The processes described there are somehow obvious. When we were confronted the first time with the ITIL framework in 2002, we found that we already did all this based on our experience and our own process improvements over many years. However, our categories were different and we used different terminology. This is why ITIL is important, even for operations teams with much experience and mature processes: it is the worldwide consistent *language* and *terminology* for system operations. Therefore we propose investing in ITIL and achieving service management certification for the key people.

It is also strongly advisable to do good bookkeeping of all changes, problems, and incidents as described in Sect. 5.7.

5.7 Making Our Own Statistics

Appendix A presents the mathematical concepts that are needed to understand and predict reliability of components and systems. The mathematical concept is important for understanding the basic theory of reliability. In particular, it defines the important terms *mean time between failures* (MTBF) and *annual failure rate* (AFR): the first is the average time until a failure happens, and the second is the average number of failures per year.

Let us apply that theory and let us come to "real" data from the field. As there is no other data source available, we have to collect our own data and make our own statistics. Following the ITIL framework, this leads to a database with the following sets of information; see also Appendix C:

Configuration management
- System name
- Vendor
- Series (i.e., a server of series S by vendor V)
- Configuration (model, patch level, system-specific, like number of CPUs, disk drives, etc.)
- Location
- Date for start of production

Change management
- System name
- Date and time of change
- Duration of change
- Type of change (use categories like "microcode upgrade")
- Reason for change (use categories like "bug-fix")
- Result (use categories like "successful," "no success – backed out")

Problem and incident management
- System name
- Date of incident
- Impact (use categories like "no," "performance degradation," "lost redundancy," "crash with x min of downtime")
- Root cause (use categories like "disk failure," "operating system panic")
- Comment with further information

There are many proprietary and open-source-based tools available that can be used to store this information. But a simple database or even a set of Excel tables (if you manage only a few systems) can do the job as well. If you decide to use commercial software, we propose checking the system's capabilities to create flexible reports (as described later). The openness of the system is also important, i.e., does it allow the export of information for further analysis.

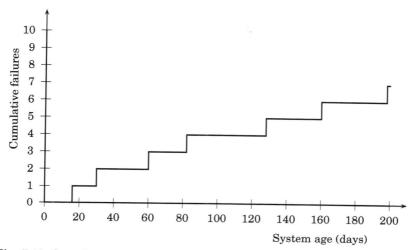

Fig. 5.12. Cumulative failures of a system as a function of system age. There is no trend – a mean time between failures number would apply

However, the challenge is not to find the best tool, it is about data quality and completeness. Our statistics are obviously only as good as the information they is based on.

Let us now assume that we collected the raw data for at least a couple of weeks (better months). The simplest thing we can do would be to calculate the MTBF for our various systems (using the problem categories "crash" or "lost redundancy"), and we can calculate the trustiness of the result. But this could be misleading, as the MTBF assumes a homogeneous distribution of failures. The MTBF can be an oversimplification, if our systems are not in the middle part of the bathtub curve, or if we have an external or a systematic root cause for the failures.

Therefore we first need to make a *cumulative plot* like that shown in Fig. 5.12. This example show a pretty constant rate; an MTBF (or AFR) number would make sense. The AFR shown of about 13 would be far too high for the failure rate of a computer system; it could represent disk failures in a large storage box of perhaps 400 disk drives. We continue using numbers of that magnitude, to simplify the discussion – to make them applicable for single components or single hosts, they need to scaled down appropriately. If this were the imaginary storage box with 400 disk drives an AFR_{disk} would be 0.0365 – consistent with Table A.2 on p. 364.

Let us now consider Fig. 5.13 on the following page, which shows the cumulative failure rate of two systems: one is at the beginning of the bathtub curve (improving), the other at its end (worsening). For both,

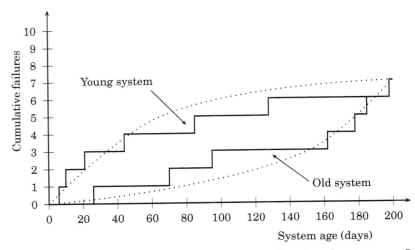

Fig. 5.13. Cumulative failures of two systems as a function of system age. One shows an improving failure rate ("early mortality"), the other a worsening rate ("end of life"). The *dotted lines* are shown to illustrate the behavior

an MTBF number does not make sense. The important information in these plots is that we *see* the changing failure probability and can act with appropriate responses.

If we have multiple systems of the same series, we can compare them in order to identify a system with anomalous behavior, as shown in Fig. 5.14 on the next page. Four of the five systems show a similar failure rate; their distribution looks homogeneous. But the fifth system's failure rate is about double and the curve's shape indicates a worsening system. For this system further analysis is required immediately.

So far we have looked into failure depending on system age. Another important diagram uses the failure dependence on *calendar date* – ignoring the system's age. This can tell us about root causes which are linked to a specific date, indicating an external reason (like environmental problems). Another reason could be that we implemented a patch on all systems on the same date. In this case the diagram can show us if the patch created new problems and, looking over longer time intervals, if it improved reliability.

Figure 5.15 on the facing page shows this behavior with bursts of failures on November 24 and May 21. This could be weekends where a change was applied to all systems. In this figure, we plotted the *mean cumulative function* (MCF) [11, 13], which is simply the average number of

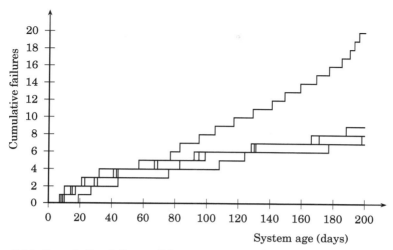

Fig. 5.14. Cumulative failures of five systems as a function of system age. One shows a significantly higher failure rate; the curve's shape indicates a worsening system

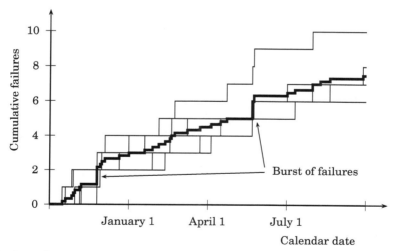

Fig. 5.15. Cumulative failures of six systems as a function of calendar date. The curves show a burst of failures on November 24, and May 21, see *arrows*. The *bold line* is the mean cumulative function

failures per system as a function of calendar date.[9] The derivative of the MCF is the recurrence rate for the population of systems in question. In this example, it shows very easily the dates when the failure bursts occur.

The MCF can and should be used for all plots with multiple systems to show the average behavior; it can also be applied using the system age as an independent variable, as we discussed before (e.g., Fig. 5.14 on the previous page).

Another important pattern to look for is the *clustering of failures*. It may happen that multiple failures occur in a short time interval, as shown in Fig. 5.17 on the facing page. This can be an indication that repair actions are not successful: the root cause for the failure was not removed by the repair action, or new failures were introduced by the repair action. The reason for this could be bad system design and missing diagnosis function or missing skills in the technical team.

It is useful to plot the *derivative* of the MCF versus age. It shows high fluctuations at the beginning (small time means a small denominator of the derivative) which should evolve into a pretty constant, horizontal, curve. If this is not the case then we have a trend, cluster(s) or burst(s) as described before. There are multiple ways to draw such a chart: lines or only dots where we calculated the derivative, we can calculate the derivatives equidistantly in time, only when failures occur; or as a sliding average over a couple of points. In Fig. 5.16 on the next page we have chosen to plot a dot whenever a failure occurred. We show the worsening system from Fig. 5.14. The fluctuations in the beginning can be ignored (days 1–90), between day 100 and day 150 the curve stabilizes, and after day 150 the worsening trend can be seen easily.

A similar analysis could be done for other dependent variables like the location of systems, specific system configurations, vendors, and system models. The last of these is important to compare the reliability of different models (and their vendors). Our experience is that the AFRs for different systems models (and different vendors) are between 0.05 and 2! This range is so large that even with statistics from only a few systems "good" models can be distinguished from "bad" ones very easily.

It is proposed to develop a set of such charts and review them monthly. In the beginning, we might not know where our problems are and what to look for. Then we need to create and review many such plots to look for all kinds of patterns and root causes. Over time we will identify those charts which are most relevant to our environment and review only those.

The influence of these activities on overall systems reliability is underestimated very often. It is a cheap and powerful method which can have a similar effect on overall reliability as a good system design! Experience

---

[9] Please note that the number of systems can change over time – the MCF for a given point in time must be calculated based on the actual number of systems at risk when failures on any system occur.

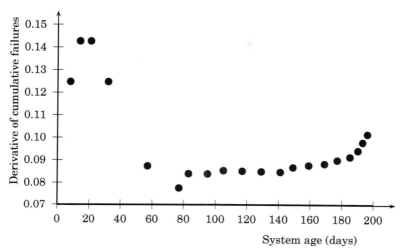

Fig. 5.16. Time derivative of the failures of the worsening system shown in Fig. 5.14. After some fluctuations in the beginning the curve stabilizes between day 100 and day 150. Later on the worsening trend can be seen easily

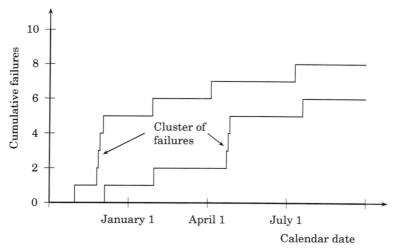

Fig. 5.17. Cumulative failures of two systems depending on calendar date. The curves show clusters of failures around November 27 and April 13, see *arrows*

shows that the overall number of problems and incidents can be reduced by more than 20%. It is motivating if we can demonstrate that our environment becomes more and more reliable. We can use it also for management reporting and future negotiations with vendors.

6

Operating Systems

Today's computer systems may have many redundant components, but are not fully redundant. Outage of a component, e.g., a CPU failure, will typically crash the operating system. The system may be restarted and might work again if the defective component is deactivated.

While redundant hardware yields many advantages, services fail for many reasons, and hardware errors are only one class. They were presented in the previous chapter to lay the foundation, but many problems occur in higher levels of our system stack. Later chapters will present concepts and methods to increase availability for middleware software, applications, and computing environments. This chapter will concentrate on complete computer systems: the conglomerate of hardware, hardware drivers, operating system, and logical storage that we call a host.

Outages on the host level occur in several flavors:

Hardware errors: Failed hardware was not redundant, or an error in redundant components happened and activation of the redundant component did not work.

Operating system errors: Process scheduling may go awry and processes may hang or may never start, or (virtual) memory management is deficient, network traffic handling may not be implemented correctly, and file systems may become corrupted.

Application errors: Memory leaks in long-running applications, deadlocks in communicating processes, or software errors that cause internal error states.

The approach presented in this chapter boils down to:

> **We increase availability through redundancy on the host level by taking several hosts and using them to supply a bunch of services, where each service is not strictly associated with a specific computer.**

Table 6.1. Cluster classification and properties

Failover cluster	Load-balancing cluster
Supports persistent data via shared storage (e.g., databases)	Application must not have a state (e.g., Web servers)
Generic solution that can be used for most applications	Specific solution that can be used for few applications
Provides recovery from failures, no scaling	Provides recovery from failures and increases also application performance (horizontal scaling)
Usually needs big servers with redundant hardware	Works typically with small and cheap servers

Being able to move services seamlessly from one host to another or provide them on several hosts from the start means that outages of one host leave the overall service functionality nevertheless intact. This approach is called *host clustering* in computer parlance.

Host clustering is not a single method but a whole class of concepts that come in different varieties:

- Failover clusters
- Server farms, also called load-balancing clusters
- Compute clusters

Compute clusters are not of relevance for this book, since they do not realize high availability or disaster recovery. There remain:

- **Failover clusters** , which allow a service to migrate from one host to another in the case of an error. They are the most used technology for high availability. Section 6.1 covers them in detail.
- **Load-balancing clusters**, which run a service on multiple hosts from the start and handle outages of a host. Section 6.2 describes this technology.

Table 6.1 shows the main usage properties of these two cluster types.

Figure 6.1 on the next page shows where cluster technology is used nowadays, and how the cluster types map to usage patterns. This graphic is for illustration of best practices only and is not meant as a definition – there are many cases where one implements the examples illustrated with different cluster technologies.

In general, host-cluster software on the operating system level does not know about session states or transactional behavior. It differs from middleware or application clusters. For example, Oracle cluster software knows about transactions and allows a client to handle them gracefully. This is not possible with clusters on the operating system level. After

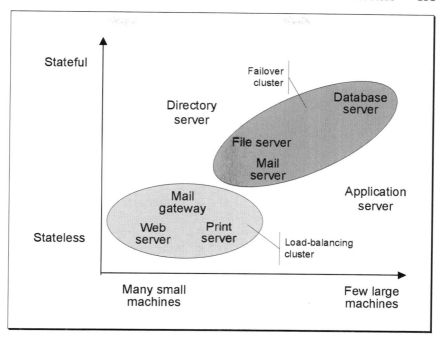

Fig. 6.1. Cluster usages. Directory servers and application servers have their own clustering capabilities and usually do not use host clustering

all, the session state is kept in the application; host clusters will not know anything about it. Therefore, on the host level, we are concerned with overall availability of a service, not with individual sessions. Forced restarts to keep a service running usually result in session termination and are thus seen by the client – except when the service is sessionless, of course. So this does not protect against loss of data, or data inconsistencies, or loss of business transactions; that task is left for upper levels or for the application software to handle.

6.1 Failover Clusters

As we noticed at the start of this chapter, the three most frequent outage causes are hardware failures, operating system (OS) crashes, and application errors. An interesting observation is then how such outages are typically handled. These are incidents and the IT staff will try to reestablish the IT service as quickly as possible. For hardware errors, the defective component is exchanged or repaired and the system is rebooted.

Table 6.2. Comparison of normal system administration and cluster reaction to failure categories

Failure category	Normal reaction	Cluster reaction
Hardware error	Repair and reboot	2nd server (no repair time and no reboot time, but failover time)
OS crash	Reboot	Service migration to other hardware (no reboot time, but failover time)
Application error	Restart, sometimes reboot	Restart, sometimes service migration to other hardware

For software errors, incident handling is most often not done by finding and resolving the root cause. Instead, the system is just rebooted in the case of an operating system crash, or the application is restarted in the case of an application error. Most of the time this is sufficient to make the service available again. Searching for the root cause of the problem can come later.

Failover clusters implement the idea that one can automate that procedure. Instead of manual service monitoring, manual hardware repair activities, and manual reboots or application restarts, we establish software that does this for us. It handles the error case when an application does not work as planned and when we can discover that misbehavior by checking the service provided. Such error situations have already been named: whole application crashes, application stalling due to egregious resource consumption, crashes of the operating system itself, hardware component outages, and others.

Instead of hardware repairs, we take a second computer system and use that in the case of component outages. The second computer system is also used in the case of operating system crashes, we do not bother with automated reboots that might go wrong. Application restarts are tried, and if they do not cure the problem, the second system is used again.

This is not a cure for these error situations; we should better call it a workaround, as it does not resolve the actual root cause of the problem. But starting anew with a clean state often makes problems disappear, even though the root cause has not been removed. Therefore, restarting and service migration to another host are no proper long-term means to handle stability and quality problems of an application; but it may well be the best short-term solution in terms of availability improvement.

Table 6.2 illustrates the relation between "normal" system administration and automated failure handling by cluster software. It shows that a cluster delivers now in an automated way what we did by hand before. Basically a failover cluster is three things:

1. Additional hardware
2. Monitoring of services
3. Automated migration of services to the other hardware

Overall, this cluster type is a kind of bastard. It fixes deficiencies of operating systems and applications by providing workarounds, but does not resolve the real causes. We need it mainly because current operating systems are not implemented well enough, and do not include that abstraction and migration functionality in the first place. The same holds for the application interface that is used here. The class of application failures handled by failover clusters should actually be resolved by improving the application – but that is wishful thinking in our cost- and new-feature-obsessed IT landscape, so we will have to live with these clusters for quite a while.

Failover clusters are suitable for applications that hold state information and where the application software has no inherent cluster functionality or where you do not want to use it. For instance, database software is a prime example. Many database software products have no cluster capability, and those that do are often quite new and are not mature yet. Also, applications are often only certified for specific releases of database software and might not allow usage of clustered databases. File servers are another example of suitable application classes.

On the other hand, Web servers most often do not keep any state information. Of course one can use failover clusters as well to raise their availability, but they are much more suitable for another cluster type, namely, load-balancing clusters, which will be introduced in Sect. 6.2 on p. 176.

▶ *Failover Clusters Need Hardware Independence*

The main task of operating systems is resource management, and providing those resources to application software with an abstracted interface. Originally, many of these resources were hardware-related, and bound to a specific piece of hardware. For example, on mainframes, one explicitly allocated files on specific cylinders on specific disk drives. But these dependencies on hardware components diminished over time; nowadays operating systems provide resource abstractions for applications:

- Processes that are started on demand, be it due to an incoming network request or triggered by another application.
- Long-running server processes (called daemon processes in Unix and services in Windows).
- Jobs, i.e., processes that are scheduled by time and started either regularly or once.
- File storage for application programs and configuration
- File storage for data
- Disk storage for data
- Network interfaces, in particular IP interfaces

Failover clusters provide these resource abstractions in a completely hardware-independent way. They are able to move allocated resources between hosts, and are thus able to migrate applications from one host to another.

This functionality needs cooperation from the application. The operating system provides the aforementioned resources named as virtual entities, and the cluster software provides the functionality to move these resources from one cluster node to the other. But hardware-specific resource access is still possible. The application must not use any other resource that is bound to the hardware, otherwise it does not work. For example, it must not use the host ID, or the host name and bind functionality to that. Section 8.1 on p. 217 spells out the requirements for applications in failover cluster environments in detail.

▶ *Failover Cluster Definition*

Let us define first more precisely what a failover cluster is and then let us look at the implementation concepts and the preconditions that are needed for such a cluster.

> A **service** is a set of applications, associated server processes and jobs, data storage, and IP network interfaces that run on one computer system at a time. Such a service is often also called a *logical host* or a *resource group*.

> A **failover cluster** is a combination of several computer systems, hardware configuration, cluster software, and the configuration of the operating system and applications that allows to move services between the computer systems of that cluster.

> These computer systems are also called **physical hosts** or just **nodes**.

Figure 6.2 on the next page illustrates this principle.

▶ *Failover Cluster Variations*

Failover clusters come in several varieties. In the most basic form there are two physical hosts and attached shared storage. This "two-node configuration" may provide one or several services. Figure 6.3 on p. 156 illustrates how services may be placed on the cluster nodes.

When only one service is provided, it will run on one cluster node and the other node is not utilized. Such an architecture is called an *active/passive cluster*. Typical examples are mission-critical big databases that need all the computing power of one node and the second node functions as a *hot-standby* or *hot-spare* system. Databases often do not degrade well performance-wise and need a minimum of available CPU and memory resources to work. If we migrated another service to the node on which the database server runs, that might reduce the available resources to an amount that makes the database unusable. Therefore active/passive clusters are a popular choice for this server type, to be on the safe side with high availability for this important service.

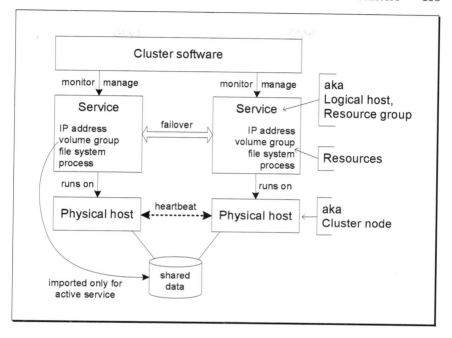

Fig. 6.2. Failover cluster

When several services run, and if they degrade gracefully in environments with reduced resources, they are normally distributed evenly over both nodes, and in the case of failures all services are migrated to one functional node. Of course, then one node must have memory and computing power to run all services, albeit often with reduced performance. Such an architecture is called an *active/active cluster* and is often used for application or file servers.

If clusters have more than two nodes, the distinction between active/active and active/passive is not as clear-cut anymore. For example, services might be distributed over $n-1$ physical hosts, and the nth host is a hot-spare node that is utilized if there are problems. All kinds of distribution of services over the physical hosts can be imagined, and happen to appear in reality.

With the advent of host virtualization for midrange servers, in the context of ever-increasing computer power in accordance with Moore's Law, this once clear-cut architectural distinction gets muddied even further. As this is quite important in its own right, these developments will be addressed later in Sect. 6.3.

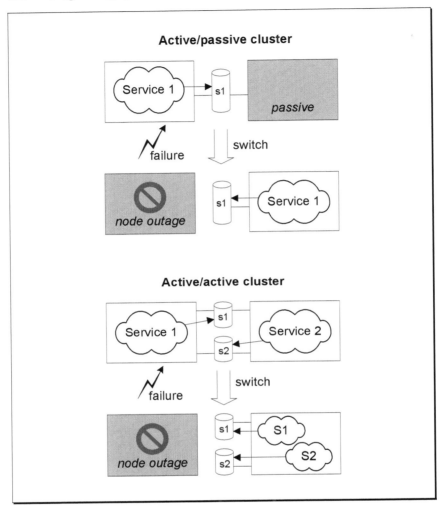

Fig. 6.3. Failover cluster variations

► *Limits of Failover Clusters*

Failover cluster technology has its limits though. There are several issues that can happen where clusters do not help:

- Failover clusters depend on shared storage facilities. Data consistency on this storage facility can be considered the single point of failure; it is not part of a failover cluster's objective to protect against logical data corruption.

- Software errors in cluster software. It is important to note that the cluster software is a single point of failure in the whole architecture of failover clusters. Cluster software errors typically cause outages of all nodes and all services.
- Single points of failure creep in (e.g., during a change) and do not get noticed.
- Components may not work in a failover cluster environment. Examples are databases where we know up-front that they cannot be restarted automatically in a reasonable time frame after a crash, or nonfunctional forced unmounts for some file-system types.
- Some components pretend to work in a cluster, but there are failure situations where they do not live up to that demand. Therefore they work "most of the time" and we still have a remaining risk of outages if we use them. As an example, for some databases the backup operation must not be interrupted; failovers during that time are not handled gracefully. On the other hand, there is no substitution for some products; often one must simply live with that problem.
- Usage of cluster software places constraints on maintenance activities. A special problem is patch management: when we deploy patches on all cluster nodes at the same time and the patch is erroneous, we run into severe trouble. No physical host of the whole cluster will work anymore.

  Therefore, it is common sense to patch one cluster system after the other. But then the application software must work both with the old and with the new patch; luckily that is almost always the case. But that one step at a time approach to patch management can only be used for system patches – application software is installed only once per cluster, and nonworking patches will render it unusable without any chance to recover. To conquer that problem, staging systems are needed that enable us to test patch application and functionality before they are put into production.

  In summary, maintenance can render a cluster nonfunctional. Good processes help to avoid that, but a cluster is not protection per se against such failure scenarios.

In addition to this list, there may be the technical problems that will be addressed in Sect. 6.1.1, where functionality of a failover cluster is explained in more technical detail.

6.1.1 How Does It Work?

Let us have a look at failover cluster functionality in more detail. First, we will check out the technical principles, then we will discuss in detail service management and associated pitfalls.

Functionality of Failover Clusters

The overall objectives of a failover cluster are:

- Retain availability of data
- Restore availability of service
- Recover from failures in an acceptable time

Potential failures are hardware errors, operating system crashes, and application errors.

The focus of a failover cluster is on data availability and overall service availability, not on sessions. Migration of sessions is a task that needs intelligence from the application level and cannot be done on the operating system level alone. Therefore, failover clusters may abort user sessions. Data consistency is not an objective, as already mentioned. This is a task that cannot be handled on the operating system level, but which must be cared for by the application.

Figure 6.4 on the next page illustrates the basic functional principle that failover clusters realize. But let us have a closer look at those principles that goes beyond a schematic representation.

▶ *Service Switch*

A failover cluster manages services that are checked for availability and can be migrated to another physical host. The technical term for such a migration is *service switch* or *logical host switch*. For that to work, we need a service declaration and lots of details must be right in handling such a service – the next section will present these details. For now, we will stick to the general view.

▶ *Preferred Node*

In almost all failover clusters, a service runs only on one physical host at a time. In active/active clusters, a service usually has a *preferred node*, i.e., a physical host on which it it preferably runs. This approach is mainly for organizational reasons – it eases planning of hardware resources needed for a cluster. Each service running on its preferred node is the "normal" state of operation that utilizes available hardware resources in the best way. Switching a service to another node needs hardware resources there and reduces available resources for other services that are already running on this physical host. As such, failovers are planned to be only temporary; when the cause of the error has been determined and eliminated, the service is switched back to its preferred node.

In active/active clusters, the nodes are sized to run their preferred services, and additional hardware resources are supplied for the hopefully special situation of a failover. This particularly works well when the service degrades gracefully under increased load. For example, a Network

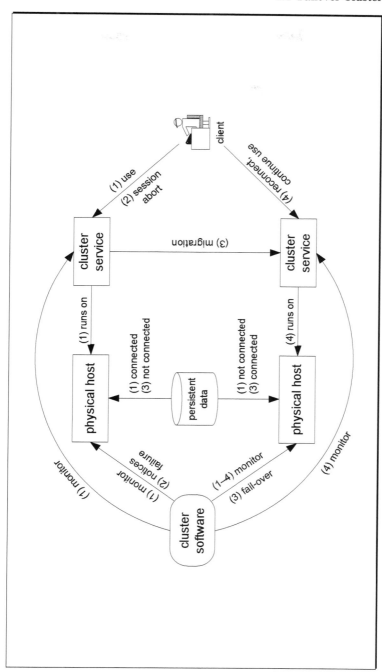

Fig. 6.4. Basics of failover cluster functionality

File System (NFS) or a Common Internet File System (CIFS) service is very easy to run in an active/active cluster, reducing available CPU and main memory resources just makes the service go slower, whereas some database systems cannot handle reduced resources at all below certain limits. Then they grind to a halt and become unusable. For such services, active/active configurations should be checked carefully to see if one physical node can really sustain all services that potentially run on it and still deliver acceptable service levels.

▸ *Shared Cluster State*

A cluster needs a shared state: it needs to know on all the physical hosts on which node each service is at the given moment. If there were a management node, this would be a single point of failure; outages of that node would break the whole cluster. Therefore each proposed service switch is communicated to all cluster nodes and is only done if the new service location is accepted everywhere. As such, service switches have a transactional behavior: either they succeed everywhere or they fail completely.

▸ *Intercluster Communication*

This intercluster communication is crucial for cluster functionality; therefore, its own dedicated communication paths are typically set up for it. Most of the time, that is just a special redundant network connection on specific network interfaces; if possible, utilizing cross cables without any intervening switch. But cluster software may also utilize other communication methods, e.g., serial lines. The stable and unchanged communication path also avoids the risk that intercluster communication is brought down by an erroneous reconfiguration, during a service switch.

▸ *Heartbeat*

But failover cluster software not only manages services and associated resources, but also coordinates physical hosts. It is a necessity for cluster software to know which physical resources are not available anymore; after all, this is often the reason for switching a service. A very special case of such hardware monitoring is the test if a physical host is still running at all. This test is done in very short intervals and is emphatically know as *heartbeat*. Hosts that answer that test are accordingly called *alive*, and hosts that do not answer are called *dead*. Heartbeat tests usually use the intercluster communication path too. Thus, the stable heartbeat communication will be part of shared state management over all physical hosts, as it should be.

▸ *Split Brain Syndrome*

By introducing the cluster heartbeat, we have introduced a new potential source of errors though. Even if the intercluster communication path is redundant, it can fail – and then we are in deep trouble. A two-node cluster illustrates that best: each node will think that the other node is dead, and will start all services to make them available again. That behavior is called a *split brain* situation. It means that the shared disk space will be accessed by both nodes, both will activate the same IP addresses on the same shared network, etc. As the minimum result, services will not work. But then you will be lucky – it may also be that persistent data is damaged beyond repair.

Some cluster products include further precautions: The *failfast* mechanism forcibly shuts down ("panics") a physical host when it detects that the node has left the cluster. This is done to ensure that no single node will start its own cluster while the others are still alive. But it is not easy to detect if one node is part of the cluster or not; further precautions are necessary to do that.

► *Quorum Devices*

Since this problem has so severe consequences, some cluster products protect against that risk by introducing yet another communication path that is used to really decide which node is part of the cluster and which is not. Shared disk devices are sometimes used for this communication path, e.g., they are called *quorum devices* by Sun and *disk heart beating* or *tie-breaker* by IBM. Serial lines or network connections are other means for the alternative communication path; but they often have distance limitations that make this requirement difficult to meet.

► *Communication with Other Systems*

It is not sufficient that a server is up. The clients or other servers must also be able to reach the server. The cluster software must not only keep a service running on a host that works, it must also check that this host does not get disconnected from the network by a switch or cabling failure.

For that reason, clusters check the reachability of important servers or other network components. Most often the reachability of the default gateway router is checked, under the assumption that this router has been made highly available itself and is a good approximation for network connectivity. (Section 9.1.3 explains how to set up highly available default gateways.)

There is more to do to assert that network communication with clients works. Cluster services use virtual IP addresses, but actual communication in an Ethernet is not based on IP addresses, it needs a Media Access Control (MAC) address. The relationship between IP and MAC addresses is stored in *Address Resolution Protocol (ARP) caches* at each communication partner and is not updated quickly. Theoretically, one could have a virtual MAC address that is one of the service resources and that is migrated as well. But most cluster software does not implement that this way; it uses the MAC address of the physical interface instead. As a consequence, ARP caches in the local Ethernet segment must be updated when a failover happens. To trigger the update, the cluster software will send an ARP broadcast after it has activated the service's virtual IP interface on the new cluster node.

▸ *Service Dependencies*

Services consist of resources (that is why they are also called resource groups). When services are started or stopped, the resources must be activated or deactivated in a specific order. This is needed because some resources are needed by others; e.g., one needs to import the volume groups to be able to mount a file system.

Some products represent the belief that is not sufficient to have resource dependencies. Instead, service or resource group dependencies are provided as well. With that ability, we can specify that a cluster service is only started if another one is active, somewhere in the cluster. As an example, we can specify that the service *database server* must be active on some cluster node before the service *messaging server* is started – supposedly because the messaging server uses the database server.

Such dependency information does not protect the service from the need to handle outages. If we look at the example from the previous paragraph, a database server outage will cause nonavailability of it for some time, namely, the failover time and maybe even the recovery time on the new node. The messaging server should handle that outage and should also know that it needs to reconnect because sessions will have been aborted during the failover. If the messaging server cannot handle this situation but needs a restart to function again, we should check if it is possible to switch products and get a better one.

Services in Failover Clusters

Now that we understand basic cluster functionality, it is time to look at cluster service management in more detail. This section will explain everything a failover cluster does with services: their declaration, activation, service checks, restarts, switches, and deactivation.

▸ *Service Declaration*

The declaration of a service is done only once, during implementation of the cluster. All other actions, like activation, deactivation, and service migration, are done repeatedly.

A service allocates a set of resources, using the cluster software. Such resources may be:

- Server processes to start that run all the time
- Jobs to start regularly or once

- Storage volume groups, with or without file systems
- Remote (network-attached storage) or storage area network (SAN) file systems
- Network IP interfaces

For each resource five actions have to be defined:

1. How to start the resource
2. How to test the resource for availability, and how often it should be tested
3. How to restart the resource
4. How to stop the resource
5. How to abort the resource, i.e., how to force it to stop

Of course, knowledge about generic services is already available in the cluster software; one does not need to specify how a file system is mounted or unmounted.

In addition, one must declare dependencies between service resources. Often, this boils down to specifying the order of starts and stops. When a server process needs a network interface to be established, the network interface is started first. Likewise with mounts of file systems and other resources.

▶ *Service Activation*

A service may be activated at boot time, or activated manually. During activation, hardware-related resources are made accessible: storage volumes are activated (sometimes called "imported"), file systems are mounted, virtual network interfaces are established. This is done by the cluster software; no service needs to supply code for this. Then server processes are started; information on how that is done is part of the resource definition.

It is important that the service start is idempotent. That means that we must be able to activate it when it is already running without causing any harm. Usually this is implemented with a semaphore that is checked at the start time to see if the service is already running. A second start is then aborted.

▶ *Service Checks*

The cluster software will now check the availability of each resource in the specified intervals. If the check delivers failure, or if the check times out, the resource is deemed inactive and the cluster will try to restore service availability.

This is important: cluster software does not know about any service or any application per se. It knows only about the registered checks for a resource, as its whole world view revolves around the registered actions. Therefore, checks must be programmed very carefully and must be very robust – otherwise a cluster might think that a service is still alive though it is not (*false positive*), or a service is thought to be defective, although it just needs a bit longer to answer the request (*false negative*).

Service checks must pay special attention to timeouts. They are needed to detect hanging processes or unresponsive hardware. But they must take into account checks on other system stack levels as well; timeouts of service checks must be coordinated with other timeouts on the computer system.

A good illustration is disk problems: when there are disk failures in a mirrored configuration, the disk drivers themselves will wait for timeouts and will attempt several retries. Only after all these retries have been unsuccessfully finished is the disk declared nonfunctional and removed from the mirror. That timeout by the disk driver might be longer than the service check timeout at the higher level – and that timeout might trigger a service migration before the defective disk has been removed from the mirror. When the disk subsystem is activated at another cluster node, the disk failure occurs again and the same error situation occurs. "Failover ping-pong" is likely to occur at this point: endless switching of the service from one cluster node to the other.

A functionality of elaborate cluster products is a framework for successive checks and associated reactions. For example, one can define a finite state automaton over test results or check output messages. If a check delivers an error or a warning, one can either trigger immediately restart or switch actions or put the check subsystem into a different state. In that new state, different checks can be made to determine the need for appropriate action.

Such service check frameworks can lead to very elaborate implementations – in the worst case, nobody except the implementor understands them. During their realization, we need to remember that the first principle for good high-availability implementations is KISS: Keep It Simple and Straightforward. It is also best practice to add a description or documentation on the server itself, in a format that can be read without access to graphical user interfaces. An ASCII file can be read from everywhere, also remotely when a system administrator is logged in via cell phone, whereas files in Word or PDF formats are often not suitable for emergency situations.

▶ *Service Deactivation*

Service deactivation is easy in principle: all resources must be stopped and deallocated:

- Server processes are shut down with either a proper command or by killing the process.
- Virtual network interfaces are brought down.
- Remote and SAN file systems are unmounted.

- Storage volume groups are deactivated. Some products call deactivation of volume groups "exporting."

Of course, the devil is in the details: quite often resources cannot be stopped easily in error situations. Section 6.1.2 on the following page discusses real-world experiences in more detail.

▶ *Service Restart*

When a service check detects that a resource is not available anymore, that resource can be restarted. A service restart can also be triggered manually. The method of restarting is known for hardware-related resources, and part of the resource definition for process resources.

Restarting means to deactivate a resource and activate it again on the same cluster node. Some cluster implementations prefer to deactivate the whole service (all resources of it) and activate it again. The aim is minimization of service migration; often a restart is sufficient to reuse a service again. This method helps again temporary exhaustion of resources, e.g., because of memory leaks.

We usually try to avoid service migration because it has its own risks associated with it. Switching over hardware resources to another cluster node might take a long time, or even might not work at all. In addition, if the other cluster node runs other services, their performance will be reduced by the additional load. Therefore, we prefer that each service stays on the node where it is usually located.

▶ *Service Migration (Aka Failovers or Switches)*

When an host is not alive anymore, or when a service restart does not result in a functional service, failover happens: the service is migrated to another node in the cluster. In principle, failovers are straightforward: all resources are stopped – server processes are stopped if they are still running, file systems are unmounted and disk volumes are deallocated, (virtual) network interfaces are brought down, etc. Then all nodes in the cluster are informed about that service migration, and the service is activated on the new node.

The migration proceeds in the following steps:

1. Shutdown the service, or do a forced shutdown, or do a failfast operation
2. Activate (import) storage volume groups with a SCSI reserve
3. Mount file systems
4. Activate IP addresses and send ARP broadcasts
5. Start services according to dependencies

If there is an error at any of these steps, the migration was not successful.

In practice, failovers always carry associated risks. Service migration might not work owing to many errors, not least that nodes within one cluster might differ owing to maintenance work and there might be problems to activate a service on the new node.

6.1.2 Failover Cluster Implementation Experiences

When a project implements a solution that utilizes a failover cluster, it must be aware of several important issues that must be resolved for successful implementations. Some of these issues are requirements for applications that shall be deployed; these are described in Sect. 8.1 on p. 217. In this section, we concentrate on the system requirements and system-level issues.

Failover Success Rates

Experience from many companies shows that a good cluster is one where only 90–95% of failovers are successful. If more than 25% fail, this is a bad cluster implementation. There have been situations where only 50% of failovers were successful; these were very bad implementations.

The difference between good and bad clusters is always the same: bad clusters have too complex setups and the quality of operations is not good. Operational quality also includes proper noncluster monitoring. It is *not* sufficient to rely on the cluster-internal monitoring. Instead we need to make sure that independent monitoring is set up – and that staff with appropriate skill check regularly that all services are running smoothly. For mission-critical servers, this should be done every day.

But still we will probably have 5–10% of failovers that do not succeed. This is a limitation that is inherent in cluster technology. The remaining failures have causes that are too complex to be handled by the cluster actions: the rather primitive approach of restart and reboot does not work for them.

In theory, one still has some time left now. At the lower end of high-availability service level agreements (SLAs), we might have 1 or 2 h to fix the problem. If the server is mission-critical, the SLAs might allow only 15–30 min to solve the problem and still count it as a major outage. If a skilled system administrator is at hand, this might even be possible – but frankly, this is an exception. In the normal case, the system administrator does not fix the problem in that half hour or might not even be on site.

Therefore, when a cluster failover fails, it is best to declare a major outage right away. Now is the time for a prepared disaster-recovery process to kick in. This does not mean that everything is migrated to the disaster-recovery system at the remote disaster-recovery site immediately. It means that the preparations for such a migration start.

Since we are now in the major outage case, our disaster recovery SLAs must be fulfilled, in particular the recovery time objective. But recovery time objective times are much longer than maximum cluster outage times: they are usually in the range of several hours. While the business owner is informed about the problem and while the decision about disaster declaration is made, system administrators can have a look at the failed system. Now, with more time on their hands, they can try to fix the problem and get the cluster running again. The big danger is that they try for too long and that migration to the disaster-recovery site is postponed so long that even the recovery time objective is not maintained any longer.

This is the reason why it must be emphasized that repair actions after failed service migrations are part of the disaster-recovery process, and not part of the normal high-availability operation. The disaster-recovery process must specify in advance how much time is allocated for the attempts to fix the problem with the primary systems, and it must specify the time when the switch to the disaster-recovery site has to be pushed with all strength. This demands human judgment and is not in the realm of automated cluster actions anymore.

Good Service Checks Are Hard to Design

Good checks are very difficult to define and realize in practice. It is always a tightrope walk to minimize the number of false negatives and false positives. One will not be able to avoid them completely, as application behavior cannot be observed and predicted in a reliable way. If there are formal SLAs, these are the best guidelines for choosing the thresholds. If the SLA defines a maximum reaction time of 60 s, our check timeout can be set to that interval and we can deem the service nonfunctional afterwards. Therefore, good resource checks always have configurable timeouts, to be adaptable to different SLAs.

Checks are done periodically. We need to assure that the same check does not run twice at the same time. For example, when a check itself needs 45 s, then starting it every minute is risky – in the case of a high load on the computer system the check might need longer than 1 min and this could lead to deadlocks or overloads.

There is also the important question of what we can and what we should check. We can check for the existence of a resource, we can check for its functionality, and even the functionality check can be on different levels. Let us consider a database server as an example:

- We can check if the database server process is running, by looking at the process list.
- We can check if the database server accepts requests, by looking to see if a process listens on the port of the service's address. Such a check might utilize the netstat command, for example. Of course, this is only possible if the database accepts requests over the network at all.

- We can check if the database server responds to requests, by making a query that is application-independent, e.g., we may query the system catalog. We need appropriate privileges for that test.
- We can check that the application data may be accessed correctly, by querying an application table. If the query succeeds, it is not necessary to check for modifications to work. This check might be expensive in terms of computing power, depending on the request. It must be realized very carefully, otherwise performance of the production system could be influenced beyond acceptable limits.

Please note that we cannot say a priori which check is best. We might want to have a very quick and resource-sparing check, then the process-existence or the port-listening check might be best. Or the server might need authentication and we do not want to store credentials in clear text in the check code or configuration; then application-level checks are out of the question. Proper selection of an appropriate check is always a matter of good cluster design.

When one selects request, response, or functionality checks, one must also consider their consequences for metrics and accounting. Service usage is usually monitored for several purposes: to create statistics about end-user usage, to create information about used capacity, and sometimes to create accounting records if the service is paid for by transaction usage.

Let us use Web servers as an example for the logging problem. Their logs are usually analyzed, to give the content owner information about usage, session duration, travel paths, transfer capacity, entry points, search engine referrals, etc. If one adds a request every minute to check for serviceability, that adds 1440 requests per day. Depending on the overall traffic, that might be negligible or not. Of course, one can avoid that error introduced by the checks: if one can identify those requests in the log, one can discard them before statistical analysis. Or one can avoid logging them in the first place.

While wrong logging is often only a nuisance, application checks can cause financial consequences when service usage is paid per transaction. Many industry pundits declare that a "public utility" model is the service model of the future; where application services are outsourced and paid for by usage, software does not need to be bought anymore. If the outsourcer is responsible for the application's availability, a failover cluster might be utilized – but then you, as the customer, do not want to pay for the internal application checks of the outsourcer's infrastructure. Then it is important if availability checks are detected and not accounted for.

Problems at Service Deactivation

The problem is quite clearly what happens when one of the stop actions does not succeed. If a server process happens to hang in a system call, it might be noninterruptible and cannot be shut down. Nothing short of a system reboot will then terminate the process.

In the same way, file systems often cannot be unmounted as long as processes still use them. Many file systems offer a *forced unmount* functionality, where one can force the unmount with the explicit risk of data inconsistencies. But then, this forced unmount happens not to work well either – sometimes, the system hangs even in that forced unmount and we need to abort the whole system with a failfast operation. Luckily, this normally is not a big problem, since journaled file systems provide quick recovery from such failure situations.

So in the end, while it is typically very easy to deactivate a service under normal circumstances, deactivation in error conditions is connected to a whole bunch of real-world problems stemming from imperfect implementations. As a result, the deactivated service resources might be in inconsistent states (e.g., unclean file systems) or it might not be possible to deactivate them completely. We are forced to invest in subsequent manual work to get a clean system again.

In the latter case, only rebooting the physical host might help. This is often a poor choice though – more services might run on this node, and they need to be migrated to another cluster node first. Cluster software will not do this automatically though, and thus rebooting a node with several services running on it is always connected with raised risk.

But there is new hope on the horizon. Advances in host virtualization are enabling usage of this technology in more circumstances than were possible in the past. Section 6.3.2 on p. 184 explains this technology in more detail. It can be put to good use for failover clusters by putting each service into a virtual host. Rebooting that virtual host then becomes practical and does not influence other services running on other virtual hosts on the same physical host. Though it must be said that at the time of writing this book, this approach has not made inroads into common cluster products and they must be configured manually.

Service Migration Must Not Take Too Long

It is usually possible to define in the cluster software how long it should wait for the first check after a service has been activated or migrated. But this time span also sets an upper limit on how long the start of the service's resources may take. The limit must not be too high, of course – the objective of a failover cluster is provision of ongoing service, after all. But it must not be too short either, since the service must finish its activation in that time span.

Long activation times can happen quickly. Let us assume that the service's file system is some terabytes that are spread over 400 disks in an enterprise-storage system or a SAN. If each disk gets its own LUN, 400 LUNs must be started. Many operating systems handle this task in a way that needs lots of time. So, it is much better to combine several disks into a few large LUNs.

But such normal-case considerations are not sufficient. This activation time limit must be thoroughly analyzed in the light of potential error situations. Of special interest are situations where the data are not consistent and must be checked in some way.

As an example, let us look at a failover cluster with a database server. When the database service needs to be switched to another node, the database content might not be consistent. The database management system will start consistency checks and recovery actions. If only some redo logs must be replayed, this will be done in a short time frame. But if indexes must be rebuilt, the recovery might need quite a long time and the service needs too long to start – leading the service check from the cluster software to fail, and the database to switch to yet another node immediately. Probably this will cause an endless loop of service migrations, from one node to the other and back again. These kinds of endless migration loops are sometimes called *failover ping-pong*.

In fact, there was a case where a database (MySQL in this case) was used first without transaction support, and where the startup consistency checks in the case of aborts needed so long that this constellation could not be operated properly in a failover cluster environment. Either we would have to compromise with the service checks (e.g., check only for running processes, and not for properly answered queries) or we would have to skip consistency checks – not a good idea, of course. In the end, the MySQL version was used that has transaction support, even though it comes with a performance penalty and needs much more space to store its data.

In summary, the system configuration must ensure that the start of all resources can be completed in the allocated activation time. This must include consistency checks, establishing consistency again.

Use Journaling Wherever Possible

The report of previous experience concerning switch times leads to a corollary. Many storage systems, be it databases or file systems, employ journaling techniques. In fact, in the context of high-availabilty systems, all operating systems and all storage options deliver that possibility.

Section 5.2 on p. 108 presented that topic in more detail. Here, it is sufficient to say that changes are written to a journal first; operations that belong together and their successful completion are marked as well. This makes for fast recovery after crashes, since the system simply has to replay completed changes and can undo uncompleted changes. Violà, the data is consistent again.

So whenever you configure your storage on the operating system level, make sure that you enabled journaling. There is no excuse for not using it.

Crashes Can Leave Garbage Behind

Suppose that your service crashed and the cluster software switched it successfully to another node. Everything's all right and in order, isn't it?

Well, in practice, it is not. *Every* switch has the potential to introduce errors that will only become visible at a later time. And we will want to switch back at some time, especially if we use the common setup of preferred nodes for services. Then these errors would be waiting for us, and that must be prevented. Sometimes crashes leave resources behind that prevent service activation. Most often the cause is a lock file that is checked during startup and prevents the start of a server process. Or some shared memory segment is allocated and not released again. There are lots of other possibilities for things that can go wrong.

This is a big difference from the operations of a normal server. When we reboot a server, that reboot most often creates a clean state. But a failover leaves the old system in the defective state and often manual rework is necessary to get it running again. Clusters are not fully automated, they must be attended to. Automation is restricted to failure discovery and workaround handling, but does not cover repairs.

Of course, most of these problems can be attributed to bad software quality. Manual intervention after crashes to be able to restart any service should not be necessary. Simple testing of the existence of a lock file is a very bad idea – nevertheless, it is used often enough that one has to ask if developers do not think about reliable operations of their software. Even worse is that there are some vendors who do not react to such problem reports and take manual intervention after crashes as granted.

The bad news is that this is something that you have to learn through experience. You can test for it by crashing your system deliberately, but you can only hope that you will hit the problematic situation during the test. After you have encountered a problem, it is worthwhile investigating the root cause of the problem and trying to change your resource start to cope with that problem. Over time, you will improve the reliability of your service switches.

Sharing Directories Between Services Is a Recipe for Disaster

Directory names should be different for all services on all nodes. No service may share directories. Only then can these directories be placed on service-specific volume groups.

There will be exceptions, and for each exception the impact must be analyzed. As long as the exception concerns only temporary files that do not keep persistent information, they are fine. Proper examples are process identifier (PID) files in /var/run – but note that it is advisable to introduce subdirectories for each service there for access rights and maintainability reasons.

All persistent information must be stored on service-specific volumes. Storing information on system volumes that are shared between several services is a no-no and must be strictly avoided. If some application demands it (e.g., insists on data files in /var) and cannot be changed, one might often utilize symbolic links to store the actual files somewhere else. But, frankly, we should not trust such an inflexible application anyhow, and should question if it is fit for enterprise-level IT deployment. With such applications, you will have many more problems in other areas as well, and you should look for a replacement immediately.

After all, sharing program files between several services introduces dependencies between these services that were not there before: they are tested with the installed version of the shared software. If that shared software is to be updated, tests with *all* services must ensure that they still work after the update. All services are also affected by the update and must be restarted, maybe data or the configuration must be migrated too. In the case of installation in the service's storage area, updates could be approached independently.

Installation and Packaging of System Tools and Configuration

Sometimes programs and configuration files for services are installed on system volumes. Configuration files in /etc are the prime example: many applications insist on that location. In that case, care must be taken that updates are done on all physical hosts to an identical state. Usually this is done properly initially; problems occur during updates. Using the operating system's packaging and installation method for self-installed software as well is a real boon that helps with coordinated roll-out of patches and program updates.

But synchronized configuration file updates are a drag. Programs exist that allow actions to be done in the same way on several hosts at the same time, e.g., the SourceForge project *clusterssh*. But often system administrators forget to use them because they want to try out the configuration first on one node and then update all the other ones. Or they have other excuses; experience shows that over time the configuration of physical hosts tends to come apart.

A possible escape from that dilemma is usage of host configuration tools like *Opsware* or *cfengine*. While these are often promoted as tools for effectively managing a large number of hosts, they can be utilized as well just for the physical hosts of a cluster. Of course, not only for system configuration, but also for configuration of an application that is installed on system volumes.

Another method for keeping system files in sync is file synchronization tools like *rsync*. This can be used both for program files and for configuration files. Mirroring program files that have been installed by a package system does not mirror the package meta-information though. Then the information about the version and installation time of an application and which files belong to a package is only available on the installation host and not on the replication targets. If the installation host breaks down, this information is lost. It is up to your management and operations principles if that bothers you. Of course, it should...

Installation package systems cause more problems. Preferably, application software should also be installed using standard software packaging methods. That procedure also delivers integration into standard system management processes. Meta-information about the software version, files that belong to a package, changes to installed files, and so on are readily available. Asset management systems, or agents for a configuration management database, just work. But this implies that all software updates are done on one specific node, the preferred node of that application. Otherwise the consistency of the package database would be destroyed. Care must also be taken for the case when the preferred node's system volumes get corrupted – while the application itself will be switched to another cluster node and will run without problems, meta-information needed for updates might get lost.

Be aware that there are often hidden parts to application configuration. For example, it may be that the application's administrator needs *sudo* rights for some commands on the cluster. These rights must be kept current on all cluster nodes; it is a usual error to update them only on the current node and then one will have surprises after switches. But these surprises often come in incident situations – and especially there they hinder proper resolution of current issues. Pay attention to such issues that are small on the surface, it is worth it.

A final note on installation: if your enterprise utilizes the IT Infrastructure Library (ITIL) or equivalent service management processes, it might have established a configuration database. Make sure that the configuration database knows how to handle failover clusters. Many simpleminded applications do not cope with the fact that configuration items can be moved freely between different hosts and must be associated with a logical host that is actually not a full machine.

System Logging Done Correctly

Logging in application-specific files is a matter of application configuration and will be looked at there. But operating systems, cluster software, and also applications often use the *syslog* service. Thus the logs by default end up on the physical host where they are created. After a crash of those physical hosts they might not be accessible anymore, and important resources for problem root cause analysis might be missing.

One has to decide for each project, if that is acceptable. If syslog information mainly consists of log entries for the physical host, or if only uninteresting parts of the application log to syslog, then you might refrain from bothering with the setup of complicated log solutions.

But if you will need those logs – and remember, logs are important for failure analysis – you are well advised to plan usage of a syslog server. If you have already a solution for a central syslog server in place, you can just use it. Most probably, that solution will provide proper reporting facilities, will have looked already at the necessary security implications, and will be a high-availability solution itself.

If you need to set up a dedicated syslog server just for your high-availability cluster, you will have to pay attention to several important issues:

- Syslog service is notoriously unsecure. There are syslog implementations available that utilize TCP and provide better authentication, or even encryption for confidentiality. Depending on the content of your logs, these alternative implementations must be deployed.
- If you have a larger cluster, or if you use a syslog server for several clusters, simple access to files may not be enough for log analysis. A proper reporting interface is needed then.
- You might need to provide views on the logs. For example, an application administrator might need to have a view of just the logs for his or her application, without confidential information like passwords.
- Logging is almost always associated with user-related information that needs special protection, for privacy or security reasons. Often, regulatory or other legal provisions exist. Retention policies, backup policies, log archiving, and rotation must be clarified and implemented.
- Your shiny new syslog server might be a single point of failure; if it fails, your logs will not be accessible anymore, and current logs will not be stored.

Of course, it is a judgment call if a syslog server must be in a high-available environment itself. For sure, this will not be an easy decision and there is no technical guidance for it. Relevance and importance of logs must be decided on a business level.

Regular Batch Jobs in a Cluster Environment

The standard tool for job management on Unix systems is *cron*. Cron does not cope well with failover clusters though. Cron jobs have no condition that guards against execution, i.e., that is checked before the job is

started. But the jobs need access to service-specific resources that might
not be there when the logical host is currently on another cluster node.

We have a simple solution for that problem. A script onloghost that
controls job execution is easy to write. It takes a logical host name and a
command as parameters, and calls the command only if the logical host is
currently activated on that cluster node. All cluster-related jobs use this
tool, and all jobs are installed on all cluster nodes. As the only drawback,
the jobs must not use I/O redirection to file systems on service volume
groups. But even if they assume that, this can be easily remedied with
small wrapper scripts.

Backup and Archiving

Backup and archiving usually associate data sets with host identification. In its configuration, it is specified which file systems, directories, or
database volumes are to be saved.

It must be assured that volume groups that are associated with services are not backed up by the physical host's configuration. Instead, each
logical host needs its own configuration where associated data is specified.

Also, each logical host needs its own backup job. In those cases where
the backup is initiated by the backup server, nothing needs to be done for
that. In that case, the backup server will contact the logical host on one of
its logical network addresses and will get the data from there. Of course,
that implies that the backup client can be started on the logical host, or
that a client-side daemon is running as part of the service's processes.

For client-initiated backup jobs, care should be taken that the service's
IP address is used for connection to the backup server. Many backup products associate data sets with hosts by means of IP addresses, and by default the physical host's address would be taken, which would lead to a
false association.

From the viewpoint of a backup system, logical and physical hosts are
the same. It is the task of system administration to configure the backup
properly, and to ensure that all relevant files are covered.

If we did not do this, backup of a physical host would save all the
data from the logical hosts that is there at that time. When a failover
happens and the next backup run is started, all these files suddenly do
not exist anymore at the old cluster node, but have sprung into existence
at the new node. First of all, this will result in lots of superfluous network
traffic that also stresses the systems without necessity. While the backup
system will delete lots of data on the first physical host's backup save set,
it will transfer and save the same data for the send host's backup.

More subtly, an important functionality of a backup system will be lost
as well: most systems allow several generations of files to be kept and

we can select the version at the restoration time. The erroneous delete-and-save-anew behavior described earlier destroys that capability as no generational information can be constructed.

It should be pointed out that backup in high-availability environments is usually only done for the convenience of users. They shall be able to restore single files or a small set of files. This is not appropriate for system error situations, not from a high-availability point of view and most often also not from a disaster-recovery point of view. If larger data sets are involved, restoration times in the case of errors will be longer than maximum outage times and the recovery time objective. Therefore backup and restoration is seldom a method that is helpful for our objectives.

Testing

Make extensive tests before you put a failover cluster into production. Do not be confident in testing situations where the cluster works. Try to produce scenarios where it does *not* work. Trigger hardware and software errors and see how the cluster software copes with it.

Be sure to retest when configuration changes are made, even though they might not seem affiliated to high-availability services at first. In one instance, an agent of some monitoring software caused a hanging cluster node when it was installed – this was not tested well enough as it was seen as low risk and not associated with the running servers. Nevertheless it was a change on all cluster nodes at the same time and led to a nonfunctional cluster. The lesson learned was every change should have failover tests.

Ideally, this is done on a test system, but often the budget does not allow hardware to be bought for a complete additional cluster. Then host virtualization, as described in Sect. 6.3.2 on p. 184, might be a method to simulate a cluster environment with restricted resources.

Of course, one must be stubborn for that. Such tests can become very expensive, and sometimes their value is not seen, especially when working under a tight budget and time restrictions as we usually do. Nevertheless, it is our task to stand up for proper work. If the service does not need such tests, the chances are high that the high-availability environment would not be needed overall and that one would be able to save even more money by not using a cluster.

6.2 Load-Balancing Clusters

Generic load-balancing clusters are used for services that do not need to keep their state between requests. They work by distributing incoming requests to a set of hosts that process these requests. All those hosts provide the same service: they are the nodes of the load-balancing cluster.

Most often the request distribution is done by a load-balancing device, but – as we will see later – there are also simplistic methods that do not need such a device.

The prototypical examples for services that are predetermined for load-balancing clusters are as follows:

WWW services as HTTP requests, being stateless, can be distributed over as many Web servers as needed. Of course, this mostly scales for static Web content. For dynamic content, application and database servers will be utilized; for them generic load-balancing technology is not appropriate. Instead, middleware clusters or failover clusters will be utilized for the back-end systems.

Directory services like Domain Name Service (DNS) and Lightweight Directory Access Protocol (LDAP). These services are characterized by high read and low write volumes. Write operations will be synchronized between the servers by application-specific means, and each server can carry out read requests on its own.

Load balancing comes in different varieties, and is made for different reasons. While we naturally want to emphasize its role for high-availability solutions, it must be made clear that most often this is not the main objective. Most of the time, load balancing is introduced to improve performance, as a solution to the problem that one system is not powerful enough to handle all requests. From this performance viewpoint, distributing requests from the network to several systems to get a balanced usage, come the alternative names of load balancing, *traffic management* or *application-level switching*.

Owing to the usual emphasis on performance and traffic management, you must be careful if you utilize load balancing in a high-availability architecture. We must assure that we do not get a single point of failure with the load balancers. We need to check that solutions are high-availability clusters themselves and that they preferably use redundant hardware. Therefore, introducing load balancing equipment can raise your failure risk, or even introduce a single point of failure in your architecture if not done properly. Always pay attention to the means to handle failures, and also for disaster recovery of load-balancing approaches.

Most of our current systems are not simple client/server systems anymore; they utilize an *n*-tier architecture, with at least a front-end tier for the user interface, a midtier for business logic and transaction management, and a back-end tier for data services. If the front-end tier utilizes Web technology – be it an HTML interface or with Web services – it is an obvious candidate for load balancing. Both application servers in the midtier and database servers in the back-end tier are stateful and need to utilize different concepts for high availability. Often, they are inherently distributed systems and support application-level clustering out of the box; this is handled in detail in Chap. 7. For database servers, failover clusters, as explained in Sect. 6.1, are also often utilized, since the database-internal clustering possibilities are still quite new and not always stable.

Load-balancing appliances sometimes come with additional functionality. They are also utilized for security improvements and scan incoming requests for validity. In addition, they can provide Secure Sockets Layer (SSL) accelerators to ease the load on Web servers and simplify key and certificate management. Especially if you provide a farm of servers for SSL-encrypted connections, such an appliance can be worth every cent as managing keys and certificates on all nodes of that server farm in a proper and secure way can be very demanding.

6.2.1 Load-Balancing Approaches

Basically, there are three architectural patterns that can be utilized when a load-balancing solution is implemented:

1. **DNS-based load balancing** is the oldest and the simplest architecture pattern. But it is also one of the most stable, has the least risk associated with it, and is very robust. Basic DNS load balancing is very cheap, whereas sophisticated appliances have their associated price tag. It is used very often, mostly in Internet or WAN environments, to enable global applications.
2. **IP load balancers** are appliances that distribute traffic on a circuit level. They usually rewrite IP addresses in the network traffic and introduce a network address translation (NAT) layer into the architecture. Since one buys a device, this approach is sometimes called *hardware-based load balancing* as well. This solution is not cheap, but functions well and is extremely efficient; its robustness is also very good most of the time. Its primary usage is in LAN environments, to balance network traffic and server utilization.
3. **Reverse proxies** implement *software-based load balancing* on the application level. As with all application proxies, they come both in transparent and in visible flavors. They can rewrite requests as they want and will provide unmatched flexibility. Reverse proxies are robust and cheap, but not fast. Their primary usage is also in LAN environments, if IP load balancers are too expensive or if extensive request rewriting is needed.

Let us have a look at each of these patterns in turn.

DNS-Based Load Balancing

Load balancing is an old technology that recently found itself in the spotlight with the increase of n-tier architectures and HTTP-based front-end access methods. Its origin was at the dawn of two-tier client-server architectures and early TCP network design.

When the DNS was designed, it had to be robust against nonreachability and network failures, i.e., high availability was one of the prime design objectives. The DNS maps names to resources, e.g., host names to IP addresses, or domain names to name servers. The DNS architects introduced early on the ability to use more than one name server for a domain, and the Internet agencies later codified that potential to be a requirement. These name servers are equally authoritative for the domain; all of them are required to have the same information. DNS servers usually give out name server information about a domain in a round-robin fashion: every request gets the next name server as the first response. Owing to this round-robin principle, over all queries, all name servers share the request load.

The same redundancy is allowed for other resource information as well. In particular it is used in the mapping from host names to IP addresses, in the so-called *A records*. A host name can have many A records, and the name server will return one of them, thus distributing the traffic for that named service to different addresses on different computer systems.

Example 1 (Load-balancing DNS configuration). Such DNS configurations are very simple. In the zone file, we only have to specify an entry for each address, using the same name. A simple load-balancing configuration of a Web server with the name www would look like

```
www     IN  A     216.239.59.99
www     IN  A     216.239.59.103
www     IN  A     216.239.59.104
www     IN  A     216.239.59.147
```

Of course, we would use our own IP addresses and not those of Google that are cited here in this example.

Violà, that is all that is needed. Load balancing on the cheap.   ∎

But most general-purpose DNS servers provide only basic implementation of this load balancing. Their behavior could probably better be called *load distribution* or *load sharing* instead, as they do not take into account the state of the request-receiving systems. They have only very limited selection of load-balancing methods, e.g., the popular BIND software – the most often used DNS server on the Internet – provides only selection methods *fixed* (in order of definition), *cyclic* (round robin), and *random* (arbitrarily chosen). Section 6.2.2 on p. 181 delves deeper into existing load-balancing methods.

Dedicated load-balancing systems for global application delivery often utilize DNS-based load balancing. Their address selection mechanism is highly configurable and takes many parameters into account:

- Current load of target system
- Geographic location of requester and server system, with the assumption that geographic nearness also implies good network connections
- Previous requests from the same client
- Past load distribution
- Others

These appliances also work with very short cache timeouts (technically called *time to live*, TTL). Usually, stable DNS entries have a high TTL and encourage aggressive caching by clients. In load-balancing environments one wants to have more control over the distribution of addresses, e.g., to quickly add some more servers or kick some server out in case of availability problems. This additional control comes at the price of reduced caching and increased DNS request traffic.

DNS-based load-balancing has one important advantage: for all its simplicity, it does not introduce an additional single point of failure into our architecture. DNS is needed anyhow for all services, and this elementary service will be deployed in a highly available infrastructure architecture anyhow. Redundant DNS servers in diverse geographic regions are a well-handled and well-understood technology that cares both for high availability and for disaster recovery without further ado. If such simple forms of load balancing are actually sufficient, it is a great solution that is easy to deploy and cheap to implement and to maintain.

Hardware-Based IP Traffic Management

IP load balancers are utilized most often for Web servers, where usual commodity hardware cannot handle millions of requests per day or even per hour, but a server farm is a cost-effective way to provide that service. These appliances originated in the network world, and are usually also high-end layer-3 switches.

As a nice by-product and of more interest for this book, they also raise the availability of the service – as long as the load-balancing appliance is functional. Current versions of such load balancers all have clustering abilities and will usually be deployed in redundant installations. But these abilities are often new and complex to configure, and mailing lists abound with questions about proper setup. Be warned that you – striving for a high-availability solution – should only implement them as a cluster and that you should get proper training for your staff to handle incidents and problem analysis.

These appliances take IP requests and forward them to the actual servers. Of course, network addresses in those IP requests and in responses are rewritten for forwarding. Introducing a NAT layer into a solution architecture can lead to problems if the application demands end-to-end authentication. But luckily, very few applications do and those are usually very dependent on the state and are therefore seldom eligible for hardware-based load balancing anyhow.

Several methods are usually available for recipient selection; they are discussed in Sect. 6.2.2 in more detail. There is also the tendency to inspect not only the IP header and information about servers for target decision, but instead the request itself is analyzed and is forwarded according to request patterns.

While IP load balancers could be utilized in WAN situations where the servers are remotely located, in practice they are placed directly beside the server farm. Otherwise, we would introduce latency and that would not square with typical performance demands.

Software-Based Reverse Proxy Solutions

It is also possible to take the incoming request on an application level and resend it to an actual server, or rewrite it. You might read that this is most often used for HTTP requests, but all other application gateways can be utilized as well. In fact, many directory services provide such reverse proxy functionality as well, e.g., DNS or LDAP servers:

Transparent proxying just forwards the request, the server sees the client's IP address and reacts to the original request, e.g., the original URL. Maybe the reverse proxy checks for request validity first.

Semitransparent proxying rewrites the request and forwards it afterwards. For example, it might substitute the host name in a URL for the server's real name. The server sees the changed URL; it is a matter of application protocol and implementation if that is revealed to the client. Owing to lots of application problems with this form of rewriting, it is seldom used; most often only as a stopgap to support legacy applications.

Visible proxying may be used in protocols that support redirection. Then a redirect is sent to the client with the real server's host name or address in it.

This load-balancing approach is either silently implemented, as in DNS or LDAP servers, where it does not get much attention, or it is available as a product add-on, most prominently in the *Apache* Web server with the mod_backhand, mod_proxy, and mod_rewrite modules.

6.2.2 Target Selection for Load Balancing

Several times we have mentioned that selection of the target system, the server that actually handles the request, is crucial for good load balancing. Target selection is independent of the approach that is used for load balancing; all the following methods and algorithms can be used in DNS-based balancers, IP load balancers, and reverse proxies:

Random: A target system is randomly selected. No attention is paid to other parameters, load is distributed but not balanced. Of course, the distribution characteristics are dependent on the random number generator chosen.

All servers should have the same capacity and all requests should need the same resources. In practice, this algorithm has the same effect as round robin, is harder to implement properly, and is therefore seldom used.

Round robin: Target systems are selected in turn, starting with the first again when the last has been used. Thus, the incoming requests are evenly distributed across the available servers. This load-balancing method is mainly for load distribution and does not consider balanced resource utilization.

As with random selection, all servers should have the same capacity and all requests should need the same resources. If that is not the case, use of round robin can cause a less powerful server to be overwhelmed by requests while another one still has resources left. But if all servers are the same, or if all servers are simply powerful enough, round robin is a simple, effective method of load distribution.

Weighted round robin: In a configuration, the capacities of all servers are defined. For example, one server is taken as a baseline and given the number 1 (or 100, if integers are used). The other servers are judged in relation to that reference server and are categorized with relative "powerfulness." That gives a weight for a server that can be used to select the frequency of request forwarding statistically.

This approach is an easy way if the capacity of each server is different but known and each request needs similar resources. In that situation, it remains a simple, effective method without the need to check for other parameters.

Fastest: Pass the request to the available server that responds the fastest, e.g., to a ping.

Least connections: For each server, a list of active connections exists. A request is forwarded to the server with the fewest active connections.

This can be used when requests pour in faster than the servers can handle them. It is an easily implemented method for basic load balancing.

Weighted least connection: As in the weighted round-robin method, the server's capacity is stored in the configuration. The weight given by that capacity configuration is combined with the least connections method to determine the target system.

In general, this is a very good method for low balancing, as it takes into account both the server's capacity and its current state, as signified by the active connections. Its main problem is the capacity configuration, which needs experience on the part of the administrator.

Adaptive balancing: Server load (fetched by Simple Network Management Protocol, SNMP), number of active connections, and request duration are input for an adaptive logic that computes actual server usage and optimizes resource usage for each server.

In newer systems, this might even use heuristics to guess the effort needed for a new request. For example, a weight that is computed from past requests is associated with each URL and server. New requests to the same URL are assumed to have similar characteristics. Further heuristics try to determine what is static content and what is dynamic content, as these use different server resources. Such advanced heuristics are still a realm of research though.

Interestingly, in practice it does not matter too much which server selection method you use. Most request loads are evenly distributed, and simple algorithms like round robin or least connections already result in great advantages. Special algorithms come into play in high-end environments with a very great number of requests that must be handled.

6.3 Cluster and Server Consolidation

In current IT environments, we have two contrary developments:

1. High availability is being demanded more and more for IT services, as those services get to be more essential for business services.
2. Cost reduction and management improvements demand consolidation of IT services fewer and fewer systems.

These developments are contradictory, since we need redundancy and service separation for high availability: important resources must be available twice or even more often, and services should not interact with each other.

6.3.1 Virtualization and Moore's Law

Owing to rapid development in hardware capacity, we cannot afford to deploy high-end server systems for each IT service. The new systems are simply too powerful (and too expensive in relation to used resources) and must be utilized for several services at the same time.

This process will even accelerate over time, according to Moore's Law. We will get ever more powerful hardware, while our software and management technology struggles to keep them deployed and used in a sensible way.

One important development is that the systems are now so powerful that we can start to utilize more virtualization techniques on a regular basis, to increase service separation while running several services on the same host at the same time.

It should be expected that future cluster software will incorporate virtualization strategies even further and will thus support better utilization of available hardware resources and keep applications highly available at the same time.

But let us have a deeper look at the most important virtualization technique in that context, host virtualization.

6.3.2 Host Virtualization

Providing complete virtual computer systems has been possible for a very long time. In fact, the term "time sharing" was originally used for this, and only later got a synonym for multitasking. Here, we can preselect the system configuration that an application runs on; including CPU count and often speed, memory, storage, and interfaces. At the same time, the application believes it has the system alone for itself, while the powerful hardware of today can easily support many virtual hosts running at the same time.

Virtual hosts are also used for stabilization and to reduce inferences of services on one host. They are an interesting method that helps enormously in disaster recovery. One can keep several disabled virtual hosts on a backup system that are enabled in case of disasters. If one succeeds in proper synchronization of the primary and the backup virtual host, switchover to the backup system will go very smoothly:

Static resource allocation is available from several vendors; the available hardware is statically separated into several subsystems and each virtual host runs on one of these subsystems. This type of virtual host is slowly diminishing, as it is far too inflexible. It can be used to consolidate several backup systems on one physical host, but when one backup system is activated, the hardware resources that are reserved for other systems cannot be reused. Therefore it is mainly a management advantage and also reduces operational computing center costs, but is not a functional enhancement compared with multiple smaller backup systems.

Dynamic resource allocation is slowly making inroads in the Unix and Windows areas. It supports definition of virtual hosts by means of system resources that might even be changed at one's whim. The virtual hosts share the hardware, but have their own file systems, network interfaces, etc. Often the CPU usage can be controlled as well, or memory restrictions can be changed, to avoid one virtual host hogging all computing resources. This is by no means easy and requires support from the underlying operating system. (For example, the operating systems must handle reduction of available memory for virtual hosts.)

Virtual machines have been available in the mainframe world for decades, and are now also in widespread deployment for C/S systems.

Each virtual host runs its own operating system, and has its own virtual CPU, disk, memory, network, interfaces, etc. No system resources are used as shared resources, and actual dispatch to the real hardware is done by a virtualization layer, the *virtual machine monitor*.

We distinguish between host-based virtual machines and native virtual machines:

- In host-based virtual machines, the virtual machine monitor (providing the environment for the "guest system") runs on top of an already installed operating system (the "host system") and uses the host system for hardware access and resource management. This has the advantage of broad hardware support, as generic operating systems that are in wide use have typically lots of hardware drivers. As a disadvantage, it adds another level that bites into performance.
- In native virtual machines, a virtual machine monitor directly runs on the bare hardware and has all necessary hardware drivers as well. For the guest systems, no differences from host-based virtual machines are visible. Native virtual machines typically have more restricted hardware support, but are faster than host-based ones.

Full virtual machines for Intel x86 (IA32) hardware are notoriously difficult to realize. Therefore the relevant products are quite recent and have appeared only in the last few years. Other hardware architectures, e.g., /360, SPARC, or PowerPC, make realization of virtual machine monitors much easier. New 64-bit architectures from AMD and Intel pick up that trend and provide similar methods.

▶ *Products*

VMware, in 2004 acquired by EMC, has both host-based and native virtual machine offerings in their portfolio. It targets the IA32 and 64-bit AMD and Intel (x64) markets. VMware Workstation and GSX Server both use Linux and Windows as the host system; ESX Server is a Linux-based native implementation. It delivers abstract hardware where few capabilities of the original hardware shine through and support all major Intel operating systems as guest systems.

ESX Server has limited hardware support, but has the best performance. To support high-availability and disaster-recovery requirements, it has the ability to move virtual hosts from one host system to another, while the guest systems are running, without any disruption. This clustering capability also provides automatic migration in the case of hardware errors; user sessions will be aborted in that case.

GSX Server is meant to be used in a client/sever environment, where thin clients access guest systems that are hosted on big servers. Of course, it can also be used to implement several servers on a physical system and has management capabilities for that task. VMware Workstation is meant for standalone deployments and does not feature the elaborate management capabilities; therefore, it is not appropriate for disaster-recovery deployments.

VMware has stable and very good products. It officially supports a wide variety of guest operating systems, from Windows to Linux to several Unix variants. For IA32 and x64 systems, it is the best in the market.

Microsoft has two host-based virtual machine offerings, Virtual PC and Virtual Server. Both run on IA32 and x64 hardware. Virtual PC targets the desktop market and is not appropriate for high-availability or disaster-recovery objectives.

Virtual Server is a mature product that should further server consolidation and migration of legacy deployments. Only Windows server operating systems are supported as guest systems. It has excellent integration into Microsoft's Windows administration framework. It comes with clustering capability that enables automatic virtual system migration in the case of host hardware errors, aborting user sessions in that case.

IBM has virtual machine products for its pSeries (logical partitioning, LPAR) and for its zSeries (z/VM). Both products realize virtual machines; they run their own operating system images. LPARs are host-based and use AIX as the host system; z/VM is a native virtual machine. As VMware, they support different guest systems at the same time.

z/VM and its predecessor VM/ESA are the most deployed virtual machine products in mission-critical environments: it does not get more solid than this old mainframe technology. LPARs represent an effort to bring mainframe capabilities to IBM's Unix servers. Up to AIX 5.1, they supported only static partitioning; since AIX 5.2 dynamic resource allocation has also been available.

Sun introduced hardware partitions for their servers, allowing these servers to be split into smaller "domains" with static resource allocation. Each domain is bound to specific hardware components; hardware cannot be shared as well. Every domain runs its own instance of Solaris. Later on, Dynamic Systems Domains allowed hardware resources to be moved from one domain to another while the system is online.

An alternative for this native virtual machine technology is Solaris Containers in Solaris 10. Containers are execution environments with limits on resource consumption; they share their operating system image. Limits can be placed on CPU usage, memory, disk space, user logins, connection time, etc. An important part of Containers is Zones, taking up the FreeBSD *jail* concept: each Zone is an isolated execution environment. Even though they share the operating system, for each application it seems as if it is running on its own own machine. One could describe Zones as *chroot on steroids*.

Containers are very lightweight and are primarily meant to separate physical hardware and logical server management. For example, network interfaces and IP numbers are assigned to Containers and cannot be changed within. As such, they make good tools for disaster recovery as well, since we want to manage several logical servers on our physical backup system.

Hewlett-Packard provides both hardware-based partitioning (nPar) and software-based virtual partitions (vPar) for its HP-UX operating system. They are host-based virtual machines which run their own operating system image. nPar resource assignments are static, like Solaris Domains. vPars can be created dynamically, and one can specify the set of resources that are assigned. Within a vPar, one can create a resource partition that allows lightweight resource control, similar to Solaris Containers and Zones.

7

Databases and Middleware

Complex IT services are usually not implemented by single programs. They have to fulfill many requirements and do so by means of software components that work together. Some of these components are written specifically for that service: these are those that we call applications in the strict sense. Others realize functionality that can be reused in many different applications, and this chapter is about the latter class of software components. Database and application servers are the most prominent examples; more will be presented in Sect. 7.1 on p. 191.

They are called *middleware* because they sit "between" the operating system and the application software. There, they either provide abstractions or adaptations of operating system functionality. (That is the origin of the term, back in 1968 at the famous NATO Software Engineering Conference). Or they provide generic functionality that is missing in operating systems but that is needed in today's enterprise-class applications.

It is a bit tricky to give an exact definition for middleware, as that term has become kind of a buzzword over the last few years. For the purpose of this book,

Middleware is the layer of software components between the operating system and the application that is independent of a specific application but needs application-specific configuration.

This rough definition captures the differences between middleware and other system stack levels. Middleware:

- Delivers functionality that is not part of the operating system
- Delivers independent services that can be used for many applications
- Must be adapted to each application and does not exist independently as infrastructure does.

These differences are not always technical.

It is hard to define what an operating system is and especially what functionality is considered part of an operating system. While that is clear for the essential parts (management of hardware resources and processes), functional outskirts like storage volume management were only recently incorporated into many operating systems. As another example, job management is available only in very rudimentary forms in most operating systems today. Therefore, the expression "functionality that is not part of the operating system" is not an inherent definition that will not change over time; it depends on the specific operating system (sometimes even on its specific version) for comparison.

Most prominently, *file server* software is sometimes part of an operating system, sometimes it is not: Common Internet File System (CIFS) and Network File System (NFS) are two protocols for remote file systems, and are either available on Windows or on Unix, but seldom on both, though this has changed with the advent of Linux. But in the end, this is more a market-oriented consideration than a technical one. Since nowadays every operating system comes with some form of network file serving, we do not consider file servers to qualify as middleware components.

At the same time, several services (in particular Web servers, sometimes even databases like MySQL) are starting to be part of many operating system default installations. Those servers have been considered separate products by many people, and still are. But this may change in the future when their availability becomes ubiquitous.

In the end, widely used middleware functionality tends to become a commodity and tends to get integrated into operating system installations. But application areas that are a niche or that cater to high-end functionality will always prevail and will be serviced by separate middleware products.

The differences between middleware and application components are sometimes vague as well. There are some products that are labeled as middleware and that are currently used by only one application. Yet, they are designed to be usable elsewhere again and they deliver functionality that is independent of that application. That alone is enough to qualify such components as middleware.

In a similar vein, the distinction from infrastructure is blurry. Network equipment (switches and routers) are usually not specifically configured for applications and thus clearly belong to the realm of infrastructure. Domain Name Service (DNS) servers are already in the gray zone since they will often be configured to provide specific service names. Nevertheless such name/address mapping is usually not seen as something application-specific and is therefore classified as infrastructure too. With email gateways, it is already becoming difficult – if receipt and sending of emails is an essential part of an application, the email server would be clearly classified as middleware for that application, whereas some outbound administrative email now and then is seen as normal application-independent service usage, and would leave the email server in the infrastructure layer.

While there is no overall agreement on the definition of the term middleware, one thing is sure: from the viewpoint of high-availability system design, middleware components are almost always a good choice. They provide application-independent behavior and one can leverage investments into high-availability designs for several IT systems at once. In effect, middleware allows us to bring standardized high-availability design parts into applications.

7.1 Middleware Categories

There are some software categories for which it is generally accepted that they can be named "middleware." Most of them are described in this chapter later in more detail.

Database servers are the prototypical and one of the oldest examples for middleware software. Most relevant for enterprise-class software are relational databases that are accessed by SQL.

Configuration for the application consists of creating databases with appropriate schemas, i.e., table structures, where data can be stored and retrieved.

High availability and disaster recovery for database servers is presented in Sect. 7.2.

Web servers are front-end systems that are used to realize the HTML user interface for an application, or for delivery of unstructured data in the form of documents or files. They are accessed via the HTTP.

Configuration for the application consists of establishing a URL mapping to the user interface or to data delivery mechanisms.

High availability for Web servers is presented in Sect. 7.3.

Application servers are components that provide ready-to-use components to realize the business logic of an application. In addition, they are a framework for the application's deployment – the application is not a program anymore, but runs within the application server.

In fact, as a runtime environment, current application servers introduce functionality that was previously provided by traditional servers, e.g., messaging or transaction management. Sometimes, that functionality is realized by wrappers that access traditional servers.

Configuration for the application consists of adding the application components and publishing the application-specific interfaces.

High availability for application servers is presented in Sect. 7.4.

Messaging servers take structured or unstructured messages from application components and assert that these messages are delivered to the receiving component, which may run on another computer system. They solve the application-independent problem that some data has been computed and must not get lost but where the application itself does not want to implement a reliable and fault-tolerant communication protocol and infrastructure.

Configuration for the application consists of definition of message formats and of communication end points that can send or receive messages.

High availability for messaging servers is presented in Sect. 7.5.

Transaction managers, also called *transaction monitors*, supply transactional behavior (that a series of actions is either completely done or not done at all) for applications. Often they control the access to database servers or to legacy mainframe systems and supply restart behavior for clients, independently of the application.

As separate middleware components, transaction monitors are like application servers: they deliver a runtime environment for application components that are not standalone programs anymore, but are loaded into the transaction monitor. Owing to that similar structure, transaction monitors cannot be used together with application servers. Instead, application servers often provide transaction management functionality, as we will see later.

Configuration for the application consists of definition of transactions and loading the application components into the runtime environment.

Some services are considered as infrastructure services in this book, even though some other publications consider them as middleware, but since their application-specific configuration is usually minimal, they do not fall under the previous definition:

- Identity management servers
- Directory servers (e.g., DNS, Lightweight Directory Access Protocol, LDAP, or Active Directory)
- Email servers
- License servers

The rest of this chapter will present most of the middleware categories already mentioned in more detail. In each section, we will present the category's basic functionality and approaches for high availability that may be typically used with such a middleware product. These approaches include product-specific clustering, data replication, and sometimes even session state replication.

7.2 Database Servers

Database Servers are the most important example of middleware components. Almost any enterprise-class software system utilizes them in some way. They are used to:

- Store most data that is essential for a business
- Query and retrieve that data
- Provide adequate performance in accessing big amounts of data
- Allow access by several users and several tasks at the same time
- Provide a robust data store
- Supply a consistent view of the data
- Help ensure consistency of stored data

Nowadays, the term database servers is more or less synonymous with *relational databases*.[1] In these databases:

- Data is stored in database tables.
- Table columns are typed, i.e., each entry in a table column has the same data type as other entries in the same column.
- A row in a table is also called a record.
- Several structural views can be defined for tables, e.g., tables can be combined or some columns or rows can be filtered out in a view.
- Definition of table structure, as well as update and retrieval of data, is done by SQL.
- Encapsulation of user actions is provided in the form of *transactions*.
- Users are always provided with a consistent view of the data.
- Consistency constraints of data can be declared and are checked by the database server automatically.
- After system crashes, a database recovers automatically and restores the data to a consistent state.

That data is stored in tables with typed columns is the reason why relational databases are said to hold structured data. There are types that just say "text" or "bytes" though. In such columns, arbitrary unstructured data can be stored, e.g., whole documents or images. For text columns, some database servers even have special operations, e.g., a full text retrieval mechanism.

When the ability to store unstructured data meets the desire to add meta-information to that data, paired with the robustness, performance, and query possibilities of a database server, then databases are used for storage of unstructured data as well. This may be email, documents and images of a content management system, CAD drawings of an engineering system, or arbitrary other data. In fact, the wide dissemination of

---

[1] The theoretical definition of relational databases is different, but that is not relevant here as we want to capture the functionality of existing software products.

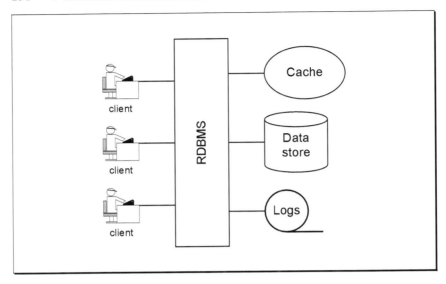

Fig. 7.1. Database server and clients. *RDBMS* relational database management system

open-source database products made it possible to use database servers for many more applications than the budget allowed before. (Of course, database vendors were always of the opinion that they supplied the best data store and that *all* information should be placed in their products.)

All database servers employ heavy caching, to provide needed performance. Besides the persistent storage for the actual table data, they also need persistent storage for auxiliary data; Fig. 7.1 illustrates that, and some terms in that figure are introduced in the next sections.

But there are many more database server categories than the relational ones. Hierarchical and network databases were prominent once and are still in use in legacy applications. Object-oriented databases were said to be the future, but never made it into the mainstream of applications. Also, some vendors were very disappointed that their special XML database servers did not receive enthusiastic and broad usage. Instead, some of the functionality of object-oriented and XML database servers was incorporated into the current crop of relational databases and is now state of the art there.

In this book, nonrelational databases are ignored; they are not relevant for most enterprise-class applications that are deployed today. In fact, the basic approach might be the same for them, but this is highly dependent on the respective product and is therefore beyond the scope of this book.

Relational Database Servers

Relational database servers consist of two parts:

1. The **relational database management system** (RDBMS) is the software that manages the databases. It has the storage functionality to decide how and where data is stored, and can add, delete, modify, sort, and display data. In addition, the query functionality allows searches for specific information in an abstract way, utilizing SQL. Many RDBMS products allow us to declare code that may be run on the server: this is called *stored procedures*.

2. The **database instances** are named collections of data sets. Each data set consists of tables with defined structure; the *Data Definition Language* (DDL) part of SQL is used to define that structure, also called the *database schema*. Part of that DDL is the definition of integrity constraints that the RDBMS shall ensure are true. Such constraints demand the existence of records that are referred to, or restrict the range of values a table column can hold.

   The table data is stored either in files or in raw disk partitions; some RDBMS products allow elaborate control of data placement to improve performance.

The RDBMS component is the same for all applications. Some of them define their own database instances, some share them. In particular, in financial applications, it is considered good style to control the database schema and make that independent of a specific application – after all, applications change often, but your account data should stay the same. On the other hand, many modern development environments take schema definition into their own hands and allege that the programmer has only to tag persistence of data. Here, the programmer or user does not touch SQL anymore.

That a user uses SQL to access a database himself or herself is not too uncommon. SQL was touted from the start as a declarative data access language that can be used by business staff as well, and the success of products like Business Object's *Crystal Reports* shows that such usage is, in fact, possible.

ACID Properties

Almost all relational databases support transactions as the basic unit of logical operation on data. A transaction is a series of low-level operations that are either all successful or not done at all. For example, a fund transfer within a bank has to withdraw (debit) money from one account and credit it to another account. Of course, the whole transaction should not be aborted while in progress, otherwise the money will be lost: either both operations are successful, or both must not be done.

These kinds of requirements led to the formulation of the ACID properties: **A**tomicity, **C**onsistency, **I**solation, and **D**urability. It is the hallmark of good database products to fulfill them:

Atomicity means that a transaction is either done completely or not at all. In our example, funds are either both withdrawn and credited, or account balances are left as they are. Completing a transaction is often called a *commit*; aborting it unsuccessfully is called a *rollback*.

Consistency means that the database instance does not violate any integrity constraints when a transaction begins and when it ends. If a constraint would be violated, the transaction is rolled back to the consistent start state.

Isolation means that every transaction behaves as if it accesses the database alone. During a transaction, intermediate or inconsistent states may be created. For example, the funds have already been withdrawn, but not yet credited. This intermediate state is not seen by any other transaction; they will always see the data in the state before or after the changing transaction.

Durability means that successful transaction results are not lost, but remain. If the user is told that the fund transfer has been successful, that transfer is not lost by later system failures.

It is clear that proper ACID support is both an advantage and a challenge for highly available database server installations. Atomicity and consistency properties allow us to handle system failures gracefully and maybe restart the user's action on a backup system. On the other hand, durability is a requirement that must be assured in the high-availability environment as well.

For disaster recovery, the durability requirement is often weakened. This is the realm of the recovery point objective that describes how much data may be lost in the case of a major outage.

Redo and Undo Logs

Atomicity and durability are realized by *write-ahead logs*, in combination with other methods that are not relevant for high availability or disaster recovery. In such logs, every data change is recorded with both the value before and the value after. The value before is the *undo* information that is used for transaction rollback. The value after is the *redo* information that is used for crash recovery. Transaction start and end (commit or rollback) information is also saved in the log. The write-ahead log is written synchronously (unbuffered) to disk, while the actual data storage might use buffered writes for performance improvements.

Example 1 (Write-ahead log function principle). Let us have a look at Fig. 7.2 on the next page. This is the write-ahead log of four transactions on a few accounts with fund transfers of $10, $20, $30, and $40,

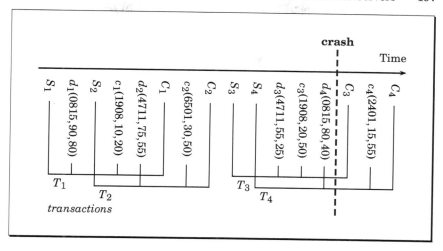

Fig. 7.2. Example of a write-ahead log

respectively. Each transaction T_i has four operations: d_i for debit and c_i for credit; S_i and C_i are start and commit.

Let us have a more detailed look at each of those operations, and write up all operations as they appear per transaction, with account number, before-value, and after-value information for debit and credit operations, as they are recorded in the write-ahead log. Please note, in our example a transaction only accesses accounts that are not in use by any other transaction; this effectively realizes the Isolation property.

$$
\begin{aligned}
T_1 &= S_1, d_1(0815, 90, 80), c_1(1908, 10, 20), C_1 \\
T_2 &= S_2, d_2(4711, 75, 55), c_2(6501, 30, 50), C_2 \\
T_3 &= S_3, d_3(4711, 55, 25), c_3(1908, 20, 50), C_3 \\
T_4 &= S_4, d_4(0815, 80, 40), c_4(2401, 15, 55), C_4
\end{aligned}
$$

To see the functionality of the write-ahead log, we need a crash scenario. Figure 7.2 sports such a crash point. Since the write-ahead log is written synchronously it will be available without problems at database restart (i.e., the content of the write-ahead log is the entries to the left of the crash line.)

We read the log from the back:

- Since T_4 has no commit entry, we need to undo the deposit if necessary, i.e., account 0815 is set to $80 if it does not have that value.
- Since T_3 has no commit entry, we need to undo both the credit and the deposit: account 1908 is set to $20 and account 4711 is set to $55. The crash recovery is not able to know that the transaction was actually

complete and just the commit tag C_3 is missing. There could have been more operations, so the transaction must be rolled back.

- Since T_2 has a commit entry, we need to ensure that credit and debit have happened: account 6501 is set to $50 and account 4711 is set to $55. (Of course, the latter was set already, so we do not actually need to do that.)
- Since T_1 has a commit entry, we need to ensure that credit and debit have happened: account 1908 is set to $20 and account 0815 is set to $80. As for T_2, there is an obvious possibility for optimization of this "redo action."

To be honest, actual implementations do not work in that simplistic way for performance reasons. But the basic principles still apply. ∎

That methodology has several consequences:

- The actual data storage can be aggressively buffered, as long as the log information is written synchronously to disk without any buffering. In our example, we mentioned that "a value must be ensured." That is because we do not know the actual value in the data store owing to buffering. But that is not a problem – in the case of a failure, all changes can be reconstructed from the log and do not need to be in persistent storage. This raises database performance by magnitudes.
- To summarize: if we have to recover from a database crash, we can take the data store and
  1. Undo all undo information of uncommitted transactions
  2. Reapply all redo information of committed transactions
  That way we get a data store with all committed transactions, atomicity and durability are asserted.
- Redo log records can be used for synchronous or asynchronous replication to another database. They are constructed at commit time as the sequence of redo information:
  - For synchronous replication, they are transmitted to another database installation and are committed there before they are committed at the primary database.
  - For asynchronous replication, they are transmitted to another database installation and are committed independently of the main database's commit.

Write-ahead logs are the traditional and easiest way to implement atomicity and durability. There exist also other means for realization, e.g., *shadow pages*, that sometimes perform better or have other advantages. All of them boil down to the principle of keeping data before and after changes. Therefore every such technology can be accommodated and adapted to the principal usage for high availability and disaster recovery that is outlined next.

7.2.1 High-Availability Options for Database Servers

For all database server products, it is possible to utilize failover clusters on the operating-system level, as explained in Sect. 6.1 on p. 151. But these cluster systems are sometimes not integrated sufficiently with the database server software, so we need to be careful.

Care must be taken to ensure that any change from the database software is really on disk, otherwise there would be no durability anymore. This means that all log records must be written synchronously to disk. In theory, this is not a problem, as the RDBMS opens the files with the *synchronous output* (O_SYNC) flag. In practice, there are quite a few pitfalls. Database files may be on network-attached storage (NAS) or on SANs, where caching might have been turned on and the O_SYNC flag is ignored. Of course, that is not a default configuration, but an overeager engineer might have turned that on to improve performance for other applications.

At the same time, at many installations performance is improved when the file system is mounted synchronously. While this does not change any access semantics (the O_SYNC flag alone is sufficient), it often discards usage of file system write buffers in the operating system and thus saves two in-memory copies of any written data.

One needs to test such installations carefully, in particular for the restart time after crashes. Some database servers run full data integrity checks after any crash, and that might take too long for a failover cluster, leading to another switch while the service start has not even finished, i.e., it is mandatory that the tests include the case of an inconsistent database to be able to assert appropriate behavior.

Typical restart times after a crash (when recovery is needed) are 1–30 min, maybe even more. This depends on database size and change rate; the times differ for each installation and must be determined in realistic tests. The recovery times must be taken into account both on the business level, for service level agreement (SLA) definitions, and on the technical level, when service checks are implemented and failover ping-pong shall be avoided.

However, a properly configured failover cluster for database servers has very good reliability and is a tried-and-tested solution for most cases.

Database Clusters with Shared Storage

For those cases where restart problems may happen, where switch times are not allowed, or where one database server is not fast enough, high-end databases provide cluster options. There, several RDBMS installations work together to provide a consistent and coherent view of one single database for any client. Those RDBMS installations work on the same database instance, i.e., they share the persistent data storage. They communicate commits instantly to all cluster nodes, to ensure that all cached data at all cluster nodes is current.

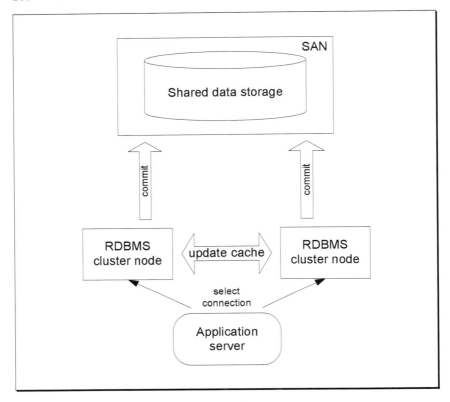

Fig. 7.3. Database clusters

Such a database cluster needs a shared storage subsystem, e.g., a SAN, that supports concurrent writes from multiple associated computers. Of course, that storage subsystem is a part of the system that exposes a risk – as in failover clusters, it contains single points of failure. In addition, the actual information is stored only once in the whole cluster; if that storage fails owing to a software error, the whole cluster will be nonfunctional, i.e., database clusters do not protect against errors in the RDBMS.

Figure 7.3 illustrates the working principle of database clusters.

Like failover clusters, node failures lead to session aborts. Data from committed transactions are not lost, but all open transactions are rolled back. The user loses all the transient state that she or he has typed in or gathered somewhere else, and the work has to be redone.

Compared with failover clusters, database clusters have a big advantage though: When a node fails, there are no failover times. Since the other cluster nodes are already up and running, there is no restart time and the cluster will be able to answer new requests immediately.

But that "no-restart-needed" capability comes with a price. Since several RDBMS installations are active at the same time, they will take requests on different IP addresses. Each address provides the same functionality; the database client (e.g., the application server) has to select one. That connection will not succeed if that cluster node is down: the client must know that it has to retry the connection with a different IP address. Similarly, when a connection is reset, the client has to reconnect to a different address.

This functionality is provided by database client libraries and does not need to be programmed anew for each database. Nevertheless, it introduces the dependency that the client programs use the right version of those libraries.

If that is not the case, these database clusters must be combined with load-balancing solutions. Load-balancing clusters were introduced in Sect. 6.2 on p. 176 and can cope with nonreachability of one cluster node. But this means that a database cluster cannot be operated on its own, but needs additional cluster support on the operating system level.

Stable and mature database clusters are a rather new development. Such products have not been on the market long, and experience in administration and operation of such clusters is still not widespread. IT staff often elect to go with the known failover cluster realization, instead of using the "new" technology of database clusters. This is particularly true when the switch-and-restart delay is not a problem for the requested SLAs, and where no advantage is seen from database clusters. While this is understandable, we should expect the usage of database clusters to broaden in the next few years, as many companies gain familiarity in pilot projects.

Multi-Master Database Clusters

Database clusters with shared storage improve on failover clusters by providing enhanced performance and no switch times. They still have the problem that the storage subsystem might have a single point of failure. That storage must support parallel-write from several cluster nodes to the same database files, and there can very well be errors in that code that render the database nonfunctional.

If overall write performance is not a problem per se, multi-master database clusters are a possible solution. In such installations, each cluster node has its own persistent data storage. Any updates are sent to a replicator component which is responsible for replicating it immediately to all cluster nodes, i.e., the node that receives a data update request does not do the update itself – all updates are always done by the replicator.

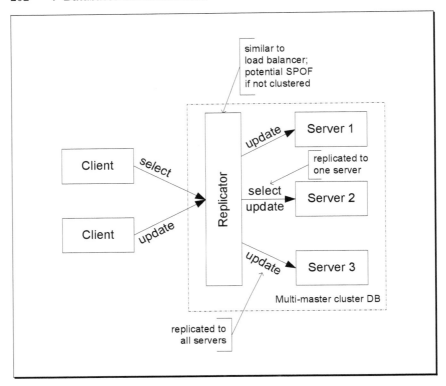

Fig. 7.4. Multi-master database clusters. *DB* database, *SPOF* single point of failure

With that method, the replicator can also handle record and table locking, otherwise the isolation property cannot be ensured for such clusters.

Since many nodes in the cluster can listen to requests, we have the problem with multiple IP addresses that we already had for database clusters with shared storage. In this case also, either the client must be able to handle it or such a solution must be combined with a load-balancing cluster.

Figure 7.4 illustrates the working principle of multi-master database clusters.

The gain achieved with such a cluster architecture is that data is stored multiple times at several independent hosts. This increased redundancy has the associated disadvantage that we have a management component, the replicator, that is most probably our new single point of failure. As so often, the redundancy management components prove that they are critical in high-availability designs.

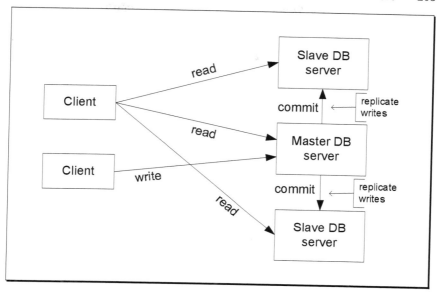

Fig. 7.5. Master-slave database clusters

Overall, it is unclear if we have to choose this design pattern or a database cluster with shared storage. It depends a lot on experience: shared storage might be a more mature technology than multi-master replicators, as it is used in other contexts as well; on the other hand, the design decision might be made obsolete be the choice of database products – not all products have all cluster options and we must face the fact that high-availability and disaster-recovery options are typically not the crucial factors for product selection.

Master-Slave Database Clusters

The last option for database clusters is a *master-slave cluster*. In this configuration, we have one node that can do write operations (the *master node*), and several nodes that handle read queries (the *slave nodes*).

This database cluster category is of interest when the application does lots of read operations and few write operations. If the write operations are done by special application parts that can be configured to use specific database connections, this cluster category is a possible design choice.

Figure 7.5 illustrates the working principle of master-slave database clusters.

Replication of data from the master to its slaves is usually not done for each write operation, but at commit time. Then all redo information can be transfered to the slaves, which can reapply it, just as they would do during crash recovery. Therefore this replication technology is sometimes called *redo log shipping*.

Master-slave replication can be done:

- Asynchronously: the master does not wait for the commits at the slaves.
- Synchronously: the commit at the master is only done when all commits at all slaves have been successfully acknowledged.

There is no predefined answer for which mode is better, asynchronous or synchronous redo log shipping. Synchronous replication makes sure that all nodes have exactly the same state. But this is bought with a high performance penalty and is often not needed. For many applications, it does not matter if a query result is a bit out of date: for them asynchronous replication is sufficient.

Example 2 (World-wide company contact information). Many companies provide Internet-based information systems that can be used to look up contacts for that company. To avoid connectivity, latency, and availability problems, the data is made available in databases at several locations around the world.

Master-slave database clusters in WANs are the obvious design choice for such a requirement. Contact information is updated and maintained in a central global database and is replicated at need to the slave servers all over the world. It does not matter if a client gets the updated informations a few minutes later.

As so often, this obvious solution has its flaws. One might not want a central global database since one wants decentralized maintenance of contact data. Then such a master-slave cluster is not appropriate and decentralized directory servers would probably be used. But if contact information is maintained in a relational database, the master-slave servers are an excellent choice for such situations.   ∎

To summarize, master-slave database clusters can be utilized in special environments where one has control over the application's write and read operation and where many more reads will happen than writes. In addition, they have a prominent place in disaster recovery, as outlined in the next section.

7.2.2 Disaster Recovery for Databases

Most disaster-recovery methods are presented in Chap. 10, but databases store the mission-critical data of your company and are therefore so important that a summary is provided here as well.

Often database clusters cannot be operated over several sites without problems. The network connection is not reliable enough, and network latency is a very big problem as replication to the cluster nodes is done synchronously. The same is true for synchronous mirroring of storage. Under such circumstances, database clusters or storage mirroring cannot be employed for many mission-critical situations.

Additionally, database clusters or storage clusters over WANs do not protect against user, administration, or software errors. But disaster recovery should protect against such failures as well.

To achieve the best disaster recovery, asynchronous redo-log shipping should be utilized, with commits delayed by the recovery point objective (RPO). That way, the redo logs can be sanitized manually in the case of human or software errors before they are applied to the data store.

This establishes a standby database on the disaster-recovery system. Management of standby databases with replication by redo-log shipping does not need to be implemented by the project team, there are ready-made products available for that, e.g., Oracle Data Guard.

7.3 Web Servers

Web servers are an essential component for many current applications. Be it that one has to interface with customers or business partners on the Internet, or be it that one wants to reduce the overhead of client management on desktops, HTML-based user interfaces are en vogue and are available for many applications. Even applications like SAP, where power users will always have their specialized client, or Exchange, where Outlook is usually used as the client, have their Web interface for users who are not at their own configured desktop or who have few actions to perform.

There is one preferred method to achieve high availability for Web servers: use a load-balancing cluster, as explained in Sect. 6.2 on p. 176. The preferred method is the usage of a redundant load-balancing appliance; if you need a low-cost solution and have the necessary skills in-house, the Linux Virtual Server Project comes in handy.

But this assumes that the state of your application is *not* kept on your Web server. If you happen to run an old-fashioned Web application that keeps its data in files on the Web server, you have two choices.

1. If you have a redundant file server, place the files with the state on that server. When you do that, you must make sure that all file access methods are supported by that server. For example, some combinations of NFS clients and servers do not support all file locking functionality, and that is probably used by the application to coordinate parallel-write accesses.
2. Migrate the data into a database. For some applications, this is the best method, but it may mean a substantial investment in the change

of an application. One needs to consider as well the applicability. While database bring you enhanced reliability and often also enhanced access performance, storing highly structured data, storing very big data blobs, or unstructured queries over many database fields are not strengths of database products.

As an example, if we have an application that serves to exchange big files with business partners over the Internet, it is questionable if one really wants to store gigabytes of data in one database blob, and if not file systems are a more adequate storage facility for such data.

3. Use a failover cluster for the Web server. This is the method to choose if you do not have a file server available, do not need the performance boost of the load-balancing cluster, and cannot change the application.

Those possibilities not withstanding, we will assume the usage of load balancers for the rest of this section.

The demanding part in a load-balancing cluster is to assure that all Web server nodes in that cluster process the requests in the same way. To do so, they must have the same content and the same Web server configuration.

▸ *Web Server Content*

Web server content usually has static and dynamic parts. Static parts are often images, style sheets, and generated or cached constant HTML pages. Dynamic parts are HTML pages that are generated per request. There is the tendency in Web server content overall that all HTML content is generated dynamically, to allow sitewide changes in style and structure. Only for performance reasons are static HTML pages generated and cached at some place.

This tendency may not be assumed to be true for Web applications as well. Here, static content may actually be server-side programs that are executed within the server context or as external programs via the server's Common Gateway Interface (CGI). On the other hand, applications that also utilize application servers often have no content at all, but only take requests and forward them to the application server. Split models are possible too. Then, a daemon runs on the Web server and processes the part of the request that does not need session state or other data, but utilizes an application server for anything else.

The challenge is now that all Web server cluster nodes must have the same static content and must access the dynamic content in the same way. In fact, dynamic content is often the easiest to manage. Each cluster node has the same installation of the program that accesses the content and creates dynamically the HTML pages. The content itself is kept in a database that runs on an external, highly available server. Update of Web server content now means update of these programs, and this happens less often than updates of content.

But what should we do with the static content that has to be on the servers as well? And the generated pages, and the coordination of this with the dynamic content in the database? We must not assume that we are able to handle that coordination manually. Instead we need to utilize *content management systems* that do that management for us.

It is not sensible to run a highly available load-balancing cluster for Web servers without a content management system.

Even if you have some, there might still be problems. For example, for some content updates, the server processes need to be restarted. Many content management systems do not support this coordination out of the box. One is well advised to establish proper automated content update support for one's clusters, otherwise one is bound to see problems during operations.

▸ *Web Server Configuration*

It is often neglected that Web server configuration is as important for request processing as content provisioning. Web servers get URLs in requests and need to map these URLs to actions that deliver the requested content.

This might be accessing a file; then the URL must be mapped to the file location. This is trivial for the simplest configuration, when a URL suffix is simply the relative path of the file. But as often one wants to keep old URLs valid while the content is at a new position already, then more and individual mappings must be introduced. These mappings must be made on all cluster nodes at the same time – and this is not supported by content management systems.

Similarly, when the URL denotes some external or internal program, there must be a mapping from that URL to the program to be called. If a program changes locations or sometimes even its name, we might need to change the server configuration.

And last, if the URL is to be processed by an external service like an application server, the proper forwarding of the HTTP request must be configured.

All this boils down to the fact that manual configuration updates are too error prone for high availability of Web server clusters. One needs to deploy Web server configuration updates by automatic means. If the server configuration is stored in files, one can utilize file replication technology like *rsync*. Some Web servers allow their configurations to be stored in a directory server, which achieves easy configuration of a whole group of servers at the same time.

▸ *Authenticated Accesses*

Many Web applications need to authenticate requests. In the most basic form, the user is asked to provide a user ID and a password and these are used for identification of the user. Other authentication schemes utilize available Windows credentials or signed public keys.

It does not matter which authentication method is used, but one thing is common among all of them: in high availability environments, the credential database must not be stored as a file on the Web server. It is near to impossible to keep it synchronized over all cluster nodes. Instead, a directory server must be utilized. Of course, that directory server must be highly available as well – without that, your Web application will not run.

It is possible to use an existing directory server that is used for authentication anyhow, like Active Directory. But then you should be aware that most Web servers do not use encryption, and basic authentication transfers the password in the clear – suddenly it becomes quite easy to capture passwords for your normal Windows accounts. Using Secure Sockets Layer (SSL) encryption for all Web accesses might not be possible for performance constraints; content-based load balancing does not work well either. (It is not possible to have one part of the page encrypted and other parts, e.g., images, unencrypted.) Therefore, the usage of existing authentication services should be planned with great care and with a thorough security analysis.

7.4 Application Servers

Many enterprise-class applications need the same basic set of functionality. Application servers provide a framework that enables sharing and (relatively) quick usage of common components.

When one uses an application server, the application is not written as a program anymore. Instead, one writes classes according to application programming interfaces (APIs) that are defined as part of the application server frameworks. These classes are "plugged into" the application server and are used when needed – the server will take requests and schedule them either to the application's objects or to other internal components, as needed.

Owing to that plug-in concept, most application servers support only applications that are written in one programming language. Microsoft's .NET framework is an exception, as it is based on the Common Language Runtime, which supports several languages.

▶ *Scaling*

Quite often, implementing the business logic needs lots of resources. Even with modern systems, this can lead to overload situations if many requests must be serviced at the same time. It is often not possible to realize that on one machine; then one needs the ability to distribute the application's business logic implementation over several systems.

Good scaling properties mean that an application can also survive unexpected growth of usage, beyond the original design. Scaling to several systems demands request scheduling. Some application servers even supply session state replication.

▸ *Database Access*

Applications want to create and access persistent information. Traditionally, that may mean access to records in a relational database. In object-oriented applications, this may also mean storage and retrieval of persistent objects.

Application servers provide a standardized interface to access relational databases. In addition, they provide methods to realize object persistency by storing and retrieving object serializations.[2]

In addition, the database access usually provides connection pooling to enhance performance of database queries and access.

▸ *Session Management*

If a session consists of several requests from a client, the requests either need to contain the context from the previous requests, or the server must keep the context. The context is the result of all previous requests, as far as it is relevant for future requests. If the application allows user-level undo capabilities, the *complete* request history must be contained in that session context.

If the session context is kept on the server, it is often called a *session object*.

▸ *Directory Interface*

Many application services need access to authentication and identity information, or to data about groups and roles. Similarly, they need information on devices. Most larger companies have such information in directory servers (NIS, LDAP servers, or Active Directory).

Application servers provide an abstract interface to such directories that hides access and implementation details.

▸ *Transaction Semantics*

The concept of transactions was introduced in Sect. 7.2 on p. 193. They are as relevant for other application parts – a user action shall either succeed or fail as a whole. Application servers provide a framework to define transactions for nondatabase actions as well. (The low-level operations of these actions need to fulfill some requirements for that; in particular, they need undo functionality.)

---

[2] An object serialization is the expression of an object state as a text string.

Transaction modules in application servers take over a role that traditionally was served by separate middleware products, namely, transaction managers.

▶ *Messaging*

Often results of one business process must be reliably transfered to another component or to another system. Messaging provides this distributed communication facility. One program component can just submit a message and rely on its delivery to the recipient. For example, when a transaction has carried out a fund transfer in a financial application, it might be necessary to notify some money-laundering check application if the amount is over a certain limit. This check does not need to be in the fund transfer application itself; that application can send a message to a separate component that handles those statutory provisions.

Messaging modules in application servers take over a role that traditionally was served by separate middleware products, namely, messaging servers or queue managers, which are described in Sect. 7.5 on p. 213.

▶ *Connectors to Legacy Applications*

IT services in companies are often supplied by legacy applications, most of them on mainframes. On the one hand, it is too expensive to move away from them; on the other hand, changing them is too much effort as well. Legacy application connectors allow us to wrap legacy software into network services and to access them by new applications.

This way, old investments are secured, while new innovative approaches are not hindered by available software environments.

▶ *Service Brokerage*

Business rules are usually expressed as sequences or alternatives of services. Such descriptions are made with abstract service names. For maintenance reasons, it is advantageous when the implementation of these rules also uses only the abstract names; this way, only a loose coupling exists between service provider and service user.

For these kinds of applications, a broker is needed that maps abstract service requests to specific implementations. The part of the application that wants to use the service can address the broker and ask for a component that implements the service. The broker delivers a reference to the implementing component where the request can be sent to afterwards.

▶ *Business Rule Engines*

The latest trend in application servers is trying to package the formulation of business rules into an XML format, mostly in *Business Process Execution Language* (BPEL) or *Business Rules Markup Language* (BRML). Such formats are supposed to be editable by business users as well as by programmers. While the usability for business users can be questioned, they surely introduce an interesting technology to ease maintenance and improve flexibility in the formulation of business processes.

Application servers provide components that interpret such specifications directly; there is no need anymore to translate them to direct imperative program code.

▶ *Shared Servers vs. Dedicated Servers*

There is the possibility to use one application server for several applications. This is often done for server consolidation and to improve server hardware utilization. In effect, this means that several sets of classes that make up an application are loaded into the server. While conventions exist that prevent the obvious conflicts like name clashes, there remains a vast potential for problems.

The different applications might need different Java releases – if not now, then a few upgrades in the future. When one application grabs memory like crazy or uses up lots of CPU resources, this affects all other applications in that application server as well. Application servers have no well-tuned possibilities for resource limitations to conquer that problem.

Therefore, dedicated application servers should be used for mission-critical applications. Shared servers should only be used for business-important or business-foundation applications. If that is a problem with hardware utilization, we can always utilize host virtualization technology; see Sect. 6.3.2. With that technology, it is possible to run several application servers on one computer system without any conflicts.

High Availability for Application Servers

Most application servers support running in a clustered configuration. In this case, several server instances run on a bunch of hosts, acting as one big server to their clients. (A client is typically a Web server, a program on the user's desktop, or another application server.)

Figure 7.6 on the following page illustrates the working principle of application server clusters. What is exceptional in the realm of high availability is that many application server cluster products do session state sharing, i.e., a session object does not only exist at one cluster node, but on all nodes – and updates are done concurrently on all nodes! To achieve that, all changes are replicated to all other nodes of the cluster.

As a result of that ability, when a cluster node goes down, the session can be continued *without aborting* at another node. No transient data is lost! This is a capability that we last saw with mirrored disk drives in this book: no outage time at all in the case of failures; no loss of transient data either.

Since this reliability is achieved with redundancy, we still have some management component. In this case, it is the client that must handle the

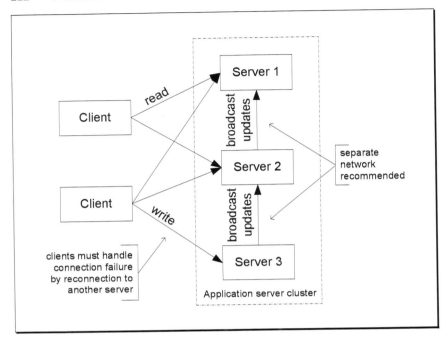

Fig. 7.6. Application server cluster

situation of the application server having multiple IP addresses where a network connection can suddenly go down and where this must not break the session, but that a reconnection to another address must be made. This requirement is not new: we encountered it when we introduced database clusters in Sect. 7.2.1 on p. 199.

State replication between application servers has consequences for the system design too. Very often, such state replication is made by broadcasts. Such broadcasts should not be on the normal network – for one, it would be received by many more systems than necessary; second, these messages have very delicate latency and bandwidth requirements and could be disturbed by other network traffic. Therefore it is recommended that intracluster node communication is done via private networks. Such networks can be created as VLANs. If one uses real network equipment for it, i.e., separate physical switches, we must not forget to set up this equipment redundantly as well.

It is important to note that application-server clusters and failover clusters do not work together. This means that it does not make sense to place one node of the middleware cluster on a logical host of a failover cluster. We have to select clustering technology on one level and stick to it.

In the end, we need to understand the products and need to know them inherently. Otherwise errors may happen that reduce availability. For example, some application server cluster products distribute configuration files automatically over all cluster nodes. We must not intervene with homemade installation and replication techniques at that point. Other pitfalls exist that can also be avoided through familiarity with products and their idiosyncrasies.

7.5 Messaging Servers

Messaging servers are used to transport information reliably from one IT system or IT component to another. Furthermore they ensure that the order of messages is not changed; when a two messages are sent subsequently from the same sender to the same recipient, they will arrive in the same order as they were sent.

The sender hands over a message to the message server and can be sure that it does not get lost and that it is delivered to the recipient eventually. Messaging servers are crucial parts of many commerce systems. For example, credit-card validation or payment may be a message. The need for high availability for such servers is obvious.

Messaging servers have persistent storage where messages are kept that have been handed over by the sender, but that have not yet been received by the recipient. This persistent storage is called the *message queue*.

Messaging servers are often used together with application servers or transaction managers. In many current developments, J2EE application servers are used; the J2EE framework contains a messaging server component named JMS. There is only one JMS server per J2EE application, unlike the applications servers. Clustering is not part of the JMS server specification and is not supported by most products. Instead, they rely on failover clusters on the operating system level. Figure 7.7 on the following page illustrates that principle.

Many JMS servers have the problem that they do not implement message queue persistency properly, and crashes can cause loss of data. One must check the functionality of products carefully to determine if their reliability is sufficient for the demands of high availability. It is also not possible to use JMS for communication outside the J2EE framework. For guaranteed database persistency and robustness, and for messaging in heterogeneous environments, specific messaging server products must be used. The market leader in that area is *MQSeries* from IBM, rebranded as *WebSphere MQ* when it was integrated into IBM's WebSphere Application Server.

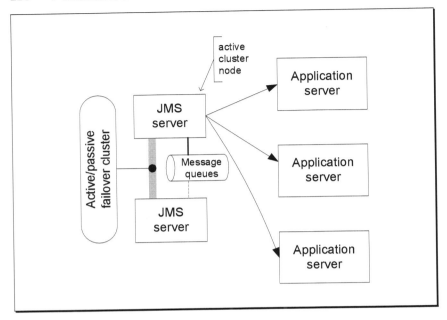

Fig. 7.7. JMS server and failover cluster

WebSphere MQ has integrated clustering capability, but with limited functionality as single points of failure remain. It is possible to create several queue managers that take over each other's work in the case of outages, but problems remain. Message queues are not replicated, multiple queue managers just serve to enable clients to dispatch messages without problems, but they do not ensure delivery of stored messages. If those messages are concerned with financial transactions, we want them delivered, of course.

Another problem is the publish/subscribe design pattern that is used quite often. There, a *broker* receives messages from clients and delivers them to subscribers that are WebSphere MQ servers themselves. Those subscribers need a unique identifier and cannot be MQ clusters, as identifiers are not shared in a cluster. Therefore MQ clustering should only be used to resolve performance problems, but not to achieve high availability. Instead, standard failover cluster technology is used for that.

8

Applications

In the previous chapters, we saw how high availability can be achieved on levels of the system stack below applications. But in the end, projects do not want to make a computer highly available; their eventual goal is high availability for applications. We will see how we can approach high-availability planning when we look at the application level in the system stack: what actions must be taken on this level to achieve end-to-end high availability for applications.

It is not the task of this chapter to repeat all the precautions and possibilities of the other chapters – all of them contribute to high availability for applications. In particular, we will not refer to high availability on the hardware level, as this is too far apart. But this does not mean that hardware high availability is not of interest in an end-to-end view, quite the contrary. It just means that we cannot contribute something new to hardware high availability in this chapter.

Each application has special requirements and one cannot easily give one-size-fits-all recommendations for how to approach application high availability in general. But painted with a very broad brush, there exist three categories of applications:

1. **Commercial off-the-shelf** (COTS) software is applications that we buy, configure, and deploy.
2. **Buy-and-modify** software represents the middle road where a COTS application is bought and adapted to local needs within the company or by a contractor. Such adaptation is more than mere configurations, but includes adding significant pieces of our own code. Some very important applications fall into this category, e.g., many complex SAP installations with their own ABAP programs.
3. **In-house** or **one-off** software is applications that we build. It does not imply that every single piece is written in-house; quite often external components are used. These external components might be large, e.g., databases or application servers; therefore, the task is not only

to build new software, but also to integrate existing components. The distinguishing factor between in-house and buy-and-modify software is the ability to decide about system design and base functionality oneself.

Clearly, there are different options that one can use to attain high availability for applications, depending on these categories. While in-house software can be especially tailored for high availability from the start, such ability does not exist for COTS software and also not for in-house applications that exist already. In any case, applications either have to bring built-in support for high availability with them, or one has to live with add-ons. For buy-and-modify software, it is even worse: similar to COTS software, one is usually not able to change the software enough to include high availability in it – but if it has high-availability options already, one needs to pay attention that one does not destroy that ability through the modifications. For example, taking up our SAP example from before, ABAP Objects is powerful enough to render high-availability precautions unusable.

But technical approaches cannot be clearly separated by those application categories. In particular, as we will see later, the most important approaches work for all categories. Therefore, the structure of this chapter will be oriented towards the technical solutions and will present them in sequence. For each technological approach, we will mention especially how this approach is used for the three application categories.

So let us start to look at approaches first that work for all categories, and then go to the approaches that are only sensible for applications developed in-house:

- **Failover clusters** are a mature method for all application categories and will be presented in Sect. 8.1.
- **Middleware** provides intrinsic capabilities to support high availability for all three application categories and will be featured in Sect. 8.2.
- **Development from scratch** is an approach that is only possible for in-house software and will be looked at in Sect. 8.3.
- **Code quality** is an important property that is needed for in-house applications and for buy-and-modify software. Section 8.4 presents the essentials, though a complete coverage of that topic is beyond the scope of this book.
- **Testing** the application for its high-availability properties is as important as testing it for functionality and is discussed in Sect. 8.5.

▶ *Beyond Technical Approaches*

The presentations in the following sections are technically focused. But we must not forget that it is as important to have prepared processes to operate the system, change it, and handle errors. For such processes, information is necessary. We need to make sure that we have an up-to-date list of:

- Process documentation (mostly incident- and escalation-related)
- System documentation (operations and administration manuals)
- Important contacts (Business owner, technical staff, escalation contacts, vendor contacts)

This list must not only be available to the project manager, it must be available to all persons who have to handle incidents.

You are advised to keep that list not only in electronic form. In the case of major outages, it might not be accessible anymore. Save it on a CD, maybe even print the most important information (e.g., the contacts) out, and store it in a safe but accessible place. Chapter 10 tells more about such commonsense precautions.

8.1 Integration in a Cluster on the Operating System Level

Section 6.1 introduced failover clusters which operate at the interface between the operating system and application programs and are especially useful for applications with persistent data storage. Section 6.2 presented load-balancing clusters for applications without a persistent state. These technologies can be used to achieve high availability for most applications; this section will explain how that is done best.

Application state and persistent data storage are the key factors for selecting the cluster technology. For applications without session states and without persistent data, load-balancing clusters can be utilized in simple setups. Proper release processes must be established to roll out new releases, change the configuration, and transfer static data to all cluster nodes, but apart from that this technology works like a charm.

Applications with session states or with persistent data need a bit more work. There we can utilize failover clusters. It is important that the data-holding component is relevant for the selection of the technology. If an application stores its data in files and these files are an inherent part of the application, then failover clusters are the right choice.

This is independent of the location of the stored data. Even if the data is stored in a database or on a network file server, failover clusters are the way to go, and a load-balancing cluster will not work. In that case, an application would need to have the ability to run multiple instances at the same time and all requests need to be done in one network connection. But that is very rare; usually we cannot start an application multiple times, have arbitrary distribution of requests to all running instances, and let them have read and write access to the database. For one, many applications cache data and that would need to be invalidated for write operations. Furthermore, many applications have several network connections per client session, in particular those that utilize HTTP.

In the rest of this section, we will leave load-balancing clusters aside. If an application can utilize them because there is no persistent data, then no further actions are needed. But a failover cluster needs to know quite a few things about the application that it covers; therefore, we will continue with the description of that technology.

In fact, usage of this mature clustering technology for application high availability is the most practical method today, for all application categories, be they COTS, in-house, or buy-and-modify software. That is not because this solution is the best, technology-wise. Quite the contrary, clusters on operating system level often have inherent problems because they have to treat applications as black boxes; therefore, often they do not know enough about the application and have to react crudely to application error situations. The most prominent example is a crash that makes persistent data inconsistent. Many cluster implementations have a hard time to handle that situation, since recovery of data consistency often needs longer than expected failover times.

On the other hand, such clusters enable limited redundancy for applications that works as long as one is able to recover from a crash and get consistent data and a working system again by restarts. Most software systems are like this, most of the time, so this strategy remains very successful in practice.

For COTS and buy-and-modify software, this approach is often the only possible solution as one cannot modify their sources anyhow. For in-house software some redundancy can be achieved through middleware clusters; we will have a more detailed look at this in Sect. 8.2. But usage of failover clusters is also a valid approach for in-house development, as it lessens the demand on the developers, who will already be busy realizing the functional requirements.

Application Requirements for Failover Clusters

As mentioned already, clusters need information about applications, and as Sect. 6.1.1 on p. 157 described, failover services place some demands on applications. The rest of this section will provide a check list of criteria that an application must fulfill before it can run in a failover cluster environment. For in-house software it is usually easy to satisfy these requirements; bought software must be checked to see if it can be configured accordingly.

The description focuses on UNIX or Linux failover clusters, which makes it possible to list specific items to look at and not just abstract principles. Similar requirements must be fulfilled for Windows clusters, as the principles are the same.

The combination of application and cluster software must meet the following objectives:

- It must be possible to control and manage the application's state: we must be able to start and stop it, must be able to see if it is running, must be able to reset it to a fresh state, etc.
- It must be possible to migrate an application from one cluster node to another. This involves shutting down the application on one node, switching programs and data storage to the new node, and starting the application there.
- It must be possible to update an application without much trouble. This is often the case for good release management and good installation policies. The more manual work must be done on several cluster nodes, the more difficult it gets to do a successful update.
- It must be possible to recover from an application crash. This does not only mean that one must be able to restart an application automatically. It also means that the recovery must turn inconsistent data into a consistent state.
- It must be possible to handle incidents quickly on a technical level. Achieving this objective is influenced by the application's code quality and robustness. Good applications that can be easily implemented in failover clusters make it easy to detect and handle failure situations.

The rest of this section describes several common requirements that must be met to fulfill these objectives. Such requirements spell out technical details that application implementations must take into account when they work in failover cluster environments.

The recommendations are the same for all application categories, be it COTS, buy-and-modify, or in-house software. If bought software does not have the necessary capabilities, adequate configuration and scripts must be supplied during implementation.

▸ *Independence from the Physical Host*

Failover cluster software does not hide the physical characteristics of a cluster node. It establishes a logical host for a service and enables migration of that service to another cluster node, but that logical host is not a contained environment. There is the danger that those who implement applications are not aware enough of that fact, and happen to use specific capabilities of the physical host, and not just of the logical host. But this prevents the failover cluster software from working, since the application would not work on other nodes.

Therefore no application must use machine-specific configurations. Particular culprits are use of

- `hostid`
- `uname -n`

- IP addresses of physical network interfaces
- Name of the physical host

The issue of network interfaces deserves special attention. For incoming requests, one does not have to worry much. TCP connections are answered with a source address where the request was received. This is important, as connection tracking firewalls would cap that TCP connection otherwise. Most UDP services do so likewise.

Services should only bind to the IP numbers of the application. They should not bind to all interfaces. If that is not possible, a thorough review should be made – after all, it is not possible anymore to supply several logical hosts with similar services in the same cluster.

Outgoing network requests (i.e., originating from the application) are another matter though. By default, they use the network interface's physical IP address and not the address of the logical host. But firewalls and intrusion detection systems analyze network traffic by associating services with IP addresses, and they should associate that traffic with the logical host, and not with the cluster's physical host. Otherwise they might block the communication. Therefore it is advisable that the application service's logical IP address is used for outgoing requests. This usually needs special configuration in the application software.

Here is a pitfall: such requests for machine-specific information may happen in libraries or in frameworks. Therefore even when no physical host information is recorded in any configuration file, still some library might make a lookup of the host name and then use the physical host's name instead of the logical host's one. This is one of the many reasons why it is mandatory for us to test failovers, to be sure of not having such surprises.

▸ *File Locations*

An application will have at least one associated volume group, or a remote file system (NAS or SAN). All data of an application must be on these volume groups.[1] Since volume groups are the migration unit in the case of a failover, this ensures that all data is migrated to the new node.

It is recommended to put program files and the application's configuration on the application's file systems as well. That way, these files will be migrated as well in the case of failovers. If we installed them on system volumes, we would need to install and configure them on all physical nodes identically. While this is quite easy for the initial installation, experience shows that updates are not made as reliably and often leave physical nodes in inconsistent states. Better to avoid that from the start and hold programs and configuration only once, on the volume group that moves.

---

[1] Either in files on file systems, or on raw volumes. Usage of raw storage volumes was common a few years ago, but is not used often anymore.

The only exception is middleware or support program files (Web servers, database servers, runtime environments for Java, Perl, Python, etc.). If these programs are shared by several logical hosts that run on one node, it might be preferable to install them once on each physical node, on system volumes. Please note that storage usage is not an input for this decision; disk storage is just too cheap for that. Section 6.1.2 on p. 166 has a longer discussion on the issues of software installation and updates in cluster environments.

Log files should be placed on the application's file systems as well. They are urgently needed for root cause analysis in problem management and thus should be available after a failover. If they are placed on system volumes, they might get lost and prevent urgent repair actions. The issue of syslog-based logging is described in Sect. 6.1.2 too.

If developers or product managers tell you that it is not possible to relocate configuration and logging files because "their location is hardwired into the application," do not believe them at first hand. Most often it is possible to install symlinks in the hardwired locations that point back to the application's file systems where the real files are placed. Of course, these symlinks must be installed on all physical hosts then – but they do not change, and they usually even do not change during updates, and thus can be installed once.

Process identifier (PID) files may be placed in or outside the application's file systems. If they are placed outside, they must be located in an existing directory, like /var/run. We recommend placing them inside though.

▶ *Provisioning*

Application installation packages must not contain or create system startup actions, like scripts in /etc/init.d or registration of application services. Service activation and deactivation is strictly a task of the cluster software; the usual operating systems methods are not used.

Services that use *inetd* need to be rewritten to use a standalone daemon process. It is not possible to utilize failover clusters for *inetd* services. During failover the service would need to be discarded from the host-global configuration file /etc/inetd.conf and would need to be inserted at the new cluster node. It is not realistic to assume that we could implement that in a reliable way.

If files or directories must be installed outside the application's file systems, several installation packages must be created. There must not be files inside and outside the application's file systems in one package. That package will be installed on the default node for this logical host. If there were files outside the application's file system, those files would only be installed on that physical node and would be missing from the other nodes. To enable installation of these files on all other nodes, it is best to put them in their own installation package and install that on all physical hosts of the cluster.

▶ *Start and Stop*

One needs start/stop/restart actions for each resource. Stop must really stop, start must really start. The stop action must handle the case where the application must be aborted because it hangs. The start action must check that the application does start, in fact, i.e., both actions should check that they were successful. Otherwise migration to another cluster node might not be possible anymore, or perpetual node switching might occur.

Reliance on pid files as semaphores (i.e., process existence marker) is bad; their only reason is to record the process ID, and their existence does not imply that the application is really running. The scripts must also assume that more than one instance of that application is running on a machine. Therefore ps/grep pipelines are not a good choice to determine the process – one needs to be very sure that one really has located the correct process to be shut down.

If the start action on booting and during normal runtime is different, the startup action should use internal discovery of that situation. One could provide a separate boot action, but internal distinction is better as it is easily done on all operating systems and is more robust.

Start actions should be idempotent: one can always call them, they detect that the resource is active and running and do not influence it. It may be that they trigger a reload of the current configuration, which is OK as variation.

Start actions must not require interactive input. They need to work completely in batch mode. This is a particular problem for encrypted services that usually need a passphrase to read the private key. Either the keys must be stored on a hardware token or they must be stored without passphrase protection. The latter often needs clearance by the security office of your company.

The restart script must assert proper stop and start of the resource. It needs to repair inconsistencies if necessary. For example, perform a database table consistency check, or other actions.

In noncluster environments, reload of a changed configuration in running service processes is often done as part of the start/stop action and is sometimes named *restart*. But this is not the restart action that we mean in the cluster context; configuration reload is not handled or supported by cluster software. It must be delivered by external means.

▶ *Batch Jobs*

If you use *cron* for job management, it is necessary to establish a method that allows all jobs on all cluster nodes to be activated. cron does not supply such a method, neither does the failover cluster software. Section 6.1.2 on p. 166 describes an easy-to-implement way of doing so by the onloghost script. Otherwise one would need to de-establish or establish cron jobs as applications are switched – and that calls for instability.

Scripts to be called by cron should be able to assume that the application is online; they must not need to check for that themselves. But they must not demand that standard I/O streams are bound to files on the cluster's file system; instead, input and output files must be determined automatically or passed as arguments.

Long-running batch jobs should have checkpoints. On restart, they should notice if they have been aborted and use the checkpoint information to save computation time.

As a last remark on cron, it should be noted that this is only usable for very basic and simple job management. When we have complex dependencies of batch hobs, it is better to use proprietary job management software products. When one goes shopping for such a product, a mandatory item on the checklist should be if it is cluster-aware.

8.2 High Availability Through Middleware

Most in-house applications that are developed now use middleware products intensively. Many of them store their data in a database, or use an application server to get lots of functionality like session handling or transaction semantics for usage in the application.

In fact, 99% of all in-house applications that need high availability should use this approach and not develop any methods from scratch. The probability that the middleware vendors got it right with better functionality than our application programmers is quite high – after all, they are specialists in that area, whereas application programmers have other skill preferences. Only in very rare circumstances, where the business requirements demand the ability to cope with many application failures and we have appropriate developer skills, are we going to use the "from scratch" approach that we present in Sect. 8.3 on p. 225.

As well, many applications that we buy deploy middleware products, and this is often still visible. So one has an Oracle database, a Web server front-end, and a BEA application server; the actual application comes in the form of Java classes that are integrated into the application server. This is especially true for buy-and-modify software.

In all these cases we can establish high availability for these middleware products, as explained in Chap. 7, and greatly improve the availability of our application this way, i.e., a load-balancing solution for the Web server will not change its behavior in any way and therefore provides a substantial improvement for high availability. The same is true for a database server and its available high-availability options.

▶ *Pitfalls and Limitations*

When we utilize middleware high-availability capabilities, we must make sure that we realize complete redundancy, until the bottom of the system stack. For example, a highly available application server is not sufficient, database and web servers must be highly available too. Since the application is integrated into an application server, one tends to care for that server first – but one must not forget the other components of the application and realize high availability for them as well.

Incidentally, there are limits to the high availability that one can achieve with middleware products. In particular, software errors in the application are often not recovered this way. These errors may be repeated and not go away at restarts, causing inconsistent data and continuous failures. Other errors are caused by too much computer resource usage (e.g., a memory leak) and the application server cluster notices that too late. An application server cluster only protects against software crashes when functionality can be restored by restarts and when the crash is not repeated immediately.

But luckily this is the common situation. We do not need to paint everything in black; most of the time aborts, recovery, and restart of applications work quite well. Since the occurrence of nonrecoverable failures is so small, the residual risk is also quite small. Therefore it is often decided that one can live with that residual risk that leads to a major outage in the case of a severe software error. Of course, if the damage would be very high for such a major outage, disaster recovery should be planned for and prepared in order to mitigate that residual risk too.

▶ *Application Servers*

But an application needs to be designed to work in a cluster environment, which does not come out of the box. If we have bought the software, we have to check with the vendor if it does so.

For in-house development, the most important consideration is the session design. The need for session state must be carefully analyzed, designed, and implemented. Often, state information that shall be replicated must be made persistent, or marked especially. Such marking comes by usage of application-server-specific APIs, e.g., by using special classes or interfaces. One must also assure that one is able to serialize those objects, a precondition for sending them across a network to synchronize the server state. This all boils down to our having to decide ourselves what information can be lost, and what must be kept in the case of a failure. This cannot be done automatically by the application server, but is a property of application design.

This means particularly that we need to decide if and when sessions can be aborted. If its not a big hassle to abort them, it becomes much easier; only transaction results have to be made permanent. If sessions should survive an outage, we need to decide if there are small dialog changes that we can ask the user to repeat and which may not be permanent.

▸ *Client Awareness*

The client must be prepared to work with a cluster as well. First of all the application server connection might break and must be reconnected. Most clients abort in such a case. Maybe the session context needs to be built anew on the client side in the case of reconnects. Maybe the user has to be told about a small problem that needs a repetition of some dialog steps.

If the client interface is realized as a Web front-end, we do not have a problem here. Web browsers have no connection state: here the Web server is the client of the application server. Almost all Web development frameworks provide proper integration between Web server clusters and application server clusters from the start – those that do not are not worth using.

8.3 High Availability From Scratch

This section starts with a word of caution. If one wants to develop an application that is inherently highly available from scratch, one must be very certain (1) that one knows the requirements, (2) that the necessary skills are available, and (3) that one has appropriate resources for that undertaking. Very often, only one or two of these necessary preconditions are true.

It is a *very rare* application that must be implemented from the ground up anew to be highly available. These are the kinds of applications where their failure would endanger lives, or where any kind of failure must be avoided at all costs. For example, the fly-by-wire control systems of civil aircrafts fall under the requirement that catastrophic failures are "not anticipated to occur over the entire operational life of all airplanes of one type" and that means a 10^{-9} probability of failure per hour [4]. Space exploration also has high requirements for software availability and reliability – after all, one cannot send one's IT staff to Mars or Venus to repair the software. Nevertheless, with all the effort, talent, skill, and resources that go into creating fault-tolerant software in these areas, failures still happen.

Most applications are better off utilizing existing middleware components, as explained in Sect. 8.2. Even when one writes a new middleware component (after all, this prefabricated high availability must come from somewhere), one should utilize existing modules and code.

With all those preliminary warnings about the difficulties, when do we use application development from scratch at all? Well, application high availability from scratch is used to implement *fault-tolerant systems,* i.e., applications that can continue to operate properly in the presence of failures and outages of component parts. Those systems are always distributed systems that run on a set of components at the same time.

Andrew Tanenbaum wrote a seminal textbook on distributed computing [10], and stated, "Distributed systems need radically different software than centralized systems do." Therefore, application developers who want to use that solution approach and who do not have sufficient experience with distributed systems already are asked to learn about it first. The textbook cited is a very good start on the senior or graduate level, as are others on this topic.

It is beyond the scope of this book to give an introduction or recommendations. But what we can do is to list some of the central terms that describe areas where development of monolithic and distributed systems are different. These are areas where distributed fault-tolerant highly-available systems need to realize requirements that are above the norm of typical application code:

Communication between physically distributed systems in the face of flaky communication links and instable systems. Different subsystems should be able to have arbitrary outages without disturbing the overall outcome.

Processes must be controlled carefully and must not stay without supervisors. If they do not work within their prescribed parameters, the supervising infrastructure processes must intervene and get them back on track.

Naming must be handled uniquely over the whole distributed system. In single-address-space systems, naming of objects is mostly easy: one just takes the address for identification, or utilizes a central ID repository for persistent objects. Single-computer systems still can utilize such a central ID system.

But a distributed system that spans over several computer systems still needs to identify its objects. When one introduces a central naming broker, that component becomes a single point of failure and introduces risks again that must not be taken for fault-tolerant systems. Therefore, decentralized approaches for object naming and identification must be utilized.

Synchronization handles the updating of objects and transaction semantics in distributed systems. In the worst-case scenario, one cannot even rely on shared time for coordination, but luckily research in distributed computing has provided mechanisms and theories even for that situation.

Consistency and replication is a whole world of problems in itself. It is not only application data that must be replicated, but usually the programs themselves as well. Most often it is necessary to run several different program versions in different subsystems, at the same time, because it is not possible to update them all together.

Caching is an important subproblem of consistency and is a research area of its own – it is very hard to balance the need between performance and correctness in the right way.

Fault tolerance is another ability that must be designed in from the start. This is the most difficult part to get right – and there is no way that one can be really sure that one was successful.

Software design diversity, i.e., writing separate applications for the same requirement is an option to achieve fault tolerance, as shown in [4]. The studies cited in this article show the advantages of this class of methods for high availability. But it should also be noted that Brilliant et al. [1] showed that while multiversion programming improves reliability by wide margins, it is still quite likely that common mistakes are made by different persons performing the same task.

Clearly, writing highly available applications from scratch is hard work, with exceptional requirements. If one needs them, one should pay utmost attention to getting really good, bright, and talented application architects, designers, programmers, and testers on board. Without a top-notch developer group, this endeavor is bound to fail.

8.4 Code Quality Is Important

If we do in-house development for an application that is to be highly available, there is one important point to remember:

Code Quality Matters!

This is independent of the development approach, if we write the application from scratch, utilize middleware components, or if these are modifications to bought software: a badly written application cannot be made highly available.

In fact, this truism holds also for bought applications. The only difference is that we cannot check for code quality of proprietary software as easily as we can for in-house developments. This is one of the advantages of open-source software, where we can get an impression ourselves of whether the software code has been written in a professional style.

Most problematic for highly available applications is resource management: memory, CPU, and disk usage. Memory is especially important. Many applications are long-running, but still have memory leaks. It is notoriously difficult to get manual memory management right for long-running programs; therefore, it is harder to develop them with C or C++. Programming languages with automatic memory management (e.g., Java or C#) help here.

Performance is not an excuse for writing a server application in C completely today. C is a language for systems programming, but not for application programming. In the case of performance problems, we can always measure to detect the hot spots, and rewrite just this function or module in C. (Most often it will be I/O problems anyhow.) Premature optimization is the cause of many errors, as the proverb says "First rule of optimization: 'Don't do it.'"

That is not to say that performance is not important. Careless programming will cost quite some performance overall – in every language. Too many allocations, memory fragmentation, and excessive overdesign with lots of superfluous layers cost performance without creating hot spots.

The best advice that can be given here is that good programmers should program and should not be put in charge with management tasks. Less qualified programmers should use other projects to enhance their skill; high-availability projects are there for the best. Also, it is important that enough time for code reviews and functional tests is allocated. Without them, the whole development is on unsafe ground.

The whole project team – project lead, architect, and programmers – should have read the *Mythical Man Month* by Frederick Brooks [2]. If it was some time ago, it is recommended to reread it. This book is a warning against hubris. It is a bit dated on technical matters, but it is not at all dated on matters related to individuals, organizations, and scale.

The most important lesson from that book is: Plan one to throw away, and write for maintenance. As the saying goes, "each engineer creates a design that is as complex as he can barely handle." – let us try to prove that proverb wrong and use a design that is simpler. Complexity costs: it is harder to think about, harder to reason about, harder to test, harder to debug, and harder to maintain.

At every step of the way, we need to remember KISS (keep it simple and straightforward), one of our basic approaches to achieve high availability. We need to ask ourselves each time: "Can it be done in a simpler way?" If not, we must write up the rationale for the complexity. We need to find out the essential complexity of our task, and shed the nonessential parts. As Albert Einstein said, "Everything should be made as simple as possible, but not simpler."

Another good precaution is courses for developers that raise the awareness of operational and implementation problems. This makes programmers see beyond their personal development environments into the environment where the application must be operated eventually. Creating an application that can be implemented easily and operated well is part of the job, and it is worth emphasizing that from time to time.

Coming back to issues of programming, it is not easily possible to give proper advice on programming methods and styles for arbitrary programming languages. But there are lots of programming-language-specific books with tips and pitfalls for good programming. Of course, high-availability projects are not good places for programmers to learn about these things: they should be acquainted with them already at the start.

But we can list some tips that are useful for essentially every programming language:

- Validate all input values, check all return values. Too many errors in software are caused by ignoring these two simple rules. This is also the reason why it is better to use a programming language with exception handling – here one is forced to define exception handlers and it is also possible to define them both globally and locally.
- Utilize proven and stable libraries, do not invent the wheel anew. Eventually, this leads to utilization of middleware components and application server frameworks.
- The appropriate architecture is important. Use design patterns, but do not overuse them. There is no need to use a J2EE framework that needs lots of resources when a simple program does it as well.

It is important that application programmers also take operational aspects into account. Too often they only care for their functional requirements. The application must be *manageable*. Properties to look for are:

- Support of restart after crashes.
- Monitoring must be supported. One should think about instrumentation of applications for better monitoring; that is not hard and pays back with lots of advantages for high-availability operations.
- Good logging facilities (not too few, not too many, good messages).
- Availability of consistency checks.

With these properties in place, good resource management, and good code quality, we will have no real problems in making our application highly available.

8.5 Testing for High Availability

The task of application testing is often to create the assurance that the application meets its functional requirements. For each *function point* a test exists that checks if the application satisfies that requirement. While this is also needed for highly available applications, it is not sufficient. In addition we also have to test for nonfunctional properties of the software and need to check if it can be operated well and if it handles failure situations gracefully. For example, we need to do end-to-end testing if an application recovers gracefully after an application or system crash, and cleans up inconsistent data states afterwards.

When we created the architecture and system design of our application, we noted objectives, requirements, and scenarios, as described in Chap. 3. Those failure scenarios are crucial for test planning as well. From them we can construct test scenarios that create such failures, see how our application reacts to them, and if it fulfills the promises of our system design to handle them.

This way, we do not only test if our application works as intended in normal circumstances, but also if it works as intended in extraordinary circumstances or failures. High-availability tests should first of all try to create failure, and not to avoid them. We are interested in the application's behavior in these borderline cases because failures are the circumstances that threaten availability, not normal operations.

Part of test goals is the detection of limits. We do not only want to know if the application runs with the available resources, but we also want to know how big the gap is, the reserve buffer, between utilized and available resources. As an example, let us take the shared buffer area of a database server. Normal tests would check if there is an overflow and would leave it at that if no problems occur. High-availability tests do not stop here, but reduce the memory size so much that errors *do* occur, to detect the configuration limits of the database server. Then we can raise the shared memory buffer size again by a sufficient amount that now represents a known buffer for this application environment, and is available for unforeseen numbers of user requests.

In the same direction, tests for application robustness have the same aims. It is not sufficient that an application behaves properly for correct input. Instead it must behave properly on invalid input as well: it must neither crash, nor must its performance be reduced to a crawl.

No high-availability application testing can be complete without *stress tests*, sometimes also called *load tests*. One generates simulated or real user requests and tests how the application behaves. Tools exist to help with request generation and automated response checks. The main difficulty with stress tests is the demand for realistic request patterns to create a realistic load simulation. For a new application, only approximations can be used; here the request patterns are often not adequate. But this is a different situation for updates of existing applications. Here we can record request/response patterns of the previous release and use them for testing the new software release. To support that, good applications are designed to output such metrics that we can use for performance and capacity planning.

When we test an application that utilizes other components, e.g., application or database servers, we should not forget to test such components on their own. During normal application tests, such dependent components are only utilized to a small degree. Erroneous situations will suddenly access parts that might fail, but it is hard to create such erroneous situations in our simulated test environments.

We can access the middleware components on our own and cause failures in their operation, to observe how the application reacts to them. For example, an application may or may not survive the failover of a database server, since session information might be lost. Tests are there to assure that this behavior is expected, and that the application's functionality in such failure situation is according to the objectives and requirements of the architecture.

9

Infrastructure

In this book, we first met the term infrastructure in Chaps. 1 and 3. Section 4.1.1 eventually provided a first definition when the system stack was introduced. Infrastructure is the box in the system stack that represents the software and hardware components that are used by application, middleware, or other categories, but are not integrated. This chapter looks into that box and attempts to present its content, the *infrastructure components*.

Like all other components, they utilize the same principles to realize high availability and disaster recovery: redundancy and robustness, as explained in Sect. 4.1. As outlined there, virtualization is an important part to realize redundancy, just like in other component categories.

"Used, but not integrated" differs from project to project – therefore we find different usages of the term infrastructure. Tongue-in-cheek, one could explain infrastructure also as "infrastructure is everything that is not one's own responsibility." This will be reflected if you just ask some arbitrary colleagues who are responsible for applications, what they think that infrastructure is. Most of the time, it is those services that they do not have to configure themselves but which they can take for granted. Invariantly, the network is mentioned, but also databases, clusters, external storage servers, and others.

Most often considered as infrastructure components are:

- Network
- Basic services like Domain Name Service (DNS), Dynamic Host Configuration Protocol (DHCP), Network Time Protocol (NTP), and others
- Backup and restoration
- Monitoring

These are also the components that will be covered in this chapter. They are mostly components or services that are needed for servers, as this is the main focus of this book. But some services, e.g., DHCP, are also about highly available infrastructure in general.

Other candidates for infrastructure components are handled at different places in this book, since they are more often involved in application-centric projects too.

Storage servers (SAN or NAS) are described in Sects. 5.2.2 and 5.2.3. They should be discussed together with other storage topics.

Failover clusters are described in Sect. 6.1. They are so important and are so involved in most high-availability projects that they almost deserve their own chapter.

Load-balancing clusters are described in Sect. 6.2, where they make up the other part of Chap. 6. They are also an integral and essential part of many high-availability projects.

Databases are handled in Sect. 7.2. They must be configured for any nontrivial application; high availability and disaster recovery for databases must be given special thought for any project, since they hold most of the essential data.

Application servers are handled in Sect. 7.4. Even though can be utilized for several applications at once, they are so intertwined with any application design that each high-availability project must look at them separately.

9.1 Network

The most important infrastructure component is the network. The ability of computers to communicate with each other is mandatory for almost all applications of today. There are few enterprise-class applications that can function without network access – most of them are big nightly batch jobs, e.g., at banks.

Some applications are explicitly designed to withstand loss of network communication for some time. Manufacturing IT systems in plants have this ability sometimes; they shall be able to control or support the plant even if the company's network has an outage; they only need a LAN connection within the plant building. The financial damage would often be too large otherwise. But this is possible because their mode of operation is localized, and no users need to access a server via a network. If they do, buffering or lead times (uploading data some time before it is actually needed) can be utilized to allow operation without a network for some time. But client/server or multi-tier applications are the norm for almost all other application areas.

Many communication protocol suites can be used on networks. ISO even produced a reference model for it, the *Open Systems Interconnection Reference Model* (OSI Reference Model or OSI Model for short). This model is very valuable for discussion of network issues, as it provides abstractions and clearly defined terminology. Table 9.1 on the next page

Table 9.1. Open Systems Interconnection (OSI) Reference Model

Layer	Name	Focus
7	Application	Network interface to application
6	Presentation	Manage representation of data, encoding of values, data compression, encryption
5	Session	Manage the data exchange between two applications: establishment, termination, checkpointing of a connection
4	Transport	Transparent transfer of data between applications, controls reliability of a link
3	Network	Transfer data between two systems that may not be on the same network, support connected networks, use logical addresses with a hierarchical addressing scheme, find the path between two computers on different networks
2	Data link	Transfer data directly between two systems that are on the network, use physical addressing with a flat addressing scheme
1	Physical	Electrical and physical properties of devices: layout of pins, voltages, termination, cable specifications, representation of signals in different media

presents its seven layers. While it is a good tool for analysis and discussion, it is not a good prescript for implementation structure; the strict separation of layers and their restricted interaction is too complicated and does not work well in practice.

The most prevalent examples of networks are Ethernet[1] and the set of communication protocols that are often referred to as *Internet protocols* or *IP protocol suite*.[2] The IP suite can also be used to show that the OSI model is good for analysis, but does not reflect the reality of protocol suites. IP is clearly on layer 3, but TCP cannot be placed on one layer exactly – it is both on layer 4, because it realizes transparent reliable transfer of data, and on layer 5, because it contains establishment and termination parts.

Very often, when we discuss network design, we take the physical layer (cabling and devices) for granted, discuss the data link and the net-

---

[1] Ethernet is just one of several protocols on the data link layer, there is also Token Ring, FDDI, HDLC, Frame Relay, ATM, Fibre Channel, SDLC, and others. Nevertheless, we will concentrate on Ethernet, as it is the most important network type that you will encounter in practice.

[2] While SNA, Windows's NetBEUI/NetBIOS, and AppleTalk are all protocol suites that one will encounter in many companies, the IP suite is the dominant communication protocol of today and convergence of the other protocol suites to IP is expected.

work layer, ignore the session layer, and lump together the presentation and application layers into the application protocol. This section will follow that discussion approach roughly:

- The **physical layer** discussion in Sect. 9.1.1 looks only at high availability for devices. Cabling is considered in Appendix B, where we discuss data centers.
- High availability for the **data link layer** (layer 2) is discussed in Sect. 9.1.2.
- The **default gateway** is an important interface between the data link and the network layer (layer 3) and is handled in Sect. 9.1.3.
- The **network layer** is handled next in Sect. 9.1.4.
- **Firewalls** do not fit in the layer scheme: they are components that are concerned with all layers above the network layer. But they are so important that they deserve their own section (Sect. 9.1.5).
- **Disaster recovery** also does not fit in the layer scheme, but gets its own Sect. 9.1.6.
- **Application-level protocols** are handled implicitly by presentation of important infrastructure services in Sect. 9.2.

In discussions about networks, we often encounter several terms that we want to explain first:

Local area network (LAN): A computer network that covers a small geographical area and that usually does not involve leased communication lines or VPNs. Usually, the network that covers a small campus or a site is named the LAN. LANs typically have both high bandwidth and very low latency for network connections.

Most LANs today are switched Ethernet networks, connected by routers, and run the IP suite. Wireless LAN (WLAN) networks are becoming increasingly popular, but are beyond the scope of this book.

Virtual LAN (VLAN): A virtualization, a network that is logically independent and that has been built on top of a physical LAN.

They are used for segmentation (to create Ethernet broadcast domains) and to be able to share equipment over several independent structures. But this is not relevant for the topics of high availability and disaster recovery – everywhere in this chapter where it reads LAN, we can say the same for VLANs.

Metropolitan area network (MAN): This is a network that covers a large campus or a city. It is made up of several site LANs that are connected by high-speed connections. Within a MAN, high bandwidth is common, and decent latency may be realized. Up to 100 Mbit/s and 100-km cable length, we can even expect low latency; only with speeds of 1 Gbit/s and above and distances of 20 km or more do we get medium latency.

MANs that are specific for a company or campus are sometimes called *corporate area networks* or *campus area networks*: both are abbreviated as CAN.

Wide area network (WAN): A network that covers a wide geographical region, larger than a city. It is made up by connection of many LANs or MANs via routers, often connected by leased lines. Though WAN bandwidth may be quite high today, it is still a magnitude smaller than that of LANs. Latency in WANs is often quite bad; applications or system designs that involve WAN usage have to take that into account.

Virtual private network (VPN): A network that is created by the connection of LANs or hosts to other LANs, using *tunneling technology* over other networks. For systems in a VPN, it works as if the connection were over a dedicated leased line.

Usually, the tunneling technology ensures confidentially and authenticity of network traffic by encryption and digital signatures. The most prominent example of such technology is IPsec, although SSL-based VPNs are currently being deployed more often.

The standard use case of a VPN is to connect an external site or a home-office worker to the Intranet via the Internet. This is much cheaper than leased lines, and often more reliable.

But VPNs may also be used over other networks. They can be used to secure WLAN connections, use a private WAN in between, or even within a corporate network to create secure "network islands" for higher confidentially and security.

Active network component: The devices that are used to build a network: switches, routers, hubs, firewalls, etc.

Intranet: The private network of a company. This can be a LAN, a MAN, or a WAN. Most often this term refers to the usage of the IP protocol suite within a company network, including the application-level protocols like HTTP and SMTP. Many intranets are connected to the Internet, but that is not necessarily the case.

Nontechnical people often use these terms to refer just to the visible services on the company network, like the internal Web site.

Intranets are the main focus of this book, as we are mainly concerned with IT services within a company, and we discuss mainly application architectures that involve the company's network.

Internet: The largest public WAN in existence, built using the IP protocol suite.

Extranet: Connection of private networks of business partners. Sometimes whole intranets are connected, but more often only part of the private networks.

Extranets are used to share information and services with suppliers and customers. The term comes from "extending one's intranet to users outside the company" and is sometimes considered a buzzword without technical meaning by networking professionals. Nevertheless, it can be used to describe the intent of network connections.

With this information, we are now ready to take on high availability for networks. We will restrict our text to Ethernet and IP communication for clarity; the principles are the same for other communication protocols.

9.1.1 Network Devices

Network devices, also called *active network components*, are the systems that consist of hardware and software and are used to create the network. They belong to the *physical layer* in the OSI model. Examples for network devices are switches, routers, and hubs. Some people also see firewalls as network devices; we will come back to them in Sect. 9.1.5.

The term *switch* is heavily misused in the realm of networks. Most of the time – also in this book – it means *layer-2 switches* or *Ethernet switches* that manage communication of connected systems with different MAC addresses. Layer-2 switches are not visible on the IP level and have no routing capabilities.

There are also devices called *layer-3 switches* or *multi-layer switches*; from an abstract functional view, they are a specialized form of router. Load-balancing clusters, which we learned about in Sect. 6.2, are sometimes called *layer-7 switches* or *content switches*, obviously to further muddy the water and spread confusion of what a switch is.

Ethernet switches are the prevalent form of network bridges. They form a meshed star topology, where computer systems are connected to switches, and switches are interconnected to each other. They create LAN segments that are connected by routers, either to other LAN segments, or to MANs or WANs. Therefore availability of switches and routers is important for the availability of the whole network; they are prototypical single points of failure for a network.

We can increase the reliability and thus the availability of switches by adding redundancy to these devices internally. Figure 9.1 on the facing page shows the dependency diagram of the internal components of a switch or a router, derived from a Cisco explanation. There is the option to double all internal components and create redundancy by managing it with the device's operating system, i.e., with software. Figure 9.2 on p. 240 shows the resulting dependency diagram.

In practice, this solution is not as robust as one would wish. Having multiple CPUs and switch fabrics is hard to manage in the software, and failovers are not always successful. They also fail very seldom, so the risk of failures in the operating system's redundancy management is sometimes higher than the risk of failures in those switch components. In any case, the software remains the single point of failure, even in an otherwise fully redundant switch.

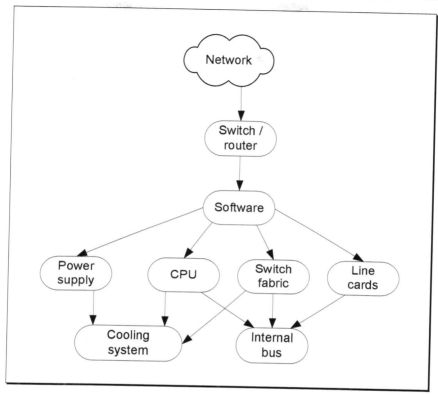

Fig. 9.1. Dependency diagram for internal components of a switch or a router

Power supply and cooling systems are different: they fail regularly. This is caused by dust, dirt, and moving parts (the fans). In addition, in many areas of the world the provision of electricity is not stable and fluctuations cause damage to power supplies. (Section B.3 gives more advice on power issues.)

Therefore many network engineers go for redundant power supplies and cooling fans, but live with the other components being single points of failure, as illustrated in Fig. 9.3 on p. 241. This is eased by the fact that we need more redundancy in the system stack anyhow, above the level of switches, as the next section will show. So, when a switch fails, we expect higher-level redundancy protections to take care of it and to handle it within the current LAN segment.

Network devices have almost no payload-based state that they need to keep. Of course, they have their configuration, but usually they do not rely on past traffic for their functionality. This gives the opportunity to realize redundancy not in a device-internal way, but to use two or more

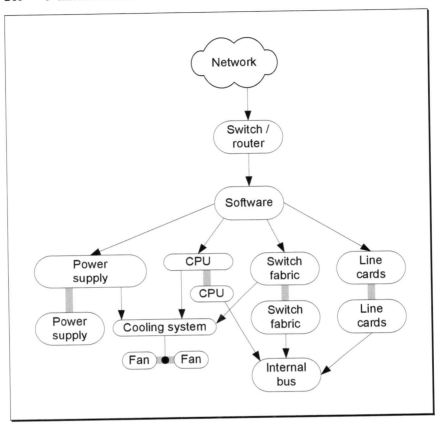

Fig. 9.2. Dependency diagram for a network device, as redundant as possible. Redundancy for software and the internal bus does not exist. Redundancy management is by software if not designated explicitly. Only one dependency is shown for redundant components

single network devices for redundancy. This option will be explored in the next few sections.

9.1.2 LAN Segments

A *data link layer network* or *layer-2 network* is a LAN segment where communication is not routed. All systems on such a network can reach each other by physical addressing. Each network interface that is connected to such a network has a physical network address called a *MAC address*. Ethernet packets contain IP packets or parts of them. Technically, a data link layer network is also called an Ethernet broadcast domain.

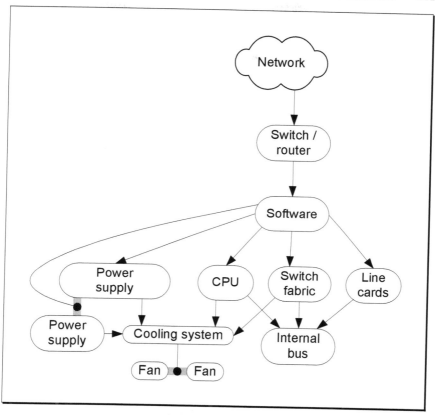

Fig. 9.3. Dependency diagram for internal components of network devices, with pragmatic redundancy

Traditionally, an Ethernet was a thick coaxial cable (also nicknamed "yellow cable") to where all packets from all connected systems were broadcast. The data link layer filtered out the packets that were addressed to the specific interface. Hubs (also called multiport repeaters) were the second wave of connection technology and are still used in small office/home office (SOHO) environments. Nowadays, Ethernets are created by using switches, to achieve higher throughput and better fault isolation.

Example 1 (Failover cluster network connection). The need for redundancy within a LAN segment is best illustrated with network connections of failover clusters. Figure 9.4 on the next page illustrates this with an example: We have two logical nodes L1 and L2, each on their preferred physical node P1 and P2, with two logical network interfaces. If these

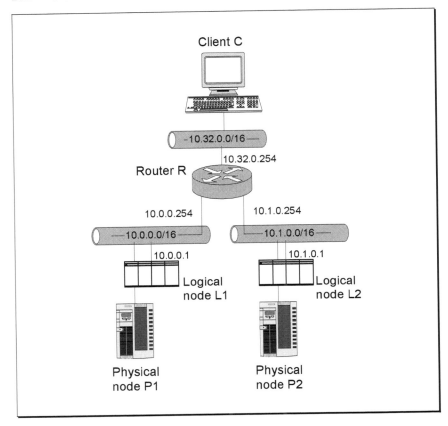

Fig. 9.4. Failover cluster on two networks

two interfaces were on different LAN segments, a client C on a third LAN segment would need to communicate via a router R with those servers.

In the case of a failure in the cluster, one logical node would switch to the other physical node. Let us assume that L2 switches to P1. Then P1 has both logical network interfaces. But without dynamic routing, the router would never know that L2 is suddenly activated on a network to which it does not belong. Since L2 has an IP address of 10.1.0.1, router R will never ask for L2's MAC address on the network 10.0.0.0/16 and will therefore not be able to communicate with L2. The whole failover is not usable, as C cannot reach L2.

Since we do not want to use dynamic routing (we will come back to that point in Sect. 9.1.3 on p. 248), both physical nodes of the cluster must be

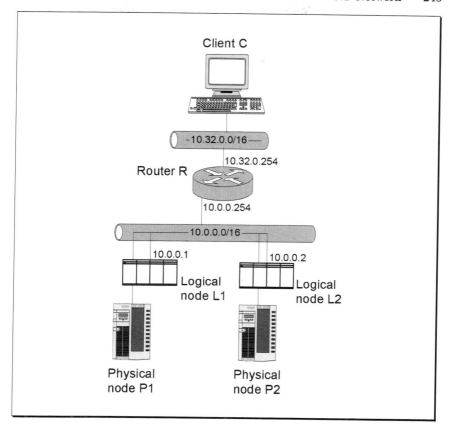

Fig. 9.5. Failover cluster on one network

on the same LAN segment, as illustrated by Fig. 9.5. It reinforces that a LAN segment itself must be redundant.

But what is a *redundant LAN segment*? Well:

- All connections are redundant.
- All switches are redundant (i.e., we duplicate switches, and not switch components).
- Redundancy management is done by software in switches and in operating systems.

Without further ado, you can have a look at Fig. 9.6 on the following page, which shows the network connection of a failover cluster on layer 2.

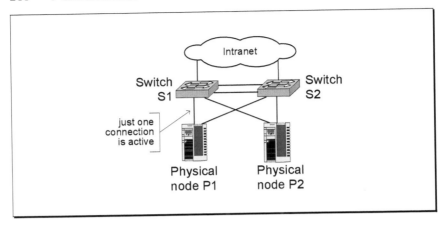

Fig. 9.6. Redundant network connection of a failover cluster

We have two switches, that have a redundant connection, i.e., two cables. Interswitch connections are described in more detail in the next section.

Both hosts are connected to either of these switches. From these connections, only one is active at a time; this is called a multipath network interface card (NIC) configuration.

This seems to be a good place for a reminder: as mentioned in Chap. 6, when failover clusters are deployed, they need to be configured to check their connectivity to other devices in the LAN segment. The default gateway is always a good candidate, but it is better to check for connectivity to more than one system. Otherwise, outage of the target system would cause failover loops.

It is also important that clusters need to send Address Resolution Protocol (ARP) broadcasts on failover. Most devices update their ARP cache when they receive a broadcast. Without that broadcast, communication partners would still have the old MAC address in the ARP cache and would not reach the logical host on the new node where it has also a new MAC address.   ∎

In the rest of this section, we address:

- Link aggregation for redundant connection of two switches
- Spanning Tree Protocol (STP) to create redundant connections of many switches.

Link Aggregation

Link aggregation is the management of the redundant connection of two switches. Without that management, every broadcast packet would result

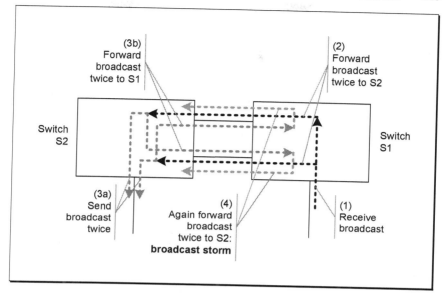

Fig. 9.7. Broadcast storm in an unmanaged duplicated switch connection

in a *broadcast storm* that would lead to outage of both switches. Let us have a look at Fig. 9.7, which illustrates the problem:

1. S1 receives a broadcast packet.
2. It forwards it to all attached ports, also to the two ports that connect it to S2.
3. S2 now receives two broadcast packets, and forwards them to all attached ports, except on the receiving port. Each packet is therefore forwarded to S1, on the other connection.
4. S1 receives them and forwards them back to S2; an endless loop is created, all the time sending broadcast packets to *all* systems that are connected to either S1 or S2. Within a short time frame, the whole LAN segment will be unusable.

Link aggregation is the IEEE standard 802.3ad that explains how to manage such duplicate connections between two systems within one LAN segment. It is also called *trunking* and creates link-specific redundancy by running both connections in parallel. In normal situations, this leads to doubled nominal bandwidth between both switches, and redundancy for the outage of one connection.

With link aggregation, the two switches know that the doubled connection should be handled as one logical connection and will not forward broadcast packets; endless loops and resulting broadcast storms are prevented.

Building-Block Approach

With link aggregation and two switches, it is possible to follow a simple network design pattern that we call the *building-block approach*: use exactly two switches per LAN segment and connect those segments by routers. The advantage of the building-block approach is that we do not need to establish redundancy for more than two switches in a LAN segment; a problem that we will cover later.

This does not mean that we need two hardware devices per LAN segment. We have already noted that all LAN information holds as well for VLANs. Here, VLANs provide a segmentation possibility that helps to create small STP domains: in VLANs, the STP is not used per VLAN and involves only those switches that are part of the VLAN. Let us assume that we have three switches and three VLANs where each of them only involves two switches – promptly we can follow the design pattern again, with three hardware devices for three LAN segments, instead of six devices (i.e., two per segment).

Building blocks can be made redundant by duplication and management on higher network layers (e.g., routing redundancy, or failover to different IP addresses by name server changes).

Spanning Tree Protocol

But the reality is usually that we do not design a network from scratch, but have to cope with existing network structures. And there the building-block approach is often not used; we encounter more than two switches per LAN segment.

And when we add a third switch to the picture, we get to another problem. Since we want to have redundant connections, we want to connect the third switch to both existing switches, otherwise outage of the middle switch would split the LAN segment and make it unusable. Figure 9.8 on the facing page illustrates the problem.

Figure 9.7 showed how broadcast storms occur with two switches that are double-connected. It is obvious that there would be similar endless loops for three switches with redundant connections as well. Just as we needed to manage the redundant connection between two switches, we also need to manage the redundant connection of more than two switches.

The aim of the management is one principle of data link layer networks:

> There must always be one and only one path at a time between two communication partners in a data link layer network. This path must not contain loops.

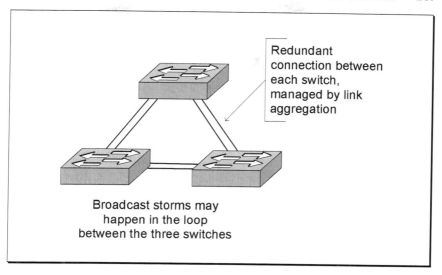

Redundant connection between each switch, managed by link aggregation

Broadcast storms may happen in the loop between the three switches

Fig. 9.8. Three switches with redundant connections

The IEEE 802.1D standard *Spanning Tree Protocol* (STP) provides this redundancy management for meshes of switches with redundant connections. Part of the IEEE 802.1 protocol suite, the 2004 edition covers multiple variants of it, the most current one is the *Rapid STP* (RSTP), which was formulated in 1998.

At the start, it selects a *root bridge* from the set of attached switches, using an election method that is guaranteed to succeed. STP selects least-cost paths to all active network components. All other switch connections are blocked, i.e., they are made inactive. Figure 9.9 illustrates this for an (admittedly trivial) example. If a switch connection fails, a blocked connection is activated to enable communication via other paths.

Recalculation of the minimum spanning tree can need up to 30 s, and during this time no network traffic will pass through involved ports, i.e., the network or the VLAN will be down in this time span for all practical purposes. The new protocol version RSTP has a faster convergence, but it can only be used if all the switches deployed in the LAN segment support it.

▶ *Inherent Problems of the Spanning Tree Protocol*

STP works with *Bridge Protocol Data Unit* (BPDU) packets that must be sent regularly. The situation can exist where no BPDU packets arrive anymore, but the switch still forwards packets, e.g., owing to CPU overload or software bugs in the switch's operating system. With unidi-

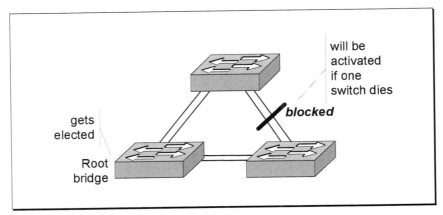

Fig. 9.9. Spanning Tree Protocol

rectional links (especially over fiber optic lines) this happens quite often. Then STP declares this switch as dead and opens a formerly blocked port. Bummer, the loop is there.

These loops block all traffic over the switches involved, and rapidly lead to the blackout of this LAN segment; nobody can transmit any data over it anymore. Therefore one should utilize only small STP domains.

The building-block approach is effectively the design pattern that takes this design objective to its logical conclusion and makes the domain so small that no loops can happen. But even when building blocks are used, the STP should be left turned on. It does not do harm, and if ever a third switch gets connected in a potential loop configuration, it will work as expected. On the other hand, turning off STP will let you detect policy infringement by addition of a third switch in a dangerous configuration immediately.

9.1.3 Default Gateway

Now that we know how to construct a highly available network on the data link layer, it is time to look beyond communication between computer systems on the same LAN segment. Ethernet networks are connected by routers. [3] One of the most basic network configurations on any server or desktop is the *default gateway*. This is a router that takes all traffic that goes beyond one's LAN segment and delivers it.

---

[3] Sometimes devices called "layer-3 switches" are used, but they are in fact just routers that are specialized for Ethernet and IP traffic.

Our task will be to provide high availability for that default gateway. Before we see how that is done, we are going to have a look at the context of this goal.

Default gateways are especially important because good network design is often seen as avoiding the need for static or dynamic routing on computer systems. Routing is the domain of special network components, be they called routers or layer-3 switches. Servers and desktops should not be concerned with routing.

That said, the default gateway is a single point of failure at first sight. When it has an outage, any communication outside the LAN segment is not possible anymore. Therefore we have reached our next task: making default gateways highly available.

We start by taking several routers. Each router gets a connection to a different switch. A router should not have multiple connections into a LAN segment, otherwise it would not know the path – and relying on the STP is dangerous, as explained before. Of course, each router connection has its own IP address.

These IP addresses must not be used at servers or clients. Several operating systems allow multiple IP addresses to be used as default gateways. But this ability is used for load balancing, initial selection during boot time, and other intentions. It cannot be used to achieve redundancy. This is not supported by operating systems and does not work.

▶ *Virtual Router Redundancy Protocol*

The canonical way to achieve redundancy of the default gateway is to use a virtual Ethernet interface, complete with a MAC and an IP address. The IP address is used as the default gateway in server and desktop configurations. In the case of a router outage, another router takes over the virtual interface and now receives the traffic that is destined for that MAC address. Figure 9.10 on the next page illustrates such a virtual interface.

Management of redundancy by a virtual Ethernet interface is done by the Virtual Router Redundancy Protocol (VRRP). Cisco devices often use the older proprietary Hot-Standby Router Protocol (HSRP), which has the same functionality. VRRP realizes a hot-standby solution. One router is the master and has the virtual interface activated. The decision of which router is the master is part of VRRP. Routers exchange heartbeats for that, via the switches. That is also needed to determine if a switch is down; then VRRP interface must be activated on the other router.

VRRP enhances the simple virtual IP interfaces that we met already with failover clusters on the operating system level: it adds virtual MAC addresses and makes switching more robust since no ARP caches must be invalidated anymore. For the case of virtual IP interfaces, an ARP broadcast is sent when failover happens, and one relies on the implementation

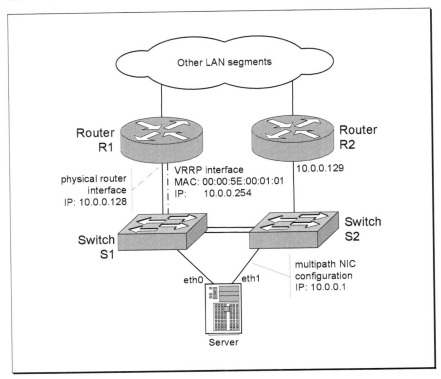

Fig. 9.10. Default gateway redundancy with a virtual Ethernet interface. *NIC* network interface card, *VRRP* Virtual Router Redundancy Protocol

of most ARP caches to invalidate a previous entry on reception of a new one. VRRP removes this dependency on implementation details.

In fact, VRRP could be used for failover clusters as well, as most server operating systems support VRRP nowadays. That simple IP interfaces are still used can be for several reasons, and we can only speculate on those – most probably "it works, why change it," which is altogether reasonable.

Availability of other components can be an input for the master selection. Often two routers are connected with vastly different bandwidth properties, e.g., a fast leased line and an ISDN dialup as shown in Fig. 9.11 on the facing page. In that situation, the slower connection shall be a backup and shall only be used in the case of failures of the leased line.

The slower line is colloquially known as the standby track connection, since Cisco's IOS uses the command standby track to configure it. Here the VRRP master selection process takes the standby configuration into

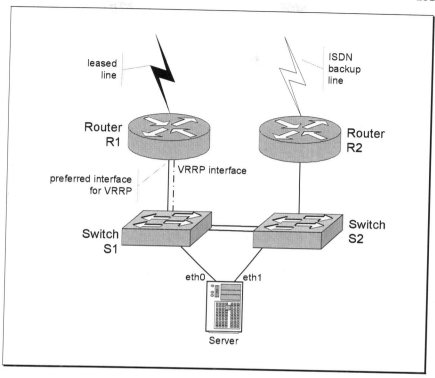

Fig. 9.11. VRRP and standby connections

account and uses preferably the router with the primary outbound connection.

▶ *Switch Optimization Is Superfluous*

There might be the temptation to coordinate the computer system's multipath NIC configuration with the active VRRP link. Let us have a look again at Fig. 9.10 on the preceding page.

When R1 has been selected as the VRRP master, one could argue that the multipath NIC configuration should choose eth0 as the active network path for the host. Then exterior packets from and to the host would just pass switch S1.

Even if such coupling of the configuration is theoretically possible, one can only advise that any thought about it be discarded. Such a configuration adds lots and lots of complexity to the configuration and therefore increases the risk of failures, just for the gain to save on (extremely fast) Ethernet frame forwarding by a switch. Robustness is one of our important design objectives, and that would be violated by such a complex configuration.

Optimization of switch usage is not needed: current switch technology is fast enough.

▸ *Passive Dynamic Routing*

Using VRRP (or HSRP from Cisco) to realize high availability for default gateways is considered best practice. Still, in some places we find another implementation method, called passive dynamic routing.

The program *routed* on Unix servers or Windows Server Multi-Protocol Routing provide the ability for servers to update their routing tables with dynamic routing protocols. These products support the *Routing Information Protocol* (RIP), which is supposed to adapt the system configuration to changes of network connectivity.

With these services activated, the two redundant routers will announce their activity and will also broadcast routing information. This information can be used by servers which will learn about the routing availability and can select their default gateway dynamically.

The servers should be configured that they do not announce routes themselves. This is known as *passive* operation and reduces the likelihood that misconfiguration of servers will influence router configuration.

There are two problems with this approach:

1. The convergence time (notification of outage and announcement of an alternative default gateway) needs up to 3 min. That is not acceptable for some high-availability requirements.
2. Desktops usually do not have RIP support. While VRRP provides high availability for desktop connectivity as well, passive dynamic routing is not available for them. This means that a router outage can separate a large group of desktops from the server and make the IT service unavailable for them.

Alternatives for RIP are dynamic routing protocols like OSPF, EIGRP, or IS-IS, which we will meet in the next section. They are also available for servers and converge faster, but are more complex to configure. Nevertheless, the desktop and robustness problems remain.

In summary, RIP or its alternatives are not *intended* to provide high availability for default gateways, but VRRP is. Misusing a protocol that is tailored for the need of router configuration for the server default gateway configuration is possible, but not recommended. It is better to stay with high-availability solutions that were designed to be so.

9.1.4 Routing in LANs and WANs

The network layer is the connection of many LAN segments into a CAN, and/or the connection to WANs. The network layer is responsible for realizing end-to-end communication between systems in such a network, whereas the data link layer only provides communication in one LAN segment. This is realized by routers or layer-3 switches. (We will handle the latter like routers – what they are, logically.)

For that the network layer introduces logical addressing by IP addresses. An IP address is called local if it is connected to the same Ethernet, and remote if it is not. Each connected system has a routing table that tells if an IP address is local, i.e., if it is connected to the same Ethernet, or if it is remote. For local IP addresses, ARP is used to determine the associated MAC address and then the information can be sent directly on the data link layer. For remote IP addresses, the routing table has an associated gateway's IP address that must be reachable. (Usually, that gateway has a local IP address as well.) The packet is then sent to the gateway that will determine a communication path for eventual delivery.

Section 9.1.3 on p. 248 explained already that computer systems should avoid large routing tables. It is best if they have just the knowledge of which IP addresses are local and the default gateway. That way, all routing configuration is delegated to the routing infrastructure, where it belongs. This is also the case that we assume in the rest of this section.

From experience, we can say that the network layer with the IP protocol suite is a mature technology that provides very good availability if properly set up. Systems can run for years without any downtime. On the other hand, if there is an outage, the available mechanisms – described later – do not have quick remedies. A network outage usually takes several minutes longer to repair and most often leads to a major outage.

That said, let us see next how we can provide a highly available infrastructure within a LAN, then we will address WANs.

Routing in LANs

As in the data link layer, we also need redundancy in the network layer. It is not acceptable to have a router outage cause disruption of IT services for many end users. Therefore all communication paths between LAN segments must be redundant; there must always be (at least) two ways to send a message from one computer system to another.

Network design now has the task to select routers, connections, and configuration in a way that:

1. Routers have multiple paths to reach a communication destination.
2. They are capable choosing an appropriate path from the multitude of available paths.

To achieve these goals, router configuration enables a *dynamic routing protocol* (also called *Interior Gateway Protocol*, IGP) that determines connectivity of other routers and allows the "best communication path" to a destination to be determined. Several such protocols exist:

Routing Information Protocol (RIP): The oldest method for routing information exchange. It is easy to configure and light on resources – but these are the only two advantages that it has. It does not scale well and needs a notoriously long time to converge in the case of changes. It is better to use it only in very rare circumstances.

We have met RIP already as a possible method to achieve high availability for default gateways, where it was also not recommended. Tongue-in-cheek, it is best to take the other meaning of that acronym and let the protocol rest in peace.

Open Shortest Path First (OSPF): The modern state-of-the-art routing protocol, tuned for IPv4 traffic. Bad link detection and rerouting is resolved in 45 s.

OSPF is very complex to handle. The risk of failures in network design is quite high; it is easy to create single points of failure by logical (mis-)design, even if physical redundancy is available.

This protocol is the most widely used IGP by Internet service providers (ISPs), but this is slowly changing to IS-IS. It is also partly used in company networks, though there EIGRP is also prevalent.

Enhanced Interior Gateway Routing Protocol (EIGRP): A proprietary protocol by Cisco that combines simplicity of protocols like RIP with the quick convergence time of protocols like OSPF or IS-IS.

This protocol is in wide use in company environments where the whole router environment is based on Cisco devices. The chances are good of finding skilled personal who have experience either in EIGRP or in OSPF, or in both.

Intermediate System to Intermediate System (IS-IS): A modern routing protocol that has a huge range of tuning options. With them, performance, efficiency, and availability can be maximized. It is also more flexible than OSPF, e.g., IPv6 support was easily added.

IS-IS is used predominantly by large ISPs. It is less well known, and documentation in the popular press is scarce. This might change if IPv6 wins more ground though. It is also more difficult to find staff with knowledge of IS-IS than of OSPF or EIGRP.

All of these routing protocols can be used to realize highly available routing infrastructures within one CAN. They are not sufficient to realize routing for several CANs, as they only provide dynamic routing within an administrative domain – for practical purposes this means outside a WAN.

All these protocols have the potential for error situations: they are not bullet-proof. Recomputation of routing information is quite computationally intensive. If a system goes down, all neighbors need to recompute their routing information. If it comes up again shortly afterwards, another recomputation is in order. This can lead to an overload situation where a router is only engaged in routing topology computation and is considered down itself by its neighbors, leading to recomputations there. After it has finished the computation it is seen to be up, leading again to recomputation at many neighbors – you get the picture. This is a known phenomenon that is called *routing meltdown*.

In summary, routing in LANs is a very mature technology and can be configured to realize highly available corporate networks. Nevertheless, failure potentials remain and major outages can happen owing to network errors.

WAN for Corporate Networks

Many companies have several sites and need WAN technology to connect these sites.

WANs are a notorious hard and complex area when it comes to high availability. With current technology:

- WANs are very stable.
- Availability is very good, but you have to shop around to find a provider that realizes SLAs in the 99.99 or 99.999% regions.
- Small glitches can be protected against.
- Medium outages can take a WAN connection down for half a day.
- Large failures can happen every few years, and may lead to major outages up of to 1 week; in the case of physical disasters, even longer.

But the main problem with high-availability requirements for WANs is that they are almost impossible to guarantee. The question remains open if these multiple connections are really independent or if they share some single point of failure.

For some it comes as surprise that even network service providers that rent leased lines often do not have enough information to answer this question. Even if the line is a real physical cable, its physical path is often not known for longer distances. Then it might very well be that it shares space in the earth or crosses a river at the same place as the other, supposedly independent cable.

Especially the last mile, i.e., the distance between the last switch site and the company's ground, is often a single point of failure – there are only so many places where one is allowed to put cables in or over public ground. The proverbial digger that destroys cable in the ground is still one of the largest dangers for highly available Internet connections – such an accident will happen very rarely, but if it happens it might lead to outages that need days or even weeks to repair.

Another problem for high-availability WAN design is the ongoing virtualization of our network backbones. Layer is added on layer, and dynamic resource allocation results in the impossibility of naming the real physical network infrastructure that is used potentially. This makes analysis and risk assessment impossible to carry out. Sad to say, service level agreements (SLAs) with network service providers do not help much either. There are many cases known where the service provider simply agreed that they did not meet the SLAs and they paid the contract penalty. But this will not help our business if we depend on that WAN connection; such contract penalties are usually not high enough to cover all our losses.

Redundancy in corporate WANs is created with the same methods as for routing in LANs. Namely, an IGP like OSPF, EIGRP, or IS-IS, more seldom also RIP, is used. These protocols are created to handle WAN connections.

WAN Connections to The Internet

Nowadays many business processes depend on a working Internet connection; such connectivities have become mission-critical for all except very small businesses. Internet connections are obtained from ISPs, who will also give out public IP addresses that are routed to our network perimeter.

Getting a good ISP is mainly a trust issue. Before we mentioned that we have to shop around to get SLAs above 99.99% (measured yearly). That is not to say that there are no companies that do not sell you contracts with such SLAs – there are even providers who will sell you a contract with an SLA of 100%, which clearly cannot be promised by anybody. These kinds of contracts have factored in the fact that the providers will pay penalties for nonperformance in situations when they do not achieve their contractual obligations. But we are not interested in contract penalties, we are interested in availability!

Therefore, many companies want to get two or more independent Internet connections and realize their redundancy themselves. First of all, we need to mention that there is a big risk involved that the connections are not as independent as they seem; we mentioned that earlier. But let us first describe summarily how such a redundant connection is made.

Redundancy for outgoing traffic is easy to realize. The outgoing router is usually our default gateway; we have explained redundancy for default gateways via VRRP already in Sect. 9.1.3 on p. 248. In fact, it is more common that the network perimeter is protected by firewalls, but that is not a big difference as you will see in Sect. 9.1.5.

Redundancy for incoming traffic is the problem. There are two ways to realize that:

1. Almost all incoming traffic is (or can be) based on Internet fully qualified domain names, i.e., the communication partner looks up the IP address of our company in the DNS. In the case of an outage, we can publish other IP addresses, and then a different communication path will be chosen.

This approach must be carefully implemented. Normally, DNS information is heavily cached. We have to reduce the *time to live* (TTL) value of the DNS records to a few minutes, to prevent caching and to give the opportunity to change addresses. This also implies that the DNS servers must be located somewhere outside our own corporate network, e.g., at the provider's location. Automated update possibilities for the DNS configuration of those outsourced servers must be available that are also functional in the face of an Internet connection outage.

2. The other approach is that we put ourselves in the role of a small ISP, get our own IP address allocation, and make several contracts as a *downstream ISP* with other providers.

   The IP protocol suite is designed to "route around problems" in WAN connectivity. On the Internet, the *Border Gateway Protocol* (BGP) is used to achieve proper routing between administrative domains, i.e., between different companies or institutions. In particular, BGP is mainly used for management of routing between providers; thus, it will also be used to manage routing for the redundant "upstream connections."

Direct WAN Connections to Other Companies

Colloquially called Extranet connections, it is often the case that corporate networks of business partners are linked via a WAN connection.

Such connections are sometimes dedicated lines, typically when a smaller business is tightly integrated into the business processes of a larger business. Such kinds of connections are especially used in manufacturing environments for suppliers or dealers.

For most other connections with business partners, site-to-site VPNs over the Internet are used nowadays. They have a better cost-to-functionality ratio for the restricted traffic they have to shoulder. Since they are made over the Internet, a redundant Internet connection is mandatory, as explained before. In addition, the VPN servers must be made redundant as well on both sides; good clustering capabilities are a feature of enterprise-class VPN solutions.

For less capable (but also much cheaper) solutions we will utilize failover clusters and will settle with the abortion of VPN connections from time to time. This is not as bad as it sounds at first; such aborts are very seldom in practice and the IP protocols beneath support reconnects transparently.

In any case, either with dedicated lines or with VPN connections, Extranet links are part of the corporate network's perimeter and are therefore secured by firewalls. In addition, it is very probable that both companies use private IP addresses in their CANs and we have to utilize network address translation (NAT) for the connection. The next section will address the possibilities to achieve high availability while using these technologies as well.

9.1.5 Firewalls and Network Address Translation

Firewalls are devices to increase security at the network perimeter. They are utilized at the connection to the Internet, in the Extranet to business partners, and for special departments in the Intranet that need higher protection and separation. They control access to and from the services on the enclosed network.

NAT is a method to map internal private IP addresses from and to external public IP addresses. It is utilized when two networks are connected that use incompatible addressing schemes. Most often it is deployed for connection of company networks to the Internet: company networks often utilize IP address ranges that are not used on the Internet (e.g., 10.0.0.0/8) and that must be mapped to public Internet addresses for every Internet connection. Such mapping also provides increased security.

Firewalls often provide NAT as one feature. They are deployed at the network perimeter and analyze IP packets anyhow and NAT is solely needed there; thus, they are the obvious place to realize it. Furthermore, both technologies have in common that they need information from and about the IP traffic to realize their functionality. This deserves more detailed explanation.

Firewalls

Firewalls come in three different flavors:

1. **Packet filters** are the most basic category of firewalls. They feature an *access control list* (ACL) that tells which IP connections are allowed to and from the network. That ACL lists source and destination IP packet characteristics and an associated action like *accept*, *reject*, or *drop*.

   The IP packet characteristics are mainly IP addresses, protocol type (e.g., TCP or UDP), and port numbers (i.e., service designations for the destination packet), but also include IP options and other information. Many packet filters have a very limited ability of connection tracking that allows them to identify TCP packets that belong to a specific TCP session, or they have heuristics to associate UDP response packets with UDP requests.[4]

   Packet filters offer the least security and the best performance. They are the only firewall technology that can operate almost at wirespeed.

---

[4] UDP has no session concept, so it is not possible in general without knowledge of the application protocol.

Nowadays, packet filters are mainly used in appliances for the SOHO and private markets. Enterprises use them only in situations where performance is of utmost importance and where stateful inspection firewalls are not fast enough.

2. **Stateful inspection** is the current mainstream of firewalls. In principal these firewalls work like packet filters, but also follow the communication's content. They have knowledge about application-level IP protocols and track connections if requests and responses stay within the constraints of the respective protocol, i.e., they observe communication between client and server. They will abort the connection if a mismatch is detected.

   While content-level checks are potentially possible with stateful inspection technology, they are seldom implemented with that category of firewall. For most products, that would be difficult to implement anyhow.

   Stateful inspection firewalls are fast enough for typical WAN connection speeds.[5] Owing to their protocol checks they have also reasonable security, and thus provide a reasonable trade-off between security and performance.

3. **Application gateways** or *proxies* utilize a different concept. They intercept the communication on the application level – the client talks to them instead of to the server; they submit the sanitized requests to the server themselves. They handle all protocol functionality and allow checks to be realized on the content level.

   Proxies can realize both transparent and nontransparent firewalling, i.e., the client might see that it is talking to the firewall and will never know about the server; or the client thinks it is talking to the server but the communication is intercepted and captured.

   Application gateways are the most secure firewall technology, but also the slowest one; therefore, they are seldom deployed, and most of the time are used for email and for high-security installations. It remains to be seen if that will change owing to the influx of Web services and the associated increased need to check communication content.

All firewall categories have one thing in common: they have an internal state that depends on past traffic, and they work only if they can see all traffic from a communication. For application gateways and stateful inspection firewalls this is clear: they cannot check content and/or protocol conformance without access to the communication's state and past. But even for packet filters this is needed in practice. Most packet filter ACLs rely on connection tracking to express rules like "accept all TCP packets of established sessions" or "accept UDP packets that are with high probability DNS responses."

---

[5] Sometimes they are said to work at wirespeed, but experience shows that they do so only in packet-filtering-only mode, without protocol checks.

This means that firewalls are inherently state-based – luckily they do not have a persistent state. We meet the usual gotchas: redundant devices can be used to recover overall functionality easily, but might abort sessions.

Packet Rewriting by NAT

IP addresses are a scarce resource. Many IP address blocks are in use already and there are very few companies who can use public Internet addresses on all their computers. Instead, companies use internal addresses on their corporate network that must not be used outside.

To do this properly, a set of address ranges has been set aside; they are called the *private IP addresses*: 10.0.0.0/8, 172.16.0.0/12, 192.168.0.0/16, and 169.254.0.0/16. These addresses will not be allocated to any company and institution; they are not valid on the Internet and must not be routed there.

When a computer system on the corporate network wants to communicate with a system on the Internet, or with a business partner's system on the Extranet, its IP address must not appear in the packets. For example, when the local system has an IP address of 10.1.2.3, that address must not be sent to the Internet. The receiving system would not know how to return the response, as this is an invalid Internet address. Similarly, if an outside system wants to send a request to an internal system, it cannot use the internal address. For that communication, a valid public Internet address must exist.

NAT rewrites packets to map private IP addresses to public ones and vice versa, i.e., in outgoing IP packets, private addresses like 10.1.2.3 are substituted with public addresses like 194.128.225.190. When the response packet to 194.128.225.190 arrives, the address is translated back to 10.1.2.3. Similarly, an incoming request to 66.54.38.9 might be translated to the new destination address 10.20.5.3, and response packets are rewritten too. Figure 9.12 on the facing page illustrates that behavior.

Although NAT is widely deployed, it also has its share of problems. In particular, there exist several application protocols that need end-to-end connectivity and knowledge of true source and destination addresses. These kinds of protocols (notably IPsec to create VPN and SIP to establish Voice-over-Internet Protocol, VoIP, connections) do not work without adaptations in a NAT environment.

On the other hand, using private IP addresses internally that are not routed on the Internet also brings advantages in terms of security. This means that only systems where we set up explicit incoming NAT mappings can be connected from the Internet – in the unsecure and hostile Internet environment of today, that is an advantage that should not be underestimated.

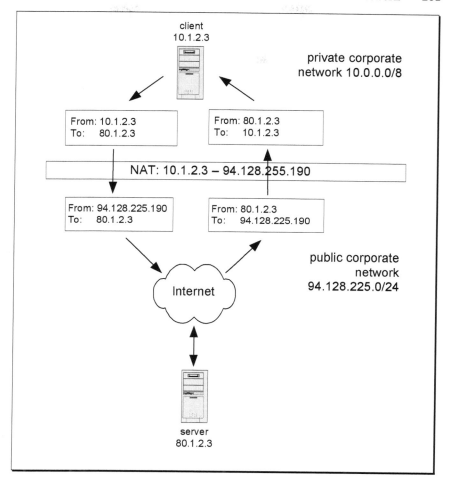

Fig. 9.12. Principles of network address translation (*NAT*)

▸ *NAT Categories*

Important for our high availability design is the question of how the mode of operation influences implementation of redundancy. There are three different categories of NAT that all have consequences for our high-availability setup:

1. **Static NAT** is the 1 : 1 mapping of internal and external addresses. Every NATed internal address is always replaced by the same external address. The port numbers of TCP or UDP connections are not changed. Static NAT supports both outgoing and incoming traf-

fic. This method is sometimes used for a limited number of computer systems in demilitarized zones.

Static NAT needs no knowledge of traffic history. It does not keep any state information about the connection, but simply rewrites addresses in every packet that needs it. Therefore, from a high-availability view, it is the easiest NAT technology when it comes to providing redundancy. For static NAT, the same redundancy methods as with routers can be used.

2. **Dynamic NAT** is the $n : m$ mapping of internal and external addresses and can only be used for outgoing connections. There is a pool of available external addresses. When an outgoing connection is initiated, an unused address from that pool is allocated and used for address rewriting of that connection. Port numbers of TCP or UDP connections are not changed.[6] This method is only available in a few firewall products and is not widely used.

   Dynamic NAT has a state where it keeps knowledge of current address mappings. Initiation and termination of sessions change that mapping. If this state information is not replicated, sessions will be aborted in the case of failure of the NAT device (i.e., the firewall or the router).

3. **Overloading NAT** is the $n : 1$ mapping of internal addresses to one external address and can only be used for outgoing addresses. This method is also called *port address translation* (PAT, mainly in Cisco-dominated environments), or *network address port translation* (NAPT), *hiding NAT* (in Checkpoint firewalls), or *IP masquerading* (mainly in open-source firewalls). The names PAT and NAPT refer to the need to rewrite port numbers in connections as well – the ports are used to identify the internal address that must be used for response packets. Overloading NAT is the most often used NAT method for Internet connections.

   Like dynamic NAT, overloading NAT needs to keep track of established connections. The only difference is that it maps internal addresses to source port numbers and vice versa. As well, overloading NAT has the danger of session aborts in the case of device failures.

As we can see, both firewalls and other NAT devices keep state information about past traffic and tracking sessions. There is no persistent state though – if we can accept session aborts, a device restart or a replacement device will enable the functionality as before. Since all NAT problems also exist for firewalls and most NAT-enabling devices are firewalls anyhow, we will use just "firewall" in the following to denote both types of systems.

---

[6] Dynamic NAT needs a stateful inspection firewall or an application gateway to support UDP communication. Otherwise it does not know about the end of sessions.

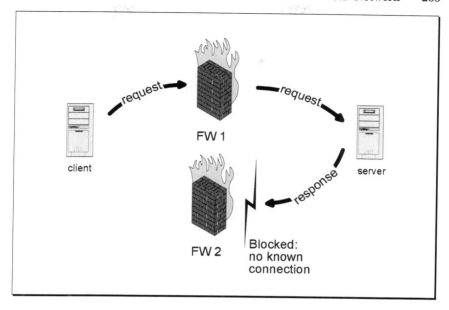

Fig. 9.13. Asymmetric routing and firewalls

Problems with Routing

Firewalls always need to see the complete traffic of any connection. This
is obvious for most NATed traffic, stateful inspection firewalls, or application gateways. But also packet filters usually need to look at the whole
traffic owing to their connection tracking.

When a network design includes *asymmetric routing*, firewalls will not
work anymore. Asymmetric routing is the situation where the communication path from system A to system B is different from that for the traffic
from system B to system A, as illustrated in Fig. 9.13.

The two firewalls F1 and F2 each see only half of the traffic and cannot
track any connection; therefore no response packet will ever be returned
to system B – F2 will block it as no session initiation has been seen.

This also means that any high-availability solution cannot just place
two firewalls in the net and let them both work without regard to routing. Their configuration and also their operations must be tuned to work
together. If dynamic routing protocols are used, it must be assured that
no asymmetric routing situation occurs, otherwise the service will not be
available anymore.

Firewall Clusters

First of all, firewalls can have internal redundancies for hardware components. This is similar to small servers and routers: if the firewall has a disk, disk redundancy is the most important. After that, fans and power supplies fail most often and redundancy should be added for them. Last, network cards can be made redundant by link aggregation or multipath configurations. More internal redundancy is questionable and often reduces robustness beyond the gains that it brings.

Therefore we want to have redundancy on the firewall device level too. Two or more firewalls are used to provide redundant and secured communication paths between computer systems, just like routers are made redundant as well.

Most often, firewalls also deliver functionality that is normally the realm of routers. The redundancy method from routers, VRRP, that we learned about in Sect. 9.1.3, is thus supported in many firewall products. This leads to installations with a hot-standby system, where one firewall is active and the other is just running idly along until an outage happens and the backup firewall takes over.

As so often, most firewall clusters lose sessions during takeover. Since they are stateful and state information is not persistent, the new cluster node will not have knowledge of sessions and will abort them, i.e., it will drop incoming packets. The clients will have to reestablish connections after a failover.

Some high-end firewall products also provide load-sharing functionality for clusters and avoid the session abort at failures. There multiple firewalls are active at the same time. Session states are shared between the nodes of such a firewall cluster by multicast messages, typically over a separate redundant network. So all nodes of that cluster have the same state – packets of a session will be processed by an arbitrarily chosen node anyhow, and in the case of an outage there is simply one cluster node less that will process packets, without loss of functionality.

9.1.6 Network Design for Disaster Recovery

The network design is usually not something a disaster-recovery project can decide alone; it must be coordinated with the networking department. There are three realistic design patterns that you can utilize.

Primary and Backup Sites Are in One LAN Segment

If the backup site is in the same town, it is often possible to have a single switched network over both the primary and the backup sites. Between the primary and the backup servers there are no routers; they are in the same segment. In modern network setups, VLANs are used to structure the network further.

In that case, the IP addresses of the primary server can be moved to the backup server in the case of disaster. Of course, such a switch, i.e., turning on the IP service addresses on the backup server, will part of preparation for disaster recovery. For the clients, there will be no changes in configuration; they will work almost immediately. (Their ARP caches might need to be updated first, but the switch to the backup server needs longer than ARP cache lifetimes anyhow.)

There is a drawback that we have to take into account: the service addresses on primary and backup systems must not be activated at the same time. This would immediately lead to IP address conflicts and neither the primary nor the backup system would be functional afterwards. In fact, this is a failure scenario that blocks both systems and is therefore a single point of failure in this design approach.

Separate LANs for Backup and Primary Sites, Move Addresses

The primary and backup sites might be in different LANs, where routers connect them. This might be one router, or several ones; there might be VPNs between the primary and backup sites. Such site-to-site VPNs are typical network infrastructure setups if primary and backup sites are wider apart and if no exclusively leased lines exist between backup and remote sites – they are the most cost-effective way to integrate several sites into one corporate network. Other reasons for different LAN segments are the avoidance of complete network outages by switch loops, as explained in Sect. 9.1.2. By separating primary and backup sites into (at least) two LAN segments, we confine any network outage to the respective site and can still work at the other one.

In the disaster case, we can move the IP service addresses from the primary to the backup site when we change the router configuration. New host routings and proxy ARPs need to be created for such a setup, but that is an easy configuration and the change can be done quickly.

This approach also has the advantage that we can activate the IP service addresses on the backup system without causing the primary system to fail – as long as there are no clients at the backup site that want to use the primary system.

The main disadvantage of that approach is the need for reconfigurations by the network group in a disaster case. This introduces another organizational dependency that may complicate recovery in the disaster case.

We might be tempted to change routing automatically by OSPF or any other dynamic routing scheme that is available on server systems via routing daemons. We advise against such configurations, as experience has shown that they are very error prone and that one does *not* want to let server configurations influence network routing.

Separate LANs for Backup and Primary Sites, Different Addresses

When the primary and backup sites are in different LAN segments, the traditional approach for the disaster case is to change the IP service addresses and let the clients access the service with the new addresses.

This assumes that a network name service – most probably DNS – is used. If any client has the service system name to IP address mapping hardcoded, or uses the IP addresses directly, this approach will not work.

Changing DNS addresses has its peculiarities as well. In a typical DNS infrastructure, we have a master server, several secondary servers, and maybe some caching servers. Changes will be propagated from master to secondary servers almost immediately, but caching servers will catch up only after the respective DNS entry has expired. Most clients also cache DNS entries locally and do not request them anew for every IP connection. Many applications also cache DNS entries (aka host lookups). The expiration of DNS entries is controlled by an attribute of the DNS entry, the *time-to-live* (TTL) duration.

If you use that approach, the DNS guys (most probably also from the network department) must agree to set the TTL of the primary service names short enough that they expire from all caches during the time that is needed for a switch to the backup system. When the backup system is up and running, caching servers and clients will have requested the new IP addresses in the meantime – if it was changed quickly enough! – and will use the new system. Shorter TTLs for DNS entries also mean more DNS traffic on your LAN, though this should be negligible for current enterprise-class intranets.

Of course, this approach introduces the organizational dependency that we need a DNS configuration change quite early after a disaster has been declared. Otherwise, the change will not have propagated by the time the backup system is ready and the clients will not use the system.

You should also be aware that there have been problems in the correct implementation of DNS expiration in caching servers and clients in the past. There are still errors in applications that simply cache the host name lookup result – the TTL is not part of that lookup, so it cannot be cached. While we cannot name deficient products here, it is well known that after DNS changes in the Internet, the old site will be accessed long after the DNS entries have expired, owing to erroneous caching behavior. Such error conditions might occur on your Intranet installation as well. As said, caching in the operating system and DNS is *not* error-prone. Other intermediate servers or applications are usually the culprit.

Therefore you need to test this design approach seriously before you engage in it – or you must be able to restart all intermediate servers and clients, to be able to get rid of cached DNS data.

9.2 Infrastructure Services

It is hard to define exactly what infrastructure services are. For the purpose of this book, we use that term to mean services that must be available to use an application, but that are not part of that application. That meaning is not precise, since there will be always "gray areas" where it is a value judgment if they belong to the application or not. In fact, quite often that decision is not a technical one, but is made for organizational and project reasons.

Nevertheless, we can name a set of services that are commonly considered to be infrastructure services. This list is not exhaustive and serves as guidance. Most of those services are actually used by applications and are not end-user services. The exceptions to that are the authentication services that are used for user login.

DHCP service	Network boot service
DNS	Windows name service
LDAP directory service	Active Directory
Kerberos authentication service	Network Information Service (NIS)
Time service	Log service
Print service	Email service

In the rest of this section, we will look at a selection of these services. They have been chosen to provide prototypical solution patterns that can be utilized for other services as well:

- **DHCP servers** are used for basic desktop configuration in most companies; they are covered in Sect. 9.2.1.
- **DNS servers** are essential for any network usage, both on the Internet and on intranets and are presented in Sect. 9.2.2.
- **Directory servers** and variants thereof are handled in Sect. 9.2.3; many of them are mainly used for user login.

Please note that network file services are absent from the list and are handled in Sect. 5.2.3, since, for this book, they are more related to storage than to infrastructure services.

9.2.1 Dynamic Host Configuration Protocol (DHCP)

Desktop systems in companies are of less use if they are not connected to the company's network. Without that, no network shares can be accessed, almost no applications work, no email or Internet access is possible, and no backup is made. For that, desktop systems need some specific information bits: first of all their network configuration, but also host name, domain name, name servers, directory servers, log server, print servers, time servers, and others.

For most companies, it is of interest that their desktop systems are centrally configured. Having the system configuration of all desktops at one central place has the big advantage that it can be changed as needed; one does not need to (physically or virtually) walk around and maintain each desktop manually. Instead, all desktop configuration data will be fetched by the systems from that central information base.

Most of the time, such configuration is needed during system boot. But sometimes desktop systems are very long running, login times may be up to months, then the configuration might need to be refreshed to reflect changes in the central configuration information. There is also the situation that a notebook is attached to a company network anew and that it should now be reconfigured to fit into the company's configuration. Technology for system configuration from a central information store must fulfill these use cases as well.

DHCP is an Internet standard protocol that supplies such a method. A system broadcasts a DHCP request on the network and a DHCP server replies with the system's configuration. The standard also spells out what are possible configuration options and the structure of the reply; it thus restricts the potential variations of configuration information.[7] The DHCP client interprets the reply and sets or alters its configuration accordingly.

The configuration can be both dynamically allocated from a pool of available resources and statically assigned. As an example, a desktop either has a fixed IP address or it can be dynamically assigned one from a pool of available IP addresses. For the static assignment, the desktop's MAC address is used to look up the configuration data in the central information store. Dynamic resource allocation implies that the DHCP server has to keep track of assignments and has a persistent state.

The ability to dynamically assign IP addresses is also used by many installations and allows for easy integration of laptops and other mobile systems. When dynamic IP address allocation is used, the DHCP service is usually coupled with DNS – then an address allocation also updates the DNS database dynamically. This is not only relevant for name lookups, but also for reverse lookup, the association of IP addresses with host names. Some servers demand that their clients resolve their IP addresses properly; coupling DHCP with dynamic DNS updates is one possibility to realize that.

---

[7] That said, most implementations use only a few of the many configuration possibilities, most of them network-related.

In contrast, DHCP is seldom used for server systems. Server systems usually demand static configuration and are manually configured and maintained anyhow. Then the advantage of a central configuration server does not play out; on the contrary, it is frustrating to have the server system configuration suddenly at two places, one part local and one part on the DHCP server. Nevertheless the network configuration is sometimes delivered by DHCP – this is usually the case if the network is managed by a particular department and that department wants to control network configuration itself and does not want to put that in the hands of system administrators.

With the same line of argument, DHCP should not be used at all for highly available servers. For one, it adds another dependency to another system that we should avoid for the sake of simplicity and robustness. Second, it is not possible to do high-availability configurations like multipath NICs or other redundancy options (e.g., link aggregation) properly with DHCP.

DHCP was selected as an infrastructure service example because it is a service where its failure might render all clients unusable. Such a service outage can have disastrous consequences and can turn a server failure into a major outage of a whole site. Therefore one is well advised to provide a highly available DHCP installation.

There exist many products that support DHCP. These products have very different implementations and there is no single high-availability approach that works for all of them. The two most important products are Internet Systems Consortium's (ISC) DHCPD and Microsoft's Active Directory. High availability for the latter is described on p. 281ff.

Case Study: High Availability for ISC's DHCPD

On Unix systems, the most often used DHCP server is DHCPD from ISC. It is open-source software that is widely used to provide DHCP service in companies.

It allows static and dynamic allocation of IP addresses and also computer host names. Pooling of configurations is also well supported, which allows different configuration policies for different classes of desktops, or for different departments, to be established.

The DHCPD configuration is traditionally stored in files. Current releases also allow the configuration to be stored on an LDAP directory server or on database back-end severs. There are several reasons why we may want to go down the LDAP road, not the least being that we can use LDAP as a back-end database for other services as well, in particular for DNS and for authentication (logging in). This allows the handling of all kinds of configuration information – not only system configuration – at one central place. Of course, then the LDAP infrastructure must be highly available as well, in addition to the DHCP service.

DHCPD has state information, namely, the database of dynamically allocated IP addresses. This is called the *lease database* and is stored in a file. To make dynamic DNS work, it is expected that this database must be preserved in the case of a server outage.

High availability for DHCP should be supported by accompanying client configurations. It is not sufficient to make our servers highly available, the objective is an end-to-end view of high availability for this service.

A well-known issue is default DHCP client configurations that are meant for easy setup, and that do not live up to the demands of company environments. Several DHCP client configuration support by default a technology that is called *Zeroconf* by Apple or *Automatic Private IP Addressing* (APIPA) by Microsoft. This technology is intended for home and small office networks and should create a usable IP network configuration without any servers.

If a Windows or an Apple client does not get a response from a DHCP server, it gives itself an IP address from the 169.254.0.0/16 network. This is not only so during boot time – when a DHCP server is not reachable for some time and a desktop cannot renew its address lease, it also falls back to such an address. This is not sensible behavior in enterprise environments, where other parts of the DHCP configuration are needed as well (e.g., routing and name servers). Here the automatic IP address configuration should be shut off.

This means that during boot time, the desktop will wait until a DHCP server is reachable and will only be usable afterwards. Since we will provide a highly available DHCP server infrastructure, that is not a big problem; maybe the user will have to wait a little longer during boot time. But this configuration advice additionally has the big advantage that desktops that *have* an address configuration – and that will be the majority of them – will not lose it. This is because most clients today simply keep their IP address if they cannot renew their address lease; they are not immediately affected by a server outage.

Thus, any corporate network with more than ten or 20 desktops on it is better served by turning off APIPA and establishing highly available DHCP servers. It is also simple: there are two options that we can choose from to realize high availability for DHCPD:

1. Failover cluster in active/active mode: ISC's DHCPD has a built-in facility for clustering with an active/active model. In DHCPD parlance, this is called a failover load-balancing configuration, i.e., both cluster nodes will have the same state information and both will answer requests from clients. State synchronization between several servers, i.e., exchange of changes to the lease database, is a capability of DHCPD.

The server configuration must name the other peers and must designate one of the servers as "primary" and the other as "secondary." The configuration is a matter of six lines in the DHCPD configuration file. The main problem is afterwards that the configuration of both cluster nodes has a shared part that must be kept synchronized – and that there is no built-in support for that synchronization. Best practice is to maintain and test that shared configuration part on some other system and deploy it with *rsync* to the production servers. Of course, if the configuration is stored in an LDAP server, that discussion is moot; then the LDAP server must provide the high availability for the DHCPD configuration.

2. Failover cluster in active/passive mode: We can use standard failover cluster technology on operating system level, as described in Sect. 6.1. The lease database file and configuration files must be on a file system that belongs to that logical node and must be switched to the backup system in the case of an outage.

   The lease database is not cached and is also changed in a way that makes corruptions very unlikely. Therefore standard cluster technology can be used.

9.2.2 Domain Name Service (DNS)

DNS is a ubiquitous service on any IP network. It is responsible for mapping host names to IP addresses and vice versa. In addition it provides information for email routing on the Internet, but this functionality is normally not needed on corporate networks.

Whenever any of your clients wants to access a server, e.g., email. example.com, it uses this name and needs a service that maps that name to an IP address. DNS is that service. DNS puts host names into hierarchically structured domains and assigns responsibility for domains or parts of them to DNS servers. Servers that are responsible for a domain are called *authoritative* for that domain.[8] In this way, DNS servers form a big distributed database of name mappings.

But DNS does not only provide names to address mapping – reverse lookup is the often overseen feature. It gives computers the ability to look up a name for an IP address. In fact, many services look up names for addresses, e.g., for logging. If no proper DNS server is authoritative for that IP address range, such a query waits until a timeout happens. An authoritative server can answer immediately with a name or with a "name unknown" response.

---

[8] That is a shortened explanation; in reality name servers are responsible for parts of domains, so-called *zones*. But that distinction is not relevant for our book, so we use domain and zone interchangeably.

In practice, timeouts are a larger problem than unresolved addresses. While one can often live with the inability to have a name for an address, waiting for lots of timeouts just for the sake of logging can have a detrimental effect on application performance, i.e., proper reverse lookup setup is needed to get performing and available applications. It is necessary to have respective definitions for all internal IP address ranges on one's internal DNS server.

With a service that is as important as DNS, it is quite clear that we want protection against outages of our DNS servers. As always, the failure can happen on many levels: the server system itself can crash, the software can have errors, and the system administrators can make errors when they manage the DNS data. The last situation is especially problematic as one error in the data can make a whole range of applications unusable. Protection against this failure is usually done by creating special tools that help to check company-specific rules before new configurations are activated. Outages that are caused by remaining errors are categorized as major outages and disaster recovery must be used if they happen.

Clients are usually configured to use a set of DNS servers; configuration happens either by DHCP or manually. Then they just query their DNS servers one after the other. DNS queries are connectionless, so there is a timeout after which the client assumes that the server is not reachable, and the same query is sent to the next server in the list. This implies that we get severe delays when the first DNS server on the client configuration list is down.

It should be noted that the DNS server has the responsibility to find out the answer to the query. That often means that it has to connect servers with the *authoritative information*, issue the query to them, and pass back the answer to the client.

A special case for each company is the question of whether they allow resolution of Internet host and domain names. For instance, do we allow any client on the company's network to resolve www.google.com? The answer depends on the policy of outbound Internet connections. If all Internet connections are done over proxies, resolving Internet names is not sensible for generic clients; this is just done at the proxy. But if all clients can access the Internet, then Internet names must be resolved and the internal DNS servers have to be able to send DNS queries to the Internet too.

It is an important distinction that the DNS system has two purposes in any network:

1. A query infrastructure where any computer system can ask for name-to-address or address-to-name mapping
2. A publishing infrastructure where one can establish these mappings

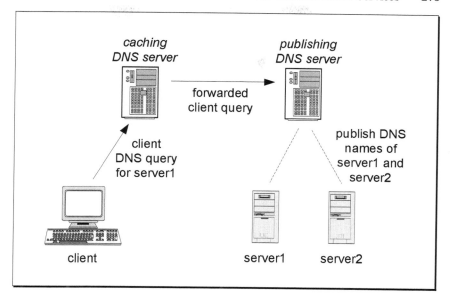

Fig. 9.14. Querying and publishing DNS information with separate servers

As Fig. 9.14 shows the servers for these two purposes may not be the same. The query infrastructure might be supplied by *caching DNS servers* that are not authoritative for any domain, but are just there for clients to answer their queries. They pass queries to publishing servers and send back the responses. As the name "caching server" implies, they also cache responses to lessen the load on the network and on the publishing servers. The complete contents of these servers are in memory; they do not have a state on any disk. They also suffer no loss of functionality if they are aborted and started anew: the cache will be empty and will be filled up over time.

In contrast, *publishing DNS servers* are able to give authoritative answers about a domain. These are also the servers that process update requests for dynamic entries from DHCP servers. Static content of these servers is stored somewhere on disk. Windows DNS server usually utilizes Active Directory, whereas Unix servers traditionally use *zone files*.

In smaller installations, both functionalities are provided by the same server. But in larger installations that have multiple domains within one company, it may very well be that these are really two different servers, as shown in Fig. 9.14.

Case Study: High Availability for ISC's BIND

Berkeley Internet Name Daemon (BIND) from ISC is the most used name server in the world: a survey from May 2004 showed it served about 70% of all Internet domains.

The case study will focus on high availability for DNS servers that will protect against system and service outages. System administrator errors (e.g., deleting the whole DNS database) are not in the scope of this description. Neither are incidents that are caused by wrong management of DNS records – they must be prevented by proper processes and good tools. It must be said that good tools are usually not predelivered with software for DNS servers, and BIND is no exception here. It is prudent to create tools that integrate tightly into company business processes and to implement safekeeping checks.

The concept of redundant servers is inherent to BIND. In fact, for Internet domains we are forced to run a redundant server infrastructure; no Internet domain name may be registered without it. As this is so easy, this is standard practice in any corporate network as well. There are three categories of configurations for domains:

1. **Master servers** hold the definitive (authoritative) content for a domain, typically in a zone file. But the content may also be stored on other storage back-ends, e.g., on an LDAP directory server. The content is maintained on this server. Master servers were formerly called *primary name servers*.

2. **Slave servers** also hold the authoritative content for a domain, but in a read-only method. All changes to domain content are replicated to slave servers; that replication is part of the DNS protocol. Slave servers were formerly called *secondary name servers*.

3. **Caching servers** hold no authoritative content, but cache responses for queries. Each DNS record has an associated lifetime (TTL) that tells how long it may be cached.

The BIND configuration file tells about zones and which ones are master and which are slave. Queries are cached automatically; this does not need to be configured. One server configuration may mix master, slave, and caching definitions for different domains.

When clients are allowed direct Internet connections, the cache servers will be configured to resolve Internet host names as well. If all clients have to use proxy servers, this is not necessary, then just the proxy will need to resolve Internet names and will do so over a separate DNS configuration. For that, it will either utilize a special cache server or it will use the ISP's DNS servers.

It is good practice for larger installations (i.e., with several thousand clients) to separate cache servers from publishing servers. This is not necessary for smaller and mid-sized installations, except when an LDAP back-end server is used for domain content storage. (The rationale for that will be provided later.)

▸ *Caching DNS Servers*

The need for high availability for caching DNS servers is often overlooked. Computer systems have a list of DNS servers that they may send queries to. They try to contact each server in turn and wait for an answer until a timeout happens, then the next server is tried. Many systems have a limit on the number of servers in that list, often three.

Outage of the first DNS server in that list does not cause nonfunctionality at the client – but the ongoing need to wait for a timeout until the second server (typically several seconds) can be questioned may well render a desktop unusable from an end-user's perspective. We just need to imagine waiting several seconds for any host name that is used in any program and we see the problem immediately.

Therefore the best solution is to establish high availability for the servers with a failover or a load-balancing cluster. Since DNS servers do not keep a state, such a cluster is very simple and easy to set up, the only resource that must be switched to the other cluster node is the IP address, and the server process must be started.

Nevertheless, clients usually have two DNS servers configured, just to be on the safe side. So even in the case of an outage of our high-availability DNS server cluster, we will still have another server to answer queries, albeit with timeouts.

▸ *Publishing DNS Servers*

For DNS queries, there is no difference between master and slave servers, both are authoritative. An authoritative server is chosen at random to answer a query. If an authoritative server cannot be reached, another server is tried; therefore, failure of a server does not render the service useless as long as other authoritative servers are still running.

Database content errors propagate with very small delay. The master server sends notification to all known slaves and slave servers fetch the updates. Slave servers also fetch updates at regular intervals; that interval is part of the zone definition and is often in the range of days. Database destruction therefore propagates more slowly.

If the master server is down, the clock starts ticking to migrate one of the slave servers to a master configuration. As explained, a DNS domain has associated expiry and refresh times that control the update interval between master and slave servers. The new master server must be established before the expiry time has passed, but this will not be a problem as this is normally a value of several days or even weeks. In such a time span we can buy and set up a whole new server.

Therefore, high availability for publishing DNS servers means establishing enough slave servers at all sites. And it means a method to update the configuration of all servers at once, and to change the address of the master server if necessary. The easiest way is to keep a backup of the master server's BIND configuration and zone files, and to restore the master configuration on one of the slave servers. Then we change all slave configurations to utilize the new master server. Of course, it is recommended to use automated provisioning for that task.

Backup and restoration of zone files is actually done to keep comments in the files. All zone files are available on slave servers as well, but there they are created by the replication that strips comments and reorders the entries.

Dynamic DNS is handled similarly. Since the zone file has been replicated, it can be taken from the slave server that becomes the new master.

Another possibility is to use an LDAP back-end server to store the DNS domain content. This is particularly of interest if we also use the LDAP back-end server for the DHCP server; then all network information can be stored on this directory server. Of course, then the LDAP infrastructure becomes mission-critical and must be highly available in itself.

Using the LDAP back-end server has one drawback though. For larger installations – and that is the case where LDAP is particularly of interest for maintenance reasons – LDAP directory servers are often not fast enough to cover the load of DNS queries. Therefore it is recommended that the master server with its LDAP back-end server is not announced as the authoritative name server. Instead, just the slave servers (which have all the content in memory and are thus fast to answer) are used as publishing infrastructure.

It is not sufficient to rely on caching DNS servers to take the load from a master server with an LDAP back-end server. Updates for a caching server are controlled by the TTL value, whereas updates for a slave server are controlled by the expiry and refresh values and by active change notifications from the master server. Very often, we want to have a low TTL to be able to change addresses for names very quickly, e.g., for disaster recovery. In such cases, slave servers can still hold the cache for a long time owing to longer refresh and expiry values.

9.2.3 Directory Server

Directory servers are systems that store named objects with various attributes and where clients can query the server for the object. They operate under the assumption that their content is very often read and, in comparison, seldom changed; they are optimized for this usage pattern.

So that was the definition of a directory server – but it is far too generic and too abstract to understand what one does with directory servers and why they are important. So, what are they good for, and where are they used?

Application Domains of Directory Servers

The oldest usage of a directory server is to hold account and user group information. Each account or user group is an object, the account or group name is the key to request that object from the server. The object's attributes are full name, office location, office phone, numeric user ID, home directory, and others. At this stage, the objects were very simple: most attributes can only appear once per object. For example, when a person had more than one office phone, it was not possible to record that properly.

Later, directory servers were also used to store information about persons beyond accounts. They serve as a phone or address book and keep information like address, phone numbers, and email, but also organizational information, like the name of the organizational unit, supervisors, proxies, colleagues, and subordinates. These directory servers cope with the fact that our information about persons is not as simple as it seems and allow most of this information to appear multiple times, i.e., it is possible to have multiple email addresses for a person (maybe designating one as the preferred or primary address), multiple addresses, multiple phone numbers, etc.

These kinds of directory services serve both as a standalone lookup tool for company staff, e.g., to replace printed phone books, or they are used in connection with email systems, where they first provided the much needed lookup facility for the email addresses of colleagues and later lookup of full contact information. (Still, the organizational information is often missing from email address books and is only available in standalone user interfaces.)

Roughly at the same time, the idea came up that one can use directory servers to store all information that one needs to manage IT systems – almost all fit the requirements of "named object, read often, change seldom." Computer information, system configurations, printer information, association of network file shares, and software installation, everything that is relevant for system management could be stored in one place, on one server, and managed consistently with one interface.

Last in this development, these different kinds of directory servers were put together and merged into one coherent infrastructure. This system management infrastructure is not easy to roll out, i.e., it comes with quite some up-front costs. But it has big advantages in reduction of system management efforts, i.e., it is a big boon for ongoing operating costs. The more systems are concerned, the higher is the return on investment – as long as we have handcrafted server installations with manually managed accounts, configuration, and software, it does not buy us an advantage. But with as few as ten similar systems, it reduces management effort dramatically – this is not only a technology for large installations of many thousands of systems.

In the future, there will be a directory server setup in any sizable Windows desktop installation. Without that directory server, no desktop will be able to function. It does not need to be emphasized how important high availability and disaster recovery are for such an elementary infrastructure service.

Important Directory Servers

The following directory servers are noteworthy; we start with the older ones.

Network Information Service (NIS): This is the traditional and basic directory server of Unix systems, first introduced by Sun under the name YP (for *yellow pages*). Owing to its inherent security weaknesses it should not be used anymore for new deployments.

NIS+: An attempt by Sun to overhaul the NIS system and make it secure and scalable. This never caught on because it was not available on other Unix systems and LDAP got the spotlight later on. No new deployment should use it either.

Novell eDirectory: Formerly called *Novell Directory Services*, this directory service has been used by many large companies for a long time. It is enterprise class and has proven its stability and manageability.

Windows NT Domain Directory: The first widespread directory server that got beyond accounts and included system configuration. While Novell's server was available earlier and is technically better, the tight integration with Windows caused deployments at many companies that would not have thought of a directory server otherwise. Nowadays, this server has been superseded by Active Directory.

Active Directory: The directory server for Windows 2000 and beyond, which has become mandatory for medium to large Windows installations. Active Directory pushed many corporations – some of them unwillingly – into the use of directory services, where they finally saw the advantages of such a service. Owing to the ubiquity of Windows desktops, it will be eventually installed in almost all companies.

Netscape Directory Server: This was the first server that provided an LDAP interface (more on access interfaces later). Development of this server was been split into two main tiers, via the iPlanet Directory Server, and resulted in Sun's Java System Directory Server and Red Hat's Fedora Directory Server. This server is said to be used for most installations on Unix systems.

OpenLDAP: The predominant open-source LDAP server. This server is preferably used in environments where the budget is tight and the number of objects is low. But even in those environments, when it comes to high availability, Red Hat's Fedora Directory Server should be taken into account first.

X.500 directory servers: These are directory servers for large institutions, often government or military, that need federated directory servers to store all kinds of information about their staff, citizens, customers, and systems. ISODE's M-Vault, eTrust from CA, and DirX from Siemens are examples of such servers. They are very complex and are usually slower than "pure" LDAP servers; therefore, they should only be deployed if X.500 back-end functionality is needed.

In summary, one can say that there are two classes of products: the PC-oriented products from Microsoft and Novell, which are tightly integrated into systems management of many desktops, and the X.500/LDAP products, which target the market of generic enterprise information systems that can *also* be used for systems management tasks.

Please note that, strictly speaking, DHCP from Sect. 9.2.1 and DNS from Sect. 9.2.2 are also directory services. We did not include them here in the overview since they have already been described in detail.

Server Categories

In the previous section some terms appeared that should be mentioned here, namely, network protocols that are used to access directory servers. These protocols are so prominent that they are often used to categorize products – though this marketing decision does much to muddy the water.

Just two server categories are of importance today, LDAP and X.500 servers. All other server categories are legacy technology that is bound to lose market share drastically and are or will be relegated to niche markets. Some of them, like Novell's eDirectory, have already migrated to LDAP, which will be the predominant directory server model of the future.

Both LDAP and X.500 servers have a shared data model in common: objects are uniquely named and are ordered into a tree hierarchy. The hierarchy can be used to restricts searches, and to delegate administration for subtrees. Therefore, different subtrees are used to store information on people and computers, maybe even further structured according to organizational units or geography.

Each object has a class: the class definition explicates which attributes an object may have. Attributes have types that are checked by the server. Classes are in an inheritance relationship, i.e., one can extend them. A set of classes, their relationship, and their attribute definitions are called an LDAP schema.

Inheritance is commonly used to add classes with new attributes to an existing LDAP schema. Most often, a set of standard X.500 and LDAP schemas are used as the core and are extended by the directory server vendor by specific classes with vendor-specific attributes. Then, each company extends the schema with its own classes and its own company-specific attributes, as needed. Generic client software will only access the core attributes; vendor-specific client software will also know about the vendor attributes. Usage of the company-specific attributes has to be integrated into applications by programming work.

Since security-relevant information is usually stored in directory servers, all products provide fine-grained access control possibilities. Access control can be both attribute-based and tree-based, and provides ample flexibility to implement any authorization scheme that one can think of. These capabilities were standardized in 2000 with LDAP version 3, which all products are converging to.

▶ *LDAP Servers*

LDAP, the *Lightweight Directory Access Protocol*, is a member of the IP protocol suite to access directory servers. The protocol includes both query and update operations; query operations can also be expressed as URLs. LDAP is already the prevalent method to access directory services; it remains be to be seen if the alternate method of using Web services (e.g., utilizing *Directory Services Markup Language*, DSML, in Simple Object Access Protocol, SOAP, requests) will catch up since it is much slower and directory service lookup performance is crucial for many applications.

All modern directory servers provide LDAP as an access protocol. Some of them have LDAP as their *only*, or at least as their preferred, protocol. Such servers are colloquially called *pure LDAP servers*. Storage of the directory data is handled directly by these servers, in varying formats (files, embedded databases, or by utilizing database middleware products).

For many other servers, be they relational databases or X.500 servers, LDAP interfaces are available. They allow these products to be used as LDAP servers as well. Sometimes an LDAP server is nothing more than a gateway that forwards the LDAP request – after an appropriate transformation – to the real data source, and relays the response back to the client.

The differentiation into pure and nonpure LDAP servers is primarily a marketing issue, and not a technical classification – for a client the access protocol's implementation quality does matter, and it does not matter if that is the preferred access method. Nevertheless, mature pure LDAP servers often have better standards compliance, better performance, and better administration tools than servers with an LDAP interface that was added on.

▸ *X.500 Servers*

X.500 servers are the heavyweights in the directory server arena. They need plenty of resources, detailed up-front planning and setup, and lots of administration work. They are suitable for very large organizations that have to keep millions or even billions of information objects, and where there must be a high degree of delegation of administration of these objects to many suborganizations, but which must also be tightly controlled for security.

X.500 directories are traditionally accessed by the *Directory Access Protocol* (DAP) that is part of ISO's X.500 protocol suite. But nowadays that protocol is losing its importance and is being replaced more and more by LDAP interfaces. Thus, X.500 servers are turning themselves more into LDAP servers with especially powerful, flexible, and complex back-ends.

Case Study: High Availability for Active Directory

Active Directory (AD) by Microsoft is one of the premier solutions for a directory server. Since it is mandatory to use it in all but the very smallest company setups for Windows desktops, virtually every company is expected to have it installed – if not now, then within the next few years.

While Active Directory is not easy to design and set up properly for a large enterprise, it comes with large savings in operational costs. It is used to store information about:

- Accounts, including groups of accounts
- Address book and contacts
- Desktops, including groups of desktops
- Desktop configuration
- Printers
- Network shares
- Location (site) of IT systems
- Software that must be installed on systems

As we can see from that list, usage of an Active Directory server in Windows environments goes way beyond the storage of account information like user IDs and groups. Windows network administrators are able to define *group policies* that describe the target state of a Windows system: which software shall be installed, what services are running, what users shall be allowed to do on the local system, what system configuration shall exist permanently or locally during a login session, which network printers and shares are connected, and loads of other configuration items. Such group policies are registered and managed in the directory server and partly stored on network shares. They are accessed at boot and login times, and also regularly in-between. That means that Active

Directory gives the Windows administrator the ability to change settings on all desktops on the fly. Such configurations can also be targeted for specific organizational units, or for specific user groups, etc.

But this also means that desktops are highly dependent on the availability of the Active Directory server. Without them, they will not boot properly, will not be able to log in to the Windows domain. Therefore, Active Directory servers are prime candidates for high-availability setups, and also for disaster-recovery protection.

Active Directory servers are effectively special-purpose database servers. Like other database servers, they have their own clustering capability. Therefore, even though it would be possible to use a generic failover cluster for Active Directory server system design, this is usually not done. Instead, an Active Directory server cluster uses an inherent clustering technology that distributes cluster nodes over a campus network. Each change in the directory is replicated to all nodes in the cluster. The clustering technology even allows changes to be processed on each cluster node; this is termed *multi-master replication*.

For these changes, no global locks exist to prevent changing the same directory object at two cluster nodes. This works well since objects are seldom changed anyhow, and this optimistic strategy leads to very few conflicts. In the case of conflicting changes, a defined conflict resolution algorithm exists.

High availability is assured by setting up multiple Active Directory servers and configuring intrasite replication for them. This works only if they are all within one LAN, owing to bandwidth and latency requirements. We need to configure them for immediate replication: usually changes are replicated in batches to save network traffic. These servers must be explicitly configured to serve the same domain, DNS records must be set up to point to those redundant directory servers, and they should also be announced as alternate servers in the LDAP configuration.

For disaster recovery, it is possible to establish an *intersite replication* to an Active Directory server on the disaster-recovery site, then systems on the disaster-recovery site can use that Active Directory server. Such replications are optimized for usage over WAN connections.

There are some Active Directory servers that have special roles, the so-called *Flexible Single Master Operation* (FSMO) roles. These roles enable those servers to make structural changes to the whole cluster or to the schema, or they check consistencies between cluster members. While this functionality is not needed during normal operations, it must not be turned off for long either. Therefore, when an Active Directory server that has such a role has an outage, processes must exist to notice that and to promote another server to take over the role. This has to be done manually.

But high availability and disaster recovery for Active Directory servers is not sufficient. Since group policy template files are stored on network shares, the network file servers must be made highly available as well. For that, standard failover cluster technology can be used.

9.3 Backup and Restore

Backup and restoration of data is one of the most important duties in any IT operations environment. Too many things can go wrong, too many possibilities for failures exist in our complex environments, for this precaution can be omitted.

As a trivial view, the task is easy: we copy data somewhere, and copy it back when they are needed. But in practice, this area is much more difficult. We do not only need to do the actual data backup, but we must also *manage our backups.*

We can distinguish three categories of backups:

1. **System backup** is the method to save installed software and configurations. This is primarily needed when release management processes do not allow a system's state to be reconstructed on a whim, i.e., if there have been manual configurations on a server where the time to track and repeat them is longer than the time to restore the system.

2. **File backup** is the elementary task of backup systems, the one that they were made for in the first place. It is possible to do full or incremental backups, and elaborate mechanisms exist to coordinate them for optimal usage of resources with maximized safety.

   Nevertheless, there are still problems that are inherent in the task. When files are opened all the time, and their content is partly cached by the operating system or the application, it is not possible to back up a consistent version of that file. We cannot back them up with normal means, but need database backups for them.

   Sometimes it is not easy to restore data in an exact state that can be used by the applications. This is particularly a problem for Windows backups of FAT partitions, as we cannot restore the short 8 + 3 name that might be used by some applications. The primary remedy for that problem is to use NTFS file systems instead – FAT should never be used in an enterprise context.

3. **Database backup** handles files or partitions that are used all the time. There, traditional backup strategies do not work. Instead, we need support from the application. Either it must be possible to demand a checkpoint that creates a consistent state of the data, or the application itself must be integrated into the backup system.

   While checkpoint functionality used to be quite common, it also often introduced the need for a system time where no changes in the database could be made. Since this is often not possible for high-availability installations, continuous backup technology by application integration has become more common.

One thing is really important for backups:

A backup is only as good as a functioning restoration.

That is an elementary issue: first, the restoration itself must work; second, it must succeed in acceptable time frames. In particular, the time to restore the data is often underestimated. Sometimes restoration management needs more time than actual data restoration; therefore, operations staff must be trained to reach best restoration performance.

▸ *Backup on Failover Clusters*

Backup systems that are used on failover clusters must support the distinction between physical and logical hosts in a cluster. Backup of the physical nodes is primarily made as a system backup, sometimes also for file backup.

This backup must not touch disk volumes that are resources for cluster services: when a failover happens that volume will not be there for the next backup. Instead, logical hosts must have their own backup definitions and those must switch together with other resources from that service.

This is sometimes a problem if the backup is not initiated by the backup server, is but on the computer system where the data is. There we either have cron jobs, they must support switching logical hosts from one cluster node to another, or some daemon runs on each cluster node and initiates the backup, then a cluster service failover must register the need for backups of the logical host with that daemon, as well as deregister the need during shutdown.

9.4 Monitoring

Monitoring is another activity at the heart of IT operations. It is the coordinated effort to check that IT services deliver their supposed functionality and that SLAs are satisfied. Coordinated means that there is a central place (or a few places) where the observations are collected and analyzed.

The ultimate goal of monitoring is to detect defects and problematic situations before they influence operations and availability. If we do not achieve that, we settle for collection and notification of failures, as well as escalation if failures are not remedied in an acceptable time range; therefore, it is a technical precondition for good incident, problem, and escalation management. In fact, failure detection is the traditional objective of monitoring, while failure avoidance is the more modern interpretation of it.

The emergence of high-availability solutions is one of the reasons for this change of objectives. Such solutions often have inherent monitoring capabilities and automated reactions. For example, monitoring of service functionality is an essential part of failover clusters, needed to detect failures that need software restarts or service migration to another cluster node. This cluster-inherent ability to detect failures and react to them makes external monitoring capabilities for outage detection less necessary.

But when we realize high availability with redundant components, we have automated automatic service recovery on a backup component. But the defective component does not repair itself automatically – and we need notice of its failure to trigger repairs. After all, after part of a redundant component fails, we usually have lost redundancy and thus high availability. So, even in cluster environments, monitoring is responsible for defect discovery – only here it is the discovery of defects in redundant components.

Another objective for monitoring in high-availability environments is the detection of major outages. By definition, high-availability solutions only cover minor outages. When several components fail at the same time, or when deadlocks occur in redundancy management, some external system must notice this and notify operational staff to look into the incident.

Redundancy management often only controls replacement or discards usage, but has no notification component. Integration of notification policies would be difficult anyhow, since this needs event compression and escalation, as explained in the following. Discovery and notification should be quick to reduce the time from outage to full redundancy recovery; remember that we have shown that shortening this interval is the best and cheapest way to improve overall availability.

Detection of a defect or an anomaly is called an *event*. Monitoring systems do not only recognize that event, they also react to it or support manual reaction. When a service or a component has a defect and is repetitively accessed to test for functionality, lots of events for a defective component will arrive at the monitoring system. Then people must not see all those events, it would hinder them in fulfilling their recovery work. Also, several events could result from one defect, e.g., a router outage could make all systems behind that router inaccessible.

Therefore events must be collected and related events must be detected. Such related events are reduced into *incidents* and an action is triggered to handle that incident. Such an action may be an automated one, but is most often the notification of operators or system administrators to look into the error.

This does not imply that after reception of one event all similar events from the same defect are discarded. It could be that this one event is overseen or gets the wrong priority. Therefore it may well be that ongoing event reception can lead to creation of another incident, where this time the associated action might be an escalation.

In high-end enterprise systems, the reduction of events to incidents and the mapping of incidents to actions is maintained in a *monitoring information system*. This system is closely coupled to incident and escalation management process definitions. Since such processes are increasingly being defined formally, we can expect to see more deployments of computer-based support for such information systems as well.

A monitoring system should also keep its monitoring results for some time, to be able to detect continuous degradation of service quality. Such issues are the first signs that defects will be more probable in the future and that problem management should look at these results. On the other hand, a monitoring system will not keep the data for a long time period; that is the task of capacity management systems to which such data might be migrated.

10

Disaster Recovery

The previous chapters focused on the principles (Chaps. 1, 3) and on the realization of high availability for systems and infrastructure (Chaps. 5–9). In this chapter, we will look at approaches to realize disaster recovery – i.e., how to recover from a major outage.

High-availability implementations handle minor outages; either they protect against them, or they provide very quick recovery. But still the issue of major outages and their associated service disruptions remains. Redundant components may fail at the same time, or a backup component may fail while the primary component is being repaired. There are also error causes that high-availability systems do not prevent against: the obvious ones are environmental disasters like earthquakes and hurricanes, en vogue is the fear of terrorist threats, and we must not forget human errors.

In our high-availability planning, we focused on failures that lead to minor outages. To achieve that we created the project-specific system stack, as outlined on p. 60ff, that discards some components that are single points of failure but are beyond the scope of high availability (e.g., the physical environment). In addition, we discarded some failure scenarios as irrelevant for high availability (see Sect. 4.2.3), typically because their probability is low.

Now, for *disaster recovery*, we consider more components and more failure scenarios. The approach and the basic principles remain the same, as we will see in Sect. 10.2 on p. 291. We have a slight shift in objectives: while high availability is concerned both with protection of and recovery from failures, disaster recovery is only about recovery, about restoration of IT service functionality in major outages.

This is an important point: we distinguish high availability and disaster recovery by the class of failures they are designed to cover. But classification of failure scenarios depends on the respective project. If we have a system design that recovers automatically from a system outage by a failover to an other system at a remote time within the minor outage service level agreement (SLA), we call that system design always highly available. For another IT service, the same failure scenario might lead to a manual recovery at a system at the same remote site that is *not* done within the minor outage SLA time. Then we call that disaster recovery, even though similar systems at the same sites are involved – the processes and objectives for service recovery are different, that is the distinguishing factor.

Typically, a phased approach is used, where services are restored gradually, until eventually all resources are available again. Disaster recovery is also concerned with a greater part of manual processes than high availability; while high availability wants to create strict automated procedures, disaster recovery works more by trusting our IT staff to assess vague error situations properly and react in a flexible and appropriate way.

Within the IT Infrastructure Library (ITIL), the disaster-recovery process is also called *IT service continuity*, to show its alignment with the business-continuity process. For the sake of this book, we use the traditional term disaster recovery though, to emphasize that we want to prepare for disasters of mission-critical or important servers.

For a business owner, definition of the term *disaster* is obviously highly context-dependent, with lots of gray areas. While destruction of a computing center by an earthquake is clearly a disaster in the eyes of everybody, system outages of 1 day may be a disaster for manufacturing companies when the production depends on them. On the other hand, many clerical tasks can survive quite a few hours without computers.

- **Definitions of related conceptual terms**, in particular "disaster," are covered in Sect. 10.1.
- Our **approach to disaster recovery** is presented in Sect. 10.2.
- The **conceptual design** in Sect. 10.3 expands the definitions and explains them in more detail.
- The **solutions** that can be used to realize disaster recovery are presented in Sect. 10.4.
- **Tests** are covered in Sect. 10.5.
- A **holistic view** goes beyond the technology issues and is presented in Sect. 10.6.
- The **prototypical system design** from Sect. 10.7.4 is a blueprint that can be used for many situations.
- **Activation of a disaster-recovery system** is another blueprint and is presented in Sect. 10.8.

But before we dive into the definitions of the concepts, let us have another look at the business need for disaster recovery that shows just how urgent it is that disaster-recovery solutions are provided at least for all our mission-critical servers. First, we will look at the most important problem that is associated with major outages, namely, data loss.

Service Loss and Data Loss

Since service loss is often accompanied with data loss, or data loss itself is the reason for service shutoffs, it is of interest to look at the consequences of data loss for a company. Several studies have been made, by accountancy companies, and by data protection and storage providers. They agree on some key facts:

- The accounting company McGladrey and Pullen reported that after serious data loss, 43% of companies must close. They also reported that 0.2% (one out of 500) computing centers have serious data losses per year.
- Toigo reports [12] that more than 10 days of computer outage cannot be recovered by most companies. Fifty percent of them go out of business within 5 years if they had outages for that long.
- According to EMC, only 2% of data loss is caused by disasters. The major cause (45% of cases) is human errors. The rest of the errors are caused by other failures, e.g., software errors.

From these numbers we see that data loss – while not identical to disaster – is clearly a major symptom, and is one of the failure consequences that we need to protect against.

It should be noted that these numbers are obviously for enterprise-class storage systems; other companies report much higher hardware defect causes for consumer-grade hardware. What is actually of interest for that data is that the common notion of disasters – earthquakes, floods, terrorist attacks, etc. – happen quite seldom. Instead, most data loss is caused for everyday reasons, but has equally disastrous consequences.

10.1 Concepts

There are some conceptual terms that are very important for disaster recovery. One of the problems of disaster recovery is that we find many vague descriptions of these terms and this leads to communication problems. Thus, to ensure that we have a common vocabulary, let us make a few definitions of the important terms first:

Major outage: A failure that impacts an IT service for end users and which cannot be repaired within the availability limits of the SLA. Major outages are also covered by SLAs, in the "Service Continuity" section, and are described with the recovery time objective (RTO) and the recovery point objective (RPO); see later. Section 2.2 introduced major outages and SLAs.

Disaster: In the context of this book, a disaster is a synonym for a major outage. Both terms are used interchangeably.

Declaration of disaster: The decision that a major outage has happened and that disaster recovery starts. This decision is usually not done automatically, but is made by IT staff and business owners together, as part of an escalation management process. Often the affirmation of executive management is necessary to declare a disaster.

Recovery time objective (RTO): The time needed until the IT service is usable again after a major outage. It starts with the declaration of disaster and is part of the SLA that describes the handling of major outages. Table 2.2 on p. 28 lists typical RTO and RPO values for different system categories.

Recovery point objective (RPO): The point in time from which data will be restored to be usable. It is typically expressed as a time span before the declaration of disaster and, like the RTO, is part of the SLA that describes the handling of major outages. In major outages, often some part of work is lost.

Disaster recovery: The process to restore full functionality in the case of major outages, including all necessary preparation actions.

Disaster-recovery planning: The management activity to define the necessary actions for disaster recovery and that governs their implementation.

Primary and disaster-recovery systems: In normal operation, the primary system supplies the IT service. A disaster-recovery system takes over functionality and supplies the service in the case of a major outage.

Primary and disaster-recovery sites: The prototypical disaster scenario is destruction of the physical environment, e.g., by floods or fire. The site where the primary IT systems are normally placed is called the *primary site*. A *disaster-recovery site* is a site where disaster-recovery systems are placed. The disaster-recovery site is at a location that is (hopefully) not covered by the disaster and can take over the role of the primary site during disaster recovery.

Primary and disaster-recovery sites are roles, not absolute descriptions. A disaster-recovery site for one service may very well be the primary site for another service, and vice versa. In fact, this is a very common setup.

At the start of this chapter, it was emphasized that high availability and disaster recovery are moored in the same ground. Both have ongoing availability of IT services as the objective, although with different SLAs. Both utilize the same approach as we will see in Sect. 10.2 on the next page.

But there is a conceptual difference that we need to note here. The goal of high availability is to provide again full functionality in a short time after a component failure. Disaster recovery is not as ambitious, and instead it puts first things first and starts to look at partial functionality for essential services. Of course, eventually full functionality will be restored, but this is an action that may take some time.

In disaster recovery, the restoration process itself is phased. First, redundant components provide (maybe reduced) functionality with a disaster-recovery system at a disaster-recovery site. Later, full functionality of the primary systems at the primary site is restored. Disaster-recovery actions also include the preparation and maintenance of the disaster-recovery systems, as well as training of staff and documentation.

This implies that disaster recovery is not an action that just happens in the case of disasters. Instead, it is an ongoing administrative and operational activity that includes preparation to mitigate the consequences of a disaster.

In addition, the availability and the cost of required resources must be taken into account. This includes nontechnical resources and organizational provisions that will be needed to handle an actual disaster-recovery event. This is valid for high availability as well, but disaster recovery is based even more on processes and procedures than on fully automated technical solutions.

10.2 Approach

The principal approach to plan and realize disaster recovery was presented in Chap. 3. It is the same approach that is also used to plan and realize high availability. Let us repeat it here, as a summary:

1. Determine objectives
   (a) Identify systems that need disaster recovery
   (b) Determine RTO and RPO
   (c) Identify users and departments that are affected
   (d) Identify responsibilities of IT staff and business owners

2. Create conceptual design (see also Sect. 10.3)
   (a) Create changes to business and IT processes that are necessary to realize and support disaster recovery
   (b) Identify and set involved system locations, i.e., primary and disaster-recovery sites
   (c) Define high-level solution approach and associated costs
   (d) Determine IT staff and vendors that are involved; create RASIC chart to define roles and responsibilities
   (e) Make a first stub at failure scenarios and failure categories, from a business point of view
   (f) Evaluate scenarios, and determine their relative probability and relative damage

(g) Determine which scenarios are already covered by high-availability technology, which must be covered by this disaster-recovery project, and which are out of scope

3. Create system design
   (a) Analyze the system components, create a project-specific system stack, and create a dependency diagram
   (b) Extend failure scenarios to cover technical component failures
   (c) Find single points of failure. Either provide recovery for them through redundancy, or provide other means to restore acceptable service within the disaster-recovery SLAs.
   (d) Review that the solution handles all relevant scenarios

4. Implement solution
   (a) Technology for implementation can be taken from Chaps. 5–9
   (b) Technology that is particular to disaster recovery is presented in Sect. 10.4
   (c) Particulars of network design for disaster recovery are described in Sect. 9.1.6

5. Define process
   (a) Create detailed disaster recovery procedures
   (b) Train people
   (c) Specify and conduct tests. Section 10.5 handles this in more detail.

6. Update design and implementation as necessary
   (a) When objectives change
   (b) When primary systems are changed or updated
   (c) When experience from other projects and problem analysis show potential improvements

This approach also gives the rough overview of the rest of this chapter. After conceptual design and technology, we will present an example for a disaster-recovery project (in Sect. 10.7) and for failover procedures (in Sect. 10.8) that can be taken as blueprints for other situations.

10.3 Conceptual Design

The conceptual model is concerned with the interface between the business and IT systems. On this level, decisions must be made that must be agreed upon both by IT (technical) and by business staff. These decisions will have a direct influence on the technical solution and will be requirements for the system design.

First, we will have a look at scenarios for major outages, and their classification with the help of the system stack. Then we will address the identification of systems, i.e., how to set the scope of disaster-recovery projects. The primary and disaster-recovery sites have been defined already, but their selection deserves a detailed explanation. There are several possible categories of primary and disaster-recovery systems with differing failure protection properties; the business owner must be involved in the basic design decision that is made with this high-level selection. Finally, we will discuss a specific part of RTO, the service recovery time; this clarification is also needed during discussion of the IT department and business owners.

10.3.1 Scenarios for Major Outages

In Sect. 4.1, we introduced the system stack, redundancy, robustness, and virtualization as basic concepts, and presented dependency diagrams as a tool to express and analyze system designs. These basic concepts and tools are as valid for disaster recovery as they are for high availability.

In particular, the system stack gives us a categorization of disaster scenarios and provides abstraction levels for failures and problems that allow us to evaluate different measures and protection activities.

As we will see, it is important to not only concentrate on the popular, but improbable case of total physical destruction of a whole site. A total solution has to protect against this worst case, but also against many other scenarios which have higher probability and more subtle results. All of them have one thing in common: classic high availability architectures like failover cluster or server farms at one site do not protect against them.

Table 10.1 on the following page brings together the system stack and examples of major outages on each stack level. And yet, this book mostly covers only errors that happen with good-willed usage. Just as important are outages from associated security risks, i.e., damage from deliberate attacks. Most software programs and installations today are still full of errors that can be exploited by hostile forces and can be used to attack several target components at the same time.

Protection against such security-related damage is beyond the scope of this book though – it needs a whole treatise of its own. Nevertheless one should note that middleware systems are attractive attack targets as they keep valuable information of companies and are widely spread. After all, the bragging undergraduate student just defacing one's Web site is not the danger anymore; today's hackers are more interested in important targets that have monetary advantages.

Therefore it is prudent to introduce processes and technology that will handle major outages – we name them *disaster recovery*. These processes will not prevent major outages, instead they will enable us to handle recovery from a major outage faster and in a reliable way.

This is a related, but different goal than that of high availability. One could argue that disaster recovery is sufficient for all outages – after all, if

Table 10.1. Examples of major outages in a system stack

System stack level	Major outage example cause
Administration environment	Human error is an all-time favorite, according Murphy's Law: "If something can go wrong, it will go wrong eventually."
	Redundancy at lower-level technical components does not help at all: all redundant components will faithfully replicate that error
Application	Software errors may leave data in an inconsistent state; no cluster protects against that.
	Some software may not be started anymore afterwards – even worse, some software may be started and may cause even bigger failures owing to the bad data!
Middleware	Data inconsistencies cause a restart to fail.
	Distributed cluster software may fail
Operating system	Failover cluster software error.
	Errors in the hardware driver code are the same on all cluster nodes. Errors in the file system corrupt shared storage beyond repair
Hardware	Firmware on redundant hardware is usually the same on all redundant components and may fail in the same way
Environment	Here are the prototypical examples for disaster causes: floods, hurricanes, earthquakes, terrorist bomb attacks.
	But there are also outages that should be prevented in the data center, but where protection failed: uninterruptible power supply (UPS) outages, or fires that got out of control

this handles disasters, it should handle minor outages as well. But there are three differences:

1. Outage times are different. That is the distinguishing factor, the difference between minor and major outages.
2. Risks and costs are different. In practice, high availability is a well-known and tried technology that has a good cost-value relationship. But implementation costs and switching costs for disaster recovery are higher. Therefore, switching to a disaster-recovery site in a disaster still costs a lot of money, even with all the preparation; the costs for a mirrored disk are negligible compared with that.
3. Processes are different. High availability strikes for automated processes to protect against or recover from well-known failures. In contrast, disaster recovery is concerned with unknown or rare incidents where automated recovery is often or is inherently not available;

therefore, disaster recovery has a greater dependency on manual processes, though they are computer-supported.

So, most of the time, outage protection or handling is established on several levels, both for minor and major outages. High availability and disaster recovery are two sides of the same coin; they complement each other.

There are exceptions to that "multiple redundancy" rule, for very special applications. The most famous one is Google, where the whole application is such a vast cluster that some redundancies on lower levels are not done anymore – if a computer breaks down, others will take over its task. In such an application architecture, big-scale redundancy was designed in up-front and one does not need to care about redundancies in single nodes anymore. But this is an exception. Mission-critical applications, run by high-availability systems, are the target of this book and they typically have not been designed as worldwide large-scale application clusters, as Google is.

To handle these problems, it is sometimes necessary to fall back to an earlier state in time. This implies that disaster recovery for some problem classes results in loss of data and therefore loss of work. Actually, we have differing requirements here: for human and software errors, we want a data and functionality state that is as close as possible to that of the original system up and running in a short time. For physical environment errors that damaged or destroyed the whole server, we want fast restoration of a previous consistent state.

To exemplify this further, a simple-minded online-mirrored system at another site is appropriate for server environment problems, but not for human or software errors since it would replicate the errors in classes immediately and we could not access the needed previous state in a short time.

Disaster recovery is only *one* piece for a total business continuity solution. However, for many businesses IT outages are among the most serious scenarios and protection against such cases is quite costly because of the high degree of physical redundancy needed. (Even though it has to be said that it is not as expensive as building a new plant of a manufacturing company; we need to see the costs in relation to each other.)

10.3.2 Disaster-Recovery Scope

As stated in Sect. 4.1, the basic concept centers around the system stack categorization, redundancy, robustness, and virtualization. The methodology is the same for high availability and disaster recovery. Our tools – in particular, dependency diagrams – are the same too. For dependency diagrams, we need to clarify where redundancy is used in the scope of disaster recovery. To answer that, we need to know our project-specific system stack first.

Disaster recovery focuses on essential business functionality and the minimum IT resources required for that. As disaster scenarios are not a common case, it will usually not be necessary to provide redundancy for full operations. Therefore some components might be declared out of scope for disaster recovery. Other components are in scope; they may be applications, computer systems, or whole sites. This section helps to identify the components of the project-specific system stack and their relationship.

In a redundant setup, the dependencies between applications, systems, and sites will become very complex. Disruptions on application, system, or site level will be as independent from each other as possible. A site that is down, either because of a disaster or because of access problems, e.g., from interruptions in WAN services, should not prevent continuation of applications originally hosted at this site. This requires careful tracking of operative states.

For disaster-recovery planning, the central questions are:

- What needs to be protected (services/data)?
- Which failures are connected with which disaster?
- What essential functionality must stay operative with the highest priority?
- What functionality must be made available again as soon as possible?
- Which minimum IT resources are required for this?

From a strategic point of view, the answers to these questions follow business demands.

From a technical point of view, however, it is not enough to know which business services shall be protected or reestablished. The more extensive the disaster is, the more possibilities exist as to which technical resources are not available anymore and in which order functionality can be restored.

Therefore, it is necessary to know which applications, servers, and sites are relevant for which business service.

▶ *Server Availability*

To handle disaster recovery for servers, the following information should be known about a server:

- Technical data: site location, architecture, capacity, maintenance contracts.
- Which applications and infrastructure services are provided for which business service?
- Which redundancy and failover solutions are available?
- Which backup strategies are available?

▸ *Application Availability*

To handle disaster recovery for applications, the following information should be known about an application:

- Which servers are involved for functionality of the application?
- For which business service is this application essential?
- Which other applications are needed for functionality?

▸ *Site Availability*

To handle disaster recovery for a site, the following information should be known:

- Which servers are located on the site?
- Which high-availability solutions (redundancy, failovers) are available?

To control the disaster-recovery process, the information just listed should be available. Preferably, it should also be available on paper – real-time monitoring may be interrupted! An essential help is a dependency diagram of the primary system that shows the dependencies between sites, servers and applications. In addition, the primary system design has important information that is needed for our analysis.

In Chap. 2, we introduced the concepts of *recovery time objective* (RTO, the time until the service should be usable again) and *recovery point objective* (RPO, the maximum data loss), which are used to specify requirements for disaster recovery. There we also introduced the basic classification of mission-critical, business-important, business-foundation, and business-edge systems and presented prototypical disaster-recovery requirements for these categories in Table 2.2 on p. 28.

10.3.3 Primary and Disaster-Recovery Sites

Since many disaster scenarios include destruction of whole computing environments (large fire, natural disasters, plane crashes, etc.), redundant components must be spread over wide areas, as noted already. In practice, this means that whole disaster-recovery systems are placed at different locations, the disaster-recovery site.

How far away the components must be placed, i.e., how far away the disaster-recovery site must be from the primary site, is first of all an organizational decision: for many scenarios, a different building is sufficient, but some installations will demand at least different parts of a city. Separating the redundant systems further from each other, in different parts of a country, or even in different countries, is very seldom needed.

Location and distance selection depends on the risks for that area. In areas with known environmental risks – earthquakes in the San Francisco Bay area and in Japan, hurricanes in Florida, etc. – one is well advised to select a disaster-recovery site outside the risk area. For example, a business in San Francisco should not select a disaster-recovery site in Berkeley. On the other hand, areas like Frankfurt in Germany have so few environmental risks associated with them that it is possible to use a disaster-recovery site in its vicinity.

We recommend that every such location analysis and decision is made together with the business owner, to ensure the business requirements are met and to achieve the best-value solution.

Besides those analyses that influence the environmental risk, an organizational decision must be made: How do we set up the disaster-recovery system organization-wise, i.e., who owns our disaster-recovery site? There are several possibilities:

One's own disaster-recovery site: This is especially sensible for large companies that run several data centers anyhow. Then disaster-recovery systems are placed in a data center abroad, and all systems, installations, and data are under one's control.

Reciprocal arrangements: Using another company's equipment as the disaster-recovery system and vice versa. This is an organizational approach to lower costs that is suitable for companies that have very strong ties and close partnerships with each other anyhow.

Most of the processes and methods presented are valid in that approach, but one needs added prearrangements. In such a situation, data security and privacy considerations are of particular importance, as well as secure access. Most of the time this results in a cold-standby approach, as it is usually not practical to operate a hot standby for each other.

Outsourcing: Using another company's equipment as disaster-recovery systems. As with reciprocal arrangements, one has to pay attention to data security, privacy, and access issues. But outsourcing companies do not do this just for you alone, and have usually standard processes in place to assure these conditions are met.

We have successfully established major outage scenarios that we need to recover from, established the project-specific system stack, and defined the scope of disaster recovery. Now it is time to look at the technical issues and see the technical requirements that we shall fulfill and the ways that we can fulfill them.

10.3.4 State Synchronization

Disaster recovery is concerned with setup, maintenance, and operation of disaster-recovery systems at disaster-recovery sites, as already outlined at the start of this chapter. To establish IT functionality on the disaster-recovery system, the system must have all applications, necessary configurations, and all data. Especially data from the primary system must

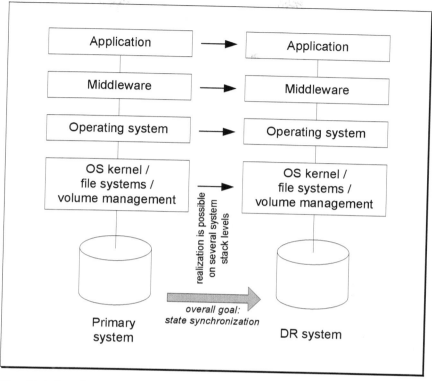

Fig. 10.1. Possible realization of state synchronization. *DR* disaster recovery, *OS* operating system

be available at the disaster-recovery system in a short time frame, otherwise too much is lost. In the end, it boils down to our wanting to replicate all changes from the primary system on the disaster-recovery system, so that the disaster-recovery system is in the same state as the primary one. In other words, we want *state synchronization* for data, installation, and configuration.

If we take up the system stack model and look at Fig. 10.1, we see that we can achieve our overall goal of state synchronization on all levels. Usually, we have to select one (or a small number) of them as the base target to implement redundancy.

In practice, state synchronization happens either on the operating system level of volume managers and mirrored disk volumes or on higher levels: many middleware servers (databases or application servers) provide replication functionality that can be utilized. Sometimes it is also possible to replicate the configuration or data if it is stored in files.

It is important to keep a consistent data state. For most data-keeping systems, this implies that some kind of transaction support must be built into the synchronization that achieves redundancy, otherwise a failover would use inconsistent data. Many systems demand the properties atomicity, consistency, isolation, and durability (ACID) that we met in Sect. 7.2. Enterprise-strength relational database management systems (RDBMS) are usually used to supply them.

This implies that disaster-recovery architecture and implementation must support failover of RDBMS operations. While this is straightforward to realize most of the time, mirroring of application data that is not in an RDBMS is often much harder. A method is needed to check the data for consistency and integrity, otherwise disk or application data mirroring might start the disaster-recovery system in an inconsistent and unrecoverable state, leading to software errors and crashes of the disaster-recovery system.

Care must also be taken to ensure that the available network bandwidth is sufficient to use the disaster-recovery system. While it is quite clear from the start that the bandwidth must be large enough to synchronize the redundant systems over a WAN, usage in the disaster case has often higher bandwidth requirements. In fact, it must be ensured that the application *can* be used over a WAN in practical situations, as many applications do not take into account the special WAN environment with high latency and low bandwidth. Network planning is an important part of disaster-recovery implementation; we learned about that already in Chap. 9.

Another important consideration is the requirement that the primary system must not be affected by the synchronization. For once, this implies that synchronous mirroring is usually not a good idea. If the disaster-recovery system went down, the mirroring would wait for timeouts and that would seriously interact with the availability of the primary system. Asynchronous mirroring is as secure in data transmission within our RPO requirements; it does so just with a small delay. But there are other implications of that requirement too. For instance, the synchronization process must not create too much load on the primary system either.

10.3.5 Shared System, Hot or Cold Standby

Since disasters are not expected to happen often, efficient resource usage is of interest. We have three basic types of disaster-recovery system designs and these are also illustrated in Fig. 10.2 on the next page:

1. **Shared systems**, where all available systems are used and the workload is distributed differently in the case of problems.
2. **Hot standby**, where an unused disaster-recovery system is ready to run all the time, and is kept on the same software, configuration, and data level as the primary system.

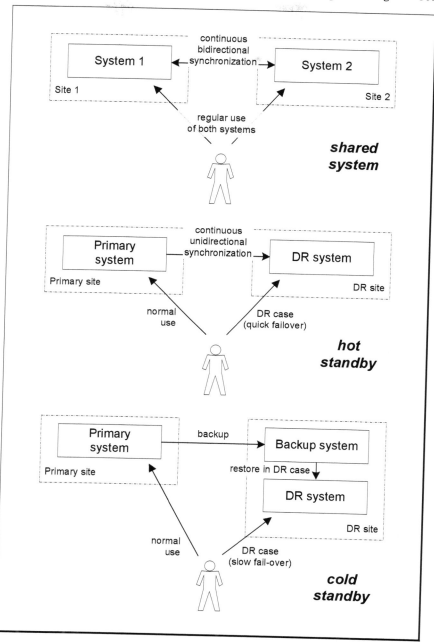

Fig. 10.2. Disaster-recovery system designs

3. **Cold standby**, where an unused disaster-recovery system is available but is not up. In the case of a disaster, the disaster-recovery system is restored from a backup system to an appropriate state and
started.

There are two subcategories of cold-standby disaster-recovery systems. The first one has systems where all the software needed is installed
already and only the data is missing. The second one uses completely unrelated systems, provisions them anew in the disaster-recovery case with
all necessary software and configurations, and then restores data from
a backup.

Design types 2 and 3 use dedicated disaster-recovery systems, while
design 1 deploys available active systems and provides for additional resources, to be used for services in the case of disasters.

The actual usage of shared systems must be analyzed in detail. At
first, they appear to be the most efficient use for the money. But by definition, they have a component in common that manages the redundancy of
the primary and the disaster-recovery system. This management component is almost always a single point of failure. In addition, shared
systems replicate all data changes immediately between primary and
disaster-recovery systems, and thus also replicate logical errors immediately. If the disaster-recovery architecture is also to cover recovery from
logical data errors due to software failures or user errors, then shared
systems are typically not an appropriate solution.

It should be noted that hardware redundancy and hardware quality
are success factors that must not be underestimated. They might make
the difference if one has one incident per week or one incident per year.
It is not enough to simply go to a well-named vendor, as all vendors have
had their share of problems with certain model ranges. As outlined in
Sect. 5.7, it is good practice to keep statistics and information from past
experience available, and maybe to exchange them in user groups or other
forums.

Again, since disasters seldom occur, failover times (i.e., the time that
is needed to migrate services from a defective component to a functional
redundant one) may be in the range of hours or even days. It is seldom
that failover times in the minutes range are really needed. (By the way,
failover times in the seconds range are marketing propaganda anyhow
and do not include failure discovery time; they are almost impossible to
deliver even in ideal conditions.)

All this boils down to the fact that a design for disaster recovery is
a compromise between the financial expenditure (the cost includes systems, licenses, staff members, etc.) and the redundancy achieved. For
example, in the case of dedicated disaster-recovery systems, it is quite
common for one disaster-recovery system to be used for several primary
systems. This increases the complexity of the installation of course: since

more than one primary system may have a problem at the same time (in fact, that is a common scenario) we must make available all services on the disaster-recovery system. In modern architectures, virtualization technologies like domains or virtual hosts help us to segregate hardware and operating system resources and make them available for separate disaster cases.

To get better usage of computer resources, cold-standby systems can be utilized as a test or a preproduction system, i.e., to analyze technical problems or to stage new releases. Within limits, this can also be done on hot-standby systems. There one needs the ability to turn off synchronization and turn it on again later without problems.

10.3.6 Time to Recovery – Failback to the Primary Site

Before, we were reminded that RTO is the time requirement to continue with a service on the disaster-recovery system. This may imply functionality restrictions and usually implies capacity and performance restrictions owing to nonidentical redundancy equipment. Depending on the importance of the service, different disaster-recovery architectures may be used that balance costs (for resources and activities to be provided beforehand) with the failover time and related costs for service interruptions, resources, and activities in the case of an event.

But it is not enough to look at RTO, i.e., at the time until the service is available again, somehow. This first step just buys time for the second step, the reestablishment of normal operations. This second step is often called *failback*. The failback time needed to recover full functionality after the disaster-recovery system went live, i.e., the time until everything runs normally again, is the *service recovery time*. Figure 10.3 on the following page illustrates that with a timeline and the relevant terms.

For physical disasters the service recovery time can be months, until a new data center is available or the old one has been repaired. For disasters that are caused by hardware errors, service recovery times range from days to weeks. Recovery of full service after major outages caused by software or human errors needs hours or days.

It is important to keep the service recovery time short too. There are several reasons for this:

- Reduced capacity/performance
- Possibly reduced functionality (only essential services are available)
- Binding of resources
- Dangers of further damage
- Backup might be limited

Binding of resources addresses both equipment and human resources. In a shared system architecture, primary and disaster-recovery systems

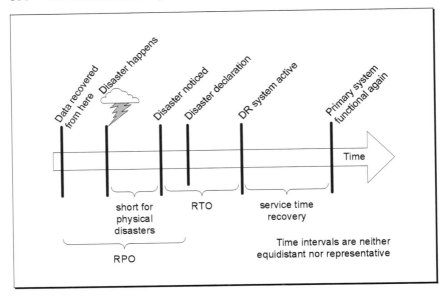

Fig. 10.3. Disaster-recovery timeline. *RPO* recovery point objective, *RTO* recovery time objective

are used all the time. During disaster recovery, disaster-recovery equipment will have more load than usual. The equipment used for disaster-recovery architectures will no longer be available for other purposes, most importantly, not for other disaster-recovery situations. In standby architectures, human resources (i.e., skilled operating center staff) have to skip regular work for setup and maintenance of disaster-recovery infrastructure, error analysis, and repair activities. This is especially true for "cold" standby architectures, where the whole disaster-recovery system has to be deployed at disaster-recovery time.

Even more problematic is the vulnerability during failover time. Normal operations include provision for failure: backups and redundancy activities take place. These are usually not available during failover time anymore. However, the normal danger of disasters still exists, maybe even more so because the reason for the current disaster may still be around. If, e.g., a software error causes data losses, switching to backup data will help to keep up reading services, but providing full access may also destroy the backup data. Also, people are more nervous, being under pressure and in an unfamiliar situation, so the risk of human errors increases.

It is important to consider backup during the system recovery time. Since that time span might be weeks or even months, we cannot afford to spend that whole time without a working backup system. The best solution is to place the backup system on the disaster-recovery site. This has the advantage that backup data is not lost if the whole primary site is destroyed. In addition, when we activate a disaster-recovery system on the disaster-recovery site, it can still use it and do its backups. When the backup system is placed on the primary site, one needs a disaster-recovery solution for it as well, for those failure scenarios where the whole primary site is destroyed or the backup system alone is destroyed.

The time frames for failover time are directly related to the disaster-recovery architecture model and the amount of automatism used: shared systems are the fastest; cold-standby systems will require most manual activity and will therefore be the slowest.

With service recovery time, this is more complex. Assuming that the actual repair times are the same for the different disaster-recovery architectures, the difference is caused by the task to failback from disaster-recovery mode to normal mode. It also depends on the kind of service that is provided during the failover time:

- A shared systems architecture will also have the techniques to add a repaired component (site/system) back into the active state. It may be assumed that with such an architecture, data does not have to be updated on the repaired component, so the failover will be fast.
- A hot- or cold-standby architecture will probably hold modified data, in which case time for data resynchronization will be needed. Resynchronization means that local changes on the disaster-recovery system are discarded and the same state as on the primary system is established again. Furthermore, the disaster-recovery infrastructure must probably be reconfigured into a default state, but this is not part of the service recovery time anymore.

Table 10.2 on the next page illustrates the relation between design categories, failover, and service recovery time. This table is not sufficient to decide on the appropriate choice of those categories – at first, it looks as if shared systems would always be better. But shared systems have other deficiencies, as we outlined in Sect. 10.3.5.

10.4 Solutions

Any disaster-recovery system design depends on a key decision that is bound to the basic RTO requirement that shall be fulfilled:

Immediate recovery refers to hot disaster-recovery systems where production is switched within 1 day – this is the main focus on this book; disaster recovery for mission-critical or important systems.

Table 10.2. System design categories, failover, and service recovery time. $+$ is a positive, ○ a medium, and $-$ a negative cost assessment. For those assessments, we assume that a cold-standby system can be used for tests or as a staging system in any case. We also assume that it is harder to use a hot-standby system for that purpose

Design type	Failover Time	Service recovery time	Low cost	Risk avoidance
Shared systems	$++$	$++$	$++$	$-$
Hot standby	$+$	○	$-$	$++$
Cold standby	$-$	○	○	○

Intermediate recovery between 1 and 3 days – this utilizes cold disaster-recovery systems and is at the edge of our focus. Even though many customers think they want faster recovery times, most often they do not need them.

Gradual recovery after about 3 days or more – some of the architectures described later do not use many resources and are therefore specially fit for this approach.

Manual workarounds until repairs are done – this approach does not fit into our scenarios of enterprise-class IT setups. While this is possible for a mom-and-pop shop, it is not a reasonable approach for mission-critical or important systems.

It is our task to analyze the real business dependencies on IT processes and their associated risks and costs. Only then can we settle on an approach. Especially for larger companies, a one-size-fits-all approach is not sensible either – it will either cost too much money when immediate recovery is made for all systems or leave too much risk when intermediate recovery is used for everything.

For each of these decisions, the approaches presented in the following have differing quality properties. It is the job of project management and architects to check the costs and work out an appropriate risk strategy. Then an associate solution approach is chosen.

In any case and independent of the ownership of the disaster-recovery site, there are a few standard solution approaches and important technologies that are used to realize disaster recovery. We will have a look at them in the next few sections.

10.4.1 Metro Cluster

This solution approach is built around a high-availability cluster where physical nodes are connected via a metropolitan area network (MAN).

Most often, they are placed in different parts of a city; thus, the term *metro cluster* was coined. Sometimes this system design is also called a *stretched cluster*.

Metro clusters are sometimes marketed as the single solution for both high availability and disaster recovery. This technology should cover both minor and major outages and handle them both equally well. At first sight that looks very good, but has very big pitfalls that one must know before one implements this solution.

The first thing that we notice is that we have different requirements for high availability and disaster recovery. While we want automatic protection against or recovery from minor outages, we prefer manual processes to recover from major outages. Even a metro cluster has higher risks associated with a switch to the disaster-recovery system; suddenly the client access goes over a MAN and that raises the probability of failures and outages. Therefore disaster-recovery switches should be explicitly decided upon and not automatically triggered.

This main issue of this technology revolves around storage. Failover clusters usually utilize redundant storage, i.e., mirrored disks, and assume that all cluster nodes have equal access to all disk mirrors. This means that writes are done synchronously and that reads are evenly spread over all mirror volumes. If disk mirroring is now spread over two sites as well, it must be assured that the increased latency and the higher risk of connection outages do not lead to problems.

To realize that, one employs two storage systems. Data mirroring between those systems can be done by the storage subsystems themselves or by the volume manager.

Mirroring with a volume manager is always done synchronously. This has the big advantage that the disaster-recovery system always has a usable state on the disk when the primary system goes down and that functionality can be achieved without additional software and thus without additional license costs. Connection problems are handled by the volume manager. But this needs timeout until the mirror is deactivated and one has to activate it again after the connection problems have been resolved. Of course, this is not a problem with the typical storage area network (SAN) connection in a local cluster environment. But owing to the higher outage probability of MAN connections, this case can happen more often for metro clusters and is therefore a typical problem in such installations.

Mirroring functionality from storage subsystems is available both in synchronous and in asynchronous form. Asynchronous mirroring allows much larger distances than synchronous mirroring. That is the main reason why this technology is used more often than mirroring by the volume manager. This functionality is supplied by special software that must also be integrated into the cluster, e.g., SRDF from EMC. The mirror volumes do not have the same properties anymore; there is now a master volume on the primary system and a slave volume on the disaster-recovery system. The slave volume can often not be accessed at all, or can just be in read-only mode. When it must be activated in the disaster case, the storage system has to be reconfigured to allow write access, introducing another complication that may lead to failure.

To make that reconfiguration less risky, an alternative system design is used from time to time. On the primary site there is an active/active cluster, with a third passive node on the disaster-recovery site. Service switches are preferably done between the two active nodes; the passive node is only used when both active nodes are not available anymore. There are two storage subsystems that mirror themselves; the disaster-recovery system is read-only. The third (passive) cluster node has a pre-pared configuration for read-write access to the disaster-recovery storage subsystem. Such reconfiguration has no consequences for the preferred cluster nodes on the primary site.

The problem with latency and disk access has been mentioned already. In practice this is not a problem with dark fiber connections up to a distance of 100 km (cable length). Then we can achieve latencies of 0.5 μs, which is sufficient for synchronous mirroring too. For other connection technologies and larger distances, one needs to check the latency from case to case. When the latency gets much higher, one must resort to asynchronous mirroring by storage subsystems.

Usually cluster software also does not take the MAN connection for heartbeat reliability. It is very hard to establish a reliable WAN connection with a guaranteed quality of service needed for the heartbeat tests but also for service availability tests. In metro cluster designs, the *split brain syndrome* must be prevented, where both sites think they are alive alone and both are automatically activated to provide the services to the end user.

In the end, larger distances between cluster nodes always decrease reliability and accessibility for the whole cluster. Owing to the inherent reduced network reliability and increased latency, the chances of unneeded failovers occurring are higher. Operations will require more effort: one needs longer to locate error causes and do repairs. This must be taken into account when a metro cluster is used in a system design. On the positive side, RTO and RPO are extremely short, which can be an advantage that recompenses for the disadvantages explained before.

Nevertheless, we must not ignore the fact that a metro cluster is only a very restricted solution for disaster recovery as it does not cover many failure scenarios. When an application or a human error occurs, it cannot be undone. That error is mirrored to the disaster-recovery site immediately. Restoration from the backup is the typical strategy for such errors in this architecture.

This failure scenario must be emphasized because it is obvious but often ignored. Metro clusters provide redundancy for a range of failure scenarios, but application, user, and administration errors are not among them. The cluster itself is another single point of failure in that system design: any error will cause the whole system to fail.

10.4.2 Fast Restore

The disaster-recovery site is located netwise near the backup server. In the disaster-recovery case, applications and user data are restored. Typical restoration speeds are 20–300 MB/s today. This depends on the restoration infrastructure (striping over multiple parallel tapes) and the backup data types (databases may be restored much faster than file hierarchies).

Thus typical restoration times for 1 TB are about 1 h; outage times will be considerable higher. On the other hand, this disaster-recovery architecture is the cheapest one: the backup infrastructure must be in place anyhow. If one plans in advance, spare machines are either available as cold standbys or may often be organized very quickly. But without such a plan, chaos is certain to ensue in the disaster case. Thorough testing is needed for this architecture: it must be assured that the service is functional after restoration. While restoring data and application software is easy, restoring the application's configuration in such a way that the disaster-recovery system can be operated must be described precisely in a process description. Otherwise the stress of a disaster-recovery case will surely cause errors during setup of the disaster-recovery system.

The big disadvantage of this architecture is that lots of work is lost in a disaster-recovery case. Typical backup intervals are daily, so the work of all users for the current day is lost. In addition, it means that users cannot work during restoration times; therefore this architecture must not be used for mission-critical applications where nonaccessibility of data and applications may severely endanger a company.

If an application or environment error is detected on the same day, fast restoration is the most often utilized technique to restore data and applications to a known working state.

10.4.3 Application-Level or Middleware-Level Clustering

Middleware clusters can rarely be used for disaster recovery. Databases, application servers, and other middleware components have their own clustering capabilities, and these were introduced in Chap. 7. An obvious idea would be to use these clusters in a MAN, just like we do with metro clusters. But compared with failover clusters, middleware clusters have very high demands on the availability of the intercluster connection that cannot be fulfilled reliably by MANs.

Application-level clustering is different if it is programmed from the start to support MAN or even WAN connections. A distributed system is likely to survive in the unfriendly operating environments of today's global networks. But sadly, there are very few such applications around, and the chances meeting some of them in normal projects are almost nonexistent.

10.4.4 Application Data Mirroring

As explained in Sect. 7.2, databases create redo logs to handle errors in transactions and to guarantee durability for their data. One can ship redo logs and replay them on a disaster-recovery system. One can also stop replaying at arbitrary times. If an application or environment error caused erroneous data deletion or alteration, replaying the redo logs that caused the problem can be skipped.

If applications store their data in files, these files may be synchronized. Synchronization tools like *rsync* handle incremental synchronization and give some freedom to choose synchronization intervals. Intervals may be in the hours range because it is problematic to synchronize file data storage with a lag of minutes: the synchronization process needs to determine the state of the file system both at the primary site and at the disaster-recovery site, and the files must be copied. This alone normally takes several minutes, maybe even hours. File synchronization is also not possible if the application keeps the files open; most often they are not in a consistent state then.

When disaster recovery is based on application-level data synchronization, the problem of application software and configuration mirroring remains. Automation of software mirroring is done easily, but often messes up release management. Software deployment is usually based on packaging systems, where a package database holds information about installed software and local changes. If we simply copy software files around, the package database and the software files become inconsistent. This might wreak havoc if automated patch management is be used because patch management often relies on a consistent package installation database.

Automation of configuration mirroring is even harder: configuration files often include data that is system-specific, like IP addresses and host names. They must be adapted to the disaster-recovery system.

Database Redo-Log Shipping

Databases are the backbone technology that stores most mission-critical structured data of any company. Most disaster-recovery projects will have to cope with database continuity. Since databases are quite large, restoration times from backup are often not sufficient. In addition, one needs all changes from the backup time until the disaster happened – daily snapshots are not enough for the target systems that we are handling here.

For disaster recovery of databases, most databases have a facility called log shipping or redo-log shipping. This allows database change logs to be transferred to a remote site where they can be "replayed" on a standby database. Database log shipping is based on the transactional behavior of RDBMSs that will keep logs about any committed changes to enable recovery in the case of crashes. Often, these logs are also used for incremental backups.

Ideally, logs may be changed manually before replay. If, for example, a database software error caused an inconsistency in the database, one could first discard the transaction that triggered the software error, before starting the replay to instantiate the disaster-recovery database. Of course, to be able to do this, one needs a database instance where the transaction can be replayed. Since such errors (by software or users) may need some time to be noticed, it is prudent to keep backups of the database and of all replay logs; thus, one can step back in time and repair the problem.

Database log shipping has also several variants:

Archive-log shipping is the method where logs are not transferred in real time, but in batches. With many database systems, redo logs cannot be accessed arbitrarily or in real time, as they are stored in an internal data area. After some time, or after some log amount has been reached, an *archive event* triggers an action, usually a command. The log data that have been collected between the last archive event and this one are made available as input for that action. The log data can now be transferred to the disaster-recovery site.

Since log data area sizes are quite large, usually in the range of several hundred megabytes, archive log shipping can still lead to lots of data loss. For mission-critical data, this might not be acceptable – a few hundred megabytes of order data can be worth millions of dollars or euros.

Redo shipping accesses the redo logs as they are written and transfers them immediately. In some database products, this is an inherent database feature, and comes both in synchronous and in asynchronous form. For disaster recovery, synchronous log transfer is most often not appropriate, as the primary site waits for successful transferal until the transaction has been successfully committed and the network latency might reduce the resulting performance in a nonacceptable way. For other database products, redo shipping is only available through third-party software or must be realized with self-written scripts.

Figure 10.4 on the following page summarizes the options for database log shipping; it uses Oracle's Data Guard realization for illustration.

Speaking of products like Oracle's Data Guard, it is time to present a selection of major database products that support log shipping in any

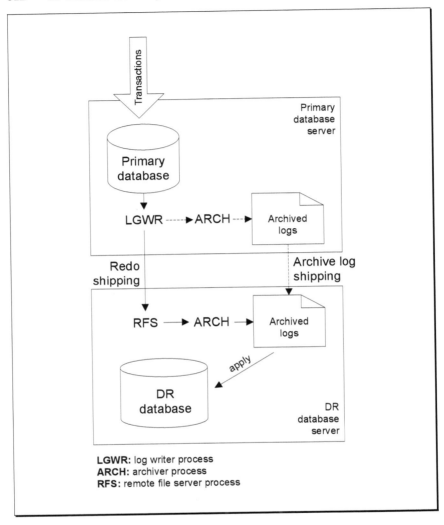

Fig. 10.4. Oracle database log shipping overview

variant. Of course, more database products exist that have this functionality as well. This selection has been made to give an impression about
representative functionality that you can buy right now.

Oracle has featured log shipping as a replication method for disaster
recovery for a long time. Up to Oracle 8i archive log shipping was supported; redo shipping needed special home-written scripts or third-party
software. Since Oracle 9i, redo shipping is integrated into core functionality where the *log writer facility* (LGWR) transfers the logs immediately to
the disaster-recovery site. To support both LAN and WAN architectures,
redo shipping can be synchronous (LGWR waits for arrival of redo logs at
the disaster-recovery site) or asynchronous (LGWR does not wait).

Oracle packages log shipping into an Oracle product, *Data Guard*, that
also supports switching the role of primary and disaster-recovery databases. That feature is important to keep the service recovery time short:
when a failover to the disaster-recovery system happened and the primary system has been repaired, Data Guard can be used to replicate the
now-changed data from the disaster-recovery system back on the primary
system.

IBM DB2 Universal Database has a *high-availability disaster-recovery*
(HADR) feature that provides the same functionality as Oracle's Data
Guard. The focus of this feature is recovery from physical disasters. In
the case of logical disasters (e.g., administrative or software errors) one
should be careful and should not use the automated failover procedures,
otherwise these errors will be replicated on the disaster-recovery system
as well.

Microsoft SQL Server has supported integrated archive log shipping
since SQL Server 2000. Self-made solutions were available with earlier
versions. No information is available about redo shipping support.

MySQL also supports archive log shipping. It writes logs as the basis
for incremental backup, which is effectively redo logs. These logs may
be shipped to the disaster-recovery site and replayed. With appropriate
caution, it is possible to realize redo shipping too.

File Mirroring

Still much data is kept in files and stored on file servers. That is particularly true if it is application data with a deep structure or it is unstructured data, like Office documents. In both cases, current database
technology does not provide enterprise-strength data storage, and special
storage capabilities are realized with files.

Configuration files are a different matter as they are often specific to
a system. They should not be handled by the methods described in the
following; we will come back to them in Sect. 10.4.6.

Figure 10.5 on the next page illustrates the difference between file
replication on the disk level (see Sect. 10.4.5) and file mirroring as pre-

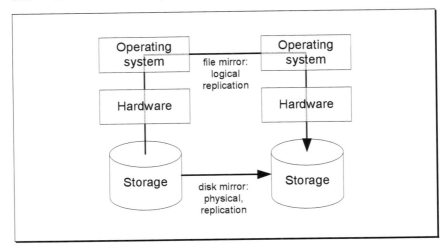

Fig. 10.5. File mirroring versus disk mirroring

sented here. While disk mirroring also replicates file data, it does not involve higher levels of the system stack. In fact, disk mirroring does not even know about files, it just replicates changes to blocks on disk volumes. Therefore no structure-related action can be integrated into disk mirroring, as we will do with file mirroring. In particular, the "delayed replay of logical changes" feature is not possible with disk mirroring – but this feature is essential for our strategy to cope with logical disasters.

For disaster recovery, all changes in a file system on the primary system must be replicated on the disaster-recovery system. Such changes include file creation, file change, metadata change (ownership, access rights, modification time), and deletion. Please note that some operating systems make it hard to replicate certain metadata; in particular, access time. If access time is needed for management or within the application, that is an additional burden. Luckily, such applications are very few.

The data change rate and the number of files at the primary site determine the replication frequency. The files must be scanned to check for changes and that needs time, both CPU time and real time. If a scan of a whole file system needs 2–4 h (and that is not unreasonable), we cannot have a replication frequency of 1 h. We only need unidirectional mirroring, not bidirectional synchronization.

Replication must have transactional semantics – either it is successful or it is aborted without remains. We do not want half-copied files; if some file copy does not succeed, it should be discarded, the old version should be kept and must be retried again in the future. Replication of changes might not succeed for several reasons; in particular, the source file might be locked, preventing access. There is also the problem of propagating changes to files that are opened by an application and are changing all the time, not being in a consistent state. These files must be seen as database files and one must find a way to replicate their content on the application level, e.g., by a procedure that is analogous to database log shipping.

To enable replication, either all changes must be recorded (related to the last replication time) or a complete inventory of existing files must be compared against the state of the disaster-recovery system. Both approaches have their problems: recording changes as they happen is only seldom used, and taking inventory of several terabytes of file space will need quite some I/O and computing resources. But it is mandatory that the performance of the primary site is not impacted for end users. Also transfer of files over the network might be bandwidth-intensive; that bandwidth is not available for primary usage and needs to be taken into account. Several protocols exist for transferring only changed parts of files, and in compressed form, to save network capacity that is needed elsewhere at the expense of CPU usage.

File mirroring can also be used to prevent accidental change or deletion of files, as shown in Fig. 10.6 on the following page. Then, deletions are deferred, deleted files are put into a "trash can area" first, and this is cleaned up at a later time. A similar thing is done with changed files: old version are placed in a backup area when new versions are replicated. Backup of metadata changes is also possible, though often overlooked. Of course, this implies the need for a retention policy that explicates when old file versions are eventually discarded – time-based, generation-based, or a mixture of both.

It might be necessary to do encrypted file transfers; this depends on the application and the data type. If the data is confidential and if the application does not leak data, file mirroring must not happen without encryption. It is not necessary for this capability to be part of the file mirroring product itself. Instead, it can be supplied by a Secure Sockets Layer (SSL) tunnel or a Secure Shell (SSH) tunnel, or by a virtual private network (VPN) that is established for the mirroring.

▸ *Products*

Vendor-supplied tools for products are very primitive and do not fulfill the requirements already set out. The most well known tools are *rdist*, a standard tool in any Unix environment, and *RoboCopy* from Microsoft's Windows Resource Kit. Both are very basic, are only capable of actual file mirroring, and provide no additional functionality as described before. Their usage for mission-critical environments should be seriously analyzed and questioned.

The current UNIX standard for file synchronization is the open-source tool *rsync*. It is available for Windows as well. It does file and metadata

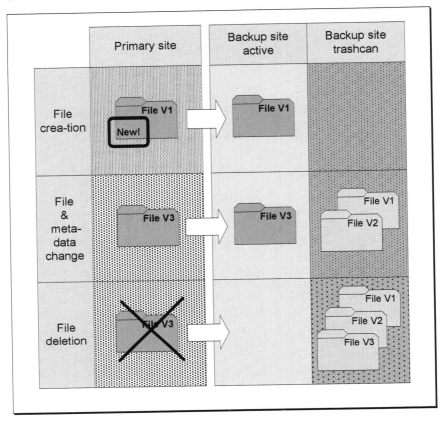

Fig. 10.6. File mirroring

replication, with bandwidth limitation and partial file transfers. Backup of deletion and changes can be made, but only for one generation, and no tool-inherent retention support is available. Both encrypted and unencrypted transfer protocols are available. rsync is a tool that compares the state of the primary site with that of the disaster-recovery site up-front, and then does the replication. But rsync also needs quite some system resources to build the file list, which might reduce primary site performance if I/O capacity is not sufficient.

In a Unix environment, it is possible to create a script-based solution that builds on rsync and adds the missing features (mostly multiversion backups, trash cans, and retention policies). Such scripts have been built multiple times in corporate environments, but none of them are known to be marketed as products or available as open-source tools.

For Windows, lots of commercial products are available that provide file synchronization.

10.4.5 Disk Mirroring

Disk mirroring is used in most disaster-recovery products. It only protects against hardware errors, as long as they do not occur on redundant disks at the same time. Any errors in the operating system or the application or user errors will be reproduced faithfully. This means that the disaster scenario of file corruption or mass deletions will simply be replicated at the disaster-recovery site. Therefore disk mirroring is appropriate for recovering from physical disasters, but not from logical ones.

Disk mirroring traditionally is used in local configurations, i.e., in one system where the disks are connected to the same bus. Therefore, most mirroring software assumes direct accessibility of storage and implements synchronous behavior. When a data item is written, the write operation is only successful if it could be written to all mirror partitions. Reading data from mirrored disks is usually done by arbitrary reads from any mirror partition. If disk mirroring is done to a disaster-recovery site, latency will often be too high for this assumption.

Disk mirroring software that we can use for disaster recovery must consider the case of higher latency and must work in this circumstance. While many applications work with asynchronous I/O, important application classes use only synchronous or direct I/O, or they synchronize the written data at the end of their operations. The timing behavior of mirroring must not be overlooked: long write times may influence directly user performance. Since reads from the local mirror partition will be much faster than reads from a remote disaster-recovery site, an equal distribution of read requests to all mirror partitions is not sensible anymore.

Special disk mirroring software for disaster recovery takes these requirements into consideration and provides the ability of a remote *slave copy* that is not read from during normal operations from the primary system. This slave copy might be accessed read-only by the disaster-recovery system though. Figure 10.7 on the next page illustrates those properties.

With all these cautious remarks in mind, disk mirroring is one of the easiest disaster-recovery technologies to implement. It is independent of applications and does not require changes in architectures if done properly. Many current proprietary disaster-recovery offerings are based on disk mirroring.

10.4.6 Matching Configuration Changes

System, middleware, and application configurations may include location-dependent information. They also are adapted to the set of services that run on a machine. If a system is moved to the disaster-recovery site,

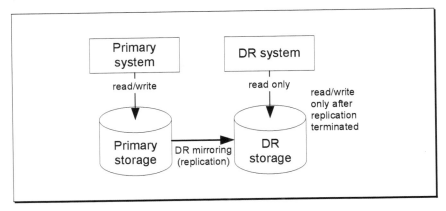

Fig. 10.7. Disk mirroring for disaster recovery

the configuration must be adapted. It is rare that 1 : 1 copying is possible. Location-dependent information like IP addresses must be updated, differences in available software must be accommodated, infrastructure services like routing, DNS servers, etc., might be different, and interdependences on other services that run on the disaster-recovery host must be considered.

Virtual hosts, as explained before, help to minimize the necessary changes. They provide isolation, and allow concentration on location-specific differences as they are not different from other services anymore. If the primary system is a failover cluster, the high-availability functionality might be of interest for the disaster-recovery system as well. Then, the disaster-recovery system can be configured as a single-node failover cluster, and can be turned on and moved around at will. The costs of failover cluster software might inhibit such an architecture though.

In many cases, configuration changes are propagated manually. If a disaster-recovery architecture selects this approach, it *must* specify regular audits that check if the configurations of primary and disaster-recovery sites are still consistent.

10.5 Disaster-Recovery Tests

Disaster-recovery tests are important, but hard to do properly and are very unpopular. To get full confidence, one has to shut down the primary system, get the disaster-recovery system up, and really use it. It is straightforward to test functionality, though one has to take care. It is much harder to test if the disaster-recovery system provides adequate performance. Most often, the disaster-recovery system is smaller than the primary system, as one cannot afford to spend all one's money on a same-sized hot-standby system. In the case of disasters, the users will surely accept lower performance – but often it is not possible to test that this lower performance is sufficient.

In addition, being off-site means that the network connection from clients to servers will not be the same; Section 9.1.6 discusses network designs for disaster recovery in detail.

Many businesses do not want to spend the effort for such thorough tests. In particular, the downtime of the primary system for disaster-recovery testing is a big issue if the system is usually used outside business hours as well. Therefore, narrowed test scenarios are often used. Then, the disaster-recovery system is activated in a virtual LAN (VLAN) or in a special laboratory environment, where also test clients are available. Measurements taken before are used to establish a typical workload pattern with the test clients to test capacity and latency.

Table 10.3 on the following page has more information on different test approaches that boil down to three categories.

1. **Hot simulation/fire drill:** No IT system will be touched in this step. Document-recovery procedures are walked through; it is checked if all people have all the required resources and information that they will need in a disaster case.
2. **Single component:** A single system is turned on and used on a restricted basis, mainly for functional tests.
3. **Complete environment:** The primary systems are turned off and all disaster-recovery systems are turned on.

Narrowed test scenarios have their risks. If the network split was not done correctly for a single component test, or if some error was made in disaster-recovery system configuration, the test clients might access partly the primary system. This could result in changing partly the disaster-recovery system's data and partly the primary system's data – which could lead to a disaster without functional backup itself being available. After all, our focus is on mission-critical services that must not be changed in an uncontrolled and in an inconsistent way.

Tests may also imply that the primary system's configuration must be changed. If synchronization is controlled on the primary system, there may be the need to turn it off during tests, otherwise lots of errors would occur at the primary system.

10.5.1 Test Goals and Categories

Disaster-recovery tests have two fundamental components.

1. Initial testing is important to verify the disaster recovery concept which was developed theoretically.

Table 10.3. Scope and objectives of test categories

Test	Requirements/scope	Result/outcome
Hot simulation	Requires limited preplanning Limited in scope and involvement Can be conducted at any time and at any location	Verification of disaster-recovery process Review existing disaster-recovery documentation (process and templates) Train on disaster-recovery procedure
Single component of disaster-recovery system	Requires extensive preplanning Requires the reservation of resources (IT staff, business owner, vendors) Requires verification of results Function restoration type test	Many components realize an IT service; a single failed component is restored A controlled recovery
Complete disaster-recovery system (all components)	Requires extensive preplanning Requires the reservation of resources (IT staff, business owner, vendors) Requires verification of results	The restoration of an entire business function from user input through return of final product to the user, at any point in time As close as you can get to a real recovery

2. Regular testing of a disaster-recovery solution is required for ongoing validation of the disaster-recovery environment and training on the disaster-recovery procedures to be prepared for a disaster.

These are different goals that we want to achieve. A complete disaster-recovery test should take place annually, while other tests can and should be scheduled more often, in particular the hot simulation. For example, hot simulations may be done three times a year, and single components are tested in simulation mode (see later) biannually. Disaster-recovery tests are also necessary after major changes.

For all disaster-recovery test cases the main issue is to ensure no impact on the productive site. For a hot simulation, there is no problem. But when we turn on the disaster-recovery system, be it a complete system or a just a single system, no client must access this disaster-recovery system in the belief that this is real. The primary system must not be made unusable involuntarily either, e.g., owing to activation of the same IP address in the same LAN segment.

Therefore extensive preplanning is required for all tests that involve activation of services. There is also the choice to run a single component test in simulation mode: the services are activated, but on test addresses and not on the primary service addresses and are tested on a basic level. This still has the high risk associated with it that we described before: one must make sure that really no conflicting resources are activated, and that the clients must not mix accesses to the primary and the disaster-recovery systems. For example, if a client accessed a disaster-recovery database and changed application files on the primary system, the application's data state might become inconsistent.

Yet another possibility is available if the disaster-recovery system is the same size as the primary system. Then we can switch to the disaster-recovery system and use that for production. Now we will see if the disaster-recovery system is really up to par.[1] After some days, one is ready to do the failback to the primary system and can test this process as well.

For basic functionality tests, one can simulate clients though. For example, one can trace which SQL requests are made by a client or which remote file accesses. Then we can activate the disaster-recovery system with a test address and access the database with an SQL client, issuing appropriate SQL commands, or we can access files the same way as the application does. If these accesses succeed, we have raised our confidence that application clients would be able to issue the same requests considerably. Such tests can be automated and are considered a kind of low-level monitoring for disaster-recovery system functionality that can be realized in an on-going and cheap way.

10.5.2 Organizational Test Context

The tests must involve the business owner. Not only technical steps should be tested, but the whole process, from problem detection to disaster declaration to failover and informing end users about changing work processes because unimportant systems are not available anymore. IT departments and business owners should discuss and agree together on a test date. Regulations like SOX and Basel II sometimes enforce regular disaster-recovery tests; one needs to pay attention to them.

All parties to that decision process are often well aware of the risks that are inherent in disaster-recovery tests; therefore, the business owner sometimes does not want the tests or wants modified tests that are enough to raise his or her confidence, but which are not real-scenario tests. Many IT staff members, especially those from the administration and operation teams, do not like those tests either: they are costly, are usually made off-hours and on weekends; abandoning the tests saves effort and money. There is a real danger that this will lead to a disaster in

---

[1] Well, this does not guarantee 100% disaster-recovery functionality. The network might be damaged as well in the case of a physical disaster and this is not the case in such a disaster-recovery test.

the disaster case; when the failover to the disaster-recovery system suddenly does not work, or when the performance is not only reduced, but unusable, etc. Even though disaster-recovery tests are not urgent, they are important.

When failover to the disaster-recovery system is successful, functional regression tests can make sure that the applications are working at the disaster-recovery system. As outlined before, performance tests can be made with the help of workload generators. This is not a simple issue: finding or constructing a good workload generator for an application is a challenge in itself. If one can emulate a proper workload, testing latency (are answers fast enough) and capacity (how many people can work with acceptable answer times) are the most important issues.

Since tests will change the disaster-recovery system's data, there is the need to synchronize data and sometimes even the application configuration back to the primary system's state. This is called *resynchronization*. During testing and resynchronization, no disaster-recovery capability is available, so it should be done quickly. Ideally, resynchronization is done automatically, without human intervention.

10.5.3 Quality Characteristics

Being able to test a disaster-recovery installation properly is a distinguishing mark that tells about the quality of a system design. Facets of that quality are:

- Being able to activate the disaster-recovery system for a test while the primary system is still active
- Being able to activate only one component on the disaster-recovery system; i.e., doing a component disaster-recovery test, or even doing disaster recovery for just this component in the case of a logical disaster
- Either no or very few changes are necessary on the primary system for tests
- Workload generator, regression tests, and test metrics are available
- Primary system downtime is not needed.
- A short time frame for resynchronization, after the test
- Business owner buy-in (suitability for business and IT processes)

10.6 Holistic View – What Is Needed Besides Technology?

This book would be incomplete if we did not also point out that many more activities must be taken into account during disaster-recovery planning.

If a serious disaster happens, very often nothing works anymore. Not just one server is affected, but a whole site does not work anymore. Then concerned and untroubled activity is needed to establish functionality of the disaster-recovery systems at the disaster-recovery site as soon as possible. These incident management activities must be planned and prepared in advance, otherwise chaos and hectic are preprogrammed and the setup time will be longer by magnitudes.

10.6.1 Command Center and War Room

Disaster-recovery planning must include the setup of a disaster command center for the disaster case. This command center is a "war room" and associated infrastructure at the disaster-recovery site. All relevant people will meet in person at this command center, and the command center's infrastructure will be the most important one to be brought on-line first.

It is important that the war room has a noncomputer infrastructure as well. Availability of a whiteboard and several flip charts is mandatory; board markers must not be forgotten too. Make yourself clear that the network or any other computer besides your local laptop might not work in the first few hours – you are without a network, without DNS, without Internet access to your information, without most planning help. "Management on walls" – pasting paper sheets with important information on walls – is still the most robust method to keep all people in the command center up to date with current developments.

Room allocation should be part of the disaster-recovery tests. We should never trust that something "just will happen," like a room will "just be available." Instead, we have to try it out to see if it really works.

10.6.2 Disaster-Recovery Emergency Pack

We mentioned this in the previous section: you must be prepared for the computer equipment at the disaster-recovery site not working in the first few hours. Most often, these are network and infrastructure problems where your network colleagues will be fully active themselves to restore services. Lots of our computers depend on available domain controllers, file servers, name servers, etc., where also the relevant information needed to restore the services is stored.

In particular, system information is crucial. Many IT shops establish a configuration management database (CMDB) that helps with our day-to-day activities by providing up-to-date information about computer systems and changes. But do not rely on that information resource being online or accessible when you are struck by a disaster. *Print out* your essential information (names, contacts, process flows) and *burn technical information on CD* (CMDB, system documentation), and put everything

Table 10.4. Content list of an Emergency Pack. *DR* disaster recovery

Information	Contacts for supplier, partners, vendors Logical and physical network plans System documentation for DR systems (with current software and patch versions)
Process descriptions	Roles and responsibilities Internal escalation procedure General disaster-recovery procedures System-specific disaster-recovery procedures
Templates	Analyze environment Contact list, roles, and responsibilities

into an executive case, and bring that *Emergency Pack* with you, to have all necessary information in the war room.

Another item for the Emergency Pack is document templates, i.e., form sheets that name the most important information that must be gathered during the first stages of disaster recovery. Again, it is a good idea to have such templates on paper and pin them on the wall. Alternatively, one could edit them on a local laptop – but then its content cannot be easily shared with the rest of the disaster-recovery team.

10.7 A Prototypical Disaster-Recovery Project

This section will present a prototypical disaster-recovery project that can be reused in many circumstances. It has been used successfully in many environments and covers the most common failure scenarios. This design can be used by you as well, with relatively small changes.

The goal of this section is to show you how the theoretical approach of the previous sections is filled with life. Here is a description of an exemplary disaster recovery for an IT service, a complete blueprint that can be cloned and adapted for your purposes.

The design has a few up-front assumptions that are quite common:

IT service exists already. Disaster recovery shall be established for an IT service that exists already.

Disaster recovery is established by a project. A team of people will work together to establish disaster recovery. They create the architecture, implement the solution, and test it. This team will then be dissolved and responsibility for the ongoing work will rest with the operations and administration staff.

High availability is not a topic. One does not need to design or realize high availability for the IT service; that has already been done.

Failure scenarios are identified. Since high availability has been realized before, failure scenarios are already available. The disaster-recovery project is concerned with establishing recovery for some failure scenarios that were classified as not applicable before.

Disaster recovery for the whole primary site is not a topic. Please take note because this is important: this blueprint does *not* describe overall disaster recovery for a whole site. Instead it focuses on disaster recovery for *one IT service* with its components and subservices.

In the design, we follow roughly the approach from Sect. 10.2. Differences are mainly due to the fact that we do not have to work out failure scenarios anymore:

System identification is done in Sect. 10.7.1, where we analyze the existing primary site. This will give us an overview of systems, available services, and dependencies.

Business requirements and project goals are described next, in Sect. 10.7.2.

Conceptual design is concerned with the disaster-recovery business view and the organizational approach used for realization of disaster recovery, and is described in Sect. 10.7.3.

System design of our blueprint presents the solutions that are used to realize disaster recovery for all our systems and services, and is covered in Sect. 10.7.4.

Implementation is described in Sect. 10.7.5 and will dive deep into technical details.

Processes for failover and for tests are the topic of Sect. 10.8. There we will build on this prototypical design and will present actual procedures for switching (both from the primary system to the disaster-recovery system and back) and for testing.

To get our feet on the ground, we will make specific technical assumptions about products and protocols and present them as a scenario that is representative of many installations. They are a remedy to formulate specific procedures, but are actually not relevant to the design: other products or other configurations will have equivalent capabilities, but the basic approach can be migrated easily.

We describe disaster recovery for a client/server system. Multi-tier architectures with application servers are also used often. While they are not covered on the surface, disaster recovery for an application server is almost identical to that for a Web server; both have no persistent state associated with them, and software and configuration must be kept consistent between redundant systems.

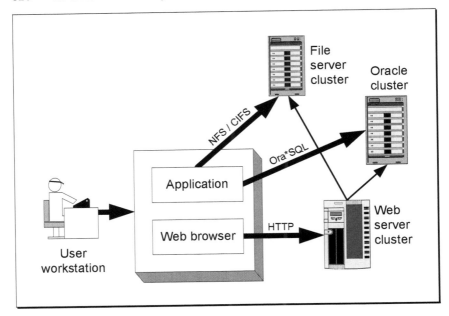

Fig. 10.8. Essential services

10.7.1 System Identification – the Primary Site

The IT service is realized by file servers, a database server, and Web servers. Figure 10.8 illustrates these servers. The IT service provides a business function for one department; there is one business owner who is easy to identify.

The bulk of application data is stored on Unix file servers. The applications are not long-running services that keep their files open all the time. Instead they are our typical run-of-the-mill applications that take some files, change them, and write them back. Clients access the files via Network File System (NFS) if the user has a Unix workstation; access from Windows desktops utilizes Common Internet File System (CIFS). The file server provides both access methods: NFS is native to Unix, CIFS is realized by *Samba*.

Some application data is structured and stored in a database. Programs on the client systems access that database server directly. To supply factual information, we will assume that Oracle is used as database product and provide specific technical information; other database products have similar procedures and capabilities.

Another access method for data is via a Web interface, i.e., a Web-based application where the user interface is accessed by a Web browser.

The application on the Web server accesses both files and the database directly.

Besides those services that are used by engineers, some infrastructure services are needed as well: none of those servers can be accessed without a functional network, and none of them will run without DNS. In addition, the applications cannot be used without licenses that are managed by license servers. For login, a running authentication service is needed which we assume to be LDAP-based without loss of generality.

All servers on the primary site are run in a high-availability environment, e.g., the file server utilizes a failover cluster. We will look at each server in more detail later.

On the file server, nightly jobs are active, e.g., files are transformed in batches, cleanup activities, etc. These jobs are aware of the high-availability environment, e.g., they are activated on all physical nodes of the cluster and check that the respective service is active before they run.

Backup is realized by Tivoli Storage Manager (TSM).[2] The TSM installation is distributed over the primary site and the disaster-recovery site. The TSM server at the disaster-recovery site does the backup of primary systems, and vice versa.

So, let us have a more detailed look at the servers and the infrastructure. We will list each system component, in turn:

- File server
- Oracle database server
- Web server
- Operating system configuration
- Infrastructure
- Related systems that are not on the primary site

For each of those components, we will look at its functionality and its requirements. Finally, we will have the dependency diagram. This will provide the information that is needed to plan the disaster-recovery system.

File Servers

Application data files are accessed via NFS (Unix file sharing) and CIFS (Windows file sharing). Several servers are run in an active/active failover cluster configuration, when a service needs to be switched the other cluster node runs two services. For NFS and CIFS services, this is acceptable. The clients will experience a performance impact, but the service will still function.

---

[2] Again, any other enterprise-class backup product could appear here instead.

A typical server configuration for such a file server has multiple CPUs, several gigabytes of main memory, and serves 10 TB of data. The data itself is stored on an external storage subsystem (e.g., from EMC).

All data is kept mirrored, i.e., the storage is configured as Raid10: mirrored and striped. Each stripe is spread over eight disks (these are four mirrored volumes); with a disk size of 146 GB this results in a LUN size of 300 GB.

This configuration is done on the storage system and not with the host's volume manager. It reduces the number of LUNs or the number of device files; this additional abstraction reduces complexity on the host side. The hosts should be able to access these virtual storage devices via several access paths; for greater redundancy, software drivers for such a feature must support it both on the storage subsystem and on the host. Usage of such storage management software often adds additional complexity and reduces robustness. For example, with *PowerPath* from EMC, every LUN exists several times as a device file; this seriously increases boot times, etc.

We mention this in this chapter, since the primary system configuration should be optimized to make disaster-recovery system configuration easier and more robust. Having very few LUNs has the advantage that there will be a smaller potential for conflicts, when several of the file servers are migrated to the same disaster-recovery host.

Oracle Database Server

Structured application data is stored in an Oracle database. The database server is also configured as a failover cluster, but in an active/passive configuration this time. One server runs the database; a second server with the same hardware configuration is kept as a hot backup node in a high-availability cluster. i.e., that second node is up and running, but is not utilized except when the Oracle resource group is switched to it. Owing to performance break-ins, it is not possible to utilize that second domain for some other service; Oracle needs all the capacity all the time and does not degrade gracefully.

Typical hardware configurations use twice as much capacity as for file servers – twice the number of CPUs and double the main memory for less data storage space. The database may be stored on the same storage subsystem that is also used for the file servers, of course on separate logical volumes. As with the file servers, Raid10 configuration is used; storage management happens on the storage box and not with the host's volume management.

To complete the description of our setup, we note that client application programs may talk directly to the Oracle database, via Oracle SQL*Net. To use one of those client application programs, a user needs a license that can be obtained from one of several license servers.

Web Server

The Web servers appear to users as one server: they are run in a load-balancing cluster. These servers are only used to host the application. The Web application holds no data and has no permanent state.

There are two load-balancing devices that are themselves a cluster too. They are run in an active/passive mode and use the router high-availability technology Virtual Router Redundancy Protocol (VRRP) for failover (see Sect. 9.1.3). If one of them has an outage, the other takes over.

Operating System Configuration

As already outlined, both the file servers and the database server run on Unix servers, as several failover clusters. Attached to the cluster are two associated external storage subsystems.

Example 1 (Example configuration of primary clusters). The servers utilize Solaris, and Sun Cluster as high-availability software. Configuration is a standard failover cluster configuration, with NFS/CIFS servers and Oracle as resource groups. EMC boxes do storage management; the management interface is ECC. PowerPath is used to enable access to EMC boxes via multiple paths.

The hosts are installed manually, with support of the configuration management system *cfengine*. Such configuration management systems allow the definition of standardized configurations that can be reproduced all the time. A Jumpstart server exists to support provisioning; automated patch management is done by scripts supplied by Sun.

There is also no need for special log management: regulatory or business demands from SOX or Basel II do not exist.   ∎

Infrastructure

As explained in Chap. 9, it is not easy to identify all infrastructure services that are used in total by an application or a system.

The servers are connected with gigabit network interfaces to the Intranet backbone, and usage of file and database servers depends on a functional network. The network itself is highly available, though there have been major outages caused by worms in the past. Common infrastructure services like DNS and Network Time Protocol (NTP) are used as well. NTP is not necessary, but without DNS, functionality cannot be delivered.

Some workstations run Unix and need an LDAP authentication service to log in. The service is also needed by file and database servers, both of them also use LDAP for authentication. The LDAP master server

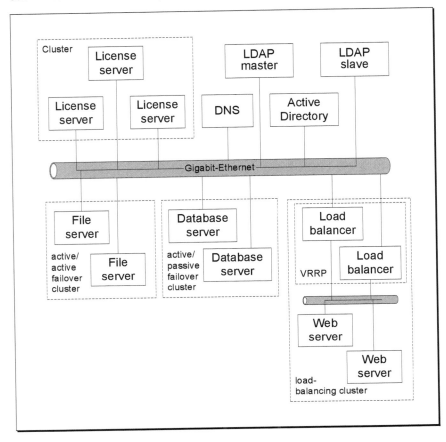

Fig. 10.9. Services and systems at the primary site

is a smaller server, and several replicated slave servers exist, both at the primary site and at the disaster-recovery site. On that master server, auxiliary administration software is used to manage the Unix accounts. Disaster recovery for the LDAP master server needs to be made available as well. This is not as critical as Oracle and file service though, as we can run without the master server for quite some time owing to existing slave servers.

Other desktops run Windows. These desktops also depend on network services, e.g., on Active Directory domain controllers. Disaster recovery for these Windows Network Services has already been established in another project; therefore, we do not need to consider them in this system design.

The licenses are maintained on three license servers, running Unix as well. The license application software already realizes a distributed operations model; these three servers run as a cluster. (The number three was taken from a FlexLM installation, where at least three servers *must* always exist.) That application-level cluster has high latency demands and cannot be operated as a metro cluster. Therefore we need to provide disaster recovery for these servers as well.

Finally, we have completed our overview of all relevant services on the primary servers and can show them in the schematic graphics of Fig. 10.9 on the facing page.

Related Systems, Not at the Primary Site

File and database backup and archiving of the primary systems is done on the TSM server at the disaster-recovery site. The TSM server recognizes the servers' identities: each node has a unique ID that is bound to the physical system. In the disaster-recovery case, there will occur problems with that knowledge; it is not possible to migrate the backup to changed physical hosts without adaptation of the state of the TSM server.

Dependency Diagram

Figure 10.10 on the next page presents the resulting dependency diagram for the primary site. As so often, several dependencies are not shown because they would make the diagram incomprehensible, e.g., all components have dependencies to the administration.

It is obvious that the application, the user environment, the administration environment, and the physical environment are single points of failure. It is not obvious that there are many more single points of failure in the components that are marked as redundant. As we explained in Chap. 3, such redundant components typically have a redundancy management part that is not redundant, though also it will not probably fail. In addition, the high-availability environment will not protect against multiple errors of dependent components; such a failure will escalate into a major outage.

10.7.2 Business Requirements and Project Goals

The servers provide mission-critical services. The disaster recovery is part of the ITIL business continuity process. It asserts that the business owner's staff can do their work even if the named primary systems that they need are damaged.

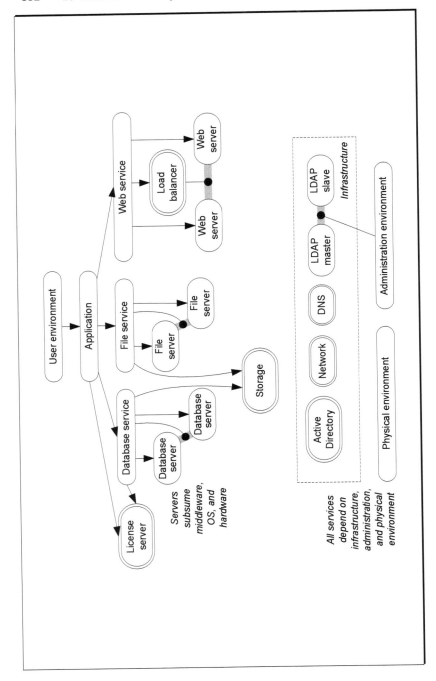

Fig. 10.10. Dependency diagram of primary systems

► *Scope*

Disasters in the client environment are not covered.

The disaster-recovery solution shall also recover from logical disasters, i.e., from major outages in upper levels of the system stack. In particular, it shall recover from software and administration errors.

► *Service Level Agreement*

The RTO is 4 h at maximum, with an expected recovery in 2 h. The RPO is 4 h for database data and 8 h for file data.

That is, the disaster-recovery systems at the disaster-recovery site *must* be up and running within 3 h.

At maximum the last 4 h of changes to the database and at maximum the last 8 h of changes to file data may be lost.

The RPO limits were chosen to be a compromise between implementation costs and business damage. Shorter RPOs would have needed more computer system resources on the primary site.

► *Process*

The disaster case must be declared explicitly. It can only be declared by a group of executives (CIO, IT lead, business manager) and their proxies that are personally named.

► *Cost Efficiency*

The disaster-recovery systems are mostly dedicated for disaster recovery. But they may also be used for testing purposes for a limited time range, e.g., to prepare for major changes like an Oracle upgrade. They are not used for any production service.

There will be fewer disaster-recovery systems than there are primary systems; one server will provide several services during disaster recovery. Those servers will also have less performance and less capacity than the primary servers. The reduced hardware equipment was set as a project goal from the start, to get a cost-effective solution. After all, the disaster-recovery systems will be idle most of the time and reduced performance can be accepted when major outages occur.

10.7.3 Business View

This section will give you information on the conceptual view, about the business entities involved, business processes, etc. It lists the business resources both of IT staff and of the business owner that are used to build the disaster-recovery solution.

Responsibilities for processes and systems often evolve over time and carry the baggage of many organizational restructure leftovers. This is not unusual, as most big and many medium-sized companies have mergers at some point, or some other drastic business changes that also influence IT management. Therefore it is hard to give a blueprint for roles and responsibilities – the allocation of roles should evolve pragmatically, and typically depends on personal relationships as well.

That said, the separation of work is typically as follows:

▸ *IT Department*

The IT department installs, configures, and maintains the servers, both the primary systems and the disaster-recovery systems. It also maintains the application. Administrative services (LDAP, license servers) are also run by the IT department. Database administration and monitoring is sometimes managed by a special subgroup; this depends on the number of IT staff. Even more often, network issues are delegated to a network department that is responsible for network and network-related infrastructure services. Both the IT system and the IT network group have vendor-support contracts.

The IT department is also responsible for the disaster-recovery preparation phase.

▸ *Disaster-Recovery Project Team*

The disaster-recovery project team is responsible for the architecture and review of major changes. It is mainly staffed from the IT department, but should also have people from the business department on board, and is often extended with subject-matter experts. Vendors are consulted by the project team, the IT staff, and also sometimes by the business owner. In theory, the IT staff or the project team provides the service and handles the connection to the supplier; there is no need for business owners to consult vendors. In practice, vendors approach them directly, and sometimes they also want to have a say on technology decisions as well.

▸ *Business Owner*

On the business owner's side, often an executive manager is directly responsible and involved; of course, he or she will get support from his or her business staff as well. At other places, responsibility for disaster declaration and disaster recovery is placed at a board support position.

As already mentioned, a disaster case can be declared by consensus of a group of executives and their proxies. This group is named personally; checking a declaration against the list of people is part of the disaster process.

Of course, there are also the end users who actually use the systems and the IT staff and business owners are responsible for servicing them.

Table 10.5. RASIC chart for disaster recovery

	IT staff		DR project		Business owner	
	System administration	Network	Project team	Vendors	Business owner	End users
Governance/IT management						
Declare disaster case	I	I	R	I	R	I
Run primary and backup systems	R		A	C	I	
Preparation						
Disaster-recovery preparation: data replication, updates, configuration	R	S	A	C	I	
Prepare for network-related disaster cases	I	R	I		I	I
Test disaster-recovery functionality	R	S	A	C	I	
Day to day						
Switch to backup system (failover) and repair primary system	R	S	S	S	I	
Failback to primary system	R	S	A		A	I
Handle network-related disaster cases	I	R	I		I	I

R responsible, *A* must approve, *S* supports, *I* must be informed, **C** consults

▸ *RASIC Chart*

A better overview of major activities and associated roles is given by the RASIC chart in Table 10.5. RASIC charts are excellent means to express the distribution of roles for an area: they express which stakeholder is responsible, must approve an action, shall support, must be informed, or consults (adds subject-matter expertise).

You are not expected to be able to use this table directly and without any changes, as there will be differences from company to company – sometimes even from project to project – of how work is distributed. Nevertheless, this table will be a good start for you. If you realize your disaster-recovery solutions with outsourcing contractors, a reduced version of this chart, together with a description of the IT processes, is the best part of the outsourcing contract.

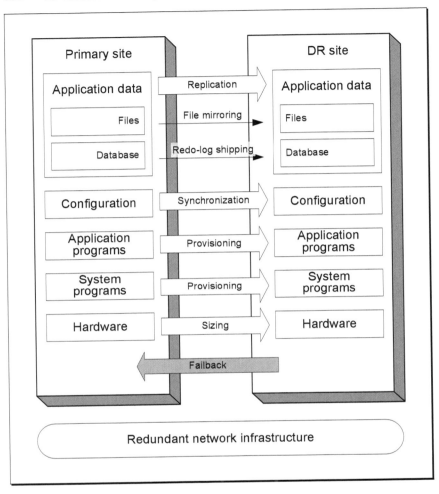

Fig. 10.11. Disaster-recovery redundancy approaches

10.7.4 System Design

The system design presents the logical view of the architecture components. It describes the components (servers and services) that are involved, what function they deliver, which hosts are involved, and which
technical processes are used to implement disaster recovery.

We need to consider redundancy on several abstractions levels, as explained in Chap. 3. Redundancy is achieved by different methods for different components, as shown in Fig. 10.11.

Table 10.6. Example hardware sizing

	Primary systems		DR systems	
	CPU	Memory (GB)	CPU	Memory (GB)
Database cluster	2 × 8	32	8	16
File server cluster	2 × 8	32	4	16
Web server cluster	2 × 2	4	1	4

We have not differentiated between application and middleware programs. The only middleware that is in use is the Oracle database; and that is provisioned in the same way as application software. If it had been deployed in a different way – e.g., if manual deployment is needed for Oracle, but automatic deployment is available for the application – we would have listed it separately. For the sake of redundancy decisions, LDAP and license servers are also considered applications. This is due to the fact that LDAP is not part of Solaris proper – for a Linux server, LDAP would have been part of the configuration.

Let us have a bottom-up look at that diagram and start with the hardware first.

Hardware of the Disaster-Recovery System

The hardware is dedicated for disaster recovery, but may also be used for limited testing purposes. The disaster-recovery system is not as large as the primary system: At the primary site, we have three servers on four systems in two clusters: two file servers on two systems in an active/active failover cluster, and one database server on two systems in an active/passive cluster.

We utilize just two systems for disaster recovery, one for file service and one for database service. In the disaster case, the two file servers will both run on one system. The system can handle outages of the database server, the file server, or both. Full functionality will be available with reduced performance.

Both servers have half the main memory of the primary servers. Table 10.6 has an example sizing that could have been used. The sizing example uses existing experience with performance data. Such performance data can be captured in the initial setup or during operations of the primary systems.

For the disaster-recovery disk storage, storage subsystems with Fibre Channel drives are used as well. To reduce costs, we use drives with higher capacity and Raid5 and thus need fewer disks. This will raise redundancy recovery times in case of disk outages, but this is sufficient for the disaster-recovery system.

The performance of the disaster-recovery system will be reduced, but the volume of work is doable. Owing to performance reduction, people might need to work longer to finish their assigned tasks; this is acceptable for the customer. You will have noticed that CPU sizing of primary and disaster-recovery systems is quite different in our example sizing. The file service (NFS or CIFS) does not break down in the case of reduced CPU performance and reduced available memory – it justs need longer to finish. As services, NFS and CIFS are very robust. Oracle is different here: if the system load goes beyond some limit, the service is not reliable anymore.

While CPU and memory have the largest influence on performance, the overall metrics not only depend on CPU and memory, but also on I/O. Owing to slower disks, I/O will be different for the primary system compared with the disaster-recovery system too. This difference cannot be analyzed in advance; one needs to do benchmark tests for sizing and check the available throughput. Initial sizing for such benchmark tests is done by senior engineers who use their past experience. Such "gut estimations" are not reliable and should not be used for contracts or for final sizing decisions.

When hardware capacity is changed at the primary site, it must be checked if sizing of the disaster-recovery system is still OK, or if an upgrade is necessary there as well.

A frame with blade servers might provide disaster-recovery systems for the LDAP server and the license server. Those servers have neither high CPU nor high memory or disk space demands. Such a server can also be used for administrative purposes, e.g., as a *JumpStart* server for provisioning Solaris software.

Figure 10.12 on the next page summarizes the disaster-recovery systems.

Programs and Configuration

System programs are Sun Solaris, EMC PowerPath, Samba, and associated administrative tools (many of them are open-source tools). On the primary system, Sun Cluster is used in addition. To reduce costs, that is not the case on the disaster-recovery system. In the case of upgrades, in particular when security-related patches are deployed, both the primary and the disaster-recovery systems must be updated. For provisioning, a JumpStart server is used. Change management processes have been adapted to assert that provisioning of the disaster-recovery systems is kept in the same state as the primary systems.

Application programs are not provisioned via the JumpStart server, as system components are. Instead, they are installed manually, in an application-specific way. Nevertheless, one can handle them similarly to system programs: each time a program change happens on the primary

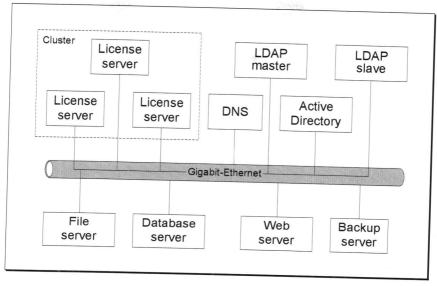

Fig. 10.12. Disaster-recovery systems

system, it must be done on the disaster-recovery system as well. It might just be a bit more complicated, if the application has no proper installation and upgrade support.

System configurations are not identical on the primary system and on the disaster-recovery system. This is mostly due to the disaster-recovery system not being a failover cluster, but is also due to hardware differences.

Clusters as Primary Systems

It is a common situation for mission-critical servers that some cluster technology is utilized for the primary servers, very often failover clusters. This brings up immediately the question of how the disaster-recovery systems will be set up, if they will be cluster systems too.

Often one will not buy several disaster-recovery systems for one service, just to run a cluster again. This is quite expensive, and that money might be better spent elsewhere. On the other hand, if we have a cluster environment at the disaster-recovery site as well, replication of the primary site gets much easier: programs, locations, and configurations can be made the same and automatic replication can be used.

We have three options to provide disaster recovery for failover clusters:

1. Utilize a cluster at the disaster-recovery site as well. Cluster products also work on single hosts: they have to function in the case of outages of the other nodes. One can set up a one-node cluster explicitly. This allows the cluster configuration to be reused and the cluster management component to start, stop, and monitor services at the disaster-recovery system.
2. In those rare cases where a single-node cluster is not possible, one can utilize virtual host technology to run several pseudo hosts on one system. They can be grouped into a cluster, and again we can reuse the primary system's setup for the disaster-recovery system.
3. One can abstain from cluster technology at the disaster-recovery site. But then one has to adapt programs, configurations, and technical processes to the different environment.

The first two options are actually rather straightforward; therefore, we will concentrate on the third option and will have a more detailed look at what happens when we do not utilize cluster technology at the disaster-recovery site of our example system design.

▶ *IP Addresses*

Section 9.1.6 presented several approaches that can be used as network design for disaster-recovery sites. Here we decided that we do not use building blocks, but implement one big VLAN that spans the primary and the disaster-recovery sites. The risk of spanning tree loops has been accepted as small enough to bear that risk. A reconfiguration of the (existing) VLAN would have brought much more complexity with it.

Since the primary systems are failover clusters, all IP addresses that are used by clients are virtual IP addresses anyhow; they must be movable between cluster nodes. The network interface cards (NICs) have different primary IP addresses, colloquially referred to as "physical host addresses." We can move those service IP addresses to the disaster-recovery system in the disaster case. This gives us two advantages: no configuration in clients or DNS must be changed; and no application configuration that records the IP address must be changed.

Care must be taken that the disaster-recovery system configuration is not activated as long as the primary system is still up. IP address conflicts would lead to problems immediately. To achieve this, no automatic activation is implemented; that needs to be done manually. Of course, not every command is issued manually; scripts have been written that provide appropriate abstractions and ease that task.

▶ *Mapping of Primary Clusters to Disaster-Recovery Systems*

On the primary system, two servers are available for file service, and two for the database. These four servers are run as two failover clusters with three services:

- The database service runs on two servers. This logical database host is so important that an unused server is used as a hot standby.
- Two file services run on the other two servers. i.e., every server has one logical file service host associated by default and will take on another one in the case of failovers.

Important system configuration, like host names, IP addresses, file system mounts, and service starts, is done by the cluster subsystem. The cron jobs also assume a cluster environment. They are activated on all cluster notes and test for active services.

On the disaster-recovery system, two servers are available: one for file service and one for the database. The two file servers from the primary system are mapped to the one disaster-recovery file service.

Since the file services do not conflict with regard to file system names or other internal configurations, it is no problem to do so. That there are no problems is inherent from failover cluster technology: they must be able to run on one cluster node anyhow.

Application Data – File and Database Services

Application data, both files and databases, are replicated. Any data change – deletion, insertion, and changes of files, metadata, or database records – is delayed by the RPO, 4 h for database data and 8 h for file data. This is the precaution against the "operator removes all data" and the "data is destroyed by software error" disasters.

Merging several NFS file servers into one server has some twists that we are lucky to avoid because the primary servers run as a failover cluster. The files are accessed as `server:/filesystem/directory/file`. If we serve two servers from the same system, they will use the same file system structure. If formerly both servers used the same file system export names, and the subdirectories therein are also named similarly or are even the same, it might be difficult to keep the filenames apart. NFS file servers cannot easily have different file system exports on different IP addresses, so one cannot establish two export namespaces. Here this shows that it is sometimes advantageous not to standardize on a common name; e.g., not to name the exported file system /export on all servers.

Merging two CIFS servers with Samba is easier. There the CIFS filename would be `//server/share/directory/file`, and the share names of different servers could conflict. But Samba allows several instances to be run with different configurations on one system that are bound to different (virtual) IP addresses. Since in contrast to NFS, the share name can be arbitrarily mapped to directories, one can always create workarounds for name conflicts.

The configuration issue goes even further: One needs ongoing access to the running disaster-recovery systems, as we need to synchronize installations and replicate data. In particular, we need a running Oracle instance for redo-log shipping; see later. Furthermore it should be possible to do functional tests without the need to shut down the primary systems; therefore, we need configured test instances of Oracle, NFS, and CIFS services on the disaster-recovery system. They must not use the same IP addresses as the primary system, but can use the disaster-recovery domain's IP addresses.

With appropriate precautions in mind, we can configure application clients to use these servers and test functionality. Those precautions are needed because we will change the server's state with these tests, and resynchronization must be assured. More will be said on test processes in Sect. 10.8.

▶ *Redo-Log Shipping*

This technology was explained in Sect. 10.4.4. It is used to replicate the database on the disaster-recovery system. Copy of redo logs to the disaster-recovery system should be done early, but replay of redo logs should be postponed by 2 h; this will enable us to handle the disaster case caused by human or software errors. Therefore, online redo-log mirroring cannot be used; we use archive log replication with the Oracle product Data Guard.

For that process, the Oracle disaster-recovery database is configured as a *standby database*, with a different IP address. Replication of data and data schemas is all done by automated archive log mirroring, but data store and configuration changes (e.g., new or changed table spaces) are replicated manually.

Usually, the database replication is just ongoing. Redo-log replay can be stopped if the database is needed for tests or other activities; as long as its content has not been changed, it can continue afterwards without any problems. If there were write accesses for tests, or if there is more than 1 week's worth of redo logs, the whole database is set up anew; this setup process is described in detail in Sect. 10.7.5.

However, we must not be too indifferent about difficulties with that solution. If the disaster is a result of human or software error and that error is detected within 2 h, there are two ways to resolve the situation:

1. One can skip the last batch of updates, i.e., lose 2 h of work.
2. One can try to identify the erroneous SQL statements in the redo log and discard them. This is risky, error-prone work, and one needs knowledge of internal application data models to be successful. Nevertheless, sometimes the gains are worth that risk.

The decision as to which of these two methods should be used is not easy and is basically a business case: Is the 2-h work worth the risk of an erroneous log repair? The decision can be wrong, especially under the pressure of a disaster case. But that difficulty cannot be resolved up-front – in the end, people need to make decisions in the disaster case and manage the risk.

If a human or a software error is discovered after more than 2 h, we need to restore the database from TSM and can then apply redo logs again. This will need longer, but will work as well as in the case of early discovery.

▸ *File Mirroring*

This is used to replicate file data. Of course, only differences are mirrored. A "trash can" feature protects against erroneous changes and deletion. Changes in content or metadata (ownerships, access rights, modification time stamp) or deleting lead to movement of the old file into the trash can area. Several generations will be held there. The mirroring will be idempotent and will not have any state besides the actual files: one can activate it as often as one likes, and if files on the disaster-recovery sys-tem are changed outside the mirroring process, they will be replicated again next time.

In the case of rollback, file instances are selected manually in the trash can area, to be moved back to the file area. This may result in inconsis-tencies in the application's data. Hopefully, the application has a method to check its data for consistency and repair it if necessary.

During implementation, several open issues must be clarified:

- Resource usage on the primary system by the file mirroring must not hinder production; i.e., the mirroring must not use "too much" CPU time, memory, disk I/O, etc. Benchmarks must be done to decide what "too much" is; this is not a conceptual question but will be decided by tests.
- The same holds for network resource usage; the bandwidth between the two sites is limited and is also used for other goals.
- It must be confirmed that the total run time of one file synchronization is not longer than 6 h. This gives us a gap of 2 h to our RPO of 8 h; this gap is needed as a safety limit if the primary system is under a heavy load or if something goes wrong during synchronization.
- Placement of the mirroring facility must be decided by benchmarks too: Is it better to push the changes (mirroring from the primary sys-tem) or to pull them (mirroring from the disaster-recovery system)?

▸ *Reestablishing the Primary System*

After disaster has been declared, the services are switched to the disaster-recovery systems. But this is not the end of disaster recovery, that is only finished when the primary systems are functional again. During the time that the primary systems are being repaired or replaced, data will be changed at the disaster-recovery system, and the data must be synchronized back to the new primary systems.

This is an important issue that has to be considered in advance in the concept. For the database, we restore a snapshot by TSM, and the incremental change is done by redo-log shipping. The files are replicated back by our file mirroring facility as explicated earlier. This has the advantage that we can first replicate data while the disaster-recovery system stays productive, and we have only a very short downtime during final resynchronization.

Web Service

There is only one Web server that replaces the Web server cluster from the primary site; therefore, no load-balancing devices are needed on the disaster-recovery site either.

Since the Web service has no permanent data, disaster-recovery preparation consists of keeping the Web application and the Web server configuration up to date. This is done by operational procedures during changes.

Infrastructure Services

LDAP disaster recovery does not need an immediate disaster-recovery system for the master server: usually one runs a large number of slave servers, for performance reasons. One can therefore rightly assume that slave servers are available on the disaster-recovery site as well. In the case of a disaster, one of them can be manually promoted to the master server without any problem. With the available slave servers and this new master server, LDAP can be used for authentication without problems and passwords can be changed as well.

Sometimes more work has to be done for account management though. Many companies utilize third-party software to manage accounts as part of their business processes (e.g., accounts might be automatically disabled when a staff member is laid off.) Special disaster-recovery preparation might be needed for such software, but this is beyond the scope of this prototypical system design.

License server disaster-recovery systems are made available easily, as these services have no state and no data beyond the configuration. Disaster recovery for these servers exists because they are mission-critical – one cannot use the application without it.

TSM backup is still available and must be deactivated in the disaster case. The logical nodes on the primary servers are systems in their own right, they do not exist on the disaster-recovery system anymore. Before their backup continues, the TSM server must learn about the changed TSM node ID.

Luckily, TSM can handle more than one node definition per physical system. Since file system names are different for all servers – as we mentioned in the file mirroring explanation – their names can be kept on the disaster-recovery system as well. There TSM can capture them when it is reactivated.

Network disaster recovery is already available and does not need to be handled in the context of this project. This also includes network services like DNS or NTP.

Dependency Diagram

We have already seen the detailed dependency diagram of the primary systems and services in Fig. 10.10. Figure 10.13 on the following page completes that picture and adds the disaster-recovery systems. For the sake of conciseness, we use less detail for the primary systems this time.

10.7.5 Implementation

This section will go deep into technical details and will present an implementation procedure for this prototypical system design. That was partly the reason why we named particular products in the design and made factual assumptions about servers. Only with such specific information can sensible technical information be given.

Oracle Redo-Log Shipping

The base of the Oracle replication is the identical physical structure of primary and disaster-recovery systems; therefore there are no differences in configuration. We need to create the standby database on the disaster-recovery system, and run it in standby mode there. Of course, we want also logs, metrics, and status reports.

▶ *Creation of Standby Database*

The creation is done in two parts: we have to create the database files, and we have to create the standby control files.

There are three possibilities to create the database files:

1. On the disaster-recovery system, restoration of a full backup from the TSM server.
2. Direct copying of the database files from the primary system. This is best done in an SQL*Plus session on the primary database, since the database server must be turned into state *backup* for that.
3. On the disaster-recovery system, direct copying of the database files from the primary system's last full backup.

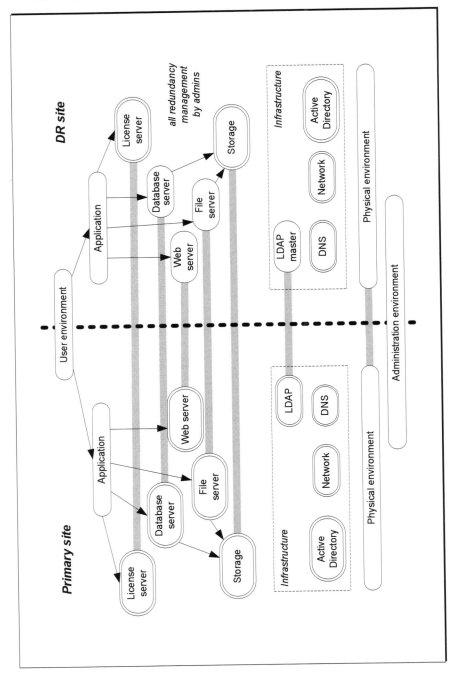

Fig. 10.13. Dependency diagram with disaster-recovery systems

This must be done for all database files. With the help of Oracle's system tables, it is easy to automate the creation of a setup script. The standby Oracle control files are created on the primary system: this is an SQL*Plus functionality. It can be copied afterwards to the disaster-recovery system.

▸ *Redo-Log Replication to the Standby Database*

Starting from the backup or from the last successful redo-log replication, all archived redo logs must be made available on the disaster-recovery system.

First, a cron job on the primary system copies all archived redo-log files to the disaster-recovery system. The script copies them from the archive directory on the primary system to the transfer directory on the disaster-recovery system. After successful action, the timestamp of the last transferred log file is saved as input for the next job.

Without log shipping, a cron job removes all redo-log files that were saved in TSM. This cron job has been changed to look at the timestamp file and prevent removal of redo-log files that have not been copied yet.

If there is a disk space shortage, removal can be forced. Then, the archived but not yet copied redo-log files must be retrieved from TSM to the disaster-recovery system manually, to keep the standby database in sync.

On the disaster-recovery system, a cron job runs that first moves all redo-log files older than 4 h (time can be changed) from the transfer directory to the archive directory of the standby database. If there is any log file to recover, the job will start the disaster-recovery database in standby mode and will activate the recovery. After the last redo-log file from the archive directory has been applied, the Oracle instance will be shut down. The recovery log file now lists the redo-log files that were applied; they can be deleted now.

▸ *Physical Database and Configuration Changes*

Physical changes in the database structure are not mentioned in the redo-log files. These changes must be replayed manually on the standby database. Not doing so will crash the database!

To add a new data file to a table space, the following activities are necessary:

1. Direct copying of the data file from the primary system (as with the original setup of the standby database, explained before)
2. Creation and transfer of new standby control files (explained before)
3. Addition of new data files to the standby database; this is done in an SQL*Plus session

When the recovery is started again, applying the redo logs will synchronize both instances.

Changes of an init parameter in the primary system has no direct consequences for the standby database. Nevertheless, the basic Oracle configuration file init.ora should be copied to the disaster-recovery system as it is changed, to enable quick turn-on times.

To help with these tasks, a script was written. It supports the following four service tasks:

1. Creation of new standby control files from the primary system and replication on the disaster-recovery system
2. Addition of new data files to the disaster-recovery database, after they have been created in the primary database
3. Replication of the configuration file init.ora on the disaster-recovery system
4. Restoration of the last TSM backup, for a new setup of the disaster-recovery database

That script is menu-based and protects the database administrator with security checks. It is not used in the disaster case, as it needs access to the primary system.

▸ *Status Reports and Replication Log Files*

The status report is created every hour by a cron job on the disaster-recovery system. It is copied to the primary system and appended to its status report; therefore all relevant reports are available in the report repository under the primary system.

The status report contains:

• An analysis of alert logs on error messages of the last 3 days that are not typical for standby databases. For control of this analysis, a test log entry is created daily as a sentinel – normally only these three entries should be seen.
• The count of the processed redo-log files of the last 3 days.
• The state of recovery (first and last redo-log file) of the current day.

An example of such a report is as follows:

```
---> Begin at Sun Sep 11 14:02:22 MEST 2005 on dbdr-ph <----
Oracle status report for Disaster Recovery server dbdr-ph
Uptime: 2:02pm up 1 day(s), 3:47, load average: 0.82, 0.36, 0.26

***********************************************
List of instances on dbdr-ph:
DB
***********************************************

Significantly Standby database ORA-errors in alert_DB.log at
the last 3 days (last 50 lines)

Sat Sep 10 10:51:51 2005
ORA-9999 *** It s the daily test error log entry - ignore it !
```

```
Sun Sep 11 10:52:55 MEST 2005
ORA-9999 *** It s the daily test error log entry - ignore it !
Count applied Redologfiles : Sep 9 = 110
-------------------------- Sep 10 = 85
Sep 11 = 54

Applied Redologfiles today
-------------------------
Start Load Archive Sun Sep 11 00:31:01 MEST 2005
from      /oraarc/DB/DBarch_0000045553.arc
until     /oraarc/DB/DBarch_0000045607.arc
Stop Load archive Sun Sep 11 14:01:53 MEST 2005

---> End at Sun Sep 11 14:02:23 MEST 2005 on dbdr-ph <------
```

The redo-log recovery scripts also write status information to log files. This makes it possible to realize when redo logs were placed in the archive directory and when they were processed. Furthermore, one can see how long the processing needed.

File Replication

The synchronization program is running on the disaster-recovery file server. *rsync* is used for all base functionality, but is not sufficient to fulfill all requirements.

Initial synchronization:
1. All previous data in target directories is deleted.
2. All data from the source directories is copied to the target directory.

Incremental synchronization:
1. Copying of the following files and directories to the target site
   - New files
   - Files with different size
   - Files with changed owner
   - Files with changed permissions
2. Run synchronization in parallel.
3. Option to save all deleted or changed data from the primary site into a "trash can" directory to have the possibility to restore an earlier state. Stop synchronization of data in case the trash can file system runs out of space to avoid propagation of unplanned deletion of data (e.g., human error or software corruption) on the primary site.

Failback synchronization:
Use the same program to copy data from the disaster-recovery site to the primary site after the primary site has been replaced.

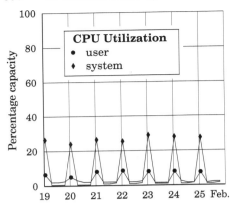

Runtime: 4 h

Data transfer:
Nine parallel streams
about 120 GB per day
(200 000 files, 18 900 000 files
inspected on primary site)

Fig. 10.14. File replication statistics from an example implementation

To fulfill these specific requirements and to provide output of metrics a wrapper script can be written. No commercial product is known that provides this functionality under Unix; some local programming is needed here.

The information of which file systems should be transferred is specified in a configuration file. Grouping in the configuration file allows parallel streams for the data synchronization. For each group one stream will be opened. The file systems to be synchronized are mounted readable from the productive server using NFS.

To meet the requirement of restoring an earlier state all changed and deleted data can be copied optionally into a disaster-recovery file system. The disaster-recovery file system has the size of the primary file system. In case the disaster-recovery file system has no space left, the synchronization program stops. For example, if for some reason (either human or software error) a couple of file systems – or in the worst case, the data of a whole server – were deleted on the production site, this feature avoids the transfer of the problem to the disaster-recovery site. The data on the disaster-recovery site is still available in the last stage.

The synchronization program runs every night. The limiting factor is the CPU on the disaster-recovery server – Fig. 10.14 provides some statistics from an example implementation.

System Configuration

For the sake of cost efficiency, we run the same operating system and application version as in production. This leaves open the risk of software errors that might be repeated at the disaster-recovery site after a restart. From experience, we judge this risk to be acceptable, compared with the cost of running and testing different software and/or different versions, i.e., for the named software, we think the chances of such failures are lower than the chances of outages due to version mismatches.

This implies that every version and configuration change on the primary systems has to be done at the disaster-recovery site as well. The same file system configuration is used as at the primary site: the same naming convention, the same UFS configuration, the same volume size. All changes to the software have to be done on the disaster-recovery system as well, either manually for the application, or using packages and patches for system software.

In fact, it is best to deploy patches first on the disaster-recovery systems. At least the database runs (for redo-log shipping); if the patch has gross errors they will be caught there. After 2 weeks, the patch can be deployed on the primary systems as well. This process does not make tests on preproduction (staging) systems irrelevant, it amends them.

In the case of file system changes (creating a new file system, deleting a file system, renaming a file system or changing the configuration) the equivalent file system on the disaster-recovery server has to be changed manually and the configuration file of the synchronization program has to be changed too.

This part of the disaster-recovery solution is the most critical because it is not automated. Since many human manual activities are required here, this is the most likely place for errors to happen.

10.8 Failover to Disaster-Recovery Site or Disaster-Recovery Systems

Now that we have seen the preparation for disaster recovery, we can cover the actual procedures to migrate IT services from primary systems to disaster-recovery systems in the case of major outages. This can be a complete outage of the primary site: in that case the whole disaster-recovery site is activated as a replacement. Or a single primary system or component might have failed: then just the respective disaster-recovery system is activated.

In this section, we will have a look at the steps that are necessary to bring a disaster-recovery system or a whole disaster-recovery site alive. These procedures are used in real disaster cases as well as in disaster-recovery tests.

10.8.1 General Approach

The assumption is that after a disaster people are available who know where to find the disaster-recovery instructions (Disaster-Recovery Emergency Pack).

▶ *Disaster Detected*

When a failure cannot be repaired within the SLA of a minor outage, it becomes a major outage. Or if a failure occurs that is not covered in the failure scenarios for minor outages and against which no high-availability precaution exists, then a major outage has happened as well.

At this point in time, we anticipate that we might have a disaster, but no "official" decision has been reached. The hypothesis of a major outage must be confirmed first.

▶ *Open Disaster-Recovery Emergency Pack*

The Emergency Pack should contain all required documentation, as listed in Table 10.4 on p. 324. The process descriptions are needed first, in particular the *internal escalation procedure* and the *roles and responsibilities* document. The latter should also contain the RASIC chart that we presented in Table 10.5 on p. 335, and an up-to-date communication plan.

These documents will help to handle the situation at hand. We must never underestimate the importance of checklists in such situations: they remind us of minute details that we are prone to forget in the hectic situation of a major outage.

We should be aware that this may not be an easy situation for many staff members. Major outages that are caused by problems in the physical environment are called disasters by right – the disaster recovery team might have to handle the death of coworkers and of friends and still have to get their work done.

▶ *Analyze Situation*

Assess the damage. There may be outages of facilities, telephones, power supplies, IT systems, networks (WAN, LAN), and human resources. It is important to get an overview of the magnitude of the outage to consider this fact for all further decisions. For example, technical skilled manpower is required to conduct a proper switch to the disaster-recovery site.

Assess the situation of the disaster-recovery system/site (facilities). Before the decision is made to start up the disaster-recovery system, it must be ensured that the disaster has not affected the disaster-recovery site, and that the disaster-recovery facilities as well as the disaster-recovery infrastructure are still ready to be used.

▶ *Make a Decision to Switch to the Disaster-Recovery Site*

After the situation has been analyzed and the impact of the disaster is known, the actual decision can be made to switch to the disaster-recovery site. The decision has to follow the decision process. Only the decision makers or their substitutes can reach a decision. It is highly recommended to include the business owner of the actual business being performed on the infrastructure as well as the business owner of the IT system in the decision process.

▸ *Establish a Command Center and a War Room*

The command center and war room should be ready at the disaster-recovery site. A location at the production site does not make sense because that might be destroyed in disaster case. Ideally the command center and war room should be close to the disaster-recovery hardware.

All hardware which is necessary to setup the disaster- recovery infrastructure has to be ready to be used and has to be independent of the production environment (e.g. user login, network).

▸ *Review the Disaster Recovery Procedure*

Before the real switch to the disaster-recovery site starts, the disaster-recovery procedure should be reviewed by a team of experts and a decision maker to ensure a successful failover, especially if the last disaster-recovery test took place a while ago.

All further steps will take place under the assumption of total damage to the primary system or site and that they cannot be recovered in an adequate time frame, and also guaranteed stability.

▸ *Preparation*

We need to communicate within our organization that we have a major outage. Everybody whose work could be affected must know about this, and everybody who might be able to help in resolving problems should be contacted too.

We also need to communicate the disaster to people outside the company. Typically suppliers, business partners, and vendors should know about this because we either need them during the next few hours or their own work will be affected. The details of whom to contact are spelled out in the escalation process part of the disaster-recovery plan.

If the disaster recovery concept is based on the minimal required hardware to provide a disaster-recovery system, special agreements/contracts with the hardware vendors are recommended to make additional hardware promptly available when a disaster occurs. The setting up of these agreements might happen during the concept phase of the disaster-recovery system. We might also have contracts in place that will ensure on-site availability of vendor technical specialists or contractors to help us achieve a working disaster-recovery switch.

▸ *Activate and Verify the Disaster-Recovery System*

This topic only covers the high-level approach of what to consider when activating a disaster-recovery system in general. For each disaster-recovery systems a separate checklist has to be developed which contains all failover steps for the specific system.

For the systems from our prototypical system design, we provide an example checklist below.

Ensure that the primary system is down and stays down
Mainly if the primary system is in an undefined state it could startup unmanaged. This has to be taken care of. Unplugging the primary system from the network should be considered to avoid any uncontrolled mixture between primary and disaster recovery services.

Stop replication between primary and disaster-recovery system
Ensuring a certain state of the data on the disaster-recovery system requires a shutdown of any data replication.

Analyze functions and services on the disaster-recovery site
Verify that the disaster-recovery site is ready to be used and all required functions and services are properly installed and configured.

Analyze data status
Check when the last synchronization ran properly. Verify the consistency of data to define potential data loss. If data corruption occurred on the primary site it is important to ensure that this problem has not been transferred to the disaster-recovery site.

Start services on the disaster-recovery system
Start all services manually and check carefully if they run. Use a test client to access the services.

Use the disaster-recovery system as the productive system
When the disaster-recovery system runs as the productive server, activation of all services has to be done only once and should start automatically after a reboot of the disaster-recovery system.

The data on the disaster-recovery server has to be backed up. For this, some changes in backup configuration might be necessary; many backup software products work with some kind of system ID that might have changed now. But with TSM that is not necessary. A new full backup is also not needed; incremental backup can continue.

▶ *Communicate That the Disaster-Recovery System Is Active*

Communicate to all parties involved that the disaster-recovery site is up and running and explain possible functional limitations and data loss.

As long as the disaster-recovery site is running as the production site it is recommended to follow a special change procedure with limited changes and and to have a special approval board.

10.8.2 Example Checklist for a Database Disaster-Recovery Server

To illustrate the kind of checklists that one needs for a specific service during a switch to the disaster-recovery system, we will look at the database service of our prototypical disaster-recovery project, from Sect. 10.7. The following list is a specific instance of the general approach list that we met in the previous section.

Activating a disaster-recovery system is a difficult and risk-prone endeavor. It should be undertaken by senior administrators who know the operating system, system software, and database by heart.

Preparation

Check the processes and procedures. Make sure that disaster recovery really should happen and that all stakeholders have the same goal:

- Approval of all parties involved must exist.
- Communication plan (roles and responsibilities) must exist and must be up-to-date.
- Detailed time plan must exist and must be agreed upon by all stakeholders.
- All operations personnel – and also the network department, if necessary – are informed about the planned activities. They must not start escalations that are caused by disaster-recovery activities just because they happen not to know about the major outage.

▶ *Clean Up Primary System If Possible*

Stop the Oracle listener at the primary system. This means that no client will be able to connect to the database anymore and no new changes will occur.

If the primary system is still running, stop the redo-log shipping. If possible and if data corruption or deletion was not the cause of the outage, transfer the last archived redo logs from the primary system to the disaster-recovery system.

▶ *Check That the Disaster-Recovery System Is Ready to Be Used*

Actually, the disaster-recovery system should be ready all the time. After all, preparation for disaster recovery made it clear that all changes on the primary systems have to be replicated on the disaster-recovery systems. But this is not always successful. In particular, during incidents, small changes are quickly made that might get forgotten. We need to make sure that the same software is available with the same versions and that data is available.

Check the state of the operating system, the system configuration, the system software, and the database software. The software must be installed, and it must be installed in the same version and with the same patch level as on the primary system. The system documentation from the Disaster-Recovery Emergency Pack lists both the software and the versions.

Check that the redo logs are up to date on the disaster-recovery system. If the major outage was caused by data corruption, manually fix the redo logs.

▶ *Check Infrastructure*

Test the network, i.e., the reachability of the disaster-recovery system by clients.

Test also the availability of DNS, authorization services (i.e., LDAP), and license servers.

Switch to the Disaster-Recovery System

After all the preparation has been done, we can continue with the actual failover.

▶ *Shut Down the Primary System If Necessary*

If the primary system is still running, stop the Oracle server at the primary system. This means shutting down the logical node in that cluster. This also disables automatically the IP address of that cluster.

Disable automatic startup of the cluster at the primary system, otherwise somebody could erroneously activate it by rebooting.

Turn off noncluster monitoring of these services, e.g., by BMC Patrol, Tivoli, Nagios, and MRTG.

▶ *Verify That the Primary System Is Down and Stays Down*

This is so important that we make it into a separate step. This step should be done by somebody other than the person who did the shutdown.

Ping the primary system (i.e., the logical hosts from the database failover cluster).

Check the process list on both physical hosts of the cluster.

Assert that the cluster is not started at boot time.

▶ *Start the Database Service on the Disaster-Recovery System*

Activate the IP address for the database server. Test it is reachable with ping – that test is best done from a client.

Recover the database, i.e., apply the latest redo logs.

Start the Oracle instance; check that the processes are running and there are no errors in the log files.

Check the Disaster-Recovery System Services

Now that the disaster-recovery system is active, the supplied services must be checked, before it can be put into production.

▶ *Check Oracle Functionality*

Check that the Oracle server is listening on its TCP/IP port, by using netstat.

Check that Oracle is working with an SQL client. That test should be prepared in advance and should be available as a script on the server. In addition, successful SQL access must be checked from a user's desktop.

An experienced database administrator must run these checks and must sign off their success.

▶ *Check Application Functionality*

Check the application's functionality from a user desktop.

Check that all cron jobs work.

Operate the Disaster-Recovery System as the Productive System

Before users can be allowed to use the disaster-recovery system, it must be made a productive system first.

▶ *Start the Database Service at Boot Time*

Establish that all necessary services and resources (e.g., the IP address) are activated at boot time. Establish all cron jobs.

▶ *Activate Operations Systems*

Backup must be reestablished. This needs reinitialization of the TSM node definition.

Cluster-external monitoring must be reestablished.

10.8.3 Failback to the Primary System

Activating a disaster-recovery system does not finish disaster recovery. Now that we have turned it into a production system, we drive without safety belts. Our goal must be to reestablish full functionality of primary systems, including high-availability setups, as quickly as possible.

When we have done so, we can switch back to the primary system, which is commonly called a *failback*. Basically that is the same process as the switch to the disaster-recovery system that we described in Sect. 10.8.1. The same replication mechanisms that were used for the disaster-recovery system can now be used to transfer data back to the primary system.

The main difference is that we do not need to detect and check the disaster. Instead, we have to deploy and test the primary systems. But the rest of the disaster-recovery plan is used just the same and provides a checklist for the failback.

For the database server, utilization of a product like Oracle Data Guard eases the failback, as it has special support for that procedure.

A

Reliability Calculations and Statistics

In this appendix we will discuss basic probabilistic and statistical coherences and quantities. Our goal is to learn how to use them in real life. The targets of our discussion are hardware components and hardware configurations. Software shows failures of different kinds which do not apply to the findings in this section.

You might say that statistics is about large numbers (of outages) – it does not apply to predicting failures which happen very seldom. Even if this is true, we can use statistics and probabilities to predict reliability when we configure a system. It also helps to identify anomalies during system operations. In particular we will address the following areas:

- In configuring a new system, there are many options. In theory, your vendor of choice should offer the *best* configuration for your needs; in practice many of your hardware vendor's presales consultants fail to do this. And technicians who assemble the systems often do it in a way such that the system works, but does not show the best possible availability. In the end, we want to achieve the best compromise between reliability, cost, and simplicity.

  To overcome this, we can do some basic computations and approximations to understand the consequences of configuration decisions like "what if we used a second power supply?" or "should we configure hot-spare disks?"

  In the following, we will discuss the reliability of disk configurations and different redundant array of independent disks (Raid) levels in detail. There are many options to protect our data and the risk of an inadequate configuration is high.

- During the lifetime of your system, problems will occur. Some will be covered by redundancy (like a drive failure in a mirrored configuration), others will have an impact (like a system crash after a CPU failure), up to real downtimes. If we monitor these occurrences, important conclusions can be drawn. We can distinguish between *good* from *bad* systems and can identify aging systems, which need to be replaced. Computer systems – like all other technology – differ in design quality as well as in manufacturing quality. There are "Monday systems" similar to cars and we need to deal with them in an appropriate way. Such statistics are typically not published: they contain too much political ammunition. Therefore the data of "your" outages is an important information source, and you know that your numbers are true.

A.1 Mathematical Basics

For the following discussion, we use some basic statistical concepts. In this section we repeat the most important formulas – if you are less interested in mathematics, skip this section and look only at the examples given. If you want more details, many undergraduate text books, such as [9], present them.

▸ *Empirical Probability*

If we execute an experiment a times, and get b times a certain event E, then b/a is the empirical probability of E. For large a, we speak of a *probability* for E and can use it for future predictions:

$$p = \frac{b}{a} \, .$$

▸ *Bernoulli Experiment*

A Bernoulli experiment has exactly two possible outcomes: the probability for event A is p, the probability for the opposite event is $\overline{p} = 1 - p$. If we execute the experiment n times and want to know the probability of getting exactly k times the result E (and $n - k$ times the opposite result $\overline{E}$), the following formula applies:

$$B_{n,p}(k) = p^k (1 - p)^{n-k} \binom{n}{k} \, . \tag{A.1}$$

▸ *Distribution Functions*

We interpret the Bernoulli formula as a distribution function $k \to B_{n,p}(k)$ with the independent variable k. It gives the probabilities that with n experiments the number of results A will be exactly $k = 0, 1, 2, \ldots, n$ times. For large n and small p we can use the following approximations to make real calculations easier. Equation (A.2) is named the *Poisson formula*, and Eq. (A.3) is named the *De Moivre–Laplace formula*;

$$B_{n,p}(k) \approx \frac{(np)^k}{k!} e^{-np}, \tag{A.2}$$

$$P(k_1 \le x \le k_2) \approx \Phi(x_2) - \Phi(x_1), \tag{A.3}$$

with

$$x_1 = \frac{k_1 - np}{\sqrt{np(1-p)}}, \qquad x_2 = \frac{k_2 - np}{\sqrt{np(1-p)}}.$$

The De Moivre–Laplace formula is used to calculate the probability for an interval of outcomes (instead of a discrete number of outcomes labeled k above). The term $\Phi(x)$ is the *Gaussian function*. It is an integral which has no elementary antiderivative; therefore, it can be calculated only numerically.

▶ *Tests of Hypothesis and Significance*

In reality, we execute only a limited number of experiments, i.e., experience a limited number of system failures during a limited time interval; therefore, the outcomes are not expected to show the given probability. We need to test the *significance* of our result to accept a given probability (e.g., if we got the probability from our system vendor). On the other hand, a given probability can be wrong as well, as its calculation is based on wrong assumptions or without enough experiments to test it.

In order to evaluate the significance of a result, a so-called hypothesis test is done. We first assume that the probability $p(A)$ for result A is correct and gives the distribution $k \to B_{n,p}(k)$. We make n experiments to test the hypothesis. We expect np times the result A, that is where $B_{n,p}(k)$ has its maximum. If the measured result deviates very much from np, then we might need to disapprove the hypothesis – the assumed probability p might be wrong. In other words, we talk about the probability that a measured result follows a given probability.

In practice this is done as follows. We calculate the sum $B_{n,p}(0) + B_{n,p}(1) + \cdots + B_{n,p}(i)$ for increasing i until the sum exceeds a given limit. Depending on the real numbers, the De Moivre–Laplace formula can be helpful. This limit describes the requested quality of our result. Typical values for this sum limit are 0.975 or 0.995. This belongs to a level of significance of 0.05 or 0.01, respectively. Using this method, we know that the probability of getting $k \ge i$ is very small (according to our earlier definition). We reject the hypothesis, when the measured result belongs to the interval $[n - i, n]$.

▶ *Confidence Interval for Probabilities*

This is a similar circumstance but from a different viewpoint: we made n experiments and experienced f failures. How close is our measured failure probability f/n to the real probability p? This question can obviously not be answered, but we can calculate an *interval of probabilities* $[p_1, p_2]$

Table A.1. Confidence levels γ and corresponding values of c

γ (%)	c
80	1.28
90	1.65
95	1.96
98	2.33
99	2.58

which contains the real probability p with a chosen confidence level γ. If we set γ very close to 1, this interval becomes very large. It depends on the number of experiments and the value chosen for γ to achieve a small enough (i.e., meaningful) interval of probabilities.

The following formula is the criterion to calculate the interval $[p_1, p_2]$. It denotes the probability Q for that interval with confidence γ:

$$Q\left(\left|\frac{f}{n} - p\right| \le c\sqrt{\frac{p(1-p)}{n}}\right) \approx \gamma = 2\Phi(c) - 1. \tag{A.4}$$

The value of c is calculated from γ, using the Gaussian function. Table A.1 gives the values of c for typical values of γ.

If we have done our experiments, measured f and n, and have chosen the confidence level γ, we use Table A.1 to get c. Then we can calculate the interval of probability $[p_1, p_2]$ by solving the following quadratic equation:

$$\left(\frac{f}{n} - p_{1,2}\right)^2 = c^2 \frac{p_{1,2}(1 - p_{1,2})}{n}. \tag{A.5}$$

This result can be interpreted as follows. If we would do many experiments, a fraction γ of the measured probabilities $\frac{f_i}{n_i}$ would be located inside the interval $[p_1, p_2]$.

A.2 Mean Time Between Failures and Annual Failure Rate

The reliability of a component (e.g., a disk drive, or a controller card) or of a whole system is measured by the *mean time between failures* (MTBF). It is the average time until a failure happens and is typically provided in hours (to make it look more authoritative) or better in years. A MTBF of 10 years means that, on average, every 10 years a failure occurs, based on a large sample. These numbers are provided in the component data sheets of the hardware manufacturers; sometimes they are also provided for whole systems.

There are two problems associated with using the MTBF:

1. The values can vary significantly, especially for components with moving parts, like disk drives. This is because the MTBF depends greatly on the quality of the individual production batch, which is far from constant. Manufacturers obviously try to detect quality problems, but this is not easy, as the manufacturing of complex components is more an art than a science. There are too many variables, like tuning of the machinery, impurities in the clean room, quality of the materials, etc. And then there is also the soft-factor microcode...

2. The appearance of failures does not follow a uniform distribution. The failure rate is high for new equipment (*early mortality*) and if equipment reaches its end of life. The time in-between is when we want to use the equipment for production. We will discuss this *bathtub curve* in Sect. A.6.

However, manufacturers often provide impressive numbers for MTBF, 10^6-h run time (about 114 years) for a disk drive is a standard value nowadays.

The inverse of the MTBF is the failure rate. The *annual failure rate* (AFR) is defined as the average number of failures per year:

$$\text{AFR} = \frac{1}{\text{MTBF}_{\text{years}}} = \frac{8760}{\text{MTBF}_{\text{hours}}}.$$

The AFR is a relative frequency of occurrence – it can be interpreted as a probability $p(A)$ if AFR < 1, where $p(A)$ means the probability that the component (or system) A fails in one year. If you multiply the AFR with the time interval you consider, you get the expected number of failures in this time interval.

For example, for a disk drive with an MTBF of 34 years, the corresponding AFR is 0.029 failures per year. If your disk subsystem contains 200 such drives, you can expect a failure every 2 months.

Even if such numbers can be discussed at length, we provide examples from our own experience based on a sample of several thousand components and hundreds of systems. These numbers should give you a rough idea of the order of magnitude and we will provide "real" examples later on. We see that all the numbers are in a similar range.

A.3 Redundancy and Probability of Failures

We consider two ways to combine components in a system or subsystem: they can back up each other, (e.g., redundant network cards, or mirrored disks), or both are needed for function of the combined components (e.g., a cable connected to a network card, or a stripe of two disks). The first

Table A.2. Typical mean time between failures (*MTBF*) and annual failure rate (*AFR*) values

Component	MTBF (h)	MTBF (years)	AFR (failures per year)
Disk drive	300 000	34	0.0292
Power supply	150 000	17	0.0584
Fan	250 000	28	0.0350
Interface card	200 000	23	0.0438

combination is obviously more reliable than its components; the second is less reliable than its weakest component.

In principle we could use such blocks to build arbitrary complex systems, and the following calculation could cover this case. However, we now concentrate on typical disk configurations and discuss first disk mirrors and stripes. This is the most important application and can easily be done in practice. More complex combinations are typically analyzed by special simulation software.

Let us start with two simple examples which set the basis for all further calculations. Let $p(A)$ be the probability that part A fails, and $p(\overline{A})$ the complementary probability that part A does not fail, $p(\overline{A}) = 1 - p(A)$. This probability is given in relation to a time interval. Let us now consider an n-way mirror. It will fail only, if all disks fail. We use the binomial distribution to calculate the probability of this failure:

$$p_{\text{mirror}} = \binom{n}{n} p(A)^n \, (1 - p(A))^0 = p(A)^n \,, \tag{A.6}$$

where $\binom{n}{n}$ is the number of possible combinations of failure.

On the other hand, a stripe of n disks will fail, when 1, 2, ..., or all n disks fail, or, the system will only work if all disks are OK:

$$p_{\text{all disks work}} = \binom{n}{n} (1 - p(A))^n p(A)^0 = (1 - p(A))^n \,.$$

That gives the failure probability that at least one disk will fail as

$$p_{\text{stripe}} = 1 - (1 - p(A))^n \,. \tag{A.7}$$

Let us go back to the two-fold redundant systems: those are systems which survive even if one disk fails, but fail if a second disk fails (in some configurations, only specific combinations of failing disks lead to a system failure). Specifically, the system only fails, if the *second* redundant disk fails during the outage of the first failed disk. This circumstance is not reflected in the general Eqs. (A.6) and (A.7). We need to consider the time intervals in question. Here a new term, the *mean time to repair* (MTTR), comes up. We divide a year (8760 h) by the time that is needed to repair the failed part, to get 8760/MTTR possible intervals of repair actions. The probability for failure during such a repair activity $p(A)$ is given by

$$p(A) = \frac{\text{AFR}}{8760/\text{MTTR}} = R,\tag{A.8}$$

where R is the *repair time failure rate*. If we look for failure during a repair interval, we have to substitute $p(A)$ in Eqs. (A.6) and (A.7) with R. Because these probabilities relate to only one interval, we have to multiply the end result with 8760/MTTR to get the average failure rate of the whole system in 1 year.

With these formulas we could calculate arbitrary configurations; however, for more complex configurations computer-modeling software is used in practice.

A.4 Raid Configurations

Section 5.2.1 on p. 109 explained how Raid, the redundancy method for disks, works. Let us now calculate the AFRs for different Raid levels: first we compare Raid10 with Raid01. Raid10 is a stripe of mirrored disks with the failure probability of Eq. (A.6); Raid01 is a mirror of two stripes, with a failure probability of Eq. (A.7). These configurations were already illustrated in Figs. 5.8 and 5.9.

The main difference is the situation after one disk has failed: in a Raid10 configuration, we now have a single point of failure which is one disk (the mirror to the failed disk); with Raid01, we have multiple single points of failure, any disk in the not failed stripe would lead to a failure of the whole system.

▸ *Raid01*

With Eqs. (A.6) and (A.7), we get for the failure rate of a Raid01 system with $2n$ disks

$$\text{AFR}_{\text{Raid01}} = \left(1 - (1 - R)^n\right)^2 \frac{8760}{\text{MTTR}}.\tag{A.9}$$

▸ *Raid10*

Using the same approach, we get

$$\text{AFR}_{\text{Raid10}} = \left(1 - \left(1 - R^2\right)^n\right) \frac{8760}{\text{MTTR}}.\tag{A.10}$$

Let us consider $\text{AFR}_{\text{Raid10}}$ and $\text{AFR}_{\text{Raid01}}$ using the Bernoulli approximation $(1-x)^n \approx 1 - nx$ for small x:

$$\text{AFR}_{\text{Raid01}} \approx n^2 R^2 \frac{8760}{\text{MTTR}},$$

$$\text{AFR}_{\text{Raid10}} \approx n R^2 \frac{8760}{\text{MTTR}}.$$

That shows that the failure rate of Raid01 increases quadratically with increasing number of disks n, whereas for Raid10 it grows only linearly.

▶ *Raid5 and Raid3*

Let us now consider a system with "normal" Raid protection. This means a system with n data disks and one additional disk taking parity information. It applies to both Raid3 and Raid5 protection: a failure occurs, if at least two disks fail simultaneously (which means the second disk fails before the repair activity of the first disk is finished). We will label both cases with *Raid5*.

Here the binomial distribution gives the solution

$$
\begin{aligned}
\text{AFR}_{\text{Raid5}} &= \left[1 - \left(\binom{n+1}{0} R^0 (1-R)^{n+1} \right. \right. \\
&\quad \left. \left. + \binom{n+1}{1} R^1 (1-R)^n \right) \right] \frac{8760}{\text{MTTR}} \\
&= \left[1 - ((1-R)^{n+1} + (n+1)R(1-R)^n) \right] \frac{8760}{\text{MTTR}}. \quad \text{(A.11)}
\end{aligned}
$$

We simplify this equation using the Bernoulli equation to second order to achieve a formula which can be used easily in practice:

$$\text{AFR}_{\text{Raid5}} \approx \frac{n(n+1)}{2} R^2.$$

Note that the failure rate increases faster than n^2 with increasing number of disks n. To calculate $\text{MTBF}_{\text{Raid5}}$ (which is the mean time to a real data loss, sometimes labeled MTTDL), we have to divide the hours of 1 year by $\text{AFR}_{\text{Raid5}}$:

$$\text{MTBF}_{\text{Raid5}} = \frac{2 \times \text{MTBF}_{\text{disk}}^2}{n(n+1)\text{MTTR}}.$$

▶ *Double Parity Raid*

Several systems introduced recently a higher protection, *double parity Raid* (also called Raid6 or RaidDP). That uses a second disk for data protection, which holds additional parity information. The system only fails, if three (or more) disks fail simultaneously. To calculate the probability, we use the same approach as before:

$$
\begin{aligned}
\mathrm{AFR_{RaidDP}} &= \left[1 - \left(\binom{n+2}{0}R^0(1-R)^{n+2}\right.\right. \\
&\quad + \binom{n+2}{1}R^1(1-R)^{n+1} \\
&\quad \left.\left. + \binom{n+2}{2}R^2(1-R)^n\right)\right]\frac{8760}{\mathrm{MTTR}} \\
&= \left[1 - (1-R)^n\right. \\
&\quad \left. \times \left(1 + nR + \frac{n}{2}R^2 + \frac{n^2}{2}R^2\right)\right]\frac{8760}{\mathrm{MTTR}}.
\end{aligned}
\qquad (A.12)
$$

From a mathematical viewpoint many more configurations are possible, and these use more disks for parity information and can recover more simultaneous single-disk failures [14]. However, none of them are implemented in products today. With current technologies we see no need to go beyond RaidDP. The additional complexity of even higher Raid levels, as well as negative performance implications (i.e., to calculate the parity information and to read/write to the additional disks) does not pay off.

Comparison of Raid Configurations

Let us now apply Eqs. (A.9)–(A.11) and (A.12) to understand the reliability of different disk configurations, and get a feeling for the numbers.

Let us first look to the dependency of $\mathrm{AFR_{system}}$ on different numbers of data disks (Fig. A.1).

"Number of data disks" means that we do not count the disks which provide redundancy. In this view the same number of disks also means the same usable data capacity. It is interesting to use it, when we want to discuss how much capacity a Raid group could or should have. For one disk, Raid01, Raid10, and Raid5 give the same number, as in this case we have one disk and one mirror disk for all Raid levels. One data disk for RaidDP means that we have a total of three disks, one for data and two additional disks for redundancy. Obviously, this leads to a much better (smaller) AFR. With increasing number of disks, the AFR increases with different slopes. Raid01 shows the worst behavior, as expected. Raid10 is better than Raid5, because with Raid5, two arbitrary disk failures will lead to data loss. With Raid10, after one disk has failed there is only one other disk which would lead to data loss if it failed.

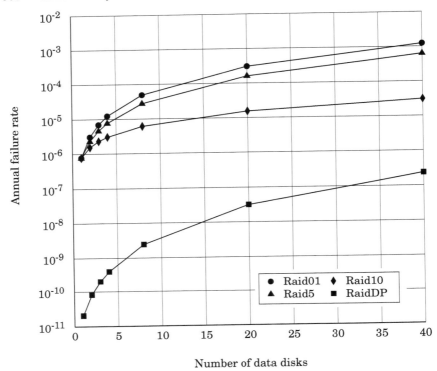

Fig. A.1. Dependence of the annual failure rate for different disk configurations on the number of data disks (see text). The annual failure rate for a single disk is 0.029; the time to repair of a single disk is 8 h (assuming a hot-spare disk – 8 h is the time for synchronizing the data)

It is not a well-known fact that Raid10 shows better protection than Raid5, and is about a factor of 10 for 20 data disks. This is an additional advantage of Raid10 besides the better performance. However, this advantage comes at the additional cost of more disks needed for redundancy, as we will see later.

RaidDP shows by far the best values, which is expected as here three disks need to fail to get data loss. But with higher numbers of data disks (some hundreds), the lines for Raid10 and RaidDP cross – then Raid10 becomes the most reliable configuration. This is when the probability that three arbitrary disks will fail becomes higher than the that for the failure of a specific pair of disks.

In the configuration considered we assume the existence of a hot-spare disk, which translates to a short time to repair a failed disk of 8 h.[1] Without a hot spare, a repair time of 48 h is realistic. This would lead to 6 times higher AFR values for Raid01, Raid10, and Raid5, and a 36 times higher value for RaidDP.

But a hot spare is not only good for improving the AFR values. It also allows the real repair action (when the technician replaces the broken disk drive) to take place on a (again) redundant configuration. This gives protection against human error, e.g., when the technician replaces the wrong disk, which happens from time to time.

Let us now review how many disks a Raid group should have. For this discussion we plot the same instances but in relation of the total number of disks, see Fig. A.2 on the following page. Here Raid5 is worst (but we need to note that Raid5 provides most disk space). RaidDP is still the best, as we expected.

Both graphs from Figs. A.1 and A.2 look at the situation from one perspective, but do not show the full picture. Let us combine the number of disks and the capacity provided in Fig. A.3 on p. 371. Assume that we want to combine eight disks into one raid group. What are the possible capacities and corresponding AFRs? Raid5 shows the most capacity, but the worst AFR. RaidDP seems to be the best compromise between (very good) AFR and capacity. The other Raid levels are not competitive in this scenario (which ignores features like performance).

If we look at Figs. A.1–A.3, all the AFR numbers look very good – why should we care at all? First, these are *averages*: in order to have a good level of confidence for the real situation, the numbers need to be much better than the average. Second, there are circumstances when multiple disks are unavailable at the same time (e.g., controller failure) – this will be discussed later. Third, there are bad batches of disks, which can show significantly higher AFR_{disk} values for the single disk than the number provided by the vendor. And, to make this worse, if you got disks from a bad batch, you can expect that many disks from that batch are in your array. How bad can AFR_{disk} be? That is hard to say, as such numbers are typically not measured or are not published. Our experience is that a factor of 20 is realistic. Figure A.4 on p. 372 is the same as Fig. A.1, but with 20 times higher AFR_{disk}. These numbers speak for themselves – we need to be careful!

---

[1] Note that the time for data synchronization to the hot-spare disk depends on the Raid level: Raid10 is fastest, here only one disk needs to be copied over to the hot-spare disk; Raid5 and RaidDP need more time, as here all disks need to be read in order to calculate the parity information. This effect will not change the general picture we describe here.

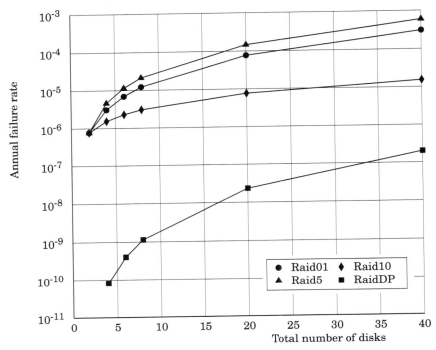

Fig. A.2. Dependence of the annual failure rate for different disk configurations on the total number of disks in a redundant array of independent disks (*Raid*) group (see text). The annual failure rate for a single disk is 0.029; the time to repair of a single disk is 8 h (assuming a hot-spare disk – 8 h is the time for synchronizing the data)

So far we have only looked at disk failures. But what happens if several disks are unavailable at the same time, caused by failure of an underlying component? Let us consider a fictitious disk array which consist of two frames with eight disk drives each. Both are independently connected to a redundant controller. Even if each frame is supposed to be redundant in itself, it can fail. Such a failure can be caused by a microcode issue, or if one disk fails in a way such that it blocks all other disks in that frame.[2] It is obviously a good idea to have the disks and their mirrors in different frames.

---

[2] This can happen, if the disks in a frame are connected with a Fibre Channel Arbitrated Loop (FCAL).

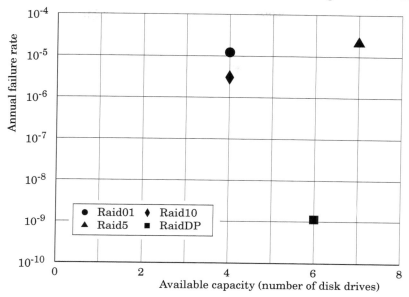

Fig. A.3. Annual failure rate for different disk configurations, all using a total of eight disk drives. The annual failure fate for a single disk is 0.029; the time to repair of a single disk is 8 h

Guidelines

At the end of this section, we give some general guidelines:

- Never use Raid01, unless you use only 2 + 2 disks.
- Always use hot-spare disks.
- The AFR for a Raid group should be smaller than 10^{-4}. This maximizes the number of disks to 8 (7 + 1) for Raid3 and Raid5, 16 (8 + 8) for Raid10, and 20 (18 + 2) for RaidDP. For more disks in one Raid group, a closer review is proposed.
- RaidDP provides the highest reliability. It should be used, if performance and hot-spare synchronization time are sufficient.
- Make a full failure mode analysis of your disk subsystem. If there are multiple failure scenarios, they all contribute to $\text{AFR}_{\text{system}}$. There is no template available for how to do such an analysis – you need to understand the architecture and the implementation on a high level and perhaps do some testing.

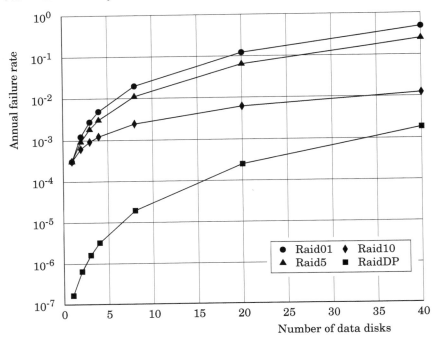

Fig. A.4. Dependence of the annual failure rate for different disk configurations on the number of data disks (see text). The annual failure rate for a single disk is 0.58 – a value for a bad charge; the time to repair of a single disk is 8 h (assuming a hot-spare disk – 8 h is the time for synchronizing the data)

A.5 Example Calculations

In this section we investigate the probability of deviations from the calculated averages. For example, assume a specific value for the AFR: How large is the probability to have one, two, or three failures in one year?

We calculate this using the Poisson formula (Eq. A.2). We use n as the time interval and $p =$ AFR.

Example 1. Let AFR = 0.0167. That means the device is expected to fail 167 times in 10 000 years, or 0.05 times in 3 years (which we assume as the lifetime of the system in question). With the given probability of 5% we do not expect the device to fail at all. But on the other hand, it could fail once, twice, or even more often. The Poisson distribution allows us to calculate probabilities for that; the result is shown in Table A.3 on the next page.

The calculation shows that the probability of getting one or more failures in 3 years is 4.9%, a possible situation. But if we experience two or

Table A.3. Probability for different number of failures.

Number of failures	Probability
0	0.951
1	0.048
2	0.0011
3	0.000019
> 0	0.049

more failures, we would disbelieve the value given for the AFR. This is according to the test method we have already described.   ∎

Example 2. We have a new – low-cost – computer cluster that consist of 512 nodes (i.e., 512 computers which perform numerical calculations). In the first month it experienced 24 failures, which corresponds to an AFR of 0.56 per node. We want to do a forecast of our expected maintenance effort and therefore we want to know the expected variation with a confidence of 95%. We solve Eq. (A.5) with $f = 24$, $n = 512$, and $\gamma = 0.95$. Then we use Table A.1 on p. 362 to get $c = 1.96$. With that we can determine the interval $[p_1, p_2] = [0.035, 0.061]$. This means that we can expect between 18 and 31 failures per month. We decide to use 30 failures per month for our cost calculation, as some kind of worst-case scenario. It is important to check the evolution of the failure rates every month, to identify possible trends (see Sect. A.6); therefore we repeat this calculation each month. But in this first month, this is the best we can do.   ∎

Example 3. We purchased a new storage system which contains 200 disk drives. Our vendor provided us with an AFR value of 0.0167 for each disk of the new system. We use the method of hypothesis tests to decide if the new system confirms the AFR value given. We want to be 95% sure about our assessment. We calculate how many disks are allowed to fail in 1 year so that we can believe the value, using a table with the following columns (refer to Eq. A.1):

$$k = \text{number of failed disks},$$

$$B_{200,0.0167}(k) = \text{probability for exactly } k \text{ disks to fail},$$

$$\sum_{i=0}^{k} B_{200,0.0167}(i) = \text{probability for a maximum of } k \text{ disks to fail.}$$
$$\text{This needs to be compared with our}$$
$$\text{confidence level, 95\%}.$$

Table A.4 on the next page shows the result: if eight or more disks fail, we can be 97.6% sure that the AFR value given was to small.

In this example we ignore the possibility that the given AFR value could be too large – as customers we are not interested in that case.   ∎

Table A.4. Verification of a given AFR value

k	$B(k)$ (%)	$\sum_{i=0}^{k} B(i)$ (%)
0	3.5	
1	11.8	15.3
2	19.7	35.0
3	22.0	57.0
4	18.4	75.4
5	12.3	87.7
6	6.7	94.4
7	3.2	97.6

A.6 Reliability over Time – the Bathtub Curve

So far, we have assumed that the probability for failures is homogeneously distributed – independent of the age of a system. This is not correct, as parts and whole systems show more failures at the beginning of their life ("early mortality"), when the so-called *burn in* takes place: Weak systems which were produced outside manufacturing tolerances fail very early. At the "end of life," systems show an increasing failure rate because their mechanical parts or electronics wear out. The probability follows a so-called *bathtub curve* as shown in Fig. A.5 on the facing page. The stable failure period is the time interval when we want to use a system in production. During this interval the weak systems have been weeded out and failures happen in a random fashion with a homogeneous distribution, as we assumed in the calculations before. It is a challenge to identify the time when our system in question approaches and leaves this "good" interval.

There is a combination of reasons for this bathtub behavior. Hardware shows early mortality because of production issues like not meeting required tolerances. Good vendors invest to identify early mortality by running the systems under stress conditions before they are delivered to customers. The "burn in" is done by running them in climate exposure test cabinets, where they run under low and high temperature, and high humidity. They run under vibration conditions to identify mechanical issues like bad contacts or bad solder joints, and also high and low voltage. The goal is to walk "down" the bathtub to the middle part before systems are delivered to clients. Such good vendors are proud of their efforts to not send early mortality systems to customers. Ask your vendor about this to find out what tests are done and if they are done for *all* systems delivered to clients, not only for some control samples.

It is hard to predict when a system is at the end of its life. A rule of thumb is that after 5 years of continuous operations, a system is expected to show more failures.

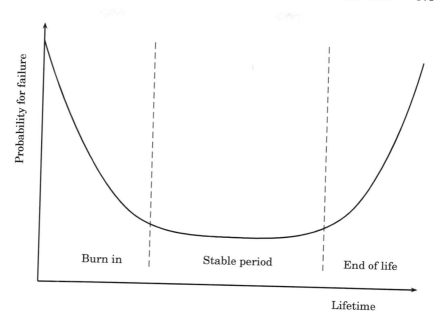

Fig. A.5. Typical bathtub curve of a system

But there is an additional reason for the bathtub behavior – perhaps equally important: the lifetime of a system is similar to or even longer than todays product cycles. If we purchase a new system, we typically want to get the best and greatest: the newest model which was just announced. The risk here is that the new, much faster and better system is not mature yet. If we purchase an early system, the vendor has no experience with it. Microcode might not be optimized for it and integration of the different components might not have been worked out well. Vendors constantly optimize their systems, based on experience in the field. Sometimes a system purchased 1 year after its introduction looks quite different from the early systems. We need to find the right compromise between product innovation and maturity.

It is hard to provide good guidance for how to deal with this situation. If a system is brand new, and the vendor announces a breakthrough from the old one, caution is required. A factor of 10 for the AFR of the newest system and the same model after 1 year of production can be expected. If we purchase such a system, we need to review the company's track record and, if possible, our own experience with that vendor. We should also review what is really new in that system design. Does it show new technologies, or just improve on existing ones? A personal relationship with the sales representative is also helpful, as he or she often has insight into the potential difficulties before and on announcement of the new system. If our system runs until the end of its product life cycle, we have also a negative effect: the system is now expected to be very mature, but it is not more in the mainstream. This means that integration tests are focused on systems from the current (newer) products; patches and microcode changes are first implemented on the new series and so on. A system from an old series in a new environment becomes more and more a contaminant, which is a reason for problems and failures.

The problem of nonconstant failure rates was tackled by the Swedish researcher *Waloddi Weibull* (1887–1979). He defined a distribution function which is widely used in the area of quality engineering which now bears his name [11].

The combination of all these effects leads to the bathtub curve. We should be conservative and stay in the mainstream: our systems should not be too young and not too old.

B

Data Centers

Data centers are facilities (rooms or complete buildings) where IT systems are placed. Such a facility must have specific installations, controls, and processes to be called a data center – otherwise it is simply a room with computers in it. Dedicated IT staff run those IT systems with specific processes to ensure proper functioning. The department that is responsible for data centers is often named IT Operations.

Even though data centers are not essential for high availability and disaster recovery, they provide good support for successful implementations. High availability and disaster recovery without data centers is possible, but requires much more effort. We will use this appendix to spell out in more detail what kinds of data center facilities will help to implement and retain high availability. Disaster recovery is supported by establishing or using a second data center at the disaster-recovery site, as described in Chap. 10.

From experience, there are four areas where errors are made most often and that cause incidents and outages:

1. **Changes** introduce errors and case failures.
2. **Air conditioning** does not work or is not sufficient.
3. **Power supply** is not successful.
4. **Fire protection** does not work (false alarm or erroneous release).

However, this is in well-run data centers. It is hard to estimate what error conditions would be the major root causes in data centers that do not follow the approach that is outlined in this appendix. For example, the potential error cause "tripping over a cable" does not appear in the list above because we do not have cables lying around that one could trip over. Therefore the list is a list of problems that one has to face in any case, even if one's preparations are good.

Data center facilities are the best form of the *physical environment* that we have met so often in the previous chapters. These are rooms and equipment that are dedicated to the task of running IT systems properly for a long time, with few outages. This appendix will not be a complete guide for how to build and operate a top-notch data center; that is beyond the scope of this book.

Broadly, data center facilities can be put up in the following categories:

- **Room installations** refer to issues around raised floors, cabling, and physical security. These issues are spelled out in Sect. B.1.
- **Heat and fire control** are crucial to keep computers operational and are described in Sect. B.2.
- **Power control** is another frequent failure area, and is handled in Sect. B.3.
- **Computer setups** are the way that computers are placed in data centers physically. This is the topic of Sect. B.4.

Let us have a look at each of those categories. But this section will provide only an overview of the most important topics, and only those that are especially relevant for high availability.

For example, the problem of grounding is not covered, even though it is a very important issue in many areas of the world. As well as the issue of water – there should be no water conduit in the room anywhere. There are more issues, and data center facility planning is such a big topic that it deserves a book of its own; we are just scratching the surface here.

B.1 Room Installation

Rooms in data centers are specifically equipped so that computer systems can be installed and run in them.

▶ *Raised Floors*

They have a raised floor system, where a second floor is installed above the actual floor. That second floor consists of removable tiles so that it is possible to access the gap everywhere. This gap is used for air circulation (as part of air conditioning, see later) and for cabling. Ideally, the gap between the base and the second floor is 60 cm (about 2 ft.), but it might be less depending on available room height.

The usage of tiles leads to the need to pay attention to the weight of computer systems and other equipment. Today the trend is towards ever higher levels of system integration. This often leads to more weight for the same volume and implies that we need to consider the impact that the weight makes on the ground at the system rack's feet.

Just as we have to pay attention to the impact of the racks, we also need to assure that the tiles that are on transport route are able to take the pressure. When one needs to reinforce the tiles at a specific place where a heavy computer system will be placed, this computer system must be transported to this place somehow. If it is transported in one piece, the tiles on the way to this place might need reinforcement as well.

When your site has a raised floor, you probably also want to consider proper drainage. Otherwise, water damage – be it from pipes or rain – might damage the power and network connections that are usually placed into the underfloor space. For example, moisture alarms could be utilized to detect problems early.

▶ *Cabling*

Proper cabling is essential for high availability. There are quite a few failure causes that can be avoided by strict cabling policies:

- When cables are lying openly on the floor, somebody can trip over them and rip them off their jack, causing power outages, network outages, or others.
- When cable/jack connection are strong, tripping over them can even result in tearing out or overthrowing the connected systems.
- Long cables can be bent or damaged otherwise. Therefore it is better to use short cables to patch panels and have structured cabling between patch panels that can be easily tested and is redundant.
- Unmarked cables are often a source of erroneous installations. Even if the initial installation goes right, using unmarked cables or forgetting to mark them when their use changes is a sure recipe for an outage. Some day somebody will unplug the cables for repairs or upgrades, and will plug them in the wrong way.

The first thing that we insist on in a data center is *structured cabling*. This term means that cabling is integrated into the structure of a building and is independent of a specific server or specific system.[1] This is realized by four principles:

- Cabling between buildings is separated; there is a definitive transfer point between interbuilding cabling and vertical cabling.
- Cabling between building levels – *vertical cabling* – is separated; there are defined transfer points to interbuilding cabling and horizontal cabling.
  Vertical cabling is best done with fiber optics cables, because that creates a galvanic separation and prevents potential differences. (The main difference of potentials is in vertical distances.) With copper cable, there might be current on the grounding.
- Cabling on a building level – *horizontal cabling* – has clear transfer points to vertical cabling and system cabling.

---

[1] Though obviously cabling is not independent of the network technology used. Cabling for Ethernet, ATM, or Token Ring will be different, of course.

- System cabling is only over very short distances. It should be possible to check a system cable completely, i.e., to make optical checks without the need to open lots of trunks or floor tiles.
  Sometimes the transfer point from system cables to horizontal cabling of the data center is not directly beside a system, then the system cables come near other systems. That should be reduced as far as possible.

Cables should be tied: for horizontal cabling at least every 50 cm; for vertical cabling more frequently.

It is a big advantage to place information about cabling in one's configuration management database (Sect. C.3). Then one can always query the tool for the connectivity of systems and get initial information about dependencies and potential error causes.

Two independent network connections for a building also means two transfer points between interbuilding and vertical cabling, as well as redundant vertical cabling. There should also be two transfer points between vertical and horizontal cabling. Each row of system racks should have connections to both transfer points to create also redundant horizontal cabling, otherwise destruction of one transfer point would cause a connectivity outage of the whole floor. Within each system rack row, several patch panels provide transfer points between the redundant horizontal and system cabling in short distances.

The transfer point between horizontal cabling and computer systems or active network components like big switches might have dozens, sometimes even hundreds of cables. It is mandatory to use an underfloor or overhead trunking system for such cabling to reduce the risks named before.

Such trunks must not be shared with power cables; there must be at least 6 cm between power and copper network cables. Use bridges to cross power and network cables, and always do so at a right angle.

▶ *Physical Security*

Major outages can be also caused by malevolent persons who get access to a computer's console – still access to the physical console has often more rights associated with it. There is also the risk of evildoers who damage computer systems physically with full intent in an act of sabotage.

Security and access control for a data center is usually established anyhow, for data security reasons. These measures are also valid precautions in the realm of high availability and will help to reduce the risk of physical sabotage. Video camera surveillance will enable faster detection of physical sabotage, or identification of the culprit after the fact.

For forensic analysis, one needs to know when somebody was in the data center and for how long, and on which systems this person worked in that time. Physical security must provide answers to these questions.

Server operations monitoring, often round-the-clock, is also sometimes integrated into physical security. For large data centers, these two functions are separate though. Even though the fully automated data center is a sought-after vision of the future, having human operators handle incidents and outages is still a valid precaution to reduce the risk to highly available installations. Appendix C presents more issues around proper operations processes.

B.2 Heat and Fire Control

Lots of computers and other devices in data centers produce lots of heat. This is so important that an acronym has been built around the need to handle this issue: HVAC for *heating, ventilation, and air conditioning*. With all this heat and with dangers of smoldering burns of electrical parts, fire is always an imminent risk in data centers.

▸ *Heat Control*

Computers, in particular high-end servers, are notoriously influenced by the temperature they operate at. Their electronic components produce so much heat that they will shut down in short time if nothing is done to reduce that heat. The heat must be dispensed and transported elsewhere.

Actually, typical IT systems will work for quite some time at higher room temperature. But even if they continue to work in warm areas, they age faster and the probability of failures will become higher (see the discussion of the bath tube curve in Appendix A.6).

Some time ago, computers had water cooling systems. They did not heat up the room themselves. Then computer systems got air cooling. Early systems relied on data centers where cold air is blown out of the floor and they emitted hot air at the top, where an air conditioning system could handle it. Nowadays, vendors build computers as they like: they ingest cold air where they want and blow out hot air where they want (most of the time not at the top).

This leads to the requirements:

- Where cold air is sucked in, there must be a cold air current.
- Where hot air is blown out, there must not be a cold air inlet of another system.

It might well be that future systems will deploy water cooling again. The trend towards ever higher system densities per volume creates heat problems as well. And water cooling needs less energy than air conditioning. Since the energy for air conditioning costs easily more than the whole server, this is an interesting aspect that would save ongoing costs and raise system availability.

Ventilation is used to dispense heat evenly within a room, but will *not* cool it. Since humans feel the windchill factor more than the real temperature, it is a high risk to depend on one's senses for room temperature. Instead, good-precision air conditioning should be used to cool down the whole room to roughly 18°C (about 64°F).

Good precision here means that the air flow in the room is observed and planned. There are sprays that emit a kind of fog that can be used to visualize air currents and help to analyze why a computer system is getting too hot. Of course, first of all one has to measure both the temperature in the computers and the temperature at multiple places in the room. Without that information one would not even know that a system gets too hot or that there are hot spots in a room.

When new computers are installed in a data center, it must ensured that the air conditioning system has enough capacity for the new equipment as well. Otherwise, availability of all systems in the data center is endangered, not just that of the new equipment.

This is an important consideration as new vendors market new systems with ever-increasing packing density, e.g., blade servers. Often, racks are planned and assembled by the IT staff and not by vendors. If one has not very strong air conditioning, one needs to pay attention to the heat production and dispensation for such dense systems. Sometimes it is necessary that one does not fill up the rack completely, but leaves some space for air circulation and less heat production.

Air conditioning is a technical system like any other, and is bound to fail as well, i.e., air conditioning can well be the single point of failure in a data center. To combat this, a backup air conditioning system should be in place, or the different components of the air conditioning should be redundant. As with all redundant technology, one needs to manage the redundancy, e.g., to monitor that the components run at all and exchange or repair them otherwise.

Such monitoring is done in a HVAC control environment. Best-of-breed installations make that control environment redundant again, with manual management in the case of failures. We might also attach the HVAC environment (both the control component and the actual air conditioning system) to the uninterruptible power supply (Sect. B.3), to protect the heat control against power outages.

But HVAC monitoring does not consist of room-temperature sensors alone. Most computer systems allow the temperature of the CPU or fans to be queried. Computer monitoring should observe such temperatures as well, with properly defined escalations when the temperature is becoming too high. (Data sheets of hardware components usually tell about their typical and best operating temperature.)

Good working air conditioning is sine qua non for high-availability installations in data centers: without it, the servers will not run.

► *Fire Protection*

Since computer equipment produces heat in exuberance, and since any electrical component is in danger of smoldering, fire is one of the most probable risks to the physical environment. Therefore, good risk mitigation strategies call for precautions to detect fire early and also to fight it without damaging all the equipment.

A very important facility is early-warning fire and smoke detection systems. They can often detect problems before fire actually breaks out. Better systems even come with sensors to do spot detection, i.e., to detect the place in the room where the smoke comes from. Sometimes they measure particles given off by hot components and trigger alarms if those particles pass thresholds. With such fire prevention systems, one can often turn off problematic devices before an actual fire breaks out.

Still, that device will be unusable from now on. But that is the known area of high-availability setups: there will be redundant components that can take over functionality. This is one example where internal monitoring of any computer component is not sufficient. Sure, we would notice that the component gets too hot and might be able to disable it. But if it has started to smolder already, disabling the component might not be sufficient; instead one has to turn it off physically, maybe even remove it from the room as soon as possible.

The early-warning fire protection system is only the first line of defense and it would be foolish to rely on it alone. The fire could break out faster than our reaction time, or it could be a spark-triggered fire without slow buildup of smoke. Then we need fire extinguishers or a fire suppression system.

Conventionally, fire suppression systems are water sprinkler systems. These are not of much use in data centers, as they damage the electrical equipment beyond repair. The same is true for foam-based fire extinguishers – if anybody uses water or foam in a data center, the chances are high that disaster recovery for the whole site will be tested in real time soon after.

Instead, data centers utilize fire suppression systems that push out or reduce oxygen in the air, so that fire cannot spread anymore. Originally, CO_2 was used, flooded from the floor. This flooding creates mechanical pressure that is so high that it damages cabling. In addition, it is acidic; with water it forms carbonic acid. Of course, it is also toxic, but almost all fire suppression materials are toxic, so that is not a differentiator.

Then halon was used often, a gas that pushes oxygen out of the room. But if people remain in the room without emergency breathing oxygen supplies, or if they are unconscious, usage of a halon-based system is often deadly. (Well, smoke and fire themselves are also often deadly.) But halon is also one of the chemicals that destroys stratospheric ozone; therefore it was banned in the EU, and in the US the EPA strongly encourages the use of non-ozone-depleting alternatives.

Today, halon alternatives like *FM-200* or *Inergen* are available. FM-200 belongs to the class of halocarbon agents that extinguish fire primarily via the absorption of heat, whereas Inergen is an inert gas agent (it consists of a mixture of argon and nitrogen) that works via oxygen depletion.

Last, but not least, fire protection zones are valuable. A fire extinguisher can operate only in those areas where fire was detected. Physical fire containment strategies are part of such a strategy and should be considered too. Fire doors or other physical firebreaks can be used to contain fire within a small physical area and confine damage to some of your highly available systems, and protect against spreading to all of them.

B.3 Power Control

Other frequent sources of computer failures are power outages or fluctuations in power frequency and power strength. It is mandatory for any data center to protect against these failures.

As a basic level of protection, we establish *uninterruptible power supplies* (UPS). These are devices that are responsible for maintaining a continuous and stable power supply for the hardware. UPS devices protect against some or all of the nine standard power problems:

1. Power failure
2. Power sag (undervoltage for up to a few seconds)
3. Power surge (overvoltage for up to a few seconds)
4. Brownout (long-term undervoltage for minutes or days)
5. Long-term overvoltage for minutes or days
6. Line noise superimposed on the power waveform
7. Frequency variation of the power waveform
8. Switching transient (undervoltage or overvoltage for up to a few nanoseconds)
9. Harmonic multiples of power frequency superimposed on the power waveform

Good data centers never connect any computer equipment directly to the power grid, but always place a UPS in-between. This it at least true for all highly available systems. A *power distribution unit* (PDU) connects the UPS devices to the computers.

As for every other device, UPS systems may be defective themselves, as well as PDUs; therefore it is necessary to monitor them all the time to detect failures early. Detecting UPS failures during power failures is bound to lead to major outages.

Installation of new hardware in the data center always has to be accompanied with an analysis of power demand changes. It must be checked that the UPS will handle changed power requirements, otherwise it must be upgraded as well (which can be quite expensive, by the way). Otherwise, the new hardware will pose a risk to all other installations in the data center; e.g., installation of an unrelated business foundation server could damage our highly available mission-critical server and lead to a major outage.

UPS devices contain batteries and will protect against short power failures in the range of a few minutes. If a power outage takes longer, one must either start disaster recovery and switch to a disaster-recovery site, or one needs to have backup generators (e.g., diesel generators) that generate power themselves.

Shortly before the batteries are dead, UPS management software will trigger automatic shutdown of attached systems since proper shutdown is much better than crashing the systems – at least the data will be in a consistent state. For high availability this might have consequences beyond the actual service: if some other system depends on this service, its availability will be affected as well; and if the dependent system is a failover cluster, it may well lead to perpetual failovers in the cluster.

Another, but more expensive, possibility to handle power outages is to get two independent power grid source connections. Then all elements of the electrical system are redundant, all servers are connected to both grids; outage of one power grid will be handled by the second grid. But we must be realistic and must see that this is very hard to realize. The problem here is not to get two power connections – any sales person of any utility company will sell that to you. The problem is the innocent term *independent*: real independence is seldom in power grid structures, and in accordance with Murphy's Law the excavator will rip apart the big grid cable in the street that is used for both input sources.

By no means does that mean that we should not strive for redundancy in our power supplies and also our power grid source connections. We can test for functional redundancy of our own installations, but will not be able to test the redundancy of grid connections.

Redundancy for internal power supplies, for UPS systems, and also for all connections is necessary for several situations. First of all, these are hardware components that wear with usage and where the probability of failures is quite high. Therefore it is advisable to protect against such failures at the cause and add redundancy already there. In particular, UPS devices use batteries that have only a limited lifetime.

Second, redundant power installations allow repair activities without disturbing the actual system usage. Maintenance work at the UPS can be done as needed if one has another UPS system that is used at this time. The same holds for power connections and power supplies.

Yet another issue to consider is the effect of powering off and on of computer systems. We need a dependency list of computer systems just for powering them off cleanly: the dependency graph shows us which systems are independent and can be shut down first. Otherwise, a cluster component could notice the shutdown and could trigger failovers of dependent components. The same holds for power-on sequences.

Powering on must be done carefully for other reasons. During power-on, most components draw much more power than in normal run situations. This can bring our overall power supply and the UPS to their limits. Therefore one should not turn on all devices at the same time. Instead, one should start them in a preplanned sequence, to play it safe both with power consumption and with service dependencies.

In summary, power outages are a risk with a high probability for highly available systems. Protection against power outages is possible, though expensive if one goes the last mile and utilizes a backup generator. At least, usage of UPS devices is mandatory, as is monitoring those devices.

B.4 Computer Setup

At first glance, the way that computer systems are physically set up is not relevant for high availability. It does not matter for the functionality if a server is a white-box medium-tower system or if it is mounted in a rack cabinet. But that first glance only looks at the failure situation and ignores the repair situation.

We should place our servers into proper rack cabinets (mostly industry-standard 19" racks). This leads to better cabling, no traps by cables or boxes, stable ventilation, and good access to the system plugs. Proper labeling of each system helps to locate it quickly in the case of necessary repairs.

Be careful when you mount systems into a rack. Racks can totter or even tumble if you pull out systems at the very top. This can have disastrous consequences for other systems in that rack and destroy their availability, i.e., maintenance work at a system with low priority can influence availability of a mission-critical system if they are in the same rack.

Such rack cabinets, as well as mainframe-type computer systems and big storage units are placed into rows in a data center. Such proper room layout also helps to identify computer systems quickly in the case of emergencies.

All these precautions will reduce the mean time to repair. One is able to locate a failed system quickly, one can access the system's components properly, and one has ordered and labeled connections that will be less probably reconnected erroneously.

Remember the start of this book – mean time to repair is the setscrew that is best to turn to raise our overall availability, as the mean time between failures cannot be changed as easily.

C

Service Support Processes

This book focuses on the principles, architecture, and implementation of high availability and disaster recovery. As such, it covers 90% of the projects that introduce those capabilities in IT environments. But as everybody knows, there is another 90% to get the job done: run the systems without deteriorating them. This is the job of the data center staff and of the system administrators who manage and maintain the systems.

The importance of the run-the-systems phase to retain high-availability and disaster-recovery capabilities is generally accepted but often not emphasized enough.

> **No tool and no automation can save you from bad operations – bad operations will make any good design fail. It is the biggest threat to high availability.**

There is a de facto standard for managing IT operations, called the *Information Technology Infrastructure Library* or ITIL for short. ITIL is a process-centric view that gives guidelines for best-practice data center management. ITIL was created[1] and is owned by the Office of Government Commerce (OGC) of the UK's Treasury.

ITIL defines the task of data center management in five areas:

1. The business perspective
2. Managing applications
3. Deliver IT Services
4. Support IT Services
5. Manage the infrastructure

IT service delivery [7] is at the heart of this whole book since it contains the descriptions of *availability management, service level man-*

---

[1] Actually, ITIL was created in the late 1980s by the Central Computer and Telecommunications Agency (CCTA), which was merged into OGC in April 2001.

agement, and *IT service continuity management* processes. We have met these processes several times throughout this book.

IT service support [6] is an area that has relevant material for the scope of this section. The area contains process descriptions of:

- Service desk
- Incident management
- Problem management
- Configuration management
- Change management
- Release management

When we apply these processes, we will have a very good chance that our run-the-systems job is improved and that the systems will stay highly available and disaster recovery will remain possible.

In the rest of this section, we will have a look at all those processes except *service desk.*

C.1 Incident Management

In ITIL terminology,

> **An 'Incident' is any event which is not part of the standard operation of a service and which causes, or may cause, an interruption to, or a reduction in, the quality of that service.**

The goal of incident management is to restore system functionality (as defined in the service level agreement) as quickly as possible.

Such an event may be a an application or hardware failure, or it may be a service request. Incident management is engaged in detection and recording of incidents, classification, initial support, and resolution.

The focus of incident management is the system's user. Its objective is to get the user working again as quickly as possible. Workarounds are perfectly valid resolutions; the underlying root cause of the incident may not be known and there is often not enough time to research it.

The cause of incidents may be obvious and can be remedied in short order. Then no further action is needed. But when the underlying cause is not known, one should try to find a workaround and transform the incident into a problem, see Sect. C.2. It is difficult to decide when this propagation is done. If it is done too often, resources will be bound that could improve the IT service otherwise (or could make operations cheaper). If it is not done often enough, structural problems are uncovered and symptoms are fought all the time in incident management, damaging service availability.

This is an important connection between incident management and high availability that is often ignored. One can learn a lot by looking at incidents that are communicated by the system's users or are triggered by automatic monitoring systems. Often these incidents give new material for failure scenarios of future projects, or they cover up deeper-level problems that should be addressed to improve availability.

But why do incidents happen at all? At first sight, high availability should ensure that no incidents happen; all are handled by the redundant systems. But that is not the case in practical terms:

- When a component fails, it must be repaired. While this might be considered as "part of the standard operation," many organizations choose to handle such failures also via their established incident management processes. After all, during the duration of repair, the missing redundancy (or the repair itself) may cause interruption of the service.
- We have seen several times that redundancy of components must be managed somehow. Time and time again we used the formulation that it may be managed by administrators. But how is this done in practical terms? Operational procedures are the answer, and here incident management enters the room. It is an established process and procedure infrastructure that can trigger resolution of failure by manually establishing the redundant component.
- Murphy's Law is true. Anything that can go wrong, will go wrong *over time*.[2] Even if the project's implementation has the best analysis, reality will bite and there will be incidents in areas where experience was not sufficient, or assumptions were wrong, etc.

In the realm of high availability and disaster recovery, it is also relevant that *escalation procedures* are part of the incident management process. Such escalations are needed when the incident cannot be handled in the normal service level agreement repair times and when it evolves into a major outage.

C.2 Problem Management

Problem management is concerned with root cause analysis of failures, and with methods to prevent them in the future. The ITIL documents define the topic of the study as follows:

> **A 'Problem' is a condition that is either identified as a result of multiple Incidents that exhibit common symptoms. Problems can also be identified from a single significant**

---

[2] Murphy's Law does not mean that every possible failure happens immediately. It means that every possible failure happens *eventually*.

Incident, indicative of a single error, for which the cause is unknown, but for which the impact is significant.

Problem management is intended to reduce the number and severity of incidents, and therefore proper implementation of this process is of high importance for high availability.

Root cause analysis (RCA) of outages and failures is the first step for continuous improvement of an IT system. Its result should:

- Enable incident management to resolve incidents faster by providing a database of known errors and appropriate resolutions
- Improve IT system implementation and operations with changes that prevent such problems in the future

This means that the goals of problem management are twofold: with the support for incident management we try to reduce the needed mean time to repair, which increases our availability. With changes to the installed systems that prevent such problems, we increase the mean time before failure, also with the result of increasing our availability.

Problem management is not only triggered by incidents. Technicians often detect problems during their normal day-to-day work. They stumble regularly over installations or configurations that *do not look right*. Such preliminary estimations are quite often correct and are grounded in solid experience. We must not forfeit that experience and must incorporate it into proactive problem management, i.e., instead of adding a "fix me" comment in some script that will soon be forgotten, system administrators should be encouraged to log the issue in a problem management database for later analysis by peers. It is best to frame such encouragement in real processes: establish metrics as to who discovered and analyzed successfully the most problems, and give out awards to your employees who are not too shy to name areas where improvements are needed. Such proactive problem management is a very valuable tool for improving availability and asserting the success of disaster recovery.

One of the biggest problems with problem management is the tendency that root cause analysis results are not followed through. Time and time again it happens that a problem is discovered and analyzed, the root cause is found, but no change is triggered owing to the inertia of the IT system that is running. "Never change a running system" is a very good approach at first, but there are limits to it. When known errors exist and cost/effort-benefit analysis for a change is positive as well, the high-availability objective should take a front seat and should enforce the change.

C.3 Configuration Management

Configuration management is concerned with management of the knowledge of our systems. Its central term is the configuration item (CI) that ITIL defines by example. Their example can be abstracted into the following definition:

> **A CI is a hardware, software, service, or documentation asset, or one of its subcomponents that is independently managed. A CI has a type, a unique identifier, and arbitrary relations to other CIs, the most important are "consists of" and "uses." A CI may have attributes (key-value pairs) that describe it further.**

You will immediately have noticed that this definition is very similar to our *component* term that we introduced in Chap. 3. So here we find a standardized process to manage components that we need to analyze systems.

Configuration management collects information about system components. It tracks actively changes and builds a knowledge base that can be used by other ITIL processes and must be kept up to date by other processes too. This knowledge base is named the *configuration management database* (CMDB).

The CMDB should keep all information:

- About configuration items
- Their attributes
- Their relationships
- Their version history
- Their configuration
- Their documentation

Sometimes, configuration and documentation are simply seen as attributes; sometimes they are mentioned to emphasize their importance.

This sounds to good to be true, doesn't it? Here we have the perfect source and storage for our architecture components, the dependency diagrams, and the redundancy information that we need so urgently in high-availability and disaster-recovery projects. Figure C.1 on the next page illustrates that goal.

Well, the reality is that existing CMDBs seldom fulfill the need of such projects, and that has several reasons, as will be shown now. A very important part of configuration management is the decision about the granularity of CIs. That decision is influenced by two factors:

1. In the ITIL model, only CIs can have relations, namely, to other CIs. It is not possible to have a relation between or to attributes. That is what distinguishes them from attributes, otherwise every attribute could be a CI itself. (The attribute name would be the CI's type, the

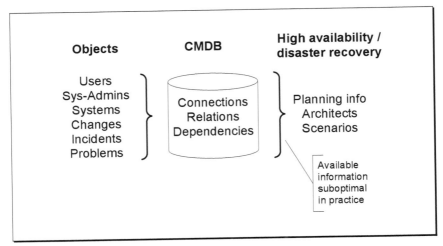

Fig. C.1. Theoretical usage of the configuration management database (*CMDB*) for high availability and disaster recovery

attribute's value would be the CI's identifier, and an "is-described" relationship would exist between the CI and these new attribute CIs.) That is, when we want to express relations in the CMDB, we need to make that component a CI. When we do not want to express relations, this component can often be modeled as an attribute.

2. CIs are the preferred unit of management by other ITIL processes, in particular change, incident, and problem management. Of course, they can and will refer to CI attributes as well, but that is more clumsy than referring directly to CIs. Depending on their demands of granularity, the CMDB model will be coarse or very fine grained.

As an example, a network interface card (NIC) may well be an attribute of a CI server and its own CI. Both are valid models:

- If change and incident management only refer to servers and describe the error message according to the server, noting the NIC existence (maybe with associated configuration information like the MAC address) is sufficient.
- Treating the NIC as its own CI allows us to express its relationship to other parts, e.g., a redundancy relationship to another NIC. It also allows us to express the exact components that are addressed by changes. On the other hand, that makes change descriptions much harder to build as one often does not know up-front what components a change will address. In fact, keeping fine-grained CIs consistent, up to date, and with a sensible history that can be assessed by people is *very* hard.

Table C.1. ITIL objectives for CMDB (excerpt). *CI* configuration item

ITIL process	CMDB support
Incident management	Automated identification of other affected CIs when any CI is the subject of an incident.
	Identification of owners, responsible IT staff, vendor contact information, support contract details
Problem management	Integration of problem management data within the CMDB, or at least an interface.
	Easy interrogation and trend analysis reports
Change management	Identification or related CIs affected by proposed change to assist with impact assessment.
	Record CIs that are affected by authorized changes.
	Maintenance of a history of all CIs.
	The ability to show graphically the configuration and input information in that graphical representation.
	Enable the organization to reduce the use of unauthorized software
Release management	Record baselines of CIs and CI packages, to which to revert with known consequences.
	Register CI status changes when releases are implemented.
	Support roll-out across distributed locations by providing information on the versions of CIs and the changes that are incorporated into a release

But our dependency diagrams that we use for high-availability and disaster-recovery design need to express their redundancy and thus needs them as CIs. Usual CMDB data schema modeling happens independently of high-availability or disaster-recovery projects, is oriented towards the need of other ITIL processes, and does not take our demands from that area into account. Therefore, the chances are low that the CMDB is really a good place to store our complete dependency and redundancy data.

According to the ITIL, the CMDB is the all-singing all-dancing data store that answers every question about our systems and their configuration. Table C.1 lists just a few of the intended usages that are already overwhelming.

Add the point that industry pundits agree that a single central CMDB is not feasible and federated CMDBs will be the way of the future. Though they do not explain in technical details how such a federation of CMDBs is supposed to work and how the CMDBs are supposed to be interlinked. (Vaguely mumbling about "Web Services" should not be seen as an explanation.)

In practice, many existing systems are quite crude and not as interlinked as the theory wants it. This may change in the future as more and more data centers orient their management procedures towards the ITIL. But good CMDBs are hard to establish, cost a lot of effort to maintain, and their benefits are not immediately visible. They are also a technical measure, and most ITIL introductions concentrate on the management and process side and leave aside radical technical improvements.

This reflection leads to the point that while configuration management and especially CMDBs could contribute a lot to our work on high availability and disaster recovery, it is not probable they will do so in the short term to the midterm.

C.4 Change Management

Good change management practice is essential to keep high availability and the ability to do disaster recovery. Change management is the process to control changes in your IT environment, be they caused by change requests or by problem management. As the ITIL says,

Change is the process of moving from one defined state to another.

Changes to your systems should be:

- Proposed with justifications; change requests without specifying cause and effect in technical details are not acceptable
- Reviewed by subject-matter experts if they introduce new single points of failure or new dependencies, to make sure that high-availability or disaster-recovery capabilities are not damaged
- Checked to see if any change in a primary system is accompanied with a change on the respective disaster-recovery system
- Approved by a *change advisory board* that evaluates their business impact and coordinates the changes with other changes

With proper change management in place, the exposure to risk is minimized. For our highly available systems and our disaster-recovery precaution, any change is surely a risk and may be a chance. This cannot be emphasized enough: *every change is a risk to availability*. A new functionality or a new component is introduced into a running IT system. Both the migration to new functionality or new components, and the new components themselves may not work. Testing will show where the functionality works, but not where it may fail. As Murphy's Law says, "anything that can go wrong, will go wrong over time."

It is thus very important that every change comes with a back-out plan, a method to revert any changes to the starting point. This back-out plan is the last resort when something goes wrong and the risk of a change manifests itself as a real failure.

On the other hand, the risk of change can be worth it. If it increases reliability of the system overall, we have exchanged the increased short-term risk of change against the decreased long-term risk of failures. That is what the reviews are for, to analyze a change request and judge the associated risk and benefit. Experience is needed for such analysis and judgment; only many years of seeing both good and bad practice gives this ability.

For mission-critical highly available servers, it is mandatory that *every* change is reviewed in detail by a senior subject-matter expert. For servers in the business-important or business-foundation categories, it is often sufficient to do summary reviews of changes and dive into detailed reviews for changes with more impact.

When you do a change to a server with disaster recovery in place, do not forget that you might have to update your Disaster Recovery Emergency Pack as well. Printing out up-to-date information is often forgotten, as it is inconvenient and seen as inefficient. But when a major outage occurs, one is glad to have material that is independent of systems that might be destroyed.

C.5 Release Management

Release management is the process to bring new software, hardware, or configurations into production. According to the ITIL,

> A *Release* describes a collection of authorized changes to an IT service. It is a collection of new and/or changed configuration items which are tested and introduced into the live environment together.

For highly available systems, this is an extremely important area. Releases must be identified, planned, and must be tested thoroughly before they are put into production. Together, change management and release management are the crucial processes that ensure ongoing availability and serviceability of IT services:

- Change management makes sure that the organizational aspects of changes – coordination with business owners, announcements, reviews, and approval – are done right.
- Release management ensures that the technological aspects of changes – planning, tests, and roll-out – are done right.

Release management has several important duties:

1. To determine the release unit
2. To testing the release unit
3. To roll out the release unit

First, we need to determine which changes are released together. This set of changes is called the *release unit*. As so often with such processes, that decision is a matter of experience. The change set must neither be too small nor too large. If it is too small, we have lots of releases and every release has associated risks that are independent of its size (e.g., the roll-out might not work). We do not want to introduce a new release for every minor change. On the other hand, if a release becomes too large, we have the issue of many independent changes that can go wrong and have often unknown interdependencies. Proper testing of large releases is very difficult and therefore error-prone. A release unit should be large enough to qualify for an improvement of the IT service, but should focus on a few improvements and should not lump together many changes from different areas.

When a release unit is tested, it must be ensured that not only functionality tests are done. This is the most common error in release unit testing: only the working functionality is tested, not the failure situations. That is, there is a description of what a change is supposed to do. Tests most often determine if the changed IT service really has the new functionality, and if the old unchanged functionality still works. In addition, back-out plans must be tested, we will look at them again later.

But it is as important to test how the new components react in the case of failures. For example, if we have utilized a new application in a failover cluster, does failover still work? In such a situation, it is not only important to start the new service on one cluster node and see if it works. It is as important to cause several failovers, abort the processes, maybe damage the data store, and check if restarts, service switches, and data consistency checks still work. Similar tests must be done when new hardware is installed. For example, a new storage unit must be thoroughly checked that redundant cabling is really done correctly, etc.

When hardware changes are rolled out, it must be checked again (this check is also done during planning) that the new hardware does not disturb the disaster-recovery concept. For example, adding new storage to the primary site usually means that we also need to add it to the disaster-recovery system. Also, replication must be established for data on the new storage system, or it must be checked that the available replication still works.

It is best to have tool support for roll-out of software releases. Installing software without package management or other software distribution tool support is a recipe for disaster. Only with tool support is it possible to check which software is installed on a system in which version, or which software a file belongs to. Both are essential capabilities that are needed during incident and problem management. Sadly, current software release tools lack support for cluster environments. Here experienced IT staff have to augment vendor-supplied mechanisms with their own developments and own procedures to keep control over their systems.

Please note that the requirements for software distribution support depend on the target system. There is a vast difference if one wants to roll-out a new Office version to a few thousand desktops, or if one installs a new Oracle release on a mission-critical server. While the first can and should be automated and the distribution should utilize a push model from a central distribution server, utilizing a fully automated push model for an Oracle update is a definitive way to get a major outage. Here the installation must be done on the server, and tool-supported installation steps are intermixed with manual checks if functionality and performance are not impacted.

As in change management, a back-out plan is an indispensable part of any release unit. The back-out plan must spell out both the organizational and the technical details of how one can roll back to a previous state. If that is not possible for technical reasons, the back-out plan must describe how a spare component can take over the service (e.g., the disaster-recovery system can be utilized). It is also necessary to specify the *point of no return*. This is the point in time when a roll back cannot be done anymore because it would need too long. At this time, the actual state of the release roll-out must be reviewed and a decision must be made as to whether one will continue successfully or whether it is better to roll back and start anew at another date.

C.6 Information Gathering and Reporting

A German proverb says, "Do good things and tell about it." This is also true for any activity in data centers. A big problem for business owners, executive managers, and fellow colleagues is that they do not know what work has been done in the past and what is planned for the future.

An important sign of a well-run data center is that information is gathered that provides metrics about the work that is done and the state of the IT system. That information should be both technical and business-oriented. As an example, it is good practice to collect information about:

- Changes
- How many incidents there are for a system
- How many changes fail
- How many changes lead to problems or incidents in a short time span
- Which releases are out, and the history of releases
- The rate of change for incidents, problems, and changes
- Failovers
- How many outages there are, and for how long
- How many and which IT systems are affected

Of interest is also a more complex analysis that gives hints to improve change and release processes. For example, consider the statistics "how many changes fail or cause problems, depending on the number of changes in a given time range." When we have ten changes at a weekend, and one of them fails – how many will we have when we have 50 changes at a weekend? The answer cannot be generalized and depends greatly on the available staff and available skills. But most often the relation is not linear, and more changes may lead to more or less error, relatively speaking.

One can improve one's statistics by creating adequate categorizations. Both change and problem categories are important. For example, let us assume that we have the (simple) change categorization:

- New installation
- Function change
- Incident repair (emergency change)
- Problem repair
- Security upgrade

Even with such a simple categorization, we can already imagine that the relation of errors to change categories is very interesting and can lead to data that tells us where we need to improve our processes, to achieve lower failure rates and thus higher availability. When the problems and incidents are also categorized (e.g., according to how many people were affected), then we can give even better input to process improvement proposals.

It is best practice to generate several reports for different target audiences that differ in information selection and level of details. For example, a report for a business owner will present different information from a report for the operations manager or the operations staff. The technical reports should always contain the information that is sent to the business owner. If she or he phones in and demands information for a specific item in her or his report, this information should be available in the operations manager's report as well.

For executive management, establishment of a *dashboard system* is sensible. Such a system collects information from many technical and business systems and condenses them into key performance indicators for essential business and IT services. Such information is typically presented on a very high abstraction level (e.g., "green/yellow/red traffic lights" for essential services) to compress the overall state of IT into one short table.

Better executive dashboards are tool-supported and also give the ability to "drill down" to more detailed information, maybe with a link to the technical information systems for the executives who are interested in technical details.

References

[1] Brilliant SS, Knight JC, Leveson NG (1990) Analysis of faults in an n-version software experiment. IEEE Trans Software Eng 16(2):238–247, DOI http://dx.doi.org/10.1109/32.44387

[2] Brooks FP (1975) The Mythical Man-Month. Addison-Wesley, Reading, NJ, USA

[3] Gibson GA (1992) Redundant Disk Arrays: Reliable, Parallel Secondary Storage. ACM Distinguished Dissertation, MIT Press, Cambridge, USA, also published twice at University of California, Berkeley, in 1992 and again as Technical Report CSD-91-613 in 1999

[4] Littlewood B, Popov P, Strigini L (2001) Modeling software design diversity: a review. ACM Comput Surv 33(2):177–208, DOI http://doi.acm.org/10.1145/384192.384195

[5] Murphy J, Morgan TW (2006) Availability, reliability, and survivability: An introduction and some contractual implications. STSC CrossTalk 3:26–29

[6] Office of Government Commerce (2000) ITIL Service Support. The Stationery Office Books, London, UK

[7] Office of Government Commerce (2001) ITIL Service Delivery Manual. The Stationery Office Books, London, UK

[8] Sowa JF, Zachman JA (1992) Extending and formalizing the framework for information systems architecture. IBM Syst J 31(3):590–616, IBM Publication G321-5488

[9] Spiegel MR (1975) Probability and Statistics. Schaum's Outline Series, McGraw-Hill, New York, USA

[10] Tanenbaum AS, Steen MV (2001) Distributed Systems: Principles and Paradigms. Prentice Hall, Upper Saddle River, NJ, USA

[11] Tobias PA, Trindade D (1995) Applied Reliability. Chapman & Hall/CRC, New York, USA

[12] Toigo JW (1989) Disaster Recovery Planning: Managing Risk and Catastrophe in Information Systems. Prentice Hall, Upper Saddle River, NJ, USA

[13] Trindade D, Nathan S (2005) Simple plots for monitoring the field reliability of repairable systems. In: Annual Reliability and Maintainability Symposium (RAMS), IEEE, Alexandria, VI, USA, pp 539–544

[14] van Lint JH (1982) Introduction to Coding Theory. Graduate Texts in Mathematics, Springer, Berlin Heidelberg New York

[15] Zachman JA (1987) A framework for information systems architecture. IBM Syst J 26(3):276–292, IBM Publication G321-5298

Index

Made in the USA
Lexington, KY
21 January 2011